"The Sea is the Body, the two Fishes are the Spirit
and the Soul"

From a manuscript of *The Book of Lambspring*

BOLLINGEN SERIES X

M. ESTHER HARDING

PSYCHIC ENERGY

Its Source and Its Transformation

WITH A FOREWORD BY *C. G. Jung*

BOLLINGEN SERIES X

PRINCETON UNIVERSITY PRESS

Published by Princeton University Press, Princeton, New Jersey

THIS IS THE TENTH IN A SERIES OF BOOKS
SPONSORED BY BOLLINGEN FOUNDATION

First Edition: *Psychic Energy: Its Source and Goal*, 1948
Second Edition, revised and enlarged, 1963

First Princeton/Bollingen Paperback Edition, 1973

11   13   15   16   14   12   10

Princeton University Press books are printed
on acid-free paper and meet the guidelines for
permanence and durability of the Committee on
Production Guidelines for Book Longevity
of the Council on Library Resources

Library of Congress Catalogue Card Number 63-10412

ISBN 0-691-01790-5 (paperback edn.)
ISBN 0-691-09817-4 (hardcover edn.)

Printed in the United States of America
Text designed by Andor Braun

PREFACE TO THE SECOND EDITION

IN THE FIFTEEN YEARS since this volume was first published, a number of books of the first importance have appeared on the subject of analytical psychology. Dr. Erich Neumann's *The Origins and History of Consciousness* (1949; English tr., 1954) gave an illuminating account of the relation of consciousness to the unconscious and showed how the consciousness of man has emerged from its hidden depths in the unconscious by definite steps, through which he has gradually freed himself from the hold of the primordial ways of nature and acquired some degree of freedom. These steps are recorded in myths found in varying form all over the world. They are stories or accounts of the ways in which the archetypal patterns of the psyche have presented themselves to man's consciousness, although the happenings they record were projected outside of man to mythic or divine beings. And only now is it becoming apparent that what was going on was a psychological and not a mythical happening. In further support of his thesis, Dr. Neumann followed this book by a study of one of the most important archetypes, *The Great Mother* (1955), using this time not myths as illustration but cult objects of all epochs gathered from all over the world. This work enlarged on the same theme that I had previously explored in my *Woman's Mysteries, Ancient and Modern* (1935, revised 1955), illustrating the meaning and function of the Eros principle of woman. Dr. Neumann later wrote a study of feminine psychology,[1] which has not yet been published in English.

1. *Zur Psychologie des Weiblichen* (Zurich, 1953).

But, to the sorrow of his many friends, the further development of his creative thought has been cut short by his untimely death.

A new study of the process of individuation in a woman undergoing analysis by the Jungian method has recently come from the pen of Dr. Gerhard Adler. In this book [2] he demonstrates the application of Jung's method of interpreting dreams and shows how the conscious problem of the individual is but the surface manifestation of a deeper underlying problem, namely, that of finding one's self as a whole individual. He shows that this can be accomplished by establishing a positive relation to the archetypal images arising from the unconscious, if they are rightly understood.

These and other works have served to clarify and enrich the field of analytical psychology. But by far the greatest contribution to the whole subject has come from Dr. Jung himself. I wrote my book during the war years when we in America were cut off from communication with Switzerland, except for rare letters, so it was not until 1948 that I was able to come into contact with the new developments of Dr. Jung's thought. During that time the *Psychology of Transference* (*Zur Psychologie der Übertragung*, 1946) was published in German, though not accessible in English till 1954; *Psychology and Alchemy* was published in English in 1953 (in German, 1944); these were followed in 1959 by *Aion* (German, 1951) and *The Archetypes and the Collective Unconscious*, and *Mysterium Coniunctionis* is promised to appear in the Collected Works in the near future.

I mention these particular books rather than give a complete list of the volumes of the Collected Works that have been appearing during this period, because these are the ones that contain the radically new work of this prolific author and set forth the core of his research into the deeper regions of the unconscious psyche.

In this new edition, a number of footnote references have been added to the text as a guide to the student who may wish to consult Jung's later works. Although the text has not been

2. *The Living Symbol* (New York and London, 1961).

materially altered, considerable additional material has been incorporated to bring the work up to date. The references have been made to conform with the published volumes of the Collected Works, and a number of new illustrations have been added, as well as a new bibliography and index.

*

Dr. Jung's concern with alchemy and his laborious work of collecting and translating rare and inaccessible texts must seem strange to those who do not understand why he has chosen to spend so much time and energy in studying this obscure and confusing material. It was only when Dr. Jung found in his patients' dreams symbols and themes resembling alchemical fantasies and ideas that he came to realize that the alchemists in their curious and often bizarre experiments were actually investigating their own unconscious contents and processes which they found projected into matter, that unknown and strange realm that fascinated them so profoundly. Their deep concern with experiments and curious chemical reactions and the fantasies they built about them really reflected the happenings within their own psyches. For the most part this was a secret the alchemists did not fathom, but some of them, especially the so-called philosophical alchemists, did realize that what went on in their retorts occurred simultaneously within themselves, for they repeatedly insisted that *"tam physice quam ethice,"* "as is the physical so is the ethical." This fact is further evidenced by the strict injunctions that occur in the literature, adjuring the alchemist to be of good moral character, and also by the urgent prayer cited by an alchemist in the *Aurora consurgens:* "Purge the horrible darknesses of our mind." [3]

However, as the alchemists did not understand that what they were concerned with was really a psychological transformation, but instead projected the *opus* into the problem of transforming matter from a base condition to a noble one, their fantasies about the reactions they observed in their retorts were reported without conscious criticism or interference. Conse-

---

3. *Aurora consurgens*, 9, 4th Parable; also *Psychology and Alchemy*, p. 259.

quently their texts give quite a naïve account of the workings of the unconscious and the unfolding of the archetypal drama in symbolic form. Their search was for the treasure beyond all treasures, the quintessentia, which they called by various names: philosophers' stone, gold, diamond, and so forth. When translated into psychological terms, this treasure would correspond to the unknown central value of the psyche that Jung has called the Self. This is really the quest with which my book also is concerned. Had I had access to Jung's later writings when I wrote it I could have given a much more inclusive account of the process. But it stands as an evidence that the road Jung follows is a genuine and true one, for it will be found that what I have to say, while far less profound than Jung's treatment of the subject, is yet in harmony with his ideas. He taught his pupils the method for studying the unconscious, and this book demonstrates that when the method is used the results tally with those of other seekers. Once again I must express my deep admiration and respect as well as my lasting affection for my teacher.

*

The news of Dr. Jung's death reached me just as I was completing work on this edition. The world has lost a great and creative personality, whose lifework has enriched our understanding of the psyche immeasurably, especially in the light he has thrown on the religious function in man; but those who knew him personally have lost as well a dearly loved friend, who will be greatly missed.

M. E. H.

New York, 1961

PREFACE TO THE FIRST EDITION

THIS BOOK was conceived during the war years, amid the din of a world cataclysm. Yet day by day I sat at my desk in utter solitude and peace, with nothing to disturb my quiet but the call of the gulls and the sound of the Atlantic breaking eternally on the rocks below my window. It seemed all but incredible that these two aspects of life could exist side by side—the surface so beautiful, the under side so terrible. But is not this a picture of life itself and, more especially, of man? The surface, the façade of civilization, looks so smooth and fair; yet beneath the cultured mask of consciousness what savage impulses, what ruthless monsters of the deep await a chance to seize the mastery and despoil the world!

These were the thoughts that gave rise to this book. Is it not possible that the primitive and unconscious side of man's nature might be more effectively tamed, even radically transformed? If not, civilization is doomed.

In the following pages this question is examined in the light that analytical psychology has thrown on the contents and processes of the unconscious. Until the first appearance of the works of Dr. C. G. Jung, the unconscious was regarded as merely the repository of forgotten or repressed experiences. In this there could be no answer to the problem of a world in the grip of a barbaric regression. But Dr. Jung discovered and opened to all explorers another aspect of the unconscious. For he penetrated to far greater depths than had ever before been reached, and found there the sources of psychological life that produce not only atavistic forms but also the potentialities for new development.

I am profoundly indebted to Dr. Jung for his work and for the teaching he has given me personally, and I take this opportunity to thank him in my own name, and also in the name of all those who have found life by following the road he has opened.

I wish also to thank him for the permission he has given me to quote from his published writings and to use the Tibetan mandala reproduced in this book.

Many thanks are due as well to Mr. Paul Mellon for much helpful criticism and for the time and interest he has devoted to the book, to Miss Renée Darmstadter for her able assistance in preparing the manuscript for the press, to Miss Hildegard Nagel for her translation of the foreword, and to my publishers for their courtesy and consideration in taking much detail work off my hands.

M. Esther Harding

New York, 1947

ACKNOWLEDGMENTS

I WANT TO EXPRESS my appreciation to the following firms for their permission generously granted me to quote extracts from copyrighted material of their publications: Ballière, Tindall and Cox, London; G. Bell and Sons, London; J. M. Dent and Sons, London; Dodd, Mead and Company, New York; E. P. Dutton and Company, New York; Harcourt, Brace and Company, New York; Harvard University Press, Cambridge, Mass.; John M. Watkins, London; Routledge and Kegan Paul Ltd., London; Macmillan and Company, London; Macmillan Company, New York; Oxford University Press, London; Rinehart and Company, New York. For quotations from the Collected Works of C. G. Jung I make grateful acknowledgment to Bollingen Foundation and Routledge and Kegan Paul Ltd.

In the preparation of chapter 6, I have availed myself of material previously published in a paper of mine, "The Mother Archetype and Its Functioning in Life," *Zentralblatt für Psychotherapie*, VIII (1935), no. 2.

The acknowledgments for the illustrations, many of which are new in the second edition, are given in the List of Illustrations. I am most grateful to the various museums for their help, and particularly to Mrs. Jessie Fraser for valuable advice.

M. E. H.

CONTENTS

LIST OF ILLUSTRATIONS

PLATES

Frontispiece. "The Sea is the Body, the two Fishes are the Spirit and the Soul." Watercolor from a manuscript of *The Book of Lambspring* (Italian, XVII century). Private collection.

I. The Corn Mother of the Pawnee Indians. Drawing from *Annual Report of the Bureau of American Ethnology* (Smithsonian Institution), XXII (1904).

II. The Slaying of the Bull. Modern drawing.

III. The Mistress of Animals. Etruscan bronze plate, VI century. Museum Antiker Kleinkunst, Munich. P: G. Wehrheim, Antikensammlungen München.

IV. The King of the Centaurs Seizes the Bride. Fragment from West Pediment of the Temple of Zeus. Archaeological Museum, Olympia. P: Deutsches Archäologisches Institut, Athens (copyright).

V. The Anima Opens the Eyes of a Child. Modern drawing.

VI. Human Sacrifice. Detail from interior panel of a silver cauldron, believed to have been made by Danube Celts, *c.* I century B.C.; found at Gundestrup, Denmark, in 1891. National Museum, Copenhagen. P: N. Elswing.

VII. Mask Representing the Animal Nature of the God. Granite statue of Sekhmet, Thebes, 19th Dynasty. Staatliche Museum, Berlin. P: Eranos Archives.

VIII. Isis Suckling Pharaoh. Limestone relief, Temple of Seti I, Abydos, 19th Dynasty. P: Eranos Archives.

IX. Two Women with a Child. Ivory, Mycenae, Bronze Age. National Archaeological Museum, Athens. P: TAP Service.

xv

TEXT FIGURES

FOREWORD

THIS BOOK presents a comprehensive survey of the experiences of analytical practice, a survey such as anyone who has spent many years in the conscientious pursuit of professional duties may well feel the need of making. In the course of time, insights and recognitions, disappointments and satisfactions, recollections and conclusions mount to such a proportion that one would gladly rid oneself of the burden of them in the hope not merely of throwing out worthless ballast but also of presenting a summation which will be useful to the world of today and of the future.

The pioneer in a new field rarely has the good fortune to be able to draw valid conclusions from his total experience. The efforts and exertions, the doubts and uncertainties of his voyage of discovery have penetrated his marrow too deeply to allow him the perspective and clarity which are necessary for a comprehensive presentation. Those of the second generation, who base their work on the groping attempts, the chance hits, the circuitous approaches, the half truths and mistakes of the pioneer, are less burdened and can take more direct roads, envisage farther goals. They are able to cast off many doubts and hesitations, concentrate on essentials, and, in this way, map out a simpler and clearer picture of the newly discovered territory. This simplification and clarification redound to the benefit of those of the third generation, who are thus equipped from the outset with an over-all chart. With this chart they are enabled to formulate new problems and mark out the boundary lines more sharply than ever before.

We can congratulate the author on the success of her attempt to present a general orientation on the problematical questions of medical psychotherapy in its most modern aspects. Her many years of experience in practice have stood her in good stead; for that matter, without them her undertaking would not have been possible at all. For it is not a question, as many believe, of a "philosophy," but rather of facts and the formulation of these, which latter in turn must be tested in practice. Concepts like "shadow" and "anima" are by no means intellectual inventions. They are designations given to actualities of a complex nature which are empirically verifiable. These facts can be observed by anyone who takes the trouble to do so and who is also able to lay aside his preconceived ideas. Experience, however, shows that this is difficult to do. For instance, how many people still labour under the assumption that the term archetype denotes inherited ideas! Such completely unwarranted presuppositions naturally make any understanding impossible.

One may hope that Dr. Harding's book, with its simple and lucid discussion, will be especially adapted to dispel such absurd misunderstandings. In this respect it can be of the greatest service, not only to the doctor, but also to the patient. I should like to emphasize this point particularly. It is obviously necessary for the physician to have an adequate understanding of the material laid before him; but if he is the only one who understands, it is of no great help to the patient, since the latter is actually suffering from lack of consciousness and therefore should become more conscious. To this end, he needs knowledge; and the more of it he acquires, the greater is his chance of overcoming his difficulties. For those of my patients who have reached the point at which a greater spiritual independence is necessary, Dr. Harding's book is one that I should unhesitatingly recommend.

C. G. Jung

Küsnacht / Zürich
July 8, 1947

And now from the Vast of the Lord will the waters of sleep
Roll in on the souls of men,
But who will reveal to our waking ken
The forms that swim and the shapes that creep
      Under the waters of sleep?
And I would I could know what swimmeth below when the tide
                                    comes in
On the length and the breadth of the marvellous marshes of Glynn.

        SIDNEY LANIER, *Hymns of the Marshes, 1870*

Be warned and understand truly
That two fishes are swimming in our sea,
The vastness of which no man can describe.
Moreover the Sages say
That the two fishes are only one, not two;
They are two, and nevertheless they are one.

NICHOLAS BARNAUD DELPHINAS, *The Book of Lambspring, 1625*

PART I

THE Source

OF PSYCHIC ENERGY

I

Introduction

*The forms that swim and the shapes that creep
Under the waters of sleep . . .*

BENEATH the decent façade of consciousness with its disciplined moral order and its good intentions lurk the crude instinctive forces of life, like monsters of the deep—devouring, begetting, warring endlessly. They are for the most part unseen, yet on their urge and energy life itself depends: without them living beings would be as inert as stones. But were they left to function unchecked, life would lose its meaning, being reduced once more to mere birth and death, as in the teeming world of the primordial swamps. In creating civilization man sought, however unconsciously, to curb these natural forces and to channel some part at least of their energy into forms that would serve a different purpose. For with the coming of consciousness, cultural and psychological values began to compete with the purely biological aims of unconscious functioning.

Throughout history two factors have been at work in the struggle to bring about the control and discipline of these nonpersonal, instinctive forces of the psyche. Social controls and the demands of material necessity have exerted a powerful discipline from without, while an influence of perhaps even greater potency has been applied from within the individual himself, in the form of symbols and experiences of a numinous character—psychological experiences that have had a powerful influence on certain individuals in every community. So powerful indeed were these experiences that they became the core of religious dogmas and rituals that in turn have influenced the large mass of the people.[1] That these religious forms have had power to curb the violence and ruthlessness of the primitive instincts to such an extent and for so long a time is a matter for the greatest wonder and amazement. It must mean that the symbols of a particular religion were peculiarly adapted to satisfy the urge of the conflicting inner forces, even lacking the aid of conscious understanding, and in many cases without the individual's having himself participated in the numinous experience on which the ritual was originally based.

So long as the religious and social forms are able to contain and in some measure to satisfy the inner and outer life needs of the individuals who make up a community, the instinctive forces lie dormant, and for the most part we forget their very existence. Yet at times they awaken from their slumber, and then the noise and tumult of their elemental struggle break in upon our ordered lives and rouse us rudely from our dreams of peace and contentment. Nevertheless we try to blind ourselves to the evidence of their untamed power, and delude ourselves into believing that man's rational mind has conquered not only the world of nature around him but also the world of natural, instinctive life within.

These childish beliefs have received not a few shocks of late. The increase in power that science has made available to man has not been equalled by a corresponding increase in the development and wisdom of human beings; and the upsurge of instinctive energies that has occurred in the last twenty-five years [2] in the political field has not as yet been adequately controlled, let alone tamed or converted to useful ends. Yet for the most part we continue to hope that we will be able to reassert the ascendancy of reasonable, conscious control without any very radical concomitant change in man himself. It

1. C. G. Jung, in *Mysterium Coniunctionis* (C.W. 14), § 604, says: " 'Religion' on the primitive level means the psychic regulatory system that is coordinated with the dynamism of instinct. On a higher level this original interdependence is sometimes lost, and then religion can easily become an antidote to instinct, whereupon the compensatory relationship degenerates into conflict, religion petrifies into formalism, and instinct is poisoned."
2. The above was written in 1946.

is of course obviously easier to assume that the problem lies outside of one's own psyche than to undertake responsibility for that which lurks within oneself. But are we justified in taking this attitude? Can we be so sure that the instinctive forces that caused the dynamic upheavals in Europe, and obliterated in a decade the work of centuries of civilization, are really limited by geographical or racial boundaries to the people of *other* nations? May they not, like the monsters of the deep, have access to all oceans? In other words, is "our sea"—the unconscious as we participate in it—exempt from such upheavals?

The force that lay behind the revolutionary movements in Europe was not something consciously planned for or voluntarily built up; it arose spontaneously from the hidden sources of the Germanic psyche, being evoked perhaps but not consciously made by will power. It erupted from unfathomable depths and overthrew the surface culture that had been in control for so many years. This dynamic force seemingly had as its aim the destruction of everything that the work of many centuries had laboriously built up and made apparently secure, to the end that the aggressors might enrich themselves in the resulting chaos, at the expense of all other peoples, meanwhile ensuring that none would be left with sufficient strength to endanger the despoilers for centuries to come.

The excuse they offered for their disregard of international law and the rights of others was that their own fundamental needs had been denied. They justified their actions on the ground of instinctual compulsion, the survival urge that requires living space, defensible frontiers, and access to raw materials—demands in the national sphere corresponding to the imperatives of the instinct of self-preservation in the individual.

The aggressors claimed that the gratification of an instinct on the lowest biological level is an inalienable right, regardless of what means are employed for its satisfaction: "My necessity is of paramount importance; it has divine sanction. I must satisfy it at all costs. Your necessity, by comparison, is of no importance at all." This attitude is either cynically egotistic or incredibly naïve. The Germans are a Western people and have been under Christian influence for centuries; they might therefore be expected to be psychologically and culturally mature. Were this the case, would not the whole nation have to be judged to be antisocial and criminal? It was not only the Nazi overlords, with their ruthless ideology, who disregarded the rights of others so foully; the whole nation manifested a naïve egocentricity akin to that of a young child or a primitive tribe, and this, rather than a conscious and deliberate criminality, may perhaps account for their gullibility and their acquiescence in the Nazi regime. Deep within the Germanic unconscious, forces that were not contained or held in check by the archetypal symbols of the Christian religion, but had flowed back into pagan forms, notably Wotanism, were galvanized into life by the Nazi call. For that which is the ideal or the virtue of an outworn culture is the antisocial crime of its more evolved and civilized successor.

The energy that could change the despondent and disorganized Germany of 1930 into the highly organized and optimistic, almost daemonically powerful nation of a decade later, must have arisen from deeply buried sources; it could not have been produced by conscious effort or by the application of rational rules either of conduct or of economics. These dramatic changes swept over the country like an incoming tide or a flood brought about by the release of dynamic forces that had formerly lain quiescent in the unconscious. The Nazi leaders seized upon the opportunity brought within their reach by this "tide in the affairs of men." They were able to do this because they were themselves the first victims of the revolutionary dynamism surging up from the depths, and they recognized that a similar force was stirring in the mass of the people; they had but to call it forth and release it from the civilized restraints that still ruled the ordinary, decent folk. If these forces had not been already active in the unconscious of the German people as a whole, the Nazi agitators would have preached their new doctrine in vain; they would have appeared to the people as criminals or lunatics, and would by no means have been able to arouse popular enthusiasm or to dominate the entire nation for twelve long years.

The spirit of this dynamism is directly opposed to the spirit of civilization. The first seeks life in movement, change, exploitation; the second has sought throughout the ages to create a form wherein life may expand, may build, may make secure. And indeed Christian civilization, despite all its faults and shortcomings, represents the best that man in his inadequacy has as yet succeeded in evolving. But the greed and selfishness of man have never been adequately dealt with. Crimes against the corporate body of humanity are constantly being perpetrated not only in overt acts but also, and perhaps more frequently, through ignorance and exclusively ego-oriented attitudes. Consequently the needs of the weak have been largely disregarded, and the strong have had things their own way.

But those who are materially and psychologically less well endowed have as large a share of instinctive desire and as strong a will to live as the more privileged. These natural longings, so persistently repressed, cannot remain quiescent indefinitely. It is not so much that the individual rebels—the masses of the people being proverbially patient—but nature rebels in him: the forces of the unconscious boil over when the time is ripe. The danger of such an eruption is not, however, limited to the less fortunate in society, for the instinctive desires of many of the more fortunate likewise have been suppressed, not by a greedy upper class but by the too rigid domination of the moral code and conventional law. This group also shows signs of rebellion and may break forth in uncontrollable violence, as has so recently happened in Germany. If this should happen elsewhere, the energies unleashed would pour further destruction over the world. But there remains another possibility, namely, that these hidden forces stirring in countless individuals the world over may be channelled again, as they were at the beginning of the Christian era, by the emergence of a powerful archetype or symbol, and so may create for themselves a different form, paving the way for a new stage of civilization.

The expansionist movement in Communism exerts a very similar threat to world order. Under the guise of offering succour to underprivileged and underdeveloped peoples the communist overlords seek world dominion and world exploitation. That their own people will support them in their ambition, in spite of the hardships entailed, speaks eloquently of the dynamic unrest in the unconscious of the mass of the people.

For this new dynamic or daemonic spirit that has sprung into being is endowed with an almost incredible energy, which has remained completely unavailable to consciousness until the present time. Can it conceivably create a new world order? So long as it continues to manifest itself only in destruction, it obviously cannot, nor can it be assimilated to that older spirit which seeks all values in terms of the established and well-tested. On the other hand, it does not look as if it could be repressed once more into the unconscious. It has come to stay. And the spirit that conserves and builds up, if it survives at all, cannot remain unaffected by the impact of so vital a force.

These two world spirits, which Greek philosophy called "the growing" and "the burning," stand in mortal combat, and we cannot foretell the outcome. The fear that they may literally destroy each other is not ended with the coming of peace. Will the revolutionary spirit triumph and become the dominant spirit of the next world age? Will war follow war, each armistice being but the excuse for another outbreak of aggression? Or dare we hope that out of the present struggle and suffering a new world spirit may be born, to create for itself a new body of civilization?

These questions only time can answer, for even in this cataclysmic epoch, world movements unfold themselves very slowly, and it is hardly probable that anyone now living will survive to see the outcome of this struggle on the global stage. Yet, since it is a conflict of philosophies, of "spirits," that is, of psychological forces within individuals and nations, perhaps the psychologist can give us a clue as to their probable development, through an understanding of the laws that govern them. For the psychologist can observe the unfolding of this same conflict in miniature in individual persons. The problems and struggles disturbing the peace of the world must in the last analysis be fought out in the hearts of individuals before they can be truly resolved in the relationships of nations. On this plane they must of necessity be worked out within the span of a single life.

In the individual, no less than in the nation, the basic instincts make a compulsive demand for satisfaction; and here too civilization has imposed a rule of conduct aimed to repress or modify the demand. Every child undergoes an education that imposes restraint on his natural response to his own impulses and desires, substituting a collective or conventional mode of behaviour. In many cases the result is that the conscious personality is too much separated from its instinctive roots; it becomes too thin, too brittle, perhaps even sick, until in the course of time the repressed instincts rebel and generate a revolution in the individual similar to that which has been threatening the peace of the world.

In the individual, as in the nation, the resulting conflict may produce asocial or criminal reactions; or, if such behaviour is excluded by his moral code, neurotic or even psychotic manifestations may develop. But no real solution of such a fundamental problem can be found except through a conscious enduring of the conflict that arises when the instincts revolt against the too repressive rule of the conscious ego. If the ego regains control, the *status quo ante* will be re-established and the impoverishment of life will continue, perhaps eventuating in complete sterility. If, on the other hand, the repressed instincts obtain the mastery, unseating the ego, the individual will be in danger of disintegrating either morally or psychologically. That is, he will either lose all moral values— "go to the dogs," as the phrase is—or he will lose himself in a welter of collective or nonpersonal, instinctive drives that may well destroy his mental balance.

But if the individual who is caught in such a problem has sufficient courage and stability to face the issue squarely, not allowing either contending element to fall back into the unconscious, regardless of how much pain and suffering may be involved, a solution of the conflict may develop spontaneously in the depths of the unconscious. Such a solution will not appear in the form of an intellectual conclusion or thought-out plan, but will arise in dream or phantasy in the form of an image or symbol, so unexpected and yet so apt that its appearance will seem like a miracle. Such a symbol has the effect of breaking the deadlock. It has power to bring the opposing demands of the psyche together in a newly created form through which the life energies can flow in a new creative effort. Jung has called this the reconciling symbol.[3] Its potency avails not only to bring the impasse to an end but also to effect a transformation or modification of the instinctive drives within the individual: this corresponds in the personal sphere to that modification of the instincts which, at least in some measure, has been brought about in the race through the ages of cultural effort.

This is something entirely different from a change in conscious attitude, such as might be brought about by education or precept. It is not a compromise, nor is the solution achieved through an increased effort to control the asocial tendencies, the outbursts of anger or the like. The conflict arose initially just because these attempts at moral control were either not successful, so that the individual remained at the mercy of his own passionate desirousness, or perhaps all too successful, so that the vital springs of life were dammed up within him and his conscious life became dry and sterile. It is only after all such conscious efforts towards a solution have failed that the reconciling symbol appears. It arises from the depths of the unconscious psyche and produces its creative effect on a level of the psychic life beyond the reach of the rational consciousness, where it has power to produce a change in the very character of the instinctive urge itself, with the result that the nature of the "I want" is actually altered.

This sounds almost incredible. Yet has not such a change taken place in very fact as a result of the cultural evolution of mankind? It represents the difference between the primitive or barbarian and the cultured man. The primitive can be taught all the arts and sciences of Western civilization, yet his deepest reactions will remain primitive: he will continue to

3. For a discussion of the *reconciling symbol*, cf. Jung, *Psychological Types*, pp. 258 ff., 478 ff., and chap. v.

be at the mercy of his unconscious impulses whenever he is subjected to any strong emotion or other stress. In contrast, the instinctive reactions of the Western man are in far greater degree related to his conscious ego and much more dependable. However, as we have good reason to know, he is by no means always civilized in this deeper sense of the word. Very many individuals have not truly achieved the psychological development that has in general profoundly affected the ideals of our civilization and the character of not a few who are, in virtue of the fact, truly cultured persons.

A historical example showing the difference in the quality of the instinctive reactions of different men under great stress will make this point clearer. When the Greely polar expedition was trapped in the far north without provisions or fuel and compelled to await the arrival of a rescue ship through a whole winter, some of the men deteriorated under the terrible hardships and uncertainties they were forced to endure. David Brainard has recorded the story in *The Outpost of the Lost*. Some of the men refused to allow a comrade to thaw himself out in the common sleeping bag after he had been out in the Arctic cold seeking food for the entire group; others began to steal from the tiny reserve of food, and more than once there was danger that some quarrel would result in murder. Yet this degeneration did not affect all the members of the party. Some, notably Brainard and Greely himself, maintained self-mastery throughout the ordeal, and sacrificed themselves as a matter of course for the welfare of the group.

What was it in them that kept them from disintegration? Was it that in these persons the conscious ego was better organized and better disciplined and therefore better able to control the primitive urges on which the human psyche is built? These men suffered just as much from hunger and cold as their fellows, and even more from anxiety than the rest. Why did they not break down or fly into uncontrollable rages? Could it be that in these two men the form of the instinctive urge had itself undergone a subtle transformation, so that the primitive man within was not so crude, not so self-centered as in their companions?

We cannot dismiss this problem simply by stating that Brainard and Greely were finer individuals than the rest, for instances are not wanting of men who at a given time, under conditions of great stress, acted in a completely selfish way in response to unrestrainable instinctive impulses, and who later, after having undergone certain never to be forgotten inner experiences, discovered to their own amazement that their spontaneous reactions to such an ordeal had changed, so that they were no longer even tempted to act asocially. In these cases one is forced to conclude that the nonpersonal impulse has been altered in character. For it is not that these individuals are more consciously heroic or more deliberately unselfish than before. The fact is that consciousness in them has changed. Their own need and their own danger simply do not obtrude themselves; thus, while they are reacting to the situation quite spontaneously, the nonpersonal instinct is no longer manifested in purely selfish ways. Such a man is freed from the compulsions of his primitive urges; his consciousness is no longer identified with the instinctive or somatic "I" but has shifted to a new centre, and consequently his whole being is profoundly changed.

Transformations of character of this kind have frequently been recorded as following religious conversion. They were indeed expected to take place as the result of the disciplines and ordeals of religious initiation; and they have been observed in individual cases after profound emotional experiences of a quite personal nature. Paul's experience on the road to Damascus is a classical example: through it his character and the whole direction of his life were altered—a change that persisted until his death. It was not simply the expression of a passing mood; nor was it an example of *enantiodromia*, that dramatic change-over to an opposite and complementary attitude which frequently occurs in the so-called conversions of popular revivals, and which can be reversed as easily as it was produced. On the contrary, the illumination that came to Paul resulted in a far-reaching and lasting transformation, affecting his whole being.

Profound psychological changes of comparable type may

occur as a result of the inner experience that Jung has named the process of individuation,[4] which can be observed in persons undergoing analysis by the method he has elaborated. This change likewise affects the very character of the basic instincts, which, instead of remaining bound to their biological goals in a compulsive way, are transformed for the service of the psyche.

These transformations observable in individual persons are similar to the psychological changes that have occurred in the race from the days of the ape man up to those of the most developed and civilized type of modern man. It is possible to trace, at least roughly, the stages by which the instinctive urges have gradually been modified and transformed in the long course of history through the increase and development of consciousness. The development of the individual follows a similar path: what has been achieved only through untold ages by the race must be recapitulated in the brief space of a few years in every man and woman if the individuals of any one generation are to attain to a personal level of consciousness suitable for their epoch. And this process must actually be accelerated if each generation is to be in a position to add noticeably to the psychological achievements of the race.

Throughout the ages various techniques have been evolved for accelerating the process in the individual. Some of these techniques worked for a time and were subsequently discarded. Sometimes a method that suited the mode of one century did not appeal to the next. None has proved universally successful. Foremost among modern methods is that evolved by medical psychologists, who made the discovery that neurotic and other psychological illnesses are often caused by an infantility or primitivity persisting in the background of the patient's psyche. Jung's work has dealt particularly with the cultural aspects and implications of the human problems

4. A detailed account of this process, based on the study of two cases, has been published by Jung in "A Study in the Process of Individuation," in *The Archetypes and the Collective Unconscious* (C.W. 9, i) and "Psychology and Religion," in *Psychology and Religion: West and East* (C.W. 11). Two other case histories, with detailed subjective material, are recorded by H. G. Baynes in *Mythology of the Soul*. Practical aspects of the process are discussed in later chapters of the present volume.

that his patients have presented to him; thus he has done more to enlarge our understanding of the processes by which consciousness develops than any of his predecessors in the field, who have been preoccupied mainly with the therapeutic aspects of their psychological work. The value and significance of these discoveries can hardly be overestimated, for Jung has demonstrated that it is indeed possible to hasten the evolution of the instinctive drives and so to assist in the cultural development of the individual, who not only gains release from his asocial compulsions but at the same time comes into possession of the energy that was formerly locked up in biological and instinctive mechanisms. Through such a transformation the man or woman becomes a truly cultured and civilized person— a worthy citizen of the world.

It may seem absurd to suggest that the attitude of the individual to his personal conflicts and problems could have any appreciable effect on an international situation involving the fate of millions, or to turn from the general problem to the personal one as if they were equivalents. Yet that is exactly what anyone with even a minimum of psychological insight is obliged to do if he seeks to understand the age in which he is living or to contribute in a conscious way towards the solution of the world problem.

The millions involved in world crises are individuals; the emotions and dynamic drives motivating the clashes of armies are engendered in individuals. These are psychic forces that dwell in individual psyches. Thousands of persons are still infected, at the present moment, with those psychic infections which so recently produced a world war. Not only have the totalitarian nations themselves suffered from this psychic disease; we too are liable to the contagion, for the simple reason that we inhabit the same world. For psychic forces know no geographical boundaries.

In the individual, as in the state, the totalitarian attitude denies the basic freedoms to a part of the whole. One part arrogates all power and all advantages to itself, while virtually enslaving or penalizing other parts if they do not agree to support the dominant element. The one-sidedness of the psychological development of Western man has been not unlike the rigid singleness of this attitude. The conscious ego has assumed rights over the whole psyche, frequently disregarding the very existence of other real needs and values. It has repressed these other aspects of the psyche, forcing them into the hidden depths of the unconscious, where they are seized upon by the dark, archaic forces that, like "the shapes that creep under the waters of sleep," forever move in the unknown reaches of the human psyche. If any further step in the psychological development of man is to be taken, the exclusive domination of the conscious ego must be terminated, and the ruthless barbarism of the primitive instincts themselves must in some way be modified, so that their energy may be made available for the cultural advancement of the individual and in this way for society as well.

When, through a study of the products of his own unconscious, an individual's awareness of the hidden realms of the psyche is increased, and the richness and vitality of that unknown world is borne in upon him, his relation to the dynamic and nonpersonal forces within himself is profoundly changed. The I, with its petty, personal desires, sinks into relative insignificance, and through his increased insight and his greater understanding of life's meaning and purpose, he is enabled to release himself from the dominance of the unconscious drives. The fact that such a change is possible in the individual may give us a clue as to the direction that must be taken if mankind is to be released from the recurrent outbreaks of violence that threaten its very existence. For the human race is endangered not by lack of material wealth or of the technical skill for using it, but only by the persistent barbarity of man himself, whose spiritual development lags so far behind his scientific knowledge and mechanical ingenuity.

2

The Transformation of the Instinctive Drives

THAT the very nature of the basic instincts can, under certain circumstances, undergo a fundamental modification or transformation, is a very strange idea, unfamiliar to most people. As a result of such a modification the instinctive drives cease to be exclusively and compulsively related to the biological aims of the organism—aims that are necessarily concerned with the survival and well-being of the individual and his immediate progeny—and are converted at least in part to cultural ends. In the present chapter this process will be further explored, and the rest of Part I will be devoted to a more detailed study of the problem as it affects the three basic instincts. Part II will centre on the discussion of the technique used in analytical psychology to further this transformation.

The instinctive drives or life urges always present themselves to consciousness in quite personal guise, as "I want," "I must have," whether it be hunger for food, or sexual satisfaction, or security, or dominance that arouses this urgent and compulsive demand. But this personalness of the need is illusory: actually the "I want" is just a personal expression of the fact that life itself "wants" in me. The urge is more correctly called nonpersonal; it is ectopsychic in origin and functions in the individual quite apart from his conscious control and not infrequently to his actual disadvantage. It is concerned only with the continuance of life and, generally speaking, with the survival of the race rather than of the individual. The individual may even be sacrificed through the blind working of such an instinctive compulsion, or may sacrifice himself for the continuance of the species—not, as we might suppose, with an altruistic purpose, but all unknowing of what his obedience to the impulse within him will involve. Thus for instance the drone flies inevitably and without choice after the nubile queen, little guessing that this flight is his last. If he is successful in the race to possess her, he will die in the consummation of his instinctive desire. If he loses, he may be too exhausted to make his way back to the hive, or on reaching it will be slaughtered on the threshold as being of no further use to the community. Nor is it only among the insects that the nonpersonal character of the instinctive drives can be observed. The strange compulsion that periodically leads lemmings to drown themselves in the ocean is of an instinctive nature; and can we say that the battle furor that ever and anon takes modern man into its grip is so very different?

The extremely personal quality that is characteristic of the instinctive urgencies is due to a lack of consciousness. An individual who has outgrown the compulsive "I want" of the infant is not unaware of his bodily needs, but he has acquired a certain degree of detachment from them. He is no longer completely identified with his hunger or sexuality or other bodily necessities, but can take them with a certain relativity and postpone satisfaction of them until conditions are adapted to their fulfilment. The infant cannot do this. If it is in bodily discomfort it screams until relieved and has no thought for the comfort or convenience of its nurse; nor will it hesitate to snatch another's food, recking little of the complications that may follow.

During the course of the child's development, some small part of this nonpersonal, instinctive energy is redeemed from its purely biological orientation and released for more conscious aims. Through this process a part of the unconscious psyche is separated from the rest, forming the personal consciousness. This personal consciousness, which the given individual calls "I," often seems to him to represent the whole psyche; but this is an illusion. It actually represents a very small part of the total psyche, which for the rest remains largely unconscious and is nonpersonal or collective in its aims and manifestations. The nonpersonal part of the psyche is not connected with the subject, the I, nor under his control; rather, its functioning happens in him as if another or something other were speaking or acting within him. For this reason Jung has called it the objective psyche. It is as much an object to the observing I as are the objects in the outer world.

To the extent to which the unconscious part of the psyche is not personal, it lacks those qualities which are characteristic of consciousness and which depend on an established I as a focus of consciousness. The conscious I sees everything from its own point of view. Things are either good or bad—for *me;* objects are near or far from, above or below *myself;* to the right or to the left, within or without, and so on, through the whole gamut of the pairs of opposites. But in the unconscious these conditions do not prevail. There forward and backward are undifferentiated, for there is no discriminating point of consciousness against which to define the movement; similarly good and bad, true and false, creative and destructive, lie side by side and, like the great fishes of the poem of Nicholas Barnaud Delphinas, "they are two, and nevertheless they are one."

When an unconscious content breaks through into consciousness, its duality becomes apparent and a conflict results. A choice has to be made. Values that seemed secure and unassailable become uncertain, issues appear confused; the solid ground, till then believed to be firm beyond any doubt, quakes and dissolves; and only after a new standpoint has been gained can a reconciliation be achieved and peace be re-established.

The average person, who assumes that his conscious ego represents the whole of his psyche, believes that he is really as civilized and cultured as he appears to be. If at times his thoughts or conduct would seem to cast a doubt on this flattering self-estimate, he condones his failure to live up to his own standard as due to an excusable fault or human weakness of no special significance.

This general complacency was sadly shaken by the researches of Freud, who demonstrated that under the seemly garment of convention there lurk in all men and women the impulses and desires of primitive instinct. This discovery was exceedingly shocking to the average man of the day. Indeed, each individual who experiences the force of primitive instinct as a prime mover in his own heart, whether as part of the analytical experience or because of some situation in life, is usually still profoundly shocked, even though the Freudian theory itself no longer appears particularly startling.

Freud's theory has popularly been supposed to apply chiefly or exclusively to the realm of sex, but it is also applicable to other aspects of life; indeed, during an analysis much attention is usually given to aggressive and vengeful impulses. For example, most people believe themselves to be peaceful folk, reasonably free from the compulsive drive of the instinct of self-preservation. In times of peace such people would say that nothing could ever bring them to kill. Yet it is well known that in the heat and fear of battle, the instinct to kill rather than be killed can take possession of one who is naturally gentle in disposition and perhaps even of pacifist tendency. Such a man may be seriously disturbed at finding a blood lust latent within him, for in ordinary civilian life we remain unaware of the strength of our primitive instincts and are blind to what lies beneath the smooth exterior in each of us. We simply do not see the jungle animal lurking in the unconscious.

Similarly, those of us who have never known want have not the remotest idea of how we should behave under conditions of starvation. Under such circumstances lying and deceit, theft, and even murder for the sake of satisfying the voracious instinct are not impossible to apparently civilized men. Crimes of passion, which form a large proportion of the more serious cases in the criminal courts, are committed not only by persons of the criminal classes but also by men and women who in all other respects are decent and respected citizens. These are examples of the way in which the control of the ego can break down before the urgent demands of an outraged instinct that on throwing off its customary restraints appears in all its naked and primitive barbarism.

The instinct of hunger and the reproductive urge, with its by-product of sexuality, are the basic manifestations of life. By their presence or absence we determine whether a given structure constitutes a living being or not. The behaviour of every organism that has not yet developed a central nervous system is completely controlled by these primordial instincts. In the earliest stage of development, the response to the stimulus of hunger or sex is automatic and compulsory, being set in motion whenever an object adapted to the satisfaction of the urge appears. With the development of a central nervous system, however, a change becomes apparent. The organism begins to acquire the capacity to exercise choice. It is no longer merely a reacting mechanism, compelled to respond to the stimulus in a purely automatic way.

This element of choice and the consequent liberation from the dominance of instinct become more marked as the central nervous system evolves, until we are obliged, in the case of the higher animals, to speak of a psychic factor separate from, though dependent on, the control of the nervous system. With the emergence of a psyche, the instincts are increasingly modified and come in some measure under the control of the individual organism. Jung has called this process the psychization [1] of the instincts.

With the development of the psyche through the centuries, control over the instincts gradually increased. Bit by bit they were changed, losing to a certain extent their automatic and compulsory character, so that the individual gained increasing freedom of choice and of action. Yet under conditions of stress he may still lose his hard-won control, temporarily or even permanently, and fall again under the arbitrary domination of instinct. This is always felt to be a regression, entailing a loss of humanness, even though it may bring with it an uprush of

1. C. G. Jung, "Psychological Factors Determining Human Behaviour," in *The Structure and Dynamics of the Psyche* (C.W. 8), p. 115.

energy and a sense of release from a restraint that has become intolerable.

That the compulsoriness of primitive instinct has been modified by the emergence of the psyche is an obvious fact accessible to daily observation, but the course by which this change has come to pass remains largely unexplained. We cannot say that the change was instituted by the conscious ego, because the conscious psyche itself arose, by some unexplained process, out of unconsciousness. If the basic urges to self-preservation and reproduction and the will to dominate were the only motivating forces in the organism, it is hardly conceivable that the psyche could have arisen. For this reason Jung differentiates three other urges motivating the psychic life of the individual organism and having the characteristic compulsoriness of instincts, namely, the drive to activity, the reflection urge, and the so-called creative instinct. He designates the last-mentioned urge as a psychic factor similar to though not identical with an instinct. He writes:

The richness of the human psyche and its essential character are probably determined by this reflective instinct. . . . [By it] the stimulus is more or less wholly transformed into a psychic content, that is, it becomes an experience: a natural process is transformed into a conscious content. Reflection is the cultural instinct *par excellence,* and its strength is shown in the power of culture to maintain itself in the face of untamed nature.[2]

As a result of this urge or necessity to reflect on experience and to relive it in drama and relate it in story, the basic instincts in man—and in him alone among all the animals—have to some extent been modified and robbed of part of their compulsive effect, thus coming to serve the growing needs of the psyche instead of remaining bound irrevocably to the needs of the nonpsychic, that is, the biological or animal life.

This transformation has occurred in the case of each of the basic instincts: sexuality, in addition to fulfilling a biological function, now serves the emotional needs of the psyche;

2. Ibid., p. 117.

the instinct of self-defence has motivated the establishment of community life, with its collective enterprises and its basic social relationships; the satisfaction of hunger, originally a purely biological activity, has come to be the focus around which human companionship is cultivated. The primitive need of the hungry animal has been so brought under the control of the psyche that satisfying hunger in common has become the most prevalent way of fostering and expressing comradely relationship with our fellow men. Elaborate rituals and customs have accrued around what was originally the simple matter of eating, and the instinct has been largely made over to serve emotional needs. We hardly feel comfortable about eating constantly alone, and experience a real need to share our delicacies with others, to make a little party of our good fortune: the feeling is, as the Chinese *I Ching* puts it, "I have a cup of good spirits; come and share it with me." [3] And when we want to express pleasure at being with a friend, we quite spontaneously mark the occasion with a meal, while even our religious festivals are celebrated with emphasis on this interest —the joyous ones with feasts, and the periods of repentance or of mourning with fasts.

When the instinct of hunger has been partly modified in the interest of the psyche, it may begin to show itself in quite different terms, as for instance in some other urgent desire characterized by insatiability. Love of money, inordinate ambition, or any other unlimited desirousness may be an expression of the hunger instinct, even though the individual in whom it occurs is completely unconscious of this fact.

The craving for food is the expression of hunger in the biological sphere; but the human being has need for sustenance in other realms—a need that can be as urgent in its demands as physical hunger and that may exert a compulsion no less inexorable. We need only note the language employed in reference to these other needs to realize how naturally and unconsciously the very terms of physical hunger are applied to them. We "assimilate" an idea or "imbibe" a thought; propaganda is "fed" to an unthinking public. The collect advises

3. Cf. *I Ching*, No. 61, p. 236.

us to "read, mark, learn and inwardly digest" the teaching. In slang phrase, we "chew over a new idea" or, rejecting it, "spit it out," saying, "I could not stomach it." Such words are almost unavoidable in talking of ideas, and the symbolism of eating and digesting is used in relation to other matters as well. For instance, the phrase "to hunger and thirst after righteousness" refers to something deeper than intellectual understanding and has nearer kinship with the ideas represented in the rituals of "eating the god," whereby the participant in the ritual meal assimilates the divine qualities. In our own Christian ritual of communion, the communicant is believed to assimilate in actual fact not only the Christ nature but Christ himself, who thenceforth will dwell in his heart "by faith."

As a result of modification and development, the hunger instinct has emerged from the purely biological realm, where it is the manifestation of a somatic or bodily need, into the realm of the psyche. There it serves the conscious ego in the form of ambition, self-esteem, or desire for possessions. But it may undergo a still further modification, and a stage may be reached in which the hunger is no longer concerned exclusively with personal possessions or aggrandizement but instead seeks, as the supreme goal, a suprapersonal or religious value.

From this brief outline it will be realized that the gradual transformation of the instinct of hunger takes place in three stages: these correspond to the three phases of development of the human being that I have elsewhere called the naïve stage of consciousness, the ego stage, and the stage of consciousness of the Self.[4] The same steps can be traced in the evolution of the other basic instincts—the urge to self-preservation, sexuality with its concomitant parental motive, and the will to power. In each of these realms, the biological needs and the instinctive impulses associated with them dominate the field of consciousness in the first stage, in which the focal centre, the I, is completely dominated by auto-erotic desires. I have

4. *The Way of All Women*, p. 6. Throughout the present volume, the term *Self*, as connoting the centre of the psyche in its totality, is thus capitalized to differentiate it from references to the personal I, which is frequently spoken of as the self—in such terms as myself, himself, etc.

called this centre the autos.[5] In the second stage the ego becomes the centre of consciousness, and the instinctive drives are modified through their relation to the new-found ego consciousness, which in its turn says "I." In the third stage the ego is displaced from its central position, becoming relative in importance to the new centre of consciousness, the Self, whose categorical imperative takes over ultimate control.

Jung uses the term Self to represent the centre of psychic awareness that transcends ego consciousness and includes in its scope all the vast reaches of the psyche that are ordinarily unconscious; it therefore is not merely a personal consciousness but a nonpersonal one as well. Achievement of this level has been regarded by most of the great religions of the world as the supreme goal. It is expressed in such terms as "finding the God within." For the Self, the centre of this new kind of consciousness, is felt to be distinct from the ego and to possess an absolute authority within the psyche. It speaks with a voice of command exerting a power over the individual as great as that of the instincts. When it functions strongly in a human being, it produces a preoccupation with the inner, subjective life that may appear to the onlooker to be auto-erotic self-absorption; but if the individual makes a clear differentiation between the personal self, the autos or the ego, and this

5. In the naïve stage of consciousness, somatic or bodily perceptions form the content of consciousness. It is this element that speaks when the individual says "I." Sometimes it is called the auto-erotic factor; but there is no term in common use to distinguish this I from the ego, which rules the next stage of consciousness. The Greek *autos* may possibly serve. It is the basis of such words as automatic, auto-erotic, autonomous, all referring to functionings of this somatic I, while the child who has never outgrown the domination of the *autos* is diagnosed as *autistic*. Freud's term "id" comes perhaps nearest to this idea of autos. Freud, however, seems to postulate that the individual speaks from the position of the ego observing the id, the instinctive drives, within himself; in my observation this differentiation is by no means always made. Not only in the young child but also in the adult, the I that speaks is often merely the voice of instinct, for no conscious ego capable of holding the auto-erotic or autonomous impulses in check has as yet been developed. For this reason I think it helpful to differentiate the autos as an early and immature centre of consciousness. The term ego can then be reserved for the next and more conscious stage of development, in relation to which such words as egocentric and egotistic are in fact used as discriminating between somatic reactions and responses connected with personal consciousness and greater sophistication.

centre of nonpersonal compelling power, the activity is certainly not auto-erotic but reflects a concern with a superordinated value of the utmost significance for the development of the psyche and therefore also for mankind.

These successive stages of development distinguish the kinds of consciousness enjoyed by different persons. An individual living entirely in the auto-erotic stage cannot conceive of the greater awareness and greater freedom of one whose consciousness has been modified by emergence of the ego. For example, a person who has never outgrown his dependence on bodily comfort cannot understand the self-discipline of one who can voluntarily lay aside the claims of ease and luxury in order to devote himself unstintingly to his work. Such a disciplined devotion is incomprehensible to the pleasure seeker, and even if he wished to do so, he would probably find it beyond his power to emulate it. For while the more evolved man is naturally aware of the claims of his body, he is no longer completely dominated by his instinctive urges. But he in turn is unable to understand the nature of that consciousness which prevails when the Self has replaced the ego even in moderate degree.

A complete replacement either of the autos by the ego, or of the ego by the Self, is as a matter of fact never observed in life. Indeed, a practical continuation of life would hardly be possible for one entirely freed from the demands of the body or completely emptied of ego desires. These urges pertain to human existence, and without them the life of the body and the life of the conscious personality would come to an end. Therefore when we speak of the pre-emption of the centre of consciousness by a nonpersonal Self, it must be remembered that this replacement means not the annihilation of biological desire but its relegation to a subservient position. Through this process the instincts, which were originally in complete control, become relative, and their compulsory character is modified by gradual psychization, that is to say, their energy is transferred in part from the biological to the psychic sphere. Part of the power of the instincts is wrested from them in this process, but only a fraction becomes available for the conscious personality of the individual; by far the larger share passes over to a new determinant of objective psychic nature.

It is interesting to observe that the Buddhists of the Mahayana sect also distinguish three stages of human consciousness, which correspond to a surprising degree to the stages we have differentiated here. The naïve stage, ruled over by the autos, in which the individual is completely dominated by his bodily needs and desires, marks the "man of little intellect." The consciousness of such a man is exceedingly narrow, being bounded by the limits of his own biological desirousness. For him, the Buddhists say, "the best thing is to have faith in the law of cause and effect." [6] He is admonished to observe the outcome of his preoccupation with his auto-erotic desires.

The man in the ego stage of development is called by the Buddhists the "man of ordinary intellect." His attention is wholly directed to controlling his environment for his personal satisfaction and advantage. He has gained some control over his instinctive drives and for him the ego is now king; he classifies everything in terms of his own wishes, taking the good and rejecting the evil, not realizing that what he discards falls into the unconscious and does not cease to exist. In this stage, the Buddhists say, "the best thing is to recognize, both within and without oneself, the workings of the law of opposites."

The state of the individual whom the Buddhists call the "man of superior intellect" corresponds to the third stage of our psychological classification. In him the identification of the ego with the supreme value has been dissolved. In consequence he experiences the inner dynamic factor as something other than the conscious ego, though definitely within the psyche. For his state, according to the Buddhists, "the best thing is to have a thorough comprehension of the inseparableness of the knower, the object of knowledge, and the act of knowing."

It must be borne in mind always that the psychological

6. W. Y. Evans-Wentz, *Tibetan Yoga and Secret Doctrines*, bk. 1, "The Supreme Path of Discipleship," p. 85.

development we are discussing does not pertain to the individual's conscious personality nor to his outer mask or persona. A man may have acquired exemplary manners, his behaviour may be courteous and correct, he may be highly educated and have all the appearances of culture, but his instinctive and natural reactions, could they be seen when he is alone, might reveal him as a very different person. Or in times of stress, physical or mental, he might astonish his friends and even himself by the undisciplined and primitive reactions that suddenly usurp the attitudes of the well-drilled persona. Such reactions do not come from the conscious part of the psyche; they arise from the nonpersonal part and reveal not the conscious character but the stage of development that the nonpersonal psyche has reached. A man's instinctive reactions, being ectopsychic in origin, are largely beyond the control of his conscious ego; their nature and character will be determined not by his conscious manners and opinions nor even by his moral convictions, but by the extent to which the instincts themselves have undergone psychic modification in him—a process depending in the first place, as noted above, on the functioning of the instinct (or urge) to reflect.

The gradual change in form of these instinctive drives reveals itself also in the evolution of religions, for the compelling and all-powerful factors of the unconscious are personified in the divine figures of the various beliefs. Man, as has been most aptly said, makes God in his own image—in the image not of his conscious self but of that objective psychological factor which rules supreme in the unconscious part of the psyche. The gradual transformation that has taken place in the religions of the world runs parallel with the slow transformation of the nonpersonal and instinctive part of man's psyche. In the earliest days the gods were conceived of as entirely external to man. They lived a life of their own in some spirit world, and the purpose of ritual was to build a bridge between mankind and these powerful and unpredictable overlords, who had to be propitiated to the end that they would grant food and protection from enemies and bestow fertility on man and beast. This signifies that the gods represented the power of nature—nature outside of man and also the instinctive nature within man.

Before he had learned to control his natural inertia and unpredictable impulses, man felt himself entirely dependent on the whim of the gods for obtaining the necessities of life. But as his psyche gradually emerged from its instinctive bondage and his power to control both himself and his environment grew greater, his religion also changed, passing through the stage in which the divine power was conceived of as a personal God concerned with the welfare of his worshippers but hating the heathen who did not serve him. This theological concept corresponds to the ego stage of psychological development. In all the more evolved religions, the central teaching has advanced beyond this stage and is concerned with the experience of a God within the psyche. Usually, however, it is reserved for the initiated, who have been prepared by special instruction and discipline, to experience revelations of this God personally. These come to the initiated as a subjective experience; they are realized as being such and are understood as emanating not from a God in the heavens but from a God within. They correspond to the objective part of the unconscious psyche. The exoteric teaching that postulates a God without, a denizen of heaven who looks down on his children from his celestial abode, caring for the bodily needs of man —and from whom "all good things do come," including spiritual thoughts, the blessing of divine grace, and redemption from sin—is usually considered more appropriate for the uninitiated worshipper.

The subjective experience of the esoteric aspect of the more highly evolved religions is expressed in varying terms. In Christianity it is the experience of Christ dwelling in the heart, to the end that "not I may live, but Christ may live in me." Throughout the centuries, Christian mystics have left records of their authentic experiences of finding this "other" within their own hearts. Sometimes the presence is called Christ, sometimes simply God. It is thought of as something other than the soul in which it comes to dwell. The initiations of the antique mystery cults sought to produce a somewhat similar experience, but here the initiate felt that he himself actually became a god and indeed was hailed as such in the ritual. In Egypt in much the same way the Pharaoh became Osiris. The thought here is that the individual is transformed into God. In the Oriental religions, the discipline is directed to producing a realization of the inner God, for the Atman is believed to have been always within, the very essence of the human being, though veiled from the consciousness of the uninitiated, so that all that is needed is to reveal him by overcoming the mists of avidya, or unknowing.

These formulations are attempts to express psychological experiences whose reality cannot be denied, even though the terms in which they are couched are foreign to the psychologist. The experiences are real [7] and must be approached with the open mind of the scientist. The dogmatic representations used to define the experiences obviously cannot be taken as objective facts but must rather be regarded as subjective expressions of inner experience.

The psychologist must ask himself in all seriousness what the nature of these experiences is. Evidently they refer to an encounter with an absolute and nonpersonal determinant within the psyche that acts with all the power and incontrovertibility of an instinct, but that is an expression of a psychic, not of a biological imperative. This factor is not connected with consciousness; it is not under the control of the conscious ego, but acts as an other within the psyche. It has always seemed to man to be a numinous phenomenon, having all the attributes of a *tremendum*. For the most part psychologists have ignored experiences of this type, on the ground that religion does not come within the field of science. It is to Jung's work that we owe whatever understanding we have of this nonpersonal factor within the psyche, which so evidently exerts a powerful influence on man's destiny.

It has been tacitly assumed in the Occident that the individual is born with either crude instincts or refined ones. He is either naturally a boor or innately a gentleman, and his con-

---

7. Jung, "Psychology and Religion," in *Psychology and Religion: West and East* (C.W. 11), p. 12.

dition is assumed to be unalterable. As the popular saying has it, "You cannot make a velvet purse of a sow's ear." A barbarian at heart will always remain barbaric, no matter how much he is trained in the traditions of gentle behaviour.

In the East, however, it is believed to be possible to achieve a transformation of these basic elements in the human being through a special training and discipline. The various forms of yoga [8] impose a physical and psychological discipline the aim of which is "to cool the fires of desire" or "to eat the world." This might be translated into psychological language as "to bring to pass a transformation of the instincts." It has not been adequately realized by Western psychology that such a radical change can take place; therefore this aspect of human development has been neglected by psychologists and pedagogues alike.

The hypothesis that such a transformation may occur was first put forward by modern depth psychologists in attempting to explain certain phenomena observed empirically in the course of analysis of the unconscious. It is now recognized that transformation is essential if the analysis is to meet with fundamental success. It is not easy, however, to present the evidence in a convincing way, because the change that takes place is so largely a subjective matter, a change in the inner reactions and impulses that arise spontaneously and constitute the background of an individual's experience of life.

The change is usually initiated by a frustration of the individual's instinctive desires, an impasse that throws him back on himself and stimulates the impulse to reflection. He reflects on his experience and so discovers the opposing elements in the situation. This leads to conflict, and in the effort to resolve the conflict, further reflection is demanded. By this process the subject's psychic energy, his libido, is turned inward upon himself and begins to exercise its creative function within him.

Individuals in whom the urge to reflect is weak are often

---

8. The yoga here referred to is of course not the popular variety displayed by the fakir and wonder-worker of the bazaars. It is the teaching practised secretly by the holy men who seek release from the bondage of desirousness through years of religious discipline. Cf. Evans-Wentz, *Tibetan Yoga and Secret Doctrines*, p. 26.

content to go through life bounded completely by the limitations of the auto-erotic stage of development. For them the satisfactions of the body suffice; if these fail, they spend their energy in complaining of their ill luck and find a perverted satisfaction in self-pity. For them the pleasure-pain principle is the criterion of right and wrong, good and bad, and by it they order their lives. Others, for whom these satisfactions have proved insufficient, or who have found it impossible invariably to choose pleasure and have therefore come into collision with unwanted pain, have found the way of ego development, which has provided an acceptable escape from the dilemma. They have disciplined the autos and discovered a new kind of satisfaction in ambition, prestige, or power; these motivations may remain on the egotistic level, or may be mobilized in the service of a highly refined idealism. This level of being accounts for perhaps the largest group of men and women in Western civilization, and very many live and die on this plane. They have learned the laws of cause and effect but have not yet realized the workings of the law of opposites within and without themselves.

But on this stage too the satisfactions may not suffice to bring happiness. The individual may discover the workings of the opposites, finding that there is no gain without a corresponding loss, that every good is balanced by an evil, or the gains themselves may pall. His capacity to pursue his aims may wane through illness or increasing age, or long-cherished hopes and ambitions may fail. And conflicts may arise within him, owing to an inner dissatisfaction—perhaps on account of a moral scruple or an unsatisfied hunger, a yearning for he knows not what—leading once more to the necessity for reflection, which is the beginning of consciousness.

For consciousness of a new stage of development is always presaged by a sense of lack. Euclid defines a point as that which has position but no length. What does consciousness limited to a point know about length? From the vantage of a point, length does not exist; it is an unknowable dimension, and the point cannot even assert that length is or is not, unless within itself there exists the latent possibility of length—an emptiness, a *bindu* point, as the Hindus would call it, that can be compensated only by something beyond its knowledge and yet dimly adumbrated within itself. It is just such a dim precursor of a higher stage of awareness that so often makes an individual dissatisfied with the good fortune he has sought wholeheartedly—or at least he has thought himself to be so doing—and creates within him that conflict which will be the turning point in his life.

Once such a conflict arises, it is likely to grow, gathering into itself a larger and larger proportion of the life energy, till it may come to occupy the major place in consciousness. No aspect of the life is free from involvement in such a conflict. Wherever the individual turns he is confronted by its antinomies, and no amount of compromise, no attempt at repression, no effort of the will suffices to release him from its impasse. This is the crucial moment, for if he can face the conflict squarely, holding both sides of it in consciousness, the reconciling symbol may arise from the depths of the unconscious and point to the hidden and unexpected way that can lead him out of his prison. This theme is a constant one in legend and myth: in the moment of the hero's final despair, the unexpected solution is brought to him by a tiny clue, a stunted or despised animal, a dwarf or a child, showing him the secret path out of his dilemma, which he himself has overlooked.

Similarly, to the ordinary man of today, caught in an inescapable problem, the solution may come perhaps through a dream or phantasy that he would usually disregard; or some small object that he finds in his path, some slight incident of no apparent importance attracting his attention, may, by the magic of the unconscious, reveal to him the one possible way out of his difficulty. Such a thing becomes for him a symbol. For it is not its obvious meaning or value that has power to release him; it is rather that this insignificant thing by some subtle suggestion releases the creative power in the unconscious whereby the opposites within him can be reconciled. Thus it becomes for him the reconciling symbol that arises from the unconscious to show the way whenever a serious conflict is faced unflinchingly.

The value of such a symbol is by no means always recognized by the layman, for its meaning is usually hidden. The ancients under similar circumstances would have consulted a seer or questioned a wise man as to its meaning. The modern way is to consult an analyst [9] when an insoluble problem brings the life to a halt. If Jung's method is used in the analysis, the change initiated by the conflict proceeds under the guidance of the individual's own unconscious. The analyst does not assume that he knows the answer to the problem but sets out with his patient to explore the unconscious and seek the solution. He is necessary to the proceeding because he has a technique for interpreting the obscure unconscious material thrown up in the dreams and phantasies; also, he is needed as a fixed point to which the patient can cling during the transition, when all values are under question and all landmarks may disappear.

The instruction given to the patient is that he become aware of what is happening in his own psyche and order his life in accordance with the truth as he finds it. The analyst makes no attempt to draw up a program similar to a course of study in college, for he himself does not know by what steps the process will unfold, nor in exactly what way the solution of the individual's life problem will emerge. The process of individuation is unique in each person and cannot be foreseen or prescribed.

In one respect, however, it does resemble a college course, for the process demands time and attention that must be withdrawn from other aspects of life in themselves wholesome and desirable, and devoted to the inner culture of the individual. To an onlooker, if he does not understand the goal and is unaware of any similar need for inner development in himself, the absorption of one following this road may seem selfish and

9. A psychoanalyst or analytical psychologist is one who practises that science of the human psyche which takes cognizance of the unconscious and explores its contents, seeking to relate them to the conscious personality.

morbid. The desire for this kind of inner experience and self-development arises from a psychic urge, a spiritual hunger—akin to the need of satisfying the hunger of the body—that is present in very different degrees in different persons. It is an expression of the instinctive drive to self-preservation on a psychic, not a biological level. Those in whom it has been aroused are compelled to strive for the satisfaction of its demands or endure the pangs of spiritual hunger and eventual starvation.

Those who do not seek release from the bondage of the instinctive drives by the road of inner development remain the slaves of their own passionate desirousness or suffer the sterility resulting from its ruthless repression. In any time of crisis these persons have no power to curb their own barbaric reactions; for though we can pass on our scientific knowledge to our children, we cannot save them from the pain and suffering caused by not-knowing in the psychological sphere.

It is recorded that Buddha was much concerned with just this problem. When, before his final enlightenment, he was meditating under the Bo Tree, he asked himself: Why are there these endlessly repeated lives? Why do people, and animals as well, go on with the senseless round of birth and suffering and death? Why does life continue exactly the same—why do men not outgrow this barbaric and immature stage? What is the cause of things? His meditation grew deeper and deeper, until at last he had a vision that revealed the answer. He saw the wheel of life, consisting of the endless round of existences, of births and deaths and rebirths, of heavens and hells, and of the earth with its many faces. In the centre were three animals, whose constant circling kept the whole wheel revolving: these were a pig, a snake, and a dove,[10] representing selfishness, anger, and lust, or, in the terms of the present discussion, greed, ego power, and sexuality.

The revelation that came to Buddha through his vision was

10. The dove as the symbol of erotic love is the constant companion of Astarte and Aphrodite, goddesses of sexual love. In later representations of the wheel, the dove is replaced by a cock as a more fitting symbol for lust.

that it is these instinct forces that motivate the endless cycle of life. So long as man seeks after the satisfaction of these, so long will mankind be bound on the wheel. These instinct powers are more ancient than the psyche of man, being rooted in the very substance and nature of the living organism, in the essence, the spirit, the life of protoplasm itself. For this reason they dominate the functioning of all living creatures, who repeat endlessly the senseless round.

In animals the instincts rule unchecked, but with the gradual awakening of consciousness man developed a psychic counterpart to the instincts. The animal acts, not knowing that he acts; man not only acts, he knows that he acts and, in addition, he retains a memory of his past actions. And even beyond this, he has developed a certain degree of free will that enables him to choose, at least to some extent, *how* he shall act. So in man a new power has arisen, the capacity to know and to understand—consciousness—that has acquired sufficient strength to set itself over against the compulsion of instinct. The coming of consciousness enabled man to create a new relation to the life spirit within him.

It is this step that marks the transition from the complete self-centredness of the autos to the beginnings of ego-consciousness. Or as the Buddhists say: the "man of little intellect" develops to the stage of the "man of ordinary intellect." The "man of little intellect" needs to learn the law of cause and effect, that is, he must observe what happens when he follows his instinctive desires unthinkingly; the one "of ordinary intellect" discovers the law of the opposites. For him the instinct drives and the psychic images—the archetypes—related to them, manifest themselves in opposites. In the following chapters we will consider these instinctual urges in their dual form, their complementary opposition. First, inertia, that manifests itself in sloth and restlessness, corresponding to the first law of Newton dealing with the inertia of physical objects; second, hunger experienced in both want and greed; third, self-defence, that produces enmity and also friendship; and, lastly, reproduction, that gives rise to both lust and love in its sexual phase, and that may be either nourishing or devouring, life-giving or death-dealing in its maternal phase.

In the later chapters we will consider the possibility of developing from this stage to that of the "man of superior intellect," who has found a way to reconcile the opposites and so has achieved consciousness of the Self.

3

Inertia

SLOTH AND RESTLESSNESS

A SYMPATHETIC Yankee once asked a Southern Negro working in a cotton field: "Sam, don't you get tired working all day in the sun?"

"No sir," replied Sam, "I don't get tired; I goes to sleep first."

In South America there are primitives who are incapable of performing even a small task unless they have what is called *gana* for it. If a boy who has been ordered to do something replies that he has no *gana*, he is exonerated until his *gana* returns. These instances are conspicuous because of the contrast between the primitives and their more civilized neighbours. But a similar condition of subservience to instinct prevails in all primitive communities. Hunting, sowing, war, all have to be prepared for by rituals—dances or magic ceremonials designed to stir up the slumbering energies of men who cannot of their own free will do what is necessary.

This seems very strange to us; for one of the chief characteristics differentiating civilized man from his more primitive brothers, and indeed from his own more primitive ancestors, is the fact that within certain limits he can do what he wants to do. He can even do things he does not want to do, if he knows that it is wise or expedient to do them. For example, he can get up in the morning despite his almost overwhelming desire to take another nap, or he can apply himself to work

37

when he would like to go fishing. In other words, some of his energy, his libido, is no longer completely at the mercy of his unconscious impulses and natural desires, but is instead at the disposal of his conscious ego. He has achieved a certain freedom from the compulsiveness of his own innate impulses, a freedom that it has taken mankind thousands of years to acquire, and that has to be won again by every individual member of the race today. This power is without question one of man's greatest and most costly attainments. In acquiring it he has gained his first taste of freedom; for now he can do what he himself wants to do, instead of being the slave of the uncontrollable forces of instinct within him. Of first importance is his new-found ability to work and create what he deems to be desirable, even though the unregenerate man in him wants to dream away the hours.

But this freedom is in fact only a partial freedom. For while most people have almost unlimited desire and energy available for following their spontaneous impulses, the amount they are able to summon to fulfill the dictates of the conscious ego is always limited—usually very limited indeed. For example, an individual sets himself a task that ordinarily would not seem too hard. But if it runs counter to his instinctive wishes, it may prove to be impossibly hard. The very idea of the task may become repugnant to him, and no sooner does he set about it than he is assailed by an intolerable heaviness and inertia. Only by the greatest effort can he keep his eyelids from closing, while mentally he is engulfed in a dark and heavy mood that weights his thoughts and chokes his desires. This is the old enemy of mankind, inertia, evidence of lack of psychological energy. The requisite energy has either never emerged from the hidden depths of the psyche, where it has its source, or else has fallen back again into those same depths. In either case it is not available for life. The light of awareness has been extinguished temporarily or has never been kindled and the psyche remains dark and heavy. For sloth is equivalent to unawareness, unconsciousness, stupidity.

The individual who is suffering from this condition may not be actually unconscious in the ordinary meaning of the word; he is not asleep, and he is probably more or less aware of what is going on around him. But nothing really penetrates his consciousness, and he remains dull and totally unaware of the *significance* of what is passing. He is unwilling or unable to arouse himself to undertake the task at hand or to feel adequate interest in it. His state is like a half waking, a half dreaming. He is sunk in his inert mood as in a swamp, and to rouse him we instinctively call on him to "wake up," as if he were asleep.

Because this condition of inertia runs counter to the cultural effort of mankind and is a regression, a pullback to a more primitive psychological condition, it has been combated by all the forces, social and religious, that seek to raise the psychological level of man. The Christian church with its moralistic attitude reckons sloth among the deadly sins. The Chinese describe it as the dark, heavy earth spirit that clings to the fleshly heart and reigns supreme whenever a man sleeps; for then the bright spirit that gives him lightness and joy sleeps in his liver and must be aroused by discipline and the work of religious meditation if he is to become free.[1]

Buddhists, with their more detached attitude, speak not of the sin of sloth but rather of avidya—unknowing, unconsciousness, or stupidity; they teach that man is held in bondage to the instincts only because he does not understand, does not realize the true meaning of things. When he has attained to insight, become conscious of the inevitable law of cause and effect, when the higher consciousness of the Atman, or Self, has been released in him, he will no longer be subject to the heavy earth-bound impulses that prevent his rising as a free individual. To achieve this he needs to extinguish or "cool" the three fires of desire—lust, anger, and stupidity. Thus he will evolve out of the torpid state of passive obedience to his unconscious instincts and become a "conqueror of existence." [2]

Even the laziest man is roused to action when he really understands that the consequences of inertia will be painful

---

1. R. Wilhelm and C. G. Jung, *The Secret of the Golden Flower: A Chinese Book of Life*, p. 114. This book is an interpretative rendering of an esoteric Taoist text dating probably from the eighth century.
2. Evans-Wentz, *Tibetan Yoga and Secret Doctrines*, p. 8.

or disastrous. A soldier exhausted beyond endurance can yet take immediate action for his own safety at the sound of approaching enemy aircraft. Dog-tired but disciplined troops will stagger into line at the command to fall in, summoning from some unknown source within them the power to go on, even though they are not personally endangered. Their obedience shows that they have achieved a considerable degree of disidentification from their natural desires. To this extent they are released from the compulsion of the instincts and enabled to bear themselves with the dignity of free human beings.

In his struggles against sloth, an individual—I refer now to the everyday problems of the everyday person—is very apt to get caught in a moralistic attitude. His heritage from puritan ancestors, who regarded sloth as a sin, makes him feel inferior and "in the wrong" when he succumbs to its lure; yet because the cause of his inertia lies hidden below the threshold of consciousness, he cannot combat it successfully without a deeper understanding. His moralistic reaction actually plays into the hands of the enemy, for nothing saps a man's energy faster than a vague and unfocused feeling of guilt. Or perhaps, being in revolt against the puritanism of his fathers, he condones his laziness as a natural and harmless indulgence, flattering himself that he can throw it off at will when the time comes. But for many persons this time never comes, or, when the need for conscious and continued effort does arise, they find themselves unable to meet life's demand, for they have not developed the necessary moral fibre.

Sloth is indeed a deadly sin if we regard the question of bondage and freedom as a moral problem, perhaps even as *the* moral problem of mankind. But to regard sloth as a problem of inner freedom is very different from taking the moralizing attitude—one "ought not" to be slothful—as if that were the end of the matter. For laziness is not overcome by a pious hope of virtue, nor is it exorcised by a statement that it ought not to be. Recognition of the shortcoming will result in the state of hopelessness and depression described above, or it will lead to an attempt to release oneself from the lower and more unconscious, instinctive side of the psyche, which is amoral—

perhaps premoral is the better term—by identifying oneself with the upper or moral side of the personality, in a futile attempt to pull oneself up by one's bootstraps. Such an attitude usually leads to a compulsive and useless activity that is the opposite of sloth, though just as unfree; or it produces a paralysing sense of guilt and inferiority that results in an inactivity not far removed from the original condition.

This is obviously the wrong way of attacking the problem, for sloth is a manifestation of a primary and primitive inertia based on an archaic attitude—a reaction appropriate to the conditions of life that prevailed on the earth in remote times. Crocodiles and other cold-blooded creatures that have not evolved much beyond the state of their remote saurian ancestors dream their lives away, lying by the hour utterly inert, seeming no more alive than the logs of wood they simulate. Even in warm-blooded animals sleep reigns over an amazingly large proportion of the twenty-four hours. Inactivity further plays an important part in self-protection in some of those animals which, like the rabbit, are not endowed with fighting weapons. When threatened they "play dead"; that is to say, their physiological reaction to danger consists in temporary paralysis—an apparent cessation of life producing a purposive though involuntary inactivity. Such reactions are adapted to the conditions these creatures have to meet, and have been developed to further life's ends.

The instinctive impulse to react in a similar way may arise in human beings, but quiescence in face of difficulties is no longer appropriate for man. An unconscious and instinctive reaction does not necessarily accord with the requirements for survival of either the individual or the race. The development of ego consciousness and the attainment of will power have brought to civilized man other means for meeting the problems of his life. The ancient tendency to passivity and inertia has become a danger that man must overcome, since otherwise he perishes.

THERE IS, however, another aspect of this problem that must not be overlooked. The attitude of passivity underlying sloth has a positive side and under certain circumstances may even be lifesaving. And beyond this it can have another value, for through it the individual may be brought in touch with the vegetative processes on which ultimately all life depends, and from which we tend to become separated through identification with the ego and its conscious aims. On the physical plane the necessity of relaxing in order to replenish the body's powers is well recognized. But because our emancipation from psychological sloth is more recent and incomplete, and therefore more precarious than the corresponding achievement in regard to physical inertia, it is not so generally recognized that a similar process may be necessary for the psyche. The bodily resources and reserves are replenished in sleep night by night, though the conscious life and all willed effort have been laid aside. In convalescence, too, the lassitude that takes possession of the field of consciousness is not only the result of the illness, which has depleted the reserves of vital energy, but also nature's beneficent gift for cure. The convalescent's reluctance to undertake any sort of exertion—a mood about which he may bitterly complain—acts as a curb on the impulses to activity arising either in response to outer demands or from an inner moral reaction to his apparent laziness. Here the natural instinct is really to be trusted, rather than the conscious opinion of the patient, for this is nature's way of safeguarding the organism against too great strain before it has had time to recuperate fully.

In the long history of the race, illness and convalescence have been experienced many hundreds of times, and the instinctive reaction is based on the unconscious wisdom thus acquired. But the individual himself may have had no previous experience of the particular illness he has suffered, and so misinterprets his own feelings. He tries to substitute book knowledge or personal opinion for the instinctive counsel of his own body, not realizing that the lassitude, arising as an expression of the completely unconscious life wisdom of the organism, is disregarded only at the peril of doing damage to it. This is a positive aspect of "laziness" that has a helpful, health-giving effect. But should an individual be faced at such a moment with a task actually essential to life, he will obviously be hampered by this instinctive reaction. Not only will he have to struggle against his physical handicap; he will also be weighed down by his lassitude. If he fights successfully against it he may be able to force himself to accomplish the task without feeling any immediate ill effects. But it is quite possible that he will unknowingly overstep the bounds of his physical endurance, and so will have to suffer for his disregard of his own instinct in a prolonged or possibly incomplete convalescence.

Thus man's ability to disregard nature's warning is at once a valuable achievement and a danger. If for instance in a crisis one is inhibited from putting out one's last ounce of strength, one may fall a helpless victim to fate; but if one continues to disregard the warnings of nature and obeys only the dictates of will, one may unwittingly drive oneself to death. It is said that it is impossible to drive a mule to death. If he has reached a certain point of fatigue, he will lie down and take any amount of beating, but he will not go on. On the other hand, a horse, an animal of far greater intelligence and development than the mule, can be overdriven. At the insistence of his rider he may go on until he drops in his tracks, perhaps even to die in harness. This we feel to be evidence of a higher development in the horse; but we must also recognize that the stubborn obedience of the mule to nature's warning has its value. The mule clings to life with true devotion, and like the man who fights and runs away, he lives to fight another day.

Among human beings it is not only in illness that inertia plays a protective role. In pregnancy, too, it is strikingly evident. The pregnant woman usually sinks into an overwhelming and placid inertia. Her psychological state resembles that of a cow or other ruminant animal. This attitude is usually felt to be not immoral or unwholesome, but rather peaceful and beneficent, a mood almost of beatitude. Meanwhile the unseen process of creation goes on within, totally cut off from any active or conscious cooperation or control. On the psychological plane a similar inertia frequently precedes creative activity; this state of mind is also called ruminating, as though the process maturing below the threshold of consciousness were indeed like that in the cow chewing her cud twice over.

The sloth or inertia experienced in conditions like these protects the vital activities from the intervention of the conscious ego at times when they are concerned with the all-important function of recuperation and the creation of physiological and psychological "children." While the hidden life forces are performing their mysterious work of transformation, the rational and willed attitude of the conscious ego can only interfere. It can neither assist nor guide. The libido [3] is withdrawn from it, and it is left high and dry. When this happens one can do nothing but await the re-emergence of the psychic energy, alert to profit by the creative work in which it has been taking part. In his "Study in the Process of Individuation" (first version), Jung writes:

What is essential to us can only grow out of ourselves. When the white man is true to his instincts, he reacts defensively against any advice that one might give him. . . .

This being so, it is the part of wisdom not to tell the white man anything or give him any advice. The best cannot be told, anyhow, and the second best does not strike home. One must be able to *let things happen.* I have learned from the East what it means by the phrase "Wu-wei": namely, not-doing, letting be, which is quite different from doing nothing. Some Occidentals, also, have known what this not-doing means; for instance, Meister Eckhart, who speaks of "sich lassen," to let oneself be. The region of darkness into which one falls is not empty; it is the "lavishing mother" of Lao-tse, the "images" and the "seed." When the surface has been cleared, things can grow out of the depths. People always suppose that they have lost their way when they come up against these depths of experience. But if they do not know how to go on, the only answer, the only advice, that makes any sense is "to wait for what the unconscious has to say about the situation." A way is only *the* way when one finds it and follows it oneself. [4]

This is the positive aspect of inertia, nondoing, *wu-wei.*

3. Following the practice of Jung, I use the term *libido* for all forms of psychological energy, manifested as interest or desire. I do not limit it to specifically sexual interest, as is more commonly done by the followers of Freud.

4. *The Integration of the Personality,* chap. ii, p. 31.

HOWEVER, while giving full weight to this helpful and constructive aspect of inertia, it is well to be on guard against its negative, slothful, and regressive aspects. For man is no longer just a child of nature. He has so well obeyed the command to increase and multiply that Mother Nature can no longer supply all of mankind with sustenance by her own unaided activity. Man's utmost industry and initiative are needed, if he is not to perish from the earth.

When an individual is caught by sloth, he loses even the awareness that he is failing to act in accordance with the demands of life. The conflict between the opposing "wants"— the "I want to get on with my task" and the "I want to laze away the day"—is lost to mind, and he slips down into the abyss of nothingness. This state is obviously far more dangerous than the condition of conflict, painful and paralysing as the latter may be.

In *The Secret of the Golden Flower*, that text of Chinese yoga translated by Wilhelm and interpreted with such depth of understanding by Jung, it is said:

> Laziness of which a man is conscious and laziness of which he is unconscious, are a thousand miles apart. Unconscious laziness is real laziness; conscious laziness is not complete laziness, because there is still some clarity in it.[5]

But when the light of consciousness itself is dimmed, it is as if there were no one left within the I to maintain a discriminating insight into the situation. Part of the individual's consciousness has fallen into the depths, and he suffers from the condition the primitives call "loss of soul." Part of his soul, or one of his souls, has left him, and what remains may not be capable of realizing what has occurred, let alone of dealing effectively with it.

What, then, can be done to meet this problem? The inertia cannot be overcome simply by action, for sloth and restless activity are a pair of opposites that frequently alternate, without producing any improvement in the underlying situation. They are both expressions of purely unconscious and undi-

5. *The Secret of the Golden Flower*, p. 47.

rected functioning belonging to the same level of psychological development. This fact is amusingly expressed in Kipling's description of the Bandar-log, the monkey people, who were always running about in great activity with intent to do something of great importance that they entirely forgot as soon as some trivial object distracted their attention. Nothing was ever accomplished, and things went on for the tribe exactly as they had gone on since the creation.

The means developed by primitive peoples to overcome the natural apathy and laziness of the individual, such as initiations, dancing, and other rituals, all have the effect of replacing the personal consciousness with a tribal or group consciousness. Through identification with the group, and through the concerted effort of all, energy otherwise inaccessible can be channelled into life. This is a technique employed almost instinctively even today whenever a difficult task must be performed. Military marches, the sailor's "heave ho" and his characteristic chanties, serve to weld individuals together into a cohesive whole. Even in more sophisticated groups it is still recognized that a concerted effort will produce a result far in excess of the sum of separate, individual contributions. Why else do we have drives or campaigns for fostering most social enterprises, whether it be the selling of war bonds, the election of a president, or the inculcation of courtesy among elevator operators?

Identification with the group is a very powerful motive, a key that can undoubtedly unlock and release imprisoned energy. The forces released, however, may be as destructive in one case as they are valuable in another. In the instances just cited, the identification is brought about for a particular purpose and is usually self-limited; in other instances, however, the identification springs from a deeper and more unconscious level. Then the outcome is quite unpredictable: a crowd may become a mob, or a group intent on self-improvement may develop into a world-shaking secret society.

In each of these cases the effect produced comes not from the conscious will of any one participant in the movement. Although one person may be selected as the leader, he, no less than his followers, is actually the pawn of the unconscious forces that have been let loose and usually their first victim. If he then becomes the prophet of the daemon that has been aroused out of the depths of the collective psyche, he will have to direct his magic upon himself before he can work magic upon the crowd. For example, a spellbinding orator always has to go through a warming-up process before he can arouse his audience so that they too will be gripped by those forces to which he has for the time being voluntarily relinquished himself. This is true of the leader of a religious revival just as much as of a Hitler. When people succumb to such a spell, the onlookers may be aware of this mechanism. If we regard the effect as beneficial, we say that they were "lifted out of themselves"; if the outcome is devilish instead of godly, we say that they were "possessed" or "beside themselves." In either case, while the influence of the daemon prevails, the individuals affected are no longer self-possessed and responsible persons. They are swayed by strange impulses, and may be capable of remarkable acts of self-devotion and heroism as far above their ordinary capacities in one case as they are beneath these in another. Such unthinkable atrocities as lynchings, witch burnings, or Jew baitings may actually be perpetrated by men and women who, when not inflamed by mob passion, are possessed of average kindliness and humanity.

Thus, while group action is certainly effective in releasing the dormant energies of the unconscious, it is always a matter of doubt whether this release will be beneficial or destructive. The man caught in such an identification loses his capacity to make an individual judgment; he relinquishes his autonomy and vests it for the time being in the group. Thus he is no longer in any real sense an individual. He is only a member of a group, identical in all respects with the other members: what they do he does, what they feel he feels, what they think he thinks, what they ignore he too ignores. The group has become the unit, the individual, and we ascribe to it powers and capacities that rightfully belong only to human beings. We say for instance that "the group says," "the group feels," "the group thinks." But these are all psychological activities that actually pertain only to individual human beings. They cannot be carried on by a group, for the group has no tongue, no heart, no brain. In such cases it is the unconscious that speaks, feels, and thinks; for the unconscious is common to all the members of the group and affects them each and all.

Where men and women meet and consciously take counsel together, coming to a decision in all soberness, the intoxication of group identity is avoided. The situation lacks the enthusiasm but it also avoids the excesses inevitably accompanying the regression from individual control to that type of group identification which Lévy-Bruhl called *participation mystique*. But capacity to do this implies a degree of personal discipline that is attained only with difficulty. Social and religious practices designed to arouse the collective energies of the unconscious, then to control them for useful ends, have usually been applied to the group as a whole. The individuals remain little more than automatons whose personal acts are governed by the taboos and sanctions of the community. For identification with the group has power to release man's latent energies and also to discipline them. But it is far more difficult for the individual man, alone and unsupported, to acquire self-mastery and freedom from the dominance of his instinctual impulses.

HINDU yogic training is concerned with this problem. The first skill that must be acquired by the neophyte is the ability to control his chit—those thoughts which flit hither and yon and are often compared to the movements of a fly or a mosquito. His thoughts must be caught and his mind brought under control, so that it will become, as they say, one-pointed. This is the first step towards overcoming avidya. In Chinese yoga, too, distraction is considered the first great stumbling block in the path of the pupil. For it is not activity but capacity for concentration that is the cure both of sloth and of restlessness. An imbecile may be inert and slothful, or he may be constantly restless, displaying a purposeless and meaningless activity. And indeed any individual—whether of the active or of the inert type—in whom no power of concentration has been developed and no inner light or self-understanding insight has been kindled, is under grave suspicion of psychological inferiority, if not of actual imbecility. For the capacity to direct and apply psychic energy is one of the most important achievements of culture, and its absence is the mark of a low level of psychological development.

Primitives have a very short attention span for anything requiring mental effort, though their capacity is much greater in regard to matters directly pertaining to their tribal culture. Half an hour's talk with an educated man, even on everyday matters, exhausts them. The attention span in civilized man has lengthened very markedly, and much of his education is directed towards further increasing it. In a young child it is as short as in the primitive, but it lengthens as the child develops; in fact, its duration is one of the criteria by which psychological development is judged.

If after his natural span has been exhausted, further attention is demanded of an individual, he becomes either restless or drowsy. A well-disciplined person may be able to overcome his boredom and fatigue sufficiently to persist in his task for a considerable time, but eventually he will relax the tension he has maintained with effort and will relapse into torpor or give way to restlessness. Or, shaking off the sense of obligation to continue the uncongenial task, he may turn with a new access of energy to a different occupation more to his taste, to find his sleepiness and fatigue disappearing as if by magic.

An illustration of this almost miraculous change can be seen on any warm afternoon in an old-fashioned schoolroom, where some of the children may be almost asleep, others fidgeting or playing with their pencils. Suddenly the bell rings. The drowsiness and restlessness vanish. All becomes purposive activity, and at a sign from the teacher the pupils stream out into the playground, full of energy and enthusiasm.

These children are not lazy: they are bored. The kind of sloth they suffer from is only a reaction to the requirement of performing an uncongenial task. There is another and far more serious kind of sloth, which persists no matter what stimulus to activity or what lure to the libido is applied, and in which no moral conviction is sufficient to arouse the individual to

PSYCHIC ENERGY: ITS SOURCE

purposive activity. This type might well be called pathological inertia. The ineffectiveness of the stimulus may be due to its inherent weakness or to a failure of the inner psychic mechanism, which does not appraise the situation rightly. If the individual fails to understand, or lacks insight, he cannot master his forces and attack the situation. His need is to realize—to make real—the situation that is challenging him. As Robert Louis Stevenson expressed it in "The Celestial Surgeon":

> Books and my food and summer rain
> Have knocked on my sullen heart in vain.

The capacity for the enjoyment of beauty and the things of the spirit has disappeared, and the individual has fallen into a dark mood of depression from which only the most drastic experience can rouse him. Stevenson indeed at the end of the poem prays for such a painful experience, lest his spirit be permanently lost in the final extinction of death:

> Lord, thy most pointed pleasure take,
> And stab my spirit broad awake.
> Or, Lord, if too obdurate I,
> Choose Thou, before that spirit die,
> A piercing pain, a killing sin,
> And to my dead heart run them in! [6]

Particular attention should be paid to the complaint here that even the desire for food has disappeared, since hunger is perhaps the sharpest goad that nature has for urging man to overcome his natural inertia.

Possibly Stevenson's lines describe one who was young and in love. In that case his indifference to food and spiritual joys is understandable, since sex is the second most potent stimulus knocking at the door of inertia. If the young man had been disappointed in love, if his eager outgoing libido had met with an overwhelming frustration, it would have been not unnatural that he should fall into depression. But there are other individuals, in whom the outgoing libido has not met with any rebuff, who nevertheless show a constant state of lethargy and depression. In these cases the life urge itself seems to be de-

6. R. L. Stevenson, *Poems*, p. 115.

ficient, or apparently it is frustrated within the psyche and turned back on itself. These individuals cannot take any adequate part in life. There are others in whom the libido seems to be dragged down into the unconscious, swallowed by the "sucking mouth of emptiness," or lured away from the light of the upper world to pine, like Persephone, in the dark realms of Tartarus. But for many who have been thus enchanted, the outcome has been less favourable than in the case of the goddess of spring.

For these persons all suffer from varying degrees of psychological illness. In some, the spark of consciousness has never been kindled. In others, the libido has withdrawn from life only temporarily, as a result of physical illness or emotional frustration. Between these two extremes will be found many degrees of mental illness, conditions of *abaissement du niveau mental*, and moods of withdrawal or of depression. Sometimes these moods are fleeting, sometimes prolonged or recurrent. Most if not all individuals have suffered in this way from time to time. Surely everyone has experienced the dimming of the light that follows frustration, or suffered the depression that accompanies physical illness or emotional loss. Who has not struggled with, or succumbed to, the sloth that creeps upon one with its cold and heavy breath when one is faced with an uncongenial task? But in many individuals a comparable or even greater depression may arise spontaneously, without awareness on their part of any frustration or unhappiness that might account for it. In such cases the libido has fallen out of consciousness through a cleft leading directly down to the unplumbed depths of the unconscious.

For the individual psyche, as we have already seen, has emerged from darkness and still floats, as it were, on those vast waters of the unknown that Jung has called the collective unconscious. And if there is a defect in the psychic mechanism that should safeguard the conscious individual from complete immersion in the collective unconscious, and relate him to it in a meaningful way, the libido can very readily leak away and be lost. Throughout the ages, this problem of the relation of the individual to the collective unconscious has been the province of religion, for the psychic realm is the spirit realm. But since the rise of the exclusively rational and intellectual approach to life, this whole field of human experience has been almost completely excluded from conscious attention. It has not been considered a valid field for research or education. Consequently all problems connected with this side of life have been left almost completely to the unconscious. Until the advent of depth psychology, we trusted that a sane and reasonable relation to the outer world would suffice for mental health and that, for the rest, nature would take care of any difficulties that might arise. It is therefore not surprising that the psychological function guarding and regulating the individual's relation to the strange world of the collective unconscious should all too frequently prove inadequate for its task, and allow gaps through which the libido can fall into unfathomable psychic depths.

Because psychological energy has disappeared from view it has not therefore ceased to be; it is still existent, even though for the time being it is inaccessible to ego consciousness. For psychological energy is apparently subject to a law similar to the principle of the conservation of energy in physics.[7] A deficiency of available conscious energy is usually due to one of two conditions: either the quantum formerly at the disposal of consciousness has dropped away again into the unconscious, or energy has never been released from its source in adequate amount but has remained bound by an attractive power of the unconscious stronger than any that consciousness can set against it.

But as energy is indestructible, some other manifestation will necessarily arise to take the place of the lapsed activity. One of the most important contributions that modern depth psychology has made towards the understanding of life is this principle of equivalence, which postulates that when energy disappears from one psychological manifestation it will reappear in another of equivalent value. In many cases, as Jung

7. Jung has discussed the whole subject of the dynamics of psychological energy very fully in "On Psychic Energy," in *The Structure and Dynamics of the Psyche* (C.W. 8), pp. 3 ff.

points out, the equivalent value is not far to seek; in regard to others, he says:

There are frequent cases where a sum of libido disappears apparently without forming a substitute. In that case the substitute is unconscious, or, as usually happens, the patient is unaware that some new psychic fact is the corresponding substitute formation. But it may also happen that a considerable sum of libido disappears as though completely swallowed up by the unconscious, with no new value appearing in its stead. In such cases it is advisable to cling firmly to the principle of equivalence, for careful observation of the patient will soon reveal signs of unconscious activity, for instance an intensification of certain symptoms, or a new symptom, or peculiar dreams, or strange, fleeting fragments of fantasy, etc.[8] ′

Jung goes on to show how these phantasy or dream pictures gradually form themselves into a symbolic image that contains the energy lost from consciousness, together with an additional amount of energy whose attracting power was responsible for the original loss. If the previous condition of inertia has been due to inability to face an uncongenial but necessary task, or perhaps to failure to solve a problem presented by life, the symbol created in the unconscious by the regressive libido will prove to be the means for overcoming the obstacle. Such a symbol cannot be formed by conscious effort and purpose; on the other hand, the formation of a creative or redeeming symbol cannot

take place until the mind has dwelt long enough on the elementary facts, that is to say until the inner or outer necessities of the life-process have brought about a transformation of energy. If man lived altogether instinctively and automatically, the transformation could come about in accordance with purely biological laws. We can still see something of the sort in the psychic life of primitives, which is entirely concretistic and entirely symbolical at once. In civilized man the rationalism of consciousness, otherwise so useful to him, proves to be a most formidable obstacle to the frictionless transformation of energy. Reason, always seeking to avoid what to it is an unbearable antinomy, takes its stand exclusively on one

8. Ibid., pp. 19-20.

side or the other, and convulsively seeks to hold fast to the values it has once chosen.[9]

In the absence of conscious work and willed concentration of attention on the images arising from the depths, the unconscious activity will remain on the level of phantasy weaving or daydreaming, and the individual will be prevented by his slothful preoccupation with his phantasy from taking an adequate part in his own life. This observation gives us a clue to the way in which sloth, inertia, and depression must be attacked. In the ordinary, everyday situation, so long as the loss of libido is not very serious, a determined summoning of all available energy may be sufficient to make a beginning on the distasteful task, and it may turn out that, as the French proverb so aptly puts it, *ce n'est que le premier pas qui coûte*. Once begun, the enterprise may go on smoothly and efficiently, bringing interest and satisfaction in its train. These are situations in which the remedy ordinarily prescribed is to ignore the problem and to "snap out of it," or if this is not possible, to seek distraction or keep oneself occupied. These measures may succeed, though at the best they evade the real issue.

But in more serious cases a prescription of this sort simply does not work. Many a patient whose life spark has seemingly gone out has been sent by his physician to roam the world like a ghost, seeking he knows not what. Had he realized that the treasure he had lost was his own soul, now dropped into the depths within, he could have made his pilgrimage in that inner universe: there, following in the steps of the legendary heroes of the past, he could have undertaken the "night journey" in quest of the "rising sun," symbol of the renewal of libido.

When the light of life dims and one is left in the darkness of depression, it is much more effective to turn for the moment from the objective task and to concentrate attention on what is going forward within, instead of forcing oneself to continue by a compulsive effort of the will. For when the libido disappears from consciousness, will power can be used effectively only to overcome the natural reluctance to follow the lost

9. Ibid., p. 25.

energy into the hidden places of the psyche by means of creative introversion. The phantasy or dream images found there will surely give the clue to the difficulty, provided one has the technical ability necessary for understanding them. For this the layman usually needs the help of an analyst trained in the interpretation of symbols.

The unconscious images will bring to light the cause of the impasse. Perhaps the inertia will prove to be an effect of regressive longing, the secret desire for death and oblivion that is latent in every human being. At times this longing may gain so much energy that it outweighs the portion available for life and its tasks. Certain people are particularly liable to the inroads of this backward-looking factor. The life problem with which they must cope has been extensively dealt with by Baynes in his brilliant study, *Mythology of the Soul*,[10] in which he calls this regressive element the "renegade." It is this component of the psyche that always refuses to co-operate in the human effort to domesticate nature, within and without, and to create a more civilized life for mankind. The renegade tendency represents the eternal outlaw, the being who wants what he wants and refuses to pay the price, always seeking to exploit the industry of others. It incorporates greed in all its many forms—greed for food, lust for sexual satisfaction or power, the demand for ease and pleasure, regardless of the cost to someone else. It is the negative aspect of the instinctual urges that keep the world moving.

The renegade is the destructive aspect of the regressive libido. It bespeaks the attitude of the child, who expects to be cared for and nourished regardless of his own unwillingness to co-operate, and who uses his powers only to demand satisfaction, never to help in creating the means for that satisfaction —as though life were an indulgent mother whose only preoccupation is her concern for the well-being of this particular child. Such an attitude may be condoned in an actual child, but in an adult it is an infantility no longer to be indulged. In his case the "mother" is not a human being who can be

10. See pp. 4, 97 ff.

coaxed or coerced, but rather Mother Nature herself, whose ways are impartial, who has no heart susceptible to appeal. Such an adult will become increasingly asocial and tyrannically demanding, until he realizes the fallacy on which his attitude has unconsciously been based.

But the backward longing of the soul for the source of its being, for its beginnings, for the mother depths, may have a different significance and so a different outcome. When it is taken in a positive way, this longing may lead the soul to renewal and rebirth. Thus the image that arises from the unconscious in a time of depression may be that of the mother in either her beneficent or her destructive form. The form of the image will be directly conditioned by the conscious attitude and will of the dreamer. If he is childish, the mother image of his dream will be threatening, it will smother him with a suffocating kindness, or it will seem to lure him to destruction. If, however, he is sincerely seeking for a renewal that will enable him to overcome the obstruction confronting him, the image presented by the unconscious will be of that Great Mother who is the source of all, and from whose womb he may be reborn.

In other cases, the symbol produced by the dream or phantasy may take one of the many forms of the father image. The father is the one who has gone before us. He tackled life and its problems before we came to conscious awareness. Throughout childhood we have experienced over and over again that "father knows how." If care is not taken to foster the child's initiative and natural creativeness, his spirit may well be crushed by being constantly forestalled. This is one of the most serious effects of the impact of civilization on primitives. When the Western man arrives, with all his mechanical devices and technical skill, it seems to the primitive no longer worth while to labour at the tasks that have been performed through the ages with the inadequate tools he has been using. His civilization simply falls to pieces, destroyed by the mere presence of a culture so far beyond anything he has ever dreamed of. Consequently he falls into sloth and depression.

The same reaction may underlie the depression of a modern adult man or woman. For when we are faced with the necessity of doing something, or of creating something for ourselves without the aid of parents, we may well be hampered by the feeling that "father could do this much better." This attitude may seem fantastic to one who has long been separated from his childhood home and his childish attitudes; but even for him the problem may not be so remote as he thinks. For quite apart from the effect of the actual parents, there remains in the psyche the image of the father as the one who can do what I, the son, cannot do. Thus when there is need for a new creation that I feel inadequate to produce, it is as if the unconscious said, "Now if only there were a father, he could meet this situation." This image of the father is therefore two-faced. On the one hand it seems to say, "Only the father can do it, therefore it is of no use for you to try," and on the other it says, "Hidden within your own psyche there speaks the voice of that creative 'old man' who has fathered every invention man has ever made. You can find him within and learn what he has to teach."

When life presents us with a new problem, a new chapter of experience for which the old adaptation is inadequate, it is usual to experience a withdrawal of the libido. For one phase of life has come to an end, and that which is needed for the new is not immediately at hand. This withdrawal will be experienced in consciousness as a feeling of emptiness, often of depression, and certainly of inertia, with an overtone of self-rebuke because of what seems like laziness or sloth. For if we do not realize that new forces must be mobilized to meet new situations, we superstitiously expect a new attitude to be available as though by magic. This new attitude, however, must arise from the unconscious before it can be made available for the life situation, and this requires a creative act that takes time.

The symbol that is produced in the unconscious will represent the new attitude needed for the next chapter of this individual life history. The acceptance of the symbol, and its gradual unfolding through such conscious work as the individual is willing to expend on it, may take years. Yet the form of the fate that results will have been foreshadowed in the dream image encountered during the period of depression. Under these circumstances it is obviously necessary to accept without self-reproach the withdrawal of the libido from consciousness, and to concentrate one's attention on the inner scene. This is the only way in which the lost energy can eventually be restored, and in which the capacity to take up the creative task of living can be renewed.

4

Hunger

WANT AND GREED

LIFE first appeared on earth, so far as we know, in the form of single living cells. From these simple origins all other life forms developed. Today the earth is covered with living organisms, constituting the whole of the vegetable and animal kingdoms. They are all descendants of those small, pregnant original cells that lived and died millions of years ago. The same physical and chemical laws that controlled the life processes of those ancestral forms still govern the physiology of the complex animals of the present day. In the psychological sphere too, far removed as this is from those simple beginnings, many reminders of the ancient life patterns still survive to affect the attitudes and habits of modern man, although he usually remains quite unaware of their influence.

Of all the characteristics that distinguish the vegetable kingdom from the animal, the most striking is the fact that the plant is stationary, subsisting on elements brought to it by the air or water in which it grows, or on the salts of the soil in which it is rooted. The plant is thus wholly dependent on its environment: if this is favourable it flourishes; if not, it languishes and dies. There is nothing it can do to change these circumstances, however unfortunate its situation may be; it cannot move to another spot, even though ideal conditions may prevail a few feet away.

Some of the most primitive animal organisms likewise are

sessile. By degrees, however, free-moving forms of life were developed, an adaptation marking a most important step in evolution. From then on, the capacity to move about in search of food and other biological necessities became characteristic of animal life.

At first the free organisms merely floated about as the currents in their environment determined; gradually, however, the ability to move of their own activity was developed. Much later, the power of purposive movement was acquired. But there remained in them a pattern of passivity, of inactivity, which was interrupted only when the need to search for food, the presence of danger, or the urge to reproduce made itself felt. These needs acted as stimuli to an activity that was at first little more than a mechanical or chemical reaction and only much later became sufficiently differentiated to form an organized reflex. At this stage passivity was the normal state, activity the unusual one.

When man found himself living under conditions not naturally adapted to his needs, and constraining him to undertake difficult enterprises in order to secure himself against starvation, the innate tendency to quiescence that he shared with all organisms took on a different aspect. From being the "natural way" it became in his case the greatest handicap to survival. Perhaps the hardest battle man has had to wage has been his struggle against his own inertia.

But Mother Nature has implanted in all her children, whether animal or vegetable, a great tenacity of life, which we call the instinct of self-preservation. This instinct is concerned with fulfilling the needs of the body so that it may be kept alive and in health. These needs are of two kinds: first, the need for food and drink; second, the need for protection from harmful external conditions, including heat and cold, injury and disease, as well as danger from hostile animals and human beings. If man was to meet these fundamental requirements, it was essential for him to overcome his primitive inertia.

The needs relating to food and drink, and to shelter and protection from enemies, are so fundamental that nature rewards their satisfaction, as it were, with bliss. To be hungry and cold brings discomfort long before life itself is threatened. To be well fed, warm, and sheltered from the elements brings pleasure. If this were not so, it is doubtful whether man and the other animals would make the effort necessary to secure conditions favourable to life, since the stimulus necessary to arouse them from lethargy would be lacking. The impulse to activity,[1] which is manifested even in very lowly animal forms, would in all probability not lead to purposive effort towards securing food and shelter were it not directed by actual discomfort or fear of discomfort resulting from their absence. These considerations obviously condition the activity of primitives, and without such a stimulus even a modern man may lack the initiative needed to overcome his lethargy and perform a necessary task, though his reason tells him that it is advisable for him to do so.

It is well known among doctors how difficult it is to induce a patient to continue treatment for a disease that no longer causes him pain or discomfort, even when he is repeatedly warned that such care is necessary and urgent. If this is true of civilized and educated people, it is hardly to be wondered at that among primitives the individual rarely makes any effort to care for his health until he is too ill to move, and delays the search for food until he is weak from hunger. And indeed quite recently some communities ostensibly not primitive could not bring themselves to make preparations for their own defence until they were actually attacked, even though their friends were already being decimated by an aggressive and warlike neighbour. These reactions show that the instinct of self-preservation has not been sufficiently modified by the impact of consciousness[2] to make it adequate to serve the complicated needs of modern life. The communities in question—comprising practically all the nations of the world—are actually far from being conscious, self-regulating organisms, but are still dependent on a crudely acting instinct for the preservation of life.

1. C. G. Jung, "Psychological Factors Determining Human Behaviour," in *The Structure and Dynamics of the Psyche* (C.W. 8), pp. 117 ff.
2. This is the process Jung calls "psychization" (cf. above, pp. 20-23).

In primitive communities, in which the spark of consciousness burns dimly and men have as yet acquired little capacity to initiate spontaneous activities to improve their condition, it is hunger primarily that forces people to throw off their innate sloth. In our own situation, in days of plenty and prosperity, it is usual to think that sexuality is the prime mover within; but this is only because the immediacy of hunger's pressure has been mitigated as a result of regulated work and ample distribution of supplies—conditions quite unknown to primitives. Thus hunger is the stern schoolmaster who has taught man to cultivate the fields and undertake many laborious tasks, quite foreign to his nature, that yield no immediate satisfactions but only supply the food he will need at a much later time.

For the Buddhists, as for ourselves, hunger or greed is represented by the pig, which devours its food with such gusto. In times of famine, however, man's need no longer presents itself to his consciousness as his own hunger; under circumstances of dire want, his inner feelings, his suffering, could not possibly be represented by the picture of a pig gorging itself on good food. A starving man feels himself to be pursued and eaten up by a demon that gnaws at his vitals and will not let him rest. Under such circumstances we find the hunger instinct represented in folk tale and myth by a wolf: hunger stalks through the land like a ravening beast and threatens to devour all living creatures. But primitive man does not realize that this wolf whom he must at all cost "keep from the door" is really his own unsatisfied instinct, seen in reversed or projected form. For when his hunger is no longer merely the friendly reminder that it is time to eat, and, because of scarcity, grows fiercely importunate, the instinct shows itself in all the strength and ferocity of a nonpersonal force. It either devours him, so that his strength fails and he dies, or it enters into him, so that the demon takes possession of him, and he is turned into a beast of prey, capable of the utmost cruelty in his search for food.

THIS DUAL ASPECT of hunger is strikingly brought out in legends and folk customs of very wide geographical range. Some of these customs relate to practices used, like the bear dance of the American Indians,[3] to summon up the energies of the tribe and focus them on the hunt. In other instances the dance is intended to conjure up magic power to hypnotize the deer so that it will allow itself to be captured, or the magic may be used to induce the herds to remain on near-by feeding grounds and not wander away to distant regions. Or, if the animal to be captured is a dangerous one, the magic ritual is designed to soothe it and convince it that man kills his "brother" only from necessity, for then it will not turn upon the hunter and destroy him. Other rites have to do with pro-pitiating the spirit of the slain animal, so that it will not haunt its murderers nor warn its brother animals to flee the neigh-bourhood. Customs of this type belong to peoples who depend largely or entirely on hunting for their food supply.

Communities that have learned to till the land, to sow and reap a harvest, and to breed domestic animals for their meat, have different customs. The earliest religious practices of peoples who engage in agriculture are rituals and magic rites connected with sowing and reaping. Frazer [4] has traced many of these from the eastern Mediterranean regions through Greece, central Europe, France, and the British Isles, among the Indians of both Americas, in Africa, the Pacific Islands, and India. Among all of these peoples, corn, that is, grain—wheat, barley, or oats in Europe, maize in America, and rice in India and other Oriental countries—is almost universally regarded as a deity. In many places it is personified as the Mother, a very natural idea; for just as the human mother is the source of the infant's first food, so corn is the source of man's bread.

An ear of wheat was in some cases itself considered to be the Mother, or a sheaf of corn was dressed in woman's clothing and venerated. In Peru, an ear of corn (maize) was dressed in rich vestments and called *Zara-Mama;* Frazer says that as Mother it had the power of producing and giving birth to maize.[5] In plate I we see an ear of maize mounted on a stake

3. J. G. Frazer, *The Golden Bough*, pp. 522 ff.
4. Ibid., pp. 393 ff.
5. Ibid., p. 412.

and adorned with a feather. It is called "The Corn Mother" and is honoured as such by the Pawnees in their Hako ceremony.

In ancient Greece, Demeter was corn goddess as well as Earth Mother. Her daughter, Persephone, who each year spent three months in the underworld, during which time the fields

Fig. 1. Demeter and Persephone

Demeter, as harvest queen, gives ears of grain to her nursling, Triptolemos (characterized by a crooked plough), who, according to legend, first planted wheat in Greece. Behind him Kore (Persephone) holds torches as queen of the underworld.

were bare, and nine months on earth—a stay corresponding with the growing season—also personified the corn. In statues of the mother and daughter they may both be seen crowned with wheat, each bearing a sheaf or sometimes a single ear of wheat in her hands, as in figure 1.

In the Eleusinian mysteries, which took place in September during the time of harvest, the story of Demeter's search for the lost Persephone was re-enacted. The last and most solemn day of the festival was given to celebration of a ritual marriage between the hierophant and a priestess impersonating the goddess. They retired to a dark cave, where the sacred marriage was consummated in symbol, for, as Hippolytus, the author of the *Philosophumena*, relates, the hierophant is "rendered a eunuch by hemlock and cut off from all fleshly generation." Immediately after, the priest came forth and silently displayed to the reverent gaze of the initiates a liknon [6] containing a single ear of wheat. Then he cried aloud, "August Brimo has brought forth a holy son, Brimos," that is, "the strong [has given birth] to the strong." [7] Thus the ear of wheat was the "child" of the corn goddess. It was called "the Strong" because bread is the source of man's strength.[8] This was the *epopteia* or epiphany, the showing forth—the supreme revelation of the goddess to her worshippers.

It is somewhat unexpected, perhaps, to find that the animal sacred to Demeter was the pig. In statues the goddess is frequently shown accompanied by a pig, which was also the animal customarily sacrificed at her festivals.[9] In all probability, the corn goddess in her earliest phase was herself a pig. First the god literally is the animal, then he is companioned by the animal, and the same animal is given to him in sacrifice. Still later, the animal is believed to represent or embody the spirit of the god. Yet it is not at first obvious why the pig, an animal notorious for its greed and destructiveness, should represent the mother goddess, giver of corn and all nourishment. Some light is thrown on the question by a strange detail in the myth of Persephone,[10] which relates that when she was lured away by Pluto, lord of the underworld and god of wealth and plenty, she fell into Hades through a chasm, and when this chasm closed again a certain swineherd named Eubuleus was also engulfed, with all his pigs. When Demeter wandered throughout the region searching desperately for her lost daughter, the footprints of Persephone were found to be obliterated by those of a pig. This story probably represents a

6. The liknon was the winnowing basket used as a cradle for the infant Dionysos, the son of Demeter.
7. Hippolytus, *Philosophumena*, trans. Legge, I, 138.
8. For a further account of these rituals cf. J. Harrison, *Prolegomena to the Study of Greek Religion*, p. 549, and Frazer, *The Golden Bough*, pp. 142 f.
9. Harrison, *Prolegomena to the Study of Greek Religion*, pp. 126, 547, illus.
10. Frazer, *The Golden Bough*, pp. 469 f.

late attempt to conceal the unpalatable fact that Persephone, the beautiful goddess of spring and of the growing corn, was originally herself a pig.

In the Thesmophoria, the autumn festival sacred to Demeter and Persephone, when the harvest and the September wheat sowing were celebrated together, the women worshippers not only imitated Demeter's sorrowing search for her daughter

Fig. 2. The Sacrifice of the Pig

The three torches indicate an offering to underworld deities.

but also partook of a solemn ritual meal consisting of the flesh of pigs. In this rite, as in many another sacramental meal, the flesh of the animal representing the god was eaten by the worshipper in order that he might become one with his god. Aristophanes makes a satirical allusion to this custom in *The Frogs*. The mystae are chanting an impassioned hymn calling the initiates to the festival, when Xanthias, in an aside to his companion, Dionysus, remarks:

> O Virgin of Demeter, highly blest,
> What an entrancing smell of roasted pig!

And Dionysus replies:

> Hush! Hold your tongue! Perhaps they'll give you some.[11]

11. Cf. Harrison, *Prolegomena to the Study of Greek Religion*, p. 540.

At this same festival, pigs and other offerings were thrown into rock clefts called "chasms of Demeter and Persephone" (fig. 2). Before it could be an acceptable gift to the goddess the pig had to be purified, and in the accompanying figure (fig. 3) we see such a rite of purification taking place. The remains of the animals were retrieved in the following spring and buried in the fields when the seed was sown. In this way,

Fig. 3. The Purification of the "Mystic" Pig

it was believed, the corn spirit, persisting in the flesh of the pig, would fertilize the seed, causing it to grow and to produce an adequate harvest.

It was not only in ancient Greece that corn, or perhaps it is more accurate to say the spirit of corn, was conceived of as a pig. Frazer reports that in Thuringia, when the wind blows over the fields, it is customary to say, "The boar is rushing through the corn." In Esthonia there is an analogous allusion to the "rye boar." In some regions, the man who brings in the last sheaf of corn, or who strikes the last blow of the flail in threshing, is chased by the other reapers, bound with a straw rope, and dubbed "the sow." He has to carry this unenviable sobriquet for the whole year, enduring as best as he can the coarse jokes of his neighbours, who pretend that he smells of the pigsty. If he tries to shift the burden of personifying the pig spirit to a comrade, which can be done by giving the latter the straw rope that figured in the rite, he risks being shut up in the pigsty "with the other pigs," and may be beaten or otherwise maltreated into the bargain.

In other places the connection between pig and harvest is preserved in less boisterous customs. In Sweden, for instance, a Yule boar is made of pastry and kept throughout the season. It represents the harvest plenty. In many localities in Europe, the Christmas boar, which is usually an actual animal roasted whole and kept on the sideboard as a cold dish for all visitors to taste, probably had a similar origin.

In these customs we see that man's hunger, indeed his greed, as personified by the pig, is closely associated with the idea of corn, which represents the mother, the provider. It is as though pig and corn together personify greed and its satisfaction. This personification has a dual implication, for while the pig eats greedily and even roots up and destroys more than it eats, it is also the most fecund and most maternal of animals. Possibly the "sow" man, whose act completes the harvest, is nevertheless maltreated and driven away because he represents not only plenty but also ravenous greed, and therefore the threat of famine.

In more remote times, human beings selected to impersonate the corn spirit were actually sacrificed at harvest, probably in an attempt to kill the negative aspect of the idea of food, which is want. Such human sacrifices [12] took place regularly each year among the Incas, the Mexican Indians, the Pawnees, and other tribes in America; they were also common in western Africa, in the Philippines, and in India, especially among the Dravidian tribes of Bengal. In each of these localities the victim was chosen some weeks in advance and was treated kindly, fed lavishly, and even venerated until he was sacrificed as the corn spirit in the harvest ritual.

In all these instances, need and greed are more or less confused in a composite idea of the corn spirit, but on the whole the emphasis is on the positive aspect, the idea of plenty. In

12. Frazer, *The Golden Bough*, pp. 431 ff.

some parts of Germany and in the Slavic countries, however, the corn spirit represents not satisfied appetite and plenty but rather their opposites, hunger and famine. For the people in these districts, when the spring winds blow over the fields, it is not a pig that rustles the corn, but a wolf. They warn their children not to go to the fields to gather flowers, "lest the wolf should eat you."

In these localities great care is taken by the reapers to "catch the wolf," for it is said that if he escapes, famine will be let loose in the land. Sometimes this wolf is represented by a handful of especially long-stalked grain, sometimes by a man who is singled out on account of some particular gesture or action. This man is then clad in a wolfskin and led into the village by a rope. In other places it is said that the wolf is killed when the corn is threshed. In olden times the man representing the corn wolf was killed in actual fact; later the killing was enacted in a ritual drama, or the man was replaced by an effigy, such as a manikin, or a loaf made in the shape of a man. In many folk customs the earlier, real killing is still represented by a symbolic game, often rude and boisterous, in which a good deal of rough handling of the victim may take place. But the origin and significance of the game have long ago been forgotten.

Sometimes, instead of an animal or a man, the last sheaf bound at harvest plays the role of the corn spirit, under the name of "the wolf." This sheaf is not threshed; it is tied up—sometimes it is wrapped in the skin of an animal—and kept intact in the barn all winter. Its "health," as they say, is carefully tended, so that its full power will be preserved. Then in the spring its kernels are mixed with the seed corn and used in the sowing. If this special store of corn should be eaten, owing to dire need or forgetfulness, the wolf will avenge himself on the farmer. He will not bring the spirit of corn—the power to grow—to the next sowing; the crops will fail and there will be famine.

These customs and beliefs apparently reflect the great difficulty man experienced in learning to reserve enough grain for seed. This was especially difficult when the harvest was too scanty to take care of the farmer's hunger during the long winter months in northern climates. Obviously the last sheaf—the wolf—must remain in the barn all winter if there is to be seed corn in the spring. This must have been one of the hardest lessons man had to learn during the transition from a food-gathering to a food-producing culture, for his instinct naturally prompted him to appease his hunger by eating all the food there was. The belief that the last sheaf contained or even actually was the corn wolf was all that restrained him. For if he ate his seed corn, then indeed the wolf of famine would be freed in the land.

The Trobriand Islanders of the Pacific have some curious ideas and customs that bear on this problem. They do not think of corn as having a life or existence of its own, inherent in the seed itself, and capable of continuation regardless of who handles it. Rather, they consider it as belonging to or appertaining to definite persons, whose life or mana it shares and without which it is powerless to grow. Each family possesses its ancestral corn, which will grow only if a member of that particular family plants it. It will not grow for anyone else. The corn is handed down from generation to generation, ownership being vested in the women of the family. If a man should allow all the corn of his family to be consumed, he could not get fresh seed, for there are strict taboos against giving seed to anyone outside the family. He would be faced with ruin, as he would be unable to plant his fields in the spring, unless he could induce a woman who had inherited seed to marry him. This belief imposes an exceedingly strict discipline on appetite, and like the custom of keeping the wolf —the last sheaf—in the barn all winter, it has a very practical significance.

When the spirit of corn was represented by the corn mother instead of the wolf, the emphasis was on the positive rather than on the negative aspect of this spirit. Yet even here the negative connotation was still present. Perhaps the difference in attitude represented by the contrast between the two symbols is related to the factor of whether it was easy or difficult in a given locale to raise an adequate crop. In fertile regions man seemed to regard the corn spirit as the mother, while in northern and barren districts, where harvests are uncertain, the wolf was the more appropriate symbol.

Where the positive aspect of the corn spirit was invoked, the sheaf personifying the corn mother was guarded during growth and venerated at harvest. It was garbed as a woman and kept in the barn all winter; there the corn mother was ceremoniously visited at intervals and asked whether she felt well and strong. If it appeared that she felt weak, she was burned, and a new corn mother was installed in her place; for unless she kept her strength she could not give birth to strong babies.

Here we see the transition from the positive to the negative aspect of the corn spirit. If she weakened, the corn mother herself had to be burned, lest she bring famine instead of plenty. Thus under certain circumstances the spirit of corn seemed to become harmful to man. Then it had to be destroyed or driven away, that is, the threat of famine had to be banished. And so the man who bound the last sheaf was made to personify this potential danger and was hounded from the village like a scapegoat. In some instances he was actually killed. Among the ancient Mexicans the corn man was regularly killed at harvest, not as a scapegoat but as a sacrifice, his body being eaten in a sacramental meal, much as the pig was eaten in the Eleusinian mysteries.

Frazer traces the gradual growth and refinement of this barbarous custom. At first it demanded actual killing and eating of the human being who was believed in very fact to embody the spirit of corn. Later the corn animal was sacrificed and eaten; Demeter's pig and the harvest boar exemplify this stage. This was followed by the eating of a loaf made of newly reaped corn and fashioned in the form of a manikin. Finally a true sacramental meal emerged, like that celebrated at the close of the rice harvest in the island of Buru, where every member of the clan was bound to contribute a little of his new rice for a meal called the "eating of the soul of the rice." [13] This name clearly indicates the ritual character of the repast.

13. Frazer, *The Golden Bough*, p. 482.

In this harvest supper we see the early beginnings of a communion meal, in which the body of the divinity is eaten in symbolic form by the worshippers, who are believed by this act to assimilate his nature and power.

THESE LEGENDS and customs surrounding the corn spirit present two aspects of man's striving to deal with the problem of his need for food. On the one hand, he attempts to control nature and so to enlarge the source of supply. On the other, he copes with the task of controlling his own nature. In addition to his innate sloth and inertia, which are born, as the Buddhists would say, of avidya, not-knowing, there is also his compulsion to satisfy his hunger of the moment, without regard to the consequences. This too is an effect of avidya; for if he were really conscious of the result of eating everything at once, he obviously would not do it. But because the pangs of today's hunger are immediate and inescapable, and the consciousness of tomorrow's hunger is remote and he can conceive it only as a faint replica of present suffering, primitive man—and the primitive in modern man likewise—does not want to become aware of the law of cause and effect, that the Buddhists say is the lesson that must be learned by those of "little intellect." [14] He prefers rather to act on the adage, "Let us eat and drink; for tomorrow we die."

Gontran de Poncins [15] reports that when he was living among the Eskimos of northern Canada, he found that they wanted to eat on the first night of a journey all the food prepared for the entire trip. He was regarded with great suspicion because he ate only a part of his store and kept the remainder in reserve. He was finally obliged to give his comrades all of his provisions at once, for fear that they would otherwise become hostile. This was particularly hard on him because at that time he had not learned to eat Eskimo food and was relying on his small store of "white man's" provisions to see him through the trip. The very presence of a store of food larger than was needed for a day at a time became a danger. For not

14. See above, p. 35.
15. Cf. *Kabloona*, pp. 90-91.

only did his companions eat his entire supply, but after their gargantuan feast they lay sleeping all the next day and refused to move, despite the fact that they had a long and hazardous journey ahead.

Among nomadic and hunting peoples like the Eskimos, the task of finding food has to be undertaken at regular intervals, and this discipline alone prevents them from sleeping away their entire time. But when a tribe settles down and begins to develop an agricultural life, it is freed in large measure from the dangers and the precarious features of a hunting economy. It can produce its food supply on its own cultivated lands, and thus is no longer dependent on the presence of game. However, a new danger to life appears in the very existence of a store of food.

Whereas the ferocity and the unaccountable comings and goings of the animals constituted the chief dangers of his former life as a hunter, man's own sloth and greed now become his principal enemies. For when a group of people for the first time reaps a harvest and possesses food in bulk, the obvious reaction is to wish to feast immediately. Indeed, in our present-day harvest festival we ourselves follow the same pattern. For while it is a thanksgiving to the Giver of the harvest, it is also an occasion for feasting, when the customary curbs on sensual indulgence are laid aside. But primitive man not only feasts at such times; he also scatters and destroys what he cannot eat. Then, when all is squandered, want inevitably follows, for in a purely agricultural community there is no possibility of replenishing the store until the next harvest.

This phase of the problem, with its consequent demand for psychological development, is represented in a legend of the corn spirit that comes from ancient Phrygia.[16] There it is related that Lityerses, son of King Midas (who, like Pluto in the Persephone myth, was lord of untold wealth), was the reaper of the corn. He had an enormous appetite, for as a bastard son he represented the shadow side or opposite, unconscious aspect of his father. For the father, Midas, represented wealth, plenty, and the bastard son, that is, the son who is not

16. Frazer, *The Golden Bough*, p. 425.

the heir, who is indeed the outsider in the family, necessarily carries all the negative aspects that the "son and heir" escapes. So Lityerses was the very personification of insatiable greed, who dissipated and devoured the wealth that his father had accumulated.

This legend is particularly instructive, for it gives a clue to the modern problem of the son who feels himself to be rejected by his father. He may not be illegitimate, as Lityerses was, but if for any reason he feels himself to be not fully accepted by one or both of his parents (if a boy especially by the father, if a girl by the mother), he is all too likely to react unconsciously, in a way corresponding to the Lityerses of the legend. Such a son will turn to his mother, he will be soft and self-indulgent. He may be and often is over-fat, lazy, demanding, and terribly jealous of any rival whose industry and self-discipline gain him the rewards of independence and the approval of the father and possibly also of the world. For if a boy's relation to his father is negative or disturbed, he is inevitably hampered in his development of the masculine values and is liable to remain a "mother's boy." If a girl feels herself to be unaccepted by the mother she will turn to the father and will develop those masculine qualities that characterize the animus. She may make a career for herself in the world or, in more serious cases where the damage has been greater, she may become an opinionated and embittered woman, one who is seemingly self-sufficient and domineering, but who underneath suffers from a sense of inferiority and insecurity on the feminine side. She cannot imagine that she might ever be attractive to men, and indeed probably men actually fight shy of her, scared away by her sharp and bitter tongue.

In the legend Lityerses was proud of his strength, and yet had to prove it to himself and to the world by repeated victories. He was accustomed to lure some passing stranger into the cornfield when he was reaping, challenging him to a contest to see which of them could reap the most. Contests of this sort are still held at harvest festivals in many localities. But while today they are merely games, in ancient times and in legend they were far more serious matters, for there might well be a sinister ending. Lityerses, the man with the limitless appetite, always won. He then bound his rival inside a sheaf of corn and beheaded him.

This legend must date from the beginning of the agricultural phase of civilization, when man had learned how to produce a crop but not how to govern his appetite. His instinct was compulsive and by no means subject to control or modification by reason. When aroused, it dominated the whole field of consciousness. No other consideration existed; for in men at this stage of psychological development, when instinct prompts to action all else is forgotten. Lityerses represents this instinctive quality in man. He is the natural man, strong and lusty and proud. The legend relates that up to the time of his encounter with Hercules no one had been able to overcome him.

The stranger who is invited to help with the reaping represents a new attitude, a developing aspect in the men of that day—the beginning of self-discipline. This new man is still, however, a stranger to the problems that cultivation of the fields and the production of harvests have let loose in the world. He has a head, it is true; he has begun to think, to recognize the law of cause and effect, as the Buddhists say,[17] but his head is not very firmly set on his shoulders, for the contest is always won by Lityerses (the instinctive man within), and the stranger (the new realization in man) loses his head. Appetite prevails, and presumably the harvest is consumed in feasting. Before sowing time comes again, the village will go hungry.

This recurrent struggle evidently went on for a very long time without much change. Then Hercules arrived on the scene, and perceiving what dire straits the village was in, undertook to reap with Lityerses. He went to the field and offered himself for the contest. The two reaped side by side, and, a thing that had never happened before, Lityerses was outstripped and Hercules won the contest. He then bound Lityerses in a sheaf, as the latter had so often done with others, killed him, and threw his body in the river. That is, the instinct

17. See above, p. 35.

factor was returned to the depths of the unconscious, just as today greed is more often repressed than transformed. Thereafter, a ritual based on this fortunate outcome of the struggle was practised yearly in Phrygia at harvest-time. A stranger chancing to pass the harvest fields was regarded by the reapers as the embodiment of the corn spirit, and as such was seized, wrapped in sheaves, and beheaded.

Obviously Lityerses is not only the spirit of corn but also the spirit of greed. He personifies insatiable appetite, which no ordinary restraint can hold in check. Yet this is an aspect of the corn spirit that must be driven out if man is to enjoy abundance the year round. At first, consciousness is too dim to enlighten the blind instinct that prompts man to go on eating as long as any food remains: in comparison to the power of his stomach's demand, the influence of his head is very feeble. But finally Hercules, the sun hero, appears and is able to overthrow the tyrant of appetite. For he represents the divine or semidivine spark of consciousness, the sun in man that enables him to make the heroic effort necessary to overcome the age-old domination of the biological urge. In this way a further step in the transformation of the instinct is taken.

This struggle against the negative aspect of the spirit of corn is also seen in the customs of driving out the "old man" or the "old woman" before the first sowing of the grain. These rites were formerly prevalent in Germany, Norway, Lorraine, the Tyrol, and in parts of England. The idea is that the spirit of corn grows weak and old during the winter; it could produce only a sickly growth in the new corn—or possibly, through the long fast during the winter, it has actually become the spirit of hunger instead of food. In the Slavic countries, this old man is called Death, and a rite practised before the first sowing is called "carrying out Death." This reminds us of the customary representation of death as a skeleton carrying a scythe. It was perhaps originally a picture of a reaper who, like Lityerses, devoured the entire harvest and so brought death by hunger and starvation. Later, this picture came to represent death from whatever cause. The allegorical interpretation of the figure of death as the reaper of man, who falls before his scythe like the grass of the field, is obviously a late conception.

This old man who must be expelled is equivalent to the wolf of the beliefs discussed above. He is often counterbalanced by a "young man," who, like Persephone, is the young corn. For instance, in ancient times in Rome it was customary on March 14—the night before the full moon that marked the beginning of sowing—to expel the old Mars, Mamurius Veturius. For Mars was a vegetation spirit as well as a god of war. In this ceremony the old Mars was treated as a scapegoat and driven out into enemy territory. It is interesting to note this dual aspect of Mars. On his positive side he is a vegetation spirit, giving his name to the spring month of March. His zodiacal house is Taurus, which is associated with the month of plenty. But in his negative aspect he is the god of war. Most wars are fought, in the final analysis, for food or food lands or their modern equivalents: fundamentally it is lack of food that makes wars. Furthermore, the anger of Mars —the blind fury that takes possession of a man, so that he loses all reason—is due as a rule to frustration of one of the basic instincts; it represents the second phase of the instinct of self-preservation, namely, the impulse to defend oneself from one's enemies.

TWO FACTORS played a part in fostering the gradual evolution of the hunger instinct—the impact of man on man, or the social factor, and man's conviction that whatever he did not understand in nature was of supernatural origin. At first this supernatural element was explained as being the mana of the creature or object or phenomenon; but gradually the mana effect was thought of as emanating from supernatural beings, gods or daemons, who controlled the world and whose good will must be cultivated if man was to survive.

We do not know the origins of the social and religious factors that have moulded man's psychological and cultural development. They were already ancient by the time man began to till the ground, and directed the evolution of instinct simultaneously along two lines that had somewhat different goals. On the one hand, man's relation to his fellow man curbed his instinctive selfishness; on the other, he recognized that although his conscious will could do much to secure his safety in the world, it was still helpless in face of the uncontrollable powers of nature. He was thus compelled to develop a relation to these powers by adopting an attitude that throughout the ages has been known as religious.

When agriculture took the place of hunting and food gathering, men began to live in larger groups, and permanent villages were established, in order that the fields and the domestic animals might be more easily protected. As a result, human relationship came to play a much greater part in each man's life. In addition, the work of tilling the fields and reaping the harvest was accomplished more satisfactorily as a community enterprise, and so again the problems of relationship increased. This led to the development of customs that had as their purpose the restraint of man's instinctive greed. His growing ego, with its desire to possess and control, had to be held in check by various social sanctions and taboos. To this day, most of our rules of politeness are based on the need to curb individual selfishness and egotism: under the code of polite table manners, for instance, one must, before beginning to eat, see that others are served with the best pieces of food, etc.

The many centuries of conformity to such regulations have established a discipline and control over the instincts of hunger and of self-preservation that have become second nature to all civilized people. For the most part these controls are valid and lasting, unless a particular strain is suddenly placed upon the conscious adaptation of a given individual or group. Then the primitive instinct may break forth and overthrow in a moment all that civilization has built up through the centuries at so great a cost.

It would seem that if there were no other means for the restraint of instinct, recurrent regressions to barbarism would be inevitable. But the second factor, namely, man's intimation that his food came from the gods, and that its supply was only in small measure under his own control, was at work from the beginning. Thus it held out at least a hope that through his relation to the gods, a real change in man's nature might be brought about. For it was through religious practices that he first learned to overcome his inertia, and it was on account of reverence for the spirit of the corn, and later for the god or goddess of the harvest, that he was able to release energy from preoccupation with the immediate satisfaction of instinct. Having accomplished this release, he began to play creatively with the deity in whom the freed libido was vested. The religious rites became more elaborate and more meaningful, while the statues and shrines of the gods grew ever more beautiful. Under the influence of this religious attitude, the libido manifested in the instincts underwent a change: it was gradually transformed for the service of the psyche instead of remaining bound to the body.

From the beginning, man was most painfully aware of his helplessness in the face of nature, and recognized that to procure a good harvest he must please the gods. The tasks that he felt compelled to undertake to propitiate them were not dictated by reason, nor were they consciously thought out, or based on observations of the actual conditions that furthered the growth of crops. They were taught him by his own intuition, or by seers and priests who had particular insight in such matters.

Sometimes these rites were fantastic and, from our point of view, utterly useless. But surprisingly often they led to activities that increased the bounds of human knowledge as well as the productivity of the fields. We need only recall the invention of the calendar on the basis of knowledge gained through the worship of the moon as harvest god. Osiris, for example, was not only the moon god but also the teacher of agriculture. While some of the rituals had a practical agricultural value, others certainly had none. But all had a further, most important effect: they increased the discipline and control of man's instinct and gave him a certain freedom of action, a disidentification from the compulsion of the blind life force within him.

The religious rites and folk customs connected with the satisfaction of hunger came into being spontaneously. They were not deliberately invented but arose of themselves, as naïve expressions of man's instinctive feeling about "the way things are." This means that in his practices concerned with magic, man was only following his intuitive perception of the ancient, archetypal images or pictures that originate in the unconscious.[18] Actually therefore these customs had to do not with a deity or daemon residing in the corn, nor even with a living spirit of corn, as their initiators believed, but with an unknown factor dwelling within man's own psyche. But since this fact was completely unsuspected by man himself, the unconscious contents that had been activated by the necessity of doing something about his need for food were projected into the external situation, where they were perceived as if they had originated in the outer world. If man was to learn how to overcome his own regressive tendencies and inertia, to progress not only in agricultural knowledge but also in psychological development, he had to find a means of coming to terms with this unknown, daemonic factor.

THE RELIGIOUS RITES and magic practices devised to increase the yield of the soil were thought of as producing an effect on the gods, beings external to man: their anger was turned aside, their indifference was overcome, their interest and benevolence were attracted. It did not dawn on man's consciousness until many centuries had passed that while his magic had no actual effect on the order of the external world, it did exert an influence on the daemonic force emanating from the depths of his own psyche. Prayers to the gods affect the inner atti-

18. The source of these images we do not know, but Jung has pointed out that the similarity of the customs and ideas that have been developed over the centuries in all parts of the world, and appear today in the dreams and phantasies of modern people as well, point to a common substrate in the psyche, a universal pattern of psychic experience and behaviour corresponding to the instinct patterns that condition the physical reactions of everyone. The elements of the psychic pattern he calls the archetypes; and just as the instincts manifest themselves in typical physical reactions, so do the archetypes manifest themselves in typical psychic forms, the archetypal images. Considerable confirmation of Jung's theory has been furnished in recent years by the observations of workers in related fields. Brain's work on the functioning of the brain, for instance, and the observations of animal psychologists and biologists, Allee, Portmann, and Lorenz among others, all point in the same direction.

tude of the petitioner, and the resulting change of attitude in him can in turn change the appearance of the world and alter the course of events. But this "belief," as well as the atheism that is its necessary precursor, are both products of a psychological insight achieved only at a much later stage in history.

The two trends, the one towards scientific exploration of the world and the other towards the psychic evolution of man himself, advanced side by side. Gradually, however, they diverged. The first gave birth to modern science; the second has been the particular province of religion. Modern psychology, with its clarification of psychological happenings, has provided a bridge between these two opposing views. Numinous experiences, the basis of metaphysical dogma, are now recognized to be due to the projection of psychic events. When this is realized, they can be accepted as valid in their own sphere, with the result that the external phenomena are released from their contamination and can be investigated objectively.

Thus there has come about a gradual change in point of view. The daemonic factor, now seen to be an expression of man's own instinctual drive, was projected into the object because he was insufficiently aware of its existence within himself. And it is hardly necessary to state that the process of man's disidentification from his inner compulsions is still only in its initial stages. It varies greatly in different individuals. Some barely realize the subjective factor in their passionate loves and hates, while others, although they are the few, are more conscious and therefore freer from such compulsive entanglements.

When the driving force within him was simply biological instinct, man's concern was the immediate satisfaction of his appetite. But as the hunger instinct was modified through increasing consciousness, two things resulted: first, man was enabled to control his food supply with ever greater certainty through self-discipline and hard work; second, he became aware of a longing not allayed by the satisfaction of his physical hunger. The corn had become merely a plant subject to natural laws: it no longer contained the life spirit, the daemon, the god. But the urgent need to be united to the unseen potency that had formerly resided in the corn still remained. Man's own spirit longed to be made one with that life spirit which animates all nature. Thus he became aware that the ritual acts to which his ancestors had felt impelled were not nonsense, but represented subjective impulses of great significance. He began to understand that the true meaning of the myths and rites could be grasped only when they were understood symbolically.

This is not the same as to say that they were taken metaphorically. A metaphor is the substitution of one known fact for another. The substitution of a manikin made of paste for a human sacrifice may well have occurred because the human sacrifice had become abhorrent to a more civilized age. If so, this would be a metaphorical use of an inanimate object in place of the animate one. Such a substitution is not a symbol in the true meaning of the word.

But when the sense of mystery, of unseen power, of numen, formerly inherent in the ritual eating of the corn man, remains—though now expressed in a strange and unknown intuition of spiritual union with God, effected under the guise of an actual meal in which, by the eating of a cake of corn, man is made one with his God—the experience is a symbolic one. For when it is clearly realized that the grain itself is not God, that the spirit, the growth, latent in the grain is not God either, and also that God is something beyond either of these things, which yet in some way represent or picture him, and when the bodily act of eating is recognized as only an analogy to the spiritual act of assimilation, an act that cannot be envisaged or represented to man's consciousness in any better way, then we are obliged to say that these objects and this act are symbols, "the best possible description, or formula, for a relatively unknown fact." [19]

These realizations produced a gradual change in man's relation to the daemonic or numinous power of the instincts. Mean-

19. Cf. Jung, *Psychological Types*, p. 473, where this distinction is discussed at length.

while, a corresponding change became apparent in his customs. The rituals connected with preserving the positive aspect of the corn spirit, or with overcoming its negative aspect, were followed by a custom of dedicating the first and best of the crop to the spirit of the corn. This spirit or daemon was now thought of in a more general form, as the god of harvest. The idea of a god of harvest is both more abstract and more personal. The container of the mana is no longer an actual ear of corn; it has been replaced by the harvest as a whole. Simultaneously the spirit becomes more personalized, and an actual deity begins to take shape. To him, or to her, offerings were made of the corn that his or her bounty had provided. Usually the first fruits, replacing the sacrificial corn man of a former time, were not eaten but were consecrated to the god of harvest.

Out of this ritual there arose another, even more meaningful one. Man began to partake of the food that was offered to the gods, not to satisfy his hunger but so that he might by this means hold communion with his god. As the corn or other food was believed to be the actual body of the god whose spirit caused the corn to grow, the communion meal was really a partaking of the actual body of the deity; thus, it was thought, man's nature was enriched by an admixture with the divine substance.

Where the corn spirit was believed to inhabit a human being, the potentiality of this transition was already latent. For when the man who carried the significance of corn spirit was killed and his flesh eaten (as happened in ancient Mexico), it was believed that his spirit—the spirit or life of corn that he personified—could be assimilated by the participants in the meal. This food was felt to have extraordinary life-giving powers; it could give health to the sick or even bring the dead to life, and those who ate it would not know hunger throughout the years.

Customs of this kind are numerous and very widespread. They vary from folkways hardly understood to practices of very similar content that have become the most important and meaningful rituals of highly developed religions, in which the implications of communion with God and of a mystical regeneration through the sacramental meal have replaced the old expectations of magic effect.

The Catholic mass in many ways resembles these early harvest meals, in that the wafer is believed to be transformed, through the ritual act of the priest, into the very body of Christ. This mystery happening of the mass, based as it is on customs and beliefs of an unreckoned antiquity, awakes an echo within the human being, for it speaks to the unconscious directly and produces its effect in a region beyond man's conscious control. One for whom this symbol still lives feels himself actually transformed by participating in the ritual. For where this central mystery has power to touch the very depths of a man's soul, it still can exert its transforming influence on his unconscious. But that power has been weakened through the development of rational thought. The psychological attitudes of mediaeval man no longer prevail, and the majority of intellectual men in consequence find themselves totally unable to accept the irrational character of the symbolic happening.

Modern man has sought to compass the whole of life with his conscious intellect, only to find that the power of the irrational life force has not been overcome, but has retreated to the unconscious and from that hidden stronghold exerts a powerful and often baneful influence on his life. The power of his primitive greed bursts forth in wars of aggression and manifests itself in asocial business practices, while the exclusive concern with outer satisfactions leaves his soul hungry and starving. For man cannot live satisfactorily, he cannot be whole, unless he is living in harmony with the unconscious roots of his being. Yet how can he be at one with himself while the barbaric impulses of unredeemed instinct continue to hold sway in the unconscious? It is just because the ideals we hold up before us do not represent the truth about mankind that the hopes of peace and progress they embody so constantly elude us. Yet we fear to admit this obvious fact and to relax our efforts at self-improvement, lest we fall again into chaos and barbarism.

Perhaps we need not be so afraid. For when all is said, the

original impulse towards psychological development and the evolution of consciousness arose not from the conscious ego (which was a result, not the cause of the development), but from the unconscious springs of life within man. It is not surprising, therefore, that its renewal should also be found in the unconscious, where the life processes manifest themselves, now as throughout human experience, in symbolic form. Through the study of this little-known part of the human psyche, it is possible to contact and in some measure to understand the symbols that arise spontaneously in dream or phantasy from the innermost depths of the individual's being. By this means he may become reconciled with his other side, because the symbols of his dream carry for him personally the value that the organized symbols of religious ritual held for his ancestors. The primitive impulses within him are profoundly affected by the concentrated work and attention he bestows upon his dreams. For the symbols themselves re-enact the ancient, ever renewed drama of spiritual regeneration or transformation. Through the experience of this inner drama, if it is rightly understood and acted upon, psychic health and inner maturity can be achieved by the modern man, just as they were found by his predecessors through participating emotionally in the symbolic drama of religious ritual.

5

Self-Defence

ENMITY AND FRIENDSHIP

T HERE is a popular illusion, rather common in the present century, that life owes us something. We feel that we "ought to be able to expect" certain things from life—as if life were a sort of supermother. We hear it said, for example, that everyone has a right to a minimum living wage, to a good education, or even to good health, while nations declare that they deserve *Lebensraum*—"a place in the sun," as it was termed in 1914. We consider such conditions in some strange way to be our due, forgetting that the majority of them must be created by man's own effort. Surely a moment's consideration will show us that this attitude of mind is based on an illusion. We have only to look back to the primordial conditions of life to realize its absurdity.

There was no mother and there was no powerful state to regulate the conditions of life for the first animal organisms, which found themselves in a world already filled with vegetable life. The older generation was as helpless as the younger in face of the inexorable conditions it faced. The predecessors of animal life, the plants, had evolved in adaptation to the various conditions of climate and soil as they actually occurred in the different regions of the world, and we cannot believe that a plant mother could arrange for her offspring to get a chance to survive. A seed that happens to fall in an unfavourable spot cannot assume that it has been denied its rights, or claim that life owes it a better chance of survival and growth. Why then should man make such an irrational assumption? Those animal forms which could adapt to the conditions in which they found themselves, survived; those which could not, perished. If a locality was unfavourable, a plant could do nothing about it; its growth was stunted, and finally, if conditions did not improve, it died. But the animals learned to move away from inauspicious sites in order to seek places better suited to their needs.

This transition required thousands of years. Meanwhile the animals were learning new ways of coping with changing conditions. This they accomplished entirely by developing new powers within themselves, not by directly altering their environment. The capacity for independent movement led to many revolutionary changes in the structure of their bodies. They developed lungs, so that they could breathe air and live on land instead of being confined to the water. They developed teeth, limbs, new kinds of digestive and reproductive organs—to mention but a few of the radical changes that increased the capacity of living forms to spread over the earth.

For many thousands of years all the new powers won by the animal kingdom were gained through physical adaptation of the organism itself. They had been attained long before the revolutionary idea of attempting to alter the conditions of life first dawned in minds that must be considered as by that time human. Up to this point the survival of the organism had depended entirely on the instinct of self-preservation, which gradually evolved to greater complexity as the organisms themselves developed. But when an attempt was to be made to change the environment, concerted effort on the part of the evolving units came to play an increasing role. Man's natural gregariousness favoured this advance, which increased his power enormously, but at the same time threatened the independent development of the individual. For the group had power that the individual had not. Consequently the individual tended to look more and more to the group as the all-powerful provider and protector, the body that "ought" to care for its members. The group or tribe became an entity in which the individuality of the separate persons was completely merged.

The survival of the living organism is threatened not only by lack of food but in many other ways as well. The dangers fall roughly into three groups—danger from the elements, danger from disease or injury, and danger from enemies. A detailed consideration of all these fields would require a history of human culture that is far beyond the scope of this book. As the main theme here is the psychological problem that man has encountered in his struggle to relate the conscious ego to his compulsive drives, our chief concern is with the danger from enemies that derives from the aggressive tendencies of man.

The instinct of self-preservation has had a very important positive effect on human society, for it has fostered the growth of relations between men. The individual life is obviously best protected when groups of men band themselves together for mutual aid. In such groups friendships readily develop. It is therefore in the sphere of man's relation to his fellow man that the most valuable as well as the most destructive aspects of this instinct can be traced; here the effort of man to tame and domesticate his compulsive instinctive reactions can be seen in its vicissitudes through the centuries. For the movement towards civilization is by no means one of steady progress. The efforts of years, even of centuries devoted to the taming and psychic modification of the instincts, have been swept away, over and over again, in a collective frenzy, a furor or madness still sweeping over mankind with a regularity that might well make one despair that the daemonic force will ever be tamed and domesticated.

Paradoxically, the instinct of self-preservation, which, like the hunger instinct, is endowed with specific energy and compulsive drive, has been responsible for some of the most uncontrollable and destructive outbursts that history records. Large regions of the earth have at times been devastated by famine or flood; plagues too have taken their toll of life, sometimes in appalling measure. In such situations men instinctively combine against the foe. But when man turns against man, there seems to be no end to the devilish ingenuity with which he devises destruction not only for his brother but for mankind as a whole. War remains the greatest evil of mankind. King David's plea that he be punished for his sin by being made to suffer plague or famine rather than defeat in war, reflected a wise choice. "Let us fall now into the hand of the Lord," he cried, "and let me not fall into the hand of man."

THE MECHANISMS of self-defence as they operate in man, guarding his life from a thousand dangers, are still largely unconscious; only to a relatively small extent are his measures for self-preservation under his own direction or control. The purely physical reflexes that maintain his well-being rarely pass the threshold of consciousness, but their ceaseless vigil goes on even during sleep. A man's stomach rejects a poison that he does not know he has eaten; his eye blinks to avoid a particle of dust so small that he has not consciously seen it. The number of the unconscious mechanisms and reflexes that daily protect him from bodily harm is almost infinite.

Other self-protective reactions are less unconscious and therefore less automatic. They are subjected to a certain amount of psychic modification through the control of the conscious ego. However, a reaction that has been brought under conscious control may fall again under the sole direction of primitive instinct if the threshold of consciousness is lowered. A pet dog who is ordinarily quite gentle may growl and snap if touched when he is sleeping. For in sleep his primitive instinct takes possession of him once more and he acts reflexly. Many human beings exhibit a similar regression to a more primitive condition when conscious control is weakened from fatigue, illness, or some drug (the outstanding example of this being the effect of alcohol). The same thing may occur when an individual is temporarily overcome by emotion or by an uprush of unconscious material flooding into the psyche and overwhelming the field of consciousness. Under such circumstances the individual may likewise respond to danger, real or imagined, with an automatic or compulsive reaction that takes no real account of the situation and is almost purely reflex in character.

However, when an automatic reaction passes the threshold of consciousness, it comes in some measure under the control of the individual and so partly loses its automatic character. The instinctive mechanism that has previously determined its release then becomes subject to the modifying influence of moral, social, and religious factors, and the process of transformation of the instinct is set on foot. This process has been greatly influenced by the tendency of the human species to congregate into groups for mutual protection and in order to facilitate the search for food. But these values were offset by their opposites, for the opportunities for theft were many, and constant quarrels resulted. Thus the development of the instinct of self-preservation has played a very large part in the problem of human relationships. Indeed it is as a result of motivations arising from this instinct that man classifies all living beings as either enemies or friends.

In man the natural weapons, teeth, claws, and fleetness, by means of which the solitary animal can generally capture its prey and protect itself against whatever threatens or hurts it, were sacrificed in the interest of specifically human qualities. Consequently man's enemies were often too powerful to be met by one individual alone, especially when there were children to be protected and fed.[1] Alliances between individuals or families, and between groups of people, assured mutual aid for offence and defence. In this movement towards social life, the modification of the instinct is already strikingly manifest; for if it had not undergone some transformation, primitive groups would have been destroyed by internecine quarrels. Men who lived in defensive bands had to learn to tolerate one another and to curb their instinctive reactions. They had to learn further how to co-operate, and to treat one man's injury as the affair of the whole community. Cain's question—"Am I my brother's keeper?"—had somehow to be answered in the affirmative.

In the course of ages man did acquire sufficient freedom from his own apathy to be able to take part voluntarily in

1. This problem was more crucial in the case of man on account of the prolonged period of immaturity and helplessness in the human young.

group action. An injury could become real to him even though he had not suffered it in his own person. Next, he learned to remember from one occasion to another; hence he could act on his own initiative and volition instead of being dependent on the stimulus of actual injury or immediate danger. Yet even today this capacity is only rudimentary in many primitive tribes. Often pantomimic dances and dramas must be undertaken to arouse the group sufficiently to go on the warpath, even though the depredations of its enemies are recent and serious. For the primitive, with his twilight consciousness, it is easier to forget a wife carried off by a neighbouring tribe, or a loved child killed by a wolf, than to overcome his own inertia. He simply cannot realize—that is, "make real" to himself—the nefariousness of the enemy who has injured him. After the pantomime has made it real, he can no more help rushing out to be avenged than he could formerly help being shackled by indifference and lethargy.

In situations like these, the majority of the tribe, the average members, are entirely dependent on the autonomous functioning of the instinct of self-preservation. There may be one man, however, who has overcome his inertia and unconsciousness. The medicine man or chief who calls for the dance, and who by his own dancing arouses the others to action, has acquired a spark of consciousness. In him the psychic modification of the instinct has progressed a stage farther, and through his development the average men are led to act in a way that cements their group alliance. In his greater psychological development and greater consciousness, this man proves himself to be a leader.

Concerted action to avenge wrong, especially in a situation that is not the immediate concern of all, implies the beginning of friendship and group loyalty. In this way enmity becomes the stimulus to friendship. The kind of friendship that develops in a community threatened by a common enemy, whether that enemy is hunger or a hostile neighbour, is based on the identification of the group members with the group as a whole. The group reacts as a unit: the individual member is no longer a separate entity but is fused with the others, and the values of the group become his values. One sheep in a flock is very much like all the other sheep, both in its appearance and in its reactions. In the same way, a primitive tribe, a civic club, a religious sect, a political party, are all composed of numbers of persons whose significance derives from the group and not from their individual and unique qualities.

Where the solidarity of the tribe is an essential for survival, special techniques are used to foster the identification of the individual with the group. First and most important are the puberty initiations in which the boys and young men are instructed in the tribal secrets, after which they are received into full membership in the tribe. The ordeals through which they must pass have also the aim of breaking up their childish dependence on their families, substituting the group affiliation as their major relationship. The rites performed in times of stress, when the village is threatened, renew this tie of membership and the sense of tribal solidarity.

Identification with the group has very obvious values, but it carries also certain disadvantages. For the unique qualities of the individual must necessarily be disregarded and sternly suppressed, with the inevitable result that he does not develop his innate capacity for initiative but depends on the group for support and defence and still more for moral guidance.

Naturally the identification of the individual with his fellow members and with the group is rarely, if ever, complete. Even among sheep in a flock there are individual differences; some few stand out from their fellows, and such differences usually make for conflict. We even speak of a rebel as a "black sheep." Those who want conformity try to impose it on the individualists; they in turn struggle for their independence. Through this struggle (perhaps not among sheep, but certainly among men) a further separation of the individual from the group takes place. If one such rebel joins with others who are like-minded, a secondary group will be formed. This process is likely to be repeated, until some, finding themselves out of sympathy with the rest, venture forth alone.

Through such a process the differences between individuals are brought more clearly into view. One person finds himself becoming differentiated from all others, even from those who in many respects are like him. To become separate can even become an aim in itself, albeit often an unconscious one. This is usually the motive behind the rebelliousness of adolescence and the argumentativeness of adults, many of whom enter into a discussion simply to clarify and differentiate their own points of view, rather than to convince their opponents or to learn from them. A similar need for clarification may motivate an individual who quarrels not about ideas but over some action or attitude that affects him emotionally, though he may be quite unaware of the nature of the unconscious motive he is obeying—namely, the urge to separate himself from someone who is too close to him or who exerts too strong an influence over him. The goal is to find himself, his own uniqueness.

In modern times the emphasis on the ego and its separateness has led to an individualism that has been erroneously regarded as individuality and that has resulted in a considerable weakening of the ties between man and his fellows. This false separateness is always challenged when the group or the nation goes to war: then it must be waived, and the individuals must be merged again into a collective entity, re-created for a common purpose. Each man is united with others through a common experience of suffering and sacrifice. A deep and satisfying sense of oneness results. For even an insignificant man is able to lay aside his concern for his own safety and comfort in loyalty to a group and to a cause beyond personal ambition; in this way unselfishness, courage, and heroism take the place of selfishness and egocentricity.

Thus the primitive instinct of self-defence, leading to hostility and conflict, can also become the motive power enabling an individual to overcome the childish bonds to his family and the traditional alliances to the group in which he was born. It may help him even to transcend his dependence on a group of his own choosing with which he feels himself to be in deepest sympathy, so that he can gain strength to separate himself from it. Having done this, he must face the world alone—a task so hard that it would not be much wonder if he ran back precipitately to the safety of the group at the first difficulty he encountered. Were it not that the door has been closed through the conflict that set him free, his triumph might prove to be but a Pyrrhic victory. But having separated himself from the group by conflict, he cannot return without renouncing the claim to his individual point of view and submitting to the rule of the majority. He has to go on.

Having left all his opponents behind him, he might expect to be at peace. For the family and the group are no longer at hand to oppose him. Little, however, does he realize the real nature of the problem. It is true that he has won the right to go his own way; but no sooner has he put a suitable distance between himself and those whose control he has rejected, than he discovers that he is not really alone. For he is of two minds. The group attitude he has opposed so strenuously is now voiced by something within himself. The whole conflict has to be taken up again—this time no longer as an external fight with an opponent outside himself, but as an inner conflict. For the group spirit is in him no less than in the other members of the community, and if he is to find his uniqueness he will have to struggle with that collective impulse within himself.

In *Flight to Arras*, Antoine de Saint-Exupéry records the inner experience of a young French pilot during the last terrible days of the Battle of France. He was a rather solitary young man who felt himself superior to the ordinary person, being isolated by the disillusioned and somewhat blasé attitude of the university student of the nineteen-thirties. When his squadron was left behind to carry out useless reconnaissance flights after the rest of the army had retreated, all the values of life, as he had known it, vanished. The emotional horizon was narrowed down to the existence of these few comrades, who were as completely separated from the rest of the world as if they had been on a lost planet; and he found himself at last emotionally one of a group.

The self-conscious egotism of the young intellectual was redeemed through this identification. For the first time in his life he was an integral part of a whole, something bigger and more significant than himself. His cynicism melted away. He found himself loving these people; and to his own great surprise he realized that he was accepted as he never had been before, not only by his comrades but also by the simple farmer's family with whom he was billeted. On his last flight, he moved a step farther in his spiritual evolution, for in those memorable hours alone above the clouds he saw that the values of humanity are merely exemplified in the group spirit. They are really to be found not in the group but in the very essence of each man: it is this that makes him human. This quality is a suprapersonal value that resides in each one and yet is not his personality, his ego. Rather, it is the spark of life within him—a divine something, yet most human too. In his solitary meditation, his experience of utter aloneness, which Saint-Exupéry recounts in simple and convincing language, the young flier touched the experience of what Jung calls the Self, the centre of consciousness that transcends the ego.

Opposition and the motive of self-defence can thus furnish the impulse necessary to bring about a separation from the group and lead to the discovery of the uniqueness of the individual. Thereby the instinct of self-defence, which contains the seeds of war and potentialities for destruction of the whole human species, shows itself to be capable of functioning in a new realm, and now its power is transferred to the quest for the supreme value within the human psyche. Through this search the primitive and barbaric forces that still slumber uneasily behind the civilized mask of modern man may be redeemed.

THE HISTORICAL evolution of this instinct proceeded in a series of fairly well-defined steps. Here and there a few individuals, as well as small groups of men, became capable of self-control and reasoned action, and thereby raised themselves above the general level of almost reflex reaction to the threat of injury. Similarly, larger groups gradually learned how to govern their mass reactions, until even nations consented to accept some discipline and control.

The aggressive instinct seems to be peculiarly difficult to transform, perhaps because, unlike the hunger instinct, it necessarily employs primitive means for its fulfillment. One individual in eating does not necessarily violate another's rights, but fighting, even in self-defence, involves the use of aggressive as well as protective mechanisms. Yet in spite of this the instinct has undergone considerable modification.

The same factors that played such an important part in the disciplining of man's instinctive greed, namely, social necessity and religious influences, were instrumental in modifying the instinct of self-defence. As the pressure of these two forces produced their characteristic effect, initiating and fostering psychic modification, the instinct came to a larger degree under control of the conscious ego. It became or seemed to become less arbitrary and compulsive. The forward steps were faltering and were often retarded by the eruption of compulsive primitive reactions whose regressive trends threatened over and over again to destroy all that civilization had wrested from the untamed reaches of the unconscious psyche.

Wherever human beings live together in groups, the primitive irascibility and belligerence of the individual will always be a threat to the life of the group. If a community is not to be decimated through internecine violence, some means of restraint must be found. The social restrictions and taboos that gradually evolved had this primary object. Through the centuries they were progressively strengthened and adapted, and as the group increased in numbers and organization, these instruments gained in power and prestige. Although aggressiveness was by these means actually tamed in some measure, the instinct of self-defence proved to be extraordinarily intransigeant. The development of mutual tolerance within the group produced a semblance of culture and reasonableness that was often exceedingly misleading. For the members of the group, restrained by fear of punishment and of disapproval from their fellows, might in public obey established laws and conventions; yet in the secrecy of their own hearts, and even in their private actions, the old primitive instinct might still have its way. For most members of a group are psychologically below the level of development represented by the group ideal and law, even though some may be above the collective standard. Thus there is often a great discrepancy between the apparent level of civilization in a community and the degree to which the primitive instinct has actually been transformed.

This discrepancy between the conventional behaviour and the reality that lurks beneath the surface of civilization is further obscured because of the great difference in accepted codes of behaviour affecting the individual in his relation to his own community on the one hand, and regulating the relations between different groups on the other. Restraint of the individual within his community usually developed more rapidly, and the rules governing his behaviour became more exacting than did the complementary rules governing the behaviour of one group in its relations with another. Man learned to respect his brother's rights long before he conceded that the foreigner had any rights at all.

The Crow Indians, for instance, formerly considered that stealing horses from a neighbouring tribe was merely a sport, to be indulged in at every opportunity, even though in their dealings with one another they had learned to be scrupulously honest. In many a community a warlike spirit is considered to have a high moral value for the group long after it has been superseded as the ideal for the individual.

In times of stress even civilized individuals, as already instanced, frequently regress to an earlier mode of behaviour. There are numerous accounts illustrating reversion to violence and murder in persons cut off from civilization and thus placed beyond the restraints of the law and public opinion. We need only recall the well-known story of the ship's crew marooned on Pitcairn Island, where the community almost totally destroyed itself in quarrels, in spite of the fact that it must have been obvious to all that the chances of survival were greater, the larger the size of the group. In contrast, there is the equally forceful illustration of the real inner development that must have been present in Adams, the man by whom the remnant of the unfortunate group was finally rallied and educated. For even today the inhabitants of Pitcairn are famed for a high level of social culture and conduct, enforced solely by their own integrity and not by a police force. That the one book which Adams possessed, and on which the education of children and adults alike was grounded, happened to be the Bible, is a fact of no small psychological importance, in view of the part the religious factor has played in the discipline and modification of the instinct of self-defence.

IN THE INFANCY of the human species, as well as in the individual infant of today, the reaction to injury is reflex and purely instinctive; it is a reaction of body, not of mind or conscious intent. And, if we can judge from our observations of animals and infants, it is not at first accompanied by the psychological experience we call feeling. But when the instinct begins to be modified, the reflex reaction is changed into an emotional one; that is, it is now a bodily reaction with a feeling overtone.

The feeling is recognized as belonging in some measure to oneself. The bodily reaction happens in one and does not have a similar quality of "my-ness." Indeed, bodily reactions that are obviously emotional may occur in us without any accompanying conscious feeling. When one feels his "gorge rising," or when one is "getting hot under the collar" or has "that sinking feeling in the pit of the stomach" which indicates disgust, anger, or fear, it is sometimes almost as though one were looking on at all this, as though it were happening to some other person. Then, if the reactions reach a certain intensity, the conscious citadel is overcome and one is invaded by the emotion and compelled to submit oneself to it, whether one wants to or not.

In some people this invasion can occur without any awareness on their part of what is happening to them. One minute the individual is apparently calm and self-possessed, and the next he is no longer in control of himself: an emotion that he may hardly recognize as his own speaks and acts through him. Others, however, are aware of the rising tide of emotion within, and although they cannot entirely control it, they can prevent themselves from committing some irrevocable act by a hasty retreat from the situation. Children especially, in whom the restraints of civilization are not as yet very firmly established, may rush from the room when they feel themselves being overwhelmed, to "have it out" by themselves. In these cases the ego, the conscious I, struggles to retain its control over that other which is not itself, that psychic force which threatens to take possession of consciousness.

Primitive man explained this other as being a god or daemon who entered into him, and we for our part use similar expressions to explain the phenomenon. We say, "He acted as if possessed," or "I don't know what got into him." We are inclined to look indulgently on invasions of this kind, as if they were natural phenomena, unfortunate perhaps, but unavoidable. Certainly when one is oneself the victim of such an uprush of primitive libido, one tends not to hold oneself entirely responsible. The loss of self-control seems in itself an adequate excuse for the outbreak. With the explanation, "I was not quite myself," or "When he spoke to me like that I saw red," or "When I struck him I hardly knew what I was doing," the violent action seems justified.

But as the conscious ego gains ability to control or repress these instinctive reactions, it begins to dominate the psyche, and man is compelled to take increasing responsibility for his own emotions: the individual is obliged to admit that it was his own anger or fear that caused the outbreak. If in spite of all his struggles to overcome his emotions, he still remains subject to attacks that override the control of his ego, he confesses that under certain circumstances he may experience anger or fear or hate beyond human measure—compulsions of daemonic energy.

It is characteristic of a certain stage of psychological development that these emotions arising from the nonpersonal part of the psyche are projected into a being outside oneself. Instead of saying that he has been possessed by a daemon, a man at this level will say that it was God who was angry. In this way he ignores his own responsibility for the anger, for he becomes merely the tool chosen by God to express divine wrath.

"Vengeance is mine; I will repay, saith the Lord": these words were spoken by the prophet of the God of wars, in whose name the Israelites had fought many a campaign. Now they were being taught that the anger belonged to God, and that when they revenged themselves they were really avenging his injuries.

> Put yourselves in array against Babylon round about: all ye that bend the bow, shoot at her, spare no arrows; for she hath sinned against the Lord. Shout against her round about: she hath given her hand: her foundations are fallen, her walls are thrown down: for it is the vengeance of the Lord: take vengeance upon her; as she hath done, do unto her.[2]

This battle cry purported to be a summons to avenge the injuries that God had suffered, but surely the injuries that God's people had suffered gave edge to their anger. Their ascription of anger to God was little more than a rationalization, or an assumption that God also suffered the emotions they felt so hot within themselves; that is to say, they projected the daemonic emotions that took possession of them into a divine figure envisaged as outside themselves. They created God in their own image.

But when we come to the Christian era, another step has been taken. Paul writes to his converts in Rome:

> Dearly beloved, avenge not yourselves, but rather give place unto wrath: for it is written, Vengeance is mine; I will repay, saith the Lord. Therefore if thine enemy hunger, feed him; if he thirst, give him drink; for in so doing thou shalt heap coals of fire on his head. Be not overcome of evil, but overcome evil with good.[3]

God is still thought of as outside the psyche; moreover, the personification has gone a step farther. It is here thought that God alone, without the co-operation of man, will bring a suitable retribution on those who have disobeyed the divine laws. This change in attitude went hand in hand with the emergence of the idea of an impersonal justice or law. It was no longer necessary for each man to be a law unto himself: the law now stood above his private feeling and judgment. To be able to submit in any real way, in his own being, to the arbitration of the law, implied a discipline of instinctive and spontaneous

2. Jer. 50:14, 15.
3. Rom. 12:19-21.

reactions that it must have taken hundreds of years to acquire. And indeed the ascendancy of the civilized man over the primitive, in any one of us, is still so precarious that we must all at times have experienced actual physical reactions indicating anger, violent anger at that, the while our conscious thoughts, words, and feelings remained perfectly balanced and under control. Who has not felt himself physically "burning" at an insult he would not dream of resenting openly, or clenching his fists during what was on the surface a perfectly friendly argument?

In times of physical danger even the most heroic may be aware that their bodies are acting as though under the influence of abject terror; the effects may be so marked that the individual may be compelled to give way to them momentarily. At the same time his mind may remain clear, and as soon as the physical reaction subsides he is able to do whatever is necessary to meet the crisis, quite regardless of personal risk. These persons could not for a moment be accused of cowardice, yet their bodily reactions are those of primitive and uncontrollable terror. Our judgment may even tell us that their courage is of a higher order than that of less sensitive persons who do not experience the impact of fear as acutely.

Conventional training insists that these violent emotions be dealt with by repression or by conscious control. In civilized countries all children are taught to control both their actions and their emotions. This lesson is learned with varying degrees of success, but all learn it in some measure. In fact, many persons become so adept at hiding their instinctive reactions, not only from others but also from themselves, that their very self-control makes them liable to another danger. For should the inner barriers be let down even slightly, through a lowering of the threshold of consciousness (as a result of fatigue or the use of alcohol or some other depressant), or should the external restraints be removed by changes in the outer conditions, the repressed reactions may burst forth unrestrainedly and prove themselves doubly destructive, just because the person in whom they occur has been so completely unaware of their presence.

If this occurs in modern persons, how much more serious must the danger have been in the beginnings of civilization. In truth, a large part of the energy of man throughout the centuries has been devoted to combating and controlling his compulsive emotions. In some civilizations, this demand for self-control has been so implacable that to show any emotion at all has meant loss of face. In others, the whole culture has been based on the disciplines of war: the national hero was the warrior, and the virtues of the warlike spirit represented the social ideal. Ancient Sparta was such a warrior state, and its name is still a synonym for an attitude of utmost fortitude and self-control. The Roman Empire likewise was founded very largely on a military ideal. Some of the American Indian tribes, such as the Iroquois, based their whole morality on war and its discipline, which accounts for the degradation that befell them when the white man would no longer allow their braves to go on the warpath. In both Germany and Japan in recent years, the prestige of an elite caste was conferred on military personnel; the qualities most esteemed were obedience, discipline, hardness, and disregard of all other values, even life itself, for the sake of military objectives.

It has even been asserted that periodic wars are necessary for the spiritual health of a nation, doubtless on account of the beneficial effect that military discipline has on the individual man. For not only can military training change a primitive man possessed by a bloodthirsty daemon into a warrior or a knight, but it can also transform an indolent and self-indulgent boy into an alert and self-reliant citizen. Furthermore, when men face a common danger together and are dependent on each other for their safety, they develop a particular kind of comradeship that has a high moral value; for it relegates personal safety and advantage to a secondary place and binds them together as perhaps no other human experience can. Also, common danger and the devotion that is engendered by war no less than by dire necessity, seem to stimulate the national life to fresh efforts. Long overdue social reforms are undertaken with enthusiasm, while scientific research takes on new life. Even the birth rate usually increases markedly. It seems as though the life of the nation were rejuvenated through the psychic forces released by war.

YET FROM THE BEGINNING of civilization it must have been obvious that the primitive resentments and murderous angers of the individual would have to be checked by something more than the discipline of the warrior band if men were to live together in villages or tribes and co-operate for purposes of self-preservation. For when the instinct to kill is aroused, it may go on working autonomously, seeking ever new victims in friend and foe alike. Therefore elaborate customs regulating war as well as quarrels between individuals are met with all over the world.

For example, certain tribes practise *rites de sortie* after battle, in addition to the *rites d'entrée* [4] designed to arouse the warlike spirit of the braves; for once the spear has tasted blood, as they say, it thirsts to taste it again, and will not care whom it kills. Thus when the young men return from the warpath they are not feted as heroes, nor are they allowed to strut about the village displaying their bloodstained weapons. Instead, they are disarmed, segregated in huts outside the village, given purgatives or sweat baths, and fed on bread and water until the spirit of war has left them and they are themselves again. They then return to the village in a chastened mood, and there is no danger of further bloodshed.

These and similar restraints upon man's aggressive instincts laid the foundation for the most important cultural development of the period extending from the tenth century over more than five hundred years, which was predominantly concerned with gaining control of the warlike spirit and the aggressive instinct. This epoch was actually named "the days of

---

4. The terms *rite d'entrée* and *rite de sortie* denote certain rituals designed respectively to induct an individual into an unusual or taboo condition and to release him from it at the expiration of the given time or function. He is thus set apart to perform certain duties that are otherwise taboo. He is believed to become imbued with the daemon or spirit whose special realm he has entered, and to remain so possessed until he is "disinfected" and released by the *rite de sortie*. The martial state in men, and the period of childbirth in women, are examples of taboo conditions requiring *rites de sortie*, while *rites d'entrée* are practised in connection not only with war but also with hunting and other activities.

chivalry" on account of the cultural achievements resulting from the disciplining of men in regard to combat. It was felt at that time that the emotions from which quarrels between individuals and wars between groups arose were valuable, and an elaborate discipline was devised to control without repressing them. For they were the true source of that courage and mettle which were so highly prized and so necessary for group survival in the unsettled state of Europe in that era.

From about the time of puberty, boys of upper-class families were trained in the school of chivalry. If they became proficient not only in the use of arms but also in the ability to handle themselves and control their emotions, they were initiated, at the end of adolescence, into the ranks of the knights, who formed an elite caste. To achieve knighthood was, indeed, the supreme accomplishment; it had a spiritual meaning in addition to the significance of graduation into manhood.

The psychological movement of which mediaeval chivalry was a part was accompanied by a profound change in the relation between the sexes. Men began to seek for an entirely new kind of association with women. From being primarily a biological object for man—the source of sexual satisfaction, the mother of his children, and the keeper of his household—woman became the focus of new and strange emotions. Romantic love began to play a prominent part in men's thoughts. The birth of this new devotion to the "fair lady" went hand in hand with the development of manly and chivalric virtues. The connection between the two ideals is clearly seen in the literature of the period—in the *Mabinogion* of the Celts and the related Arthurian cycle, or in early French romances such as *Aucassin et Nicolette*. It is interesting to observe that the somewhat earlier *Chanson de Roland* is an epic of chivalry devoted entirely to feats of war and the friendships of comrades-in-arms, while the theme of the fair lady is practically absent.

The association between discipline and control of the warlike instinct and the beginnings of romantic love is no accident. From the psychological point of view, man, instead of being merely the puppet of the unconscious, had become in some measure his own master. There had come into being a psychic function that related his conscious personality in a meaningful way with those dark sources of psychic energy which had formerly held him in their grip. This psychic function was maintained by his unknown, other side, his feminine counterpart or soul, which Jung has called the anima.[5] To become acquainted with this "fair lady," to rescue her from the power of dragon and tyrant—personifications of the untamed instinctive drives —and to serve her, became his chief spiritual necessity. Naturally he could not see this process directly. It sprang from a cultural movement, a process taking place in the unconscious of hundreds of persons and moulding the very spirit of the times. The individual always perceives these unconscious soul happenings in projected form, that is to say, his attention is caught by and riveted on an outer happening that derives its fascination from the unconscious energy it symbolizes and reflects. The soul of man, his anima, came into being when he succeeded in separating himself from complete identity with the unconscious drives; being feminine, it was projected into an actual or ideal woman, and so was personified.

When the individual man was in danger of being sucked back into a more primitive condition, his anima appeared as threatening. Then he envisaged woman as bestial or devilish. But as he gradually succeeded in dissolving the identification with his compulsive instincts, his anima likewise changed and began to appear in desirable guise. The projection then fell on a woman who was also seen as desirable. In her aloof bearing, in the subtle attraction of her otherness, her difference from man, woman carried some of the mana, the glamour, the mysterious potency that had functioned in uncivilized man as concomitants of blind passion. The spell that woman's allure put upon man now aided him in his struggle with the barbaric elements in his nature. For the fair lady's sake he would undergo any discipline, no matter how rigorous; or he would undertake a quest in the name of the "destresséd damsel," whom, in the legends at least, he unfailingly rescued. We, with

5. See C. G. Jung, *Two Essays on Analytical Psychology* (C.W. 7); M. E. Harding, *The Way of All Women*; E. Bertine, *Human Relationships: in the Family, in Friendship, in Love.*

our greater psychological insight, recognize this quest as the journey into the inner world in search of his soul, perpetually awaiting his arrival.

The interest of the whole community was focused on the exploits of the elite caste of chivalry. They lived their lives ritually, as it were, not only for themselves but for the group as well. They were set apart in order that they might fulfill this imperative of life. Private acts of vengeance were replaced by tournaments and duels, fought and won before an audience of the entire community. A knight was not permitted to redress a wrong by an immediate retaliation: to do so was considered barbarous and unworthy. He had to wait until a time could be set for a formal meeting with his enemy. Even when they did meet they could not plunge into a murderous brawl but had to restrain themselves and act according to prescribed forms, under the direction of umpires. Gradually the skill of the combatants came to have a greater importance than the amount of bodily injury they could inflict on each other by brute strength. Friends would challenge each other at a tournament to see which was the better man, and the observance of the rules came to be spoken of as "fair play." The deadly fight had now become play!

In the days of chivalry, when the tournament held such an important place in the education and civilizing of men and in the tempering of their instinct of self-defence, obedience to the rules and the carrying out of the ritual became an aim in itself. This aim interposed itself between the combatants and their immediate goal of killing each other. Consequently, the primitive urge of the instinct was deflected from its primary objective and found at least partial satisfaction in another realm. This modification was fostered by the regulations governing knightly combat. In the first place, time was allowed to intervene between the injury and the retribution, so that passions cooled in the interim; further, as the emphasis came to be placed on skill, the combatant who was more successful than his rival in keeping cool had a definite advantage. When brute force counts most, emotion is helpful, for it lends strength to the blow; but when prowess depends on dexterity, the balance is otherwise. The man who has himself in hand, who is not the helpless servant of his own passion, has the advantage over a less disciplined opponent.

When the encounter took place in open tournament, a secondary objective came into the picture. For part of the combatant's concern was diverted from the effort to injure his opponent to the desire to please the onlookers by playing, in its every detail, the role of the ideal warrior. In this way, satisfaction of his anger and of his desire for revenge was gained on a different plane. A knight who had been insulted or dishonoured felt himself to be reinstated as much through the approval of the community as by the shedding of his opponent's blood. Later it was considered a sufficient satisfaction to gain this public approval, even though the opponent suffered a defeat that inflicted only a token injury or merely hurt his prestige while leaving his person uninjured.

The tales of the *Mabinogion* and of the entire Arthurian literature show the transformation thus wrought upon the instinct of self-defence. Instead of fighting only to avenge bodily or material injury, a man might fight to defend his honour or to reinstate himself in the eyes of his lady, who represented ideal womanhood. These goals reflect the more refined aspects of ego striving. Or perhaps his courage was dedicated to a more impersonal image, such as the Holy Sepulchre, or the Holy Grail, for which many a knight of the Middle Ages risked his life. For to him these were symbols of inestimable worth, surpassing even the claims of his personal safety and honour.

To what extent this change was really effective in mediaeval man we have no means of knowing. The stories of the Round Table are undoubtedly idealized accounts, or perhaps wholly fictitious. Yet because they show a change in the ideal of the times, they are valid evidence that a real psychological transformation was taking place. Individual men may never have attained the heroic level attributed to the knights of Arthur's court; but that generations of people preserved or even invented such tales indicates that man was capable of conceiving of such a modification of the instinct and of admiring it. Indeed, from that time on the very name of knight came to have new significance. It no longer meant merely warrior or soldier: "knightly virtue," "a chivalrous act," are concepts that to this day carry the hallmark of devotion to a suprapersonal motive.

THE FIRST LESSON a candidate for knighthood had to learn was to overcome himself. The ideal of self-mastery, and the obligation to overcome the animal instinct in one's nature, is also represented in the ritual of the Spanish bullfight. Brutal and disgusting as this survival from a barbarous age is in the opinion of most Western people, it is nevertheless very instructive. It demonstrates that a symbol containing *in potentia* all the factors necessary for the redemption of primitive energy may yet produce no change in the psychology of either the participants or the onlookers, because it remains merely an outer spectacle. If it were realized to be a symbolic act, the drama of the bull ring might perhaps serve to set on foot an inner conquest of brute instinct and a change in the unconscious of the Spanish people.

The bull, being the largest, most powerful, and most dangerous of the domesticated or semidomesticated animals, represents the bull-like, only partially tamed instincts and passions of man. The ritual begins with a procession in which the bull, garlanded with flowers, has the place of honour. Just as in an older day the bull was deified, so here too homage is paid to his indomitable power and energy, which are recognized as suprahuman, even divine.

When the fight begins, the bull is attacked first by men on foot, then by men on horseback, who fail to overcome him. This shows his superiority to the average human, to collective man; that is, instinct is recognized as being stronger than ego. At last the matador, the hero, makes his appearance, alone and on foot. It is his task, as the embodiment of the heroic quality in man, to face the enraged bull and overcome him. But this is not an ordinary killing, the slaughter of a dangerous beast. It is a ritual act, and the matador must carry out the rite in every detail, even at the risk of his own life. The bull must be killed in a particular manner; any matador who dispatched his antagonist in a slovenly and unskillful fashion would be hissed from the ring. His task is not to butcher the animal but to demonstrate a certain attitude towards it: for the bull is the carrier or representative of a suprapersonal value—an essence that is both blind emotion and a god—and through its death man is redeemed from subjection to his own passion.

The majority of people who attend bullfights are quite unaware of what is happening before their eyes, though the action holds them and moves them, indeed transports them completely beyond themselves. It obviously touches a root deep in the unconscious and full of vitality and power. Were the symbolic drama understood, it surely would have a profound psychological influence. When such a drama is enacted and not understood, it has a brutalizing effect on actors and spectators alike, serving merely to sanction indulgence of a crude and brutal blood lust.

If, however, the bullfight were to be perceived as a symbolic portrayal of the age-old need to overcome the animal instinct in man himself, the actual combat would be replaced by a ritual drama. It might then become an experience by which man could learn that he must control his blind and compulsive instinct and release himself from its dominance. Such a transformation would be in line with the evolution of the rituals of redemption in many religions; these rites usually have their roots in ancient and brutal sacrifices analogous to the bullfight. For the matador is the symbol of the fact that it is only by a heroic act, indeed a heroic attitude, that man can quell his passions. If he is able to remain cool and to maintain his self-possession in face of the onrush of his own angers and brute instincts, he will perhaps be a match for them, in spite of the fact that they dispose over far more energy than is available to his new-found ego consciousness. Skill, self-discipline, and a ritual or religious attitude, are the factors that turn the scales in his favour.

This aspect of the ritual combat with the animal was practised in ancient Crete, where captured youths, men and maidens, were trained to "play" with the bulls, and finally to kill them, in order to demonstrate the power of discipline over blind instinct represented by the bull. In figure 4 such a ritual sacrifice is depicted. It comes from a gold bead seal, found in a Mycenean rock tomb, near Thisbê.

When in the course of psychological analysis an individual is confronted with the problem of having to deal with power-

Fig. 4. A Cretan Bull Sacrifice

ful instincts newly aroused through the confrontation with his shadow [6] the problem may be represented in dreams as a fight with a wild and powerful animal. A modern woman, who was faced with a problem of this nature, dreamed that a primitive man was attacked by a fierce bull. There ensued a desperate struggle but finally the man killed the bull by a stab behind the shoulder, which strangely corresponds to the wound inflicted ritually, so long ago, in Crete. (See plate II.)

There are many legends and stories as well as actual historical events that exemplify the emergence of such a heroic attitude. A highly instructive instance is the legendary encounter between David and Goliath. The armies of the Israel-

6. See below, note, p. 295.

ites and the Philistines were encamped over against each other, and day after day Goliath, a giant of enormous size and strength, came out before the army of the Philistines and challenged the Israelites to send over a champion to meet him in single combat. The outcome of the encounter was to decide the battle, though the custom of the time was to fight to the last man, with the victor annihilating the vanquished foe and despoiling his country. To the children of Israel this was a sacred duty imposed by the voice of Jehovah, for he was a warlike God and embodied the unconscious drives of a people who had only recently fought their way to a land in which to live. Then came the battle with the Philistines, who were more firmly established and held superiority in power. Their champion, Goliath, represented their reliance on brute strength. David, who volunteered to meet him as champion of the Israelites, was, in marked contrast, a youth—hardly more than a boy. Yet he overcame his huge opponent by skillful use of a weapon of no intrinsic strength, his shepherd's sling, devised to drive off the wild animals that threatened the flock at night. This victory signified that force was no longer the most powerful factor in the world. The Lord of Hosts was changing his character. As David said: "The Lord saveth not with sword and spear." A time was approaching when these predatory tribes would be obliged to settle down, when skill would have to replace might.

IN THIS STORY, whether it is legend or historical fact, David and Goliath engage in actual combat, but their duel foreshadows a change in attitude that led by degrees to the substitution of a ritual encounter for the actual one. Thus the very nature and meaning of the combat underwent a change. Man's struggle against his foe became a drama representing his conquest of brute instinct itself, perhaps even of the spirit of passion—anger or hostility—personified in the enemy. In the episodes of the Arthurian cycle, the opponent—whether legendary knight, magician, or dragon—was, to the hero of the Round Table, the very personification of evil: to destroy him was to rid the world of an accursed thing. At that stage in psychological development, the evil lurking in the unconscious was projected into the "enemy" and hated and attacked as if it had no connection with the protagonist other than that he felt himself destined to struggle with and overcome this menace or die in the attempt. But in a still later stage, man came to realize that it was the barbaric spirit within himself that he had to overcome, albeit still in the person of an outward opponent.

In the tournaments, where the embodiment of the inimical force was not an actual foe, but might be a friend chosen to play the role, the realization of the ritual nature of the encounter hovered just below the threshold of consciousness. It was only a short step farther to the recognition that the real enemy was not a person but a destructive instinct, a psychological force, a spirit—not of course a daemon or ghost, a spirit in the primitive sense, but rather a psychological factor of nonpersonal origin, much in the sense in which we speak of the warlike spirit, or the spirit of adventure. Yet when such a motive force arises from the unconscious and acts compulsively and autonomously in the individual, it is almost as if he were possessed by a daemon or spirit in the antique sense of the term. As Paul says, "We wrestle not against flesh and blood, but against the powers of darkness in high places."

The idea of the struggle against evil is frequently represented in the terms of actual warfare—the "soldiers of Christ" are urged to "fight the good fight," etc.—and indeed it is a battle. But only too often this combat is not recognized as a contest that should be waged in the subjective realm, within a man's own heart. Instead, he sees the forces of evil only outside himself: they are projected and thus personified in another being as the mortal enemy.

This psychological mechanism of projection has been the cause of many brutalities throughout the centuries. Religious persecutions—inquisitions, pogroms, and crusades—have been carried out by men who believed themselves to have all of the truth, with the consequence that the enemy had only its opposite, all the error. Such a one-sided and fanatical attitude always denotes complete ignorance of what lies in one's own unconscious. It seems to the zealot that God himself demands that the evil in the other man be attacked and overcome. Campaigns against evil, of the most brutal and barbarous type, have been undertaken, over and over again, at the instigation of God—or so their perpetrators believed—a God who like the God of Hosts of Old Testament days could brook no opposition. This was but one of the many gods of battle whom men have worshipped and in whose name they have indulged their own barbaric impulses. Ishtar of Babylon was goddess of hosts as well as Magna Mater, giver of nourishment and embodiment of vegetation. Mars was god of war and at the same time the spirit of spring. And many another deity has represented the negative-positive energies that have their origin in man's own instinctive drives.

To realize that the god is indeed only the personification of that spirit power which rules in man's unconscious requires insight that was beyond the psychological range of the man of antiquity. To him it seemed rather that his god was an external being of most arbitrary disposition. He did not suspect that this angry, jealous, undependable god, who gave life and plenty at one moment only to blast and destroy at the next, was really a projection of the powerful and unaccountable forces within himself.

However, even the character of gods may change; that is to say, the instinctive drives deep-buried in the unconscious of man are subject to an evolutionary psychic development or transformation that is mirrored in the transformation of the character of God. I have already referred briefly to the change that took place in the Israelites' concept of Jehovah. From being a bloodthirsty God of battles when the Israelites were predatory tribes who had descended upon the land of Canaan, he became a far more spiritual God, the Shepherd of Israel, a God of morality, for whom justice was more than vengeance. A similar transformation took place in the character of the Greek gods. Finally a time arrived when man began to understand that the gods really represented a law within himself.

In earliest antiquity, Zeus was the Thunderer hurling his bolts at all who offended him, whether man or beast. He represented the power of brute instinct. But there came a time when he made a differentiation. His law for the beasts was still that they must be guided by their instincts. They remained under the law of Zeus the Thunderer. But man had now to learn a different law. Conflict for him was to result not in violence but in justice. "Fishes and beasts and fowls of the air devour one another," writes Hesiod, "but to man, Zeus has given justice. Beside Zeus on his throne, Justice has her seat." [7]

THE NEGATIVE ASPECT of enmity is obvious; its positive fruits are not so readily recognized. Courage, self-sacrifice, and the other virtues mobilized by war grow in proportion to the dangers that threaten. For danger can rouse an individual or a nation to such profound recognition of essential values that private welfare is forgotten, at least while the peril lasts.

But beyond these lies another potential value of entirely different dimension. For the dynamic forces that the instinct of self-defence has power to arouse are of an intensity that overrides the boundaries of the conscious part of the psyche. We could hardly have believed at the beginning of this century that passions and qualities we thought long ago outgrown were only slumbering beneath the surface of our complacency and *laisser aller* attitude. Little pleasures, little comforts, well-bounded ambitions and ideals, expressed our philosophy of life. Then came in rapid succession two world wars, let loose by men who despised small virtues and little pleasures and threw open the doors to unlimited, unbounded desirousness and brutality. The day of the small things was past.

Just over twenty years ago,[8] in a lecture before a small group of people, Jung remarked that when the forces of the unconscious slumber, man lives a petty life concerned merely with little things. He lives on the personal level only. But if a big idea awakens in such a man, be it an idea of good or of evil, it arouses energies belonging to the nonpersonal level, and he begins to live beyond himself. He becomes the tool, the mouthpiece of a force greater than his ego. He becomes in

7. *Works and Days*, ll. 276-81. Cf. Evelyn-White trans., pp. 23-25.
8. This was written in 1947.

fact the soldier of an idea, and as such he can change the face of the world. Here is another value of war, which can be positive, but may on the other hand precipitate the greatest of tragedies.

It is perhaps not possible for the group, for collective man, to advance beyond the stage that Hesiod depicts. If the nations can reinstate Justice beside Zeus upon his throne, much will have been accomplished. If any further transformation of the aggressive instincts is to take place, we shall have to look to the individual, in whom alone psychological understanding and development can be achieved. I have already spoken of the part that conflict plays in separating the individual from the dominance of the group and from his own dependence on its support, and of the fact that when he finds himself alone and unsupported by the group approval and morality, he is likely to fall into conflict again as soon as he is confronted with any situation that arouses an instinctive emotional response. At such a moment he will find himself flooded with involuntary reactions threatening to drag him back to an old behaviour pattern. If this regression is to be avoided, a further step must be taken to enable him to understand his own psyche and to adapt or modify the instinct itself.

The psychological insight that Hindu religious thought brings to this problem is most illuminating. The *Bhagavad-Gita* tells the story of a hero, Arjuna, who was about to engage in a battle of vengeance against a kinsman. His every instinct was against the inevitable slaughter of his relatives, but his duty, according to the law of the day, was to do battle. In the greatest conflict and depression, he went a little apart to struggle with himself and try to see his situation more clearly. As he sat in his chariot, the god Krishna came to him in the guise of the charioteer and taught him the meaning of the battle. The god pointed out to him that as he was of the warrior caste his role was to fight and carry out the obligations of a warrior. Thus and thus only could he fulfill his own karma, or fate. Then the teaching touched a more profound level. Krishna explained that the evil kinsman whom Arjuna must defeat really represented his own shadow, the powers of aggression and egotism within himself. In fighting the actual battle he was fighting a symbolic one as well, for the enemy was also himself. By overcoming his kinsman he himself would be released from the karma of a warrior.

The cycle is thus completed. The individual first projects the evil of which he is unconscious. Then in his anger and resentment towards that evil he separates himself from unconscious identification with the group and at long last comes to recognize that it is his own evil that he has been fighting. Through this recognition a little more of the nonpersonal energy of the instinct becomes available for redemption from the depths, and the individual is released to move a step forward in his psychological development.

6

Reproduction

I. SEXUALITY: *Lust and Love*

THE INSTINCT of self-preservation safeguards the life and well-being of the individual: the well-being of the race is served in a similar way by an instinct for race preservation. This instinct, however, operates not in the race as a whole but in the individuals comprising it. At the same time, since the life of the race precedes the life of the current generation, and will continue long after the latter has perished, it is, as an entity, something greater than the sum of the lives of its living members. Consequently, the impulse that ensures the continuance of the race will function regardless of the self-interest of the individual. It may be detrimental to his personal interests, may even destroy him. Thus at times an opposition can arise between the two great impulses that guard life.

In a purely natural existence, in which the instincts have complete control, this conflict can readily be observed. Whenever it arises, the instinct for race preservation seems to take precedence over the instinct for individual preservation. For example, it is said that a fruit tree affected by disease or injury may produce a bumper crop. When its life is threatened, the tree produces more fruit than before, regardless of the fact that it thereby squanders the vital energies needed for its recuperation. By a similar reaction, the number of bees in a hive will increase when the colony is threatened by shortage of food. It is as though nature were making a last desperate attempt to carry on the life of the community by sheer weight of numbers, regardless of how many perish of starvation. The bees carry out this suicidal policy themselves, though they will also on occasion ruthlessly kill off large numbers of their fellows, if the welfare of the hive seems to require the sacrifice. It would seem that nature is greatly concerned with the survival of the race and relatively less concerned about the welfare of the individual.

When, however, the original condition is modified by the active intervention of individuals who have come to realize themselves consciously, the natural course of events is disturbed. These humans seek to conserve their individual lives, often in preference to serving the collective life of the race. For when ego consciousness comes on the scene and the instincts lose some of their compulsory character through psychic transformation, the balance between the instinctual forces changes.

Nature gives precedence to the race; from the point of view of the ego, the well-being of the individual is obviously the essential value. The ego would say, "What would happen to the life of the race if the individuals that make it should perish?" Or, as the Negro spiritual puts it, "It's me, it's me, it's me, O Lord." In the struggle between the two instincts, the scales can occasionally be turned, by conscious intervention, in favour of personal survival; yet man's power to change the natural order for his own benefit is not as great as he thinks. For the law of instinct functions within him; it is not a rule imposed from without. And nature's ancient way usually prevails.

It is possible for a woman afflicted with a grave disease, such as cancer, to go through a normal pregnancy. The child may be born healthy and well-nourished, even though the mother's illness progresses more rapidly. In the case of such an unfortunate pregnancy, the child is formed and develops at the cost of the mother's life, regardless of her own wishes in the matter. Here nature makes the choice. On the other hand, a mother may consciously choose to save her child, even though the decision costs her own life. Or a woman may deliberately allow herself to become pregnant even though her conscious judgment warns her that it is folly, perhaps even fatal folly, to do so.

The force of the instinctive mechanism that works to preserve the race even at the expense of the individual is particularly demonstrated in wartime. The marked rise in the birth rate that generally occurs in such periods indicates that the impulse to reproduce grows stronger when the life of the race is threatened, even though from the point of view of the individual the advisability of assenting to it is open to serious question.

The reproductive instinct manifests itself in two aspects, sexuality and parenthood. Discussion of the parental instinct has been reserved for the following chapter; the analysis here will centre upon the sexual instinct.

The fundamental importance of sexuality in the psychological make-up of modern men and women has been brought into the open through the researches of Freud and his followers. The demonstration that creative activities of many kinds, cultural, artistic, and scientific, depend for their energy *au fond* on the sexual instinct, no longer shocks us as it did our immediate forebears. The instinctive roots of erotic and romantic love have been made abundantly clear to us by Freud. It remained for Jung to demonstrate the developmental trend inherent in this fundamental instinct.[1]

The tendency to psychic modification of the biological instincts, which is innate in the human being, has produced a wealth of cultural achievements whose origin can be traced back, by a process of reductive analysis, to instincts hardly more differentiated than the rudimentary reflexes from which they arose: yet we cannot conclude from such an analysis that the final cultural product is nothing but a displaced sexual gesture. For creative work has been expended upon the crude impulse, with the result that a cultural value has been produced, and in addition that the instinct itself has been transformed for the use of society.

It is with this aspect of the process that Jung has been

1. See C. G. Jung, *Symbols of Transformation* (C.W. 5).

especially concerned. He was impressed with the fact that the tendency to evolution is inherent in the living organism. It is not something imposed from without, nor is it an invention of consciousness. Living forms have evolved quite apart from any conscious aim. The aim, if aim there was, came from a source of which the organism was completely unaware—that is, the motivation was unconscious. Furthermore, this "aim" was apparently passed on from one generation to another; for most of the adaptations that have actually been achieved have required many generations for their evolution. In his researches in regard to the unconscious background of the human psyche, Jung observed contents that could not be satisfactorily explained on the basis of the Freudian theory of repression; their meaning became apparent only when they were teleologically interpreted. The evidence supporting this point of view is not rare nor inaccessible. It is available to anyone who has the means of understanding the happenings that go on in the background of his own psyche. In the depths of the unconscious, the old, long-established life patterns are eternally repeated; at the same time, nature is also continually producing new forms, undertaking new experiments. This we recognize to be so in the biological sphere; a study of the unconscious demonstrates that it is true in regard to the psychological realm as well.

It is comparatively easy to trace the steps of an evolutionary process upon which we look back. It is much harder to credit the idea that there are still embryonic, unfinished structures to be found within the living individual of the present day, and that these, far from being meaningless, actually bear the germs of significant new forms whose nature we cannot even guess. Yet, unless we assume that the evolutionary process has come to an end with our own era, and that man today stands at the apex of his development for all time, we must admit that unfinished structures now in process of evolution do actually exist both in the body and in the psyche. If we do not accept this, we are tacitly assuming that twentieth-century man is less, far less than his predecessors; for has he not lost their greatest potentiality, namely, the power to initiate new forms? If so, modern man is not at the peak of evolution; he is a long way down on the other side of the mountain, and must shortly be replaced by a more virile organism retaining the power to evolve. It is with the evidence of this power to evolve, as it is manifested in the psychological sphere, that Jung and his followers are so particularly concerned.

The original impulse expressing the sexual instinct is bound up with gratification of the organism's own physical need. At this level of development, interest in the sexual object is limited to the consideration of its suitability as stimulus and adjuvant to the act. On the animal level, there is apparently no awareness that the sexual partner is moved by impulses similar to the subject's own and seeks similar satisfactions; nor is there any awareness of the consequences of the sexual act in terms of reproduction. It was not until the process of psychic transformation of the instinct had progressed considerably that awareness of these two factors came into consciousness. Among the most primitive tribes, even adults do not seem to be aware of them, while in civilized societies, children may be moved by sexual impulses long before they have any consciousness of the meaning of such feelings or any realization of their goal. Moreover, the compulsory effect of the instinct is such that too often mere knowledge has little connection with behaviour.

Ancient tribal rituals and taboos pertaining to the sexual function had as their aim the release of the individual from the dominance of his sexual impulses. Participation in these rites initiated the process called psychization [2]—a change marked by development of the power to control to some extent the automatic response to sexual stimulation. With the increase of this power came the ability to choose a mate instead of being at the mercy of an uncontrollable physical reaction to any chance stimulus.

When man came to realize the connection between sexuality and reproduction, a new phase in the psychic modification of the instinct was inaugurated. The idea arose that there was a connection between his own reproductive power and the fertility of his fields and herds: to him both were the work

2. See above, pp. 20-23.

of a "spirit of fertility." [3] Through the use and discipline of his own impulses he hoped to influence the fertility of the land. The magic ceremonies and religious rituals that grew out of this idea had an enormous influence on man's relation to his sexual instinct. Not only did these ritual practices help him to disidentify himself in some measure from the insistent demand of the instinct; they also made him realize that although the sex desire arose in his body and seemed to be an expression of his most intimate self, it was in a sense also something separate from himself—a daemonic force or spirit that used him or operated in him.

There are thus in the sexual instinct, as in the instinct of self-preservation, two trends, one having a social and the other a religious goal. The social component of the *libido sexualis* moves towards the goal of human relationship. Love of mate and offspring, and the urge to form a family unit and a home within the community, are the products of this trend. The religious component leads towards the goal of unification within the individual himself, through a union or marriage of the male and female elements within the psyche. For the religious mystic, throughout the ages, this inner marriage has been a symbol of the union of the soul with God. For the psychologist, it signifies the union of the conscious personality with the unconscious part of the psyche, whereby the individual is made whole.

THIS GRADUAL DEVELOPMENT or transformation of the sexual instinct can be traced in the history of the race and must be recapitulated in the experience of each individual, if he is to attain psychological maturity. At first, the sexual instinct is merely a bodily urge unrelated to any knowledge of its possible results in reproduction or to love of a partner. It is merely an urge akin to other biological impulses, such as hunger, the desire to eliminate, and the inclination to sleep. So far as we know, there are no tribes on earth so primitive and unconscious that they know nothing of the meaning

3. See M. E. Harding, *Woman's Mysteries*, for Spirit of Fertility and associated sexual rites.

of this bodily urge; there are still some, however, like the Aruntas of Australia, who profess not to know the connection between intercourse and pregnancy.[4] It is probable, however, that they do really know it, while their formal belief, based on tradition, does not take cognizance of it. They will state that a woman became pregnant because she slept under a particular tree or drew water from a certain spring, or because the light of the moon fell upon her: these are the accepted explanations of pregnancy. If one can get the informant to be more frank, he will admit that she probably also had relations with a man. This is an example of the way in which traditional teaching takes the place of thinking among primitive peoples.

In many myths and traditional stories of primitives we can find the traces of early attitudes towards the sexual function. There is for instance the story of Trickster, a mythical hero of the Winnebago tribe of American Indians.[5] Trickster is a strange fellow, a newcomer among the tribal heroes, who never quite understands what is going on. He blunders along, breaking taboos and flouting the sacred ways. He is like Sung the monkey in Chinese mythology, who surely represents the earliest beginnings of human consciousness. Sung typifies man, the clever fool, who is never content, like the other animals, to obey the ancient law of nature, but must be always investigating, improvising, and devising new ways.

The legend goes that Trickster was burdened with a huge and ponderous phallus, which he was compelled to carry on his back. He did not know what it was, or what it was for, nor why he should be so burdened. The other animals laughed at him, saying that he was at the mercy of this thing and could not put it down. But Trickster retorted that he could put it down as soon as he wanted to; he just did not want to, for by carrying it he could show how strong he was. In turn he derided the other animals, saying that none of them was strong enough to carry so large a burden. This went on for

4. See B. Spencer and F. J. Gillen, *The Northern Tribes of Central Australia*, p. 265. Cf. also R. Briffault, *The Mothers*, II, 46.

5. This account was given in a lecture by Paul Radin. Cf. P. Radin, *The Trickster*, with commentaries by C. J. Jung and K. Kerényi, passim, for other versions of Trickster's attitude to portions of his body.

a long time, until Trickster began privately to be a little worried. He realized that he had carried this bundle as long as he could remember and had never laid it down. So he went to a quiet place in the woods where he could be alone, and tried to remove his load. But he found to his great anger that he could not do so. Then he struggled to wrench off the phallus, but each effort hurt him horribly and threatened to tear him in half. His burden was part of himself.

This story is obviously an account of man's gradual awakening to consciousness of his own sexuality. In the beginning, its demands are considered an asset, a strength, a source of pride. But as consciousness grows, the biological urge is recognized as a burden, a daemon whose service demands time and effort and energy that might be used for more valuable tasks. Then man begins to struggle with his daemon. His conscious self and the nonpersonal daemon are no longer in harmony, and in trying to rid himself of the compulsion within him man finds that he is being torn apart.

The burden of sexual instinct that woman carries manifests itself in a different form. Male sexuality is essentially outgoing, a pursuit of the object in order to obtain relief from tension and discomfort through physical contact. It produces an urge to activity, a restlessness and drive that can be stilled only by detumescence. In contrast to this, woman's sexuality manifests itself in a yearning passivity, a desire to have something carried out upon her; it produces a burden of inertia that is the exact counterpart of man's instinctive drive.

Woman is therefore burdened with two measures of inertia, the primal sloth of unconsciousness that is the common lot of man and woman, and an additional quota that is the effect of unconscious and unrealized sexuality. Just as Trickster had to struggle with his phallic bundle, so woman has to struggle with her inertia if she is to be freed from identification with her daemon of biological instinct. It is this aspect of feminine psychology that is responsible for the heavy sensuousness of the cowlike woman. It is personified in dreams not infrequently as the "white slug" woman. It signifies not merely sloth but unrecognized sexuality. When Trickster knew what his burden was, he could begin to free himself. In the same way, the modern woman who recognizes that her inertia may be due to sexuality rather than to sloth is in a position to begin to detach herself from it.

A human being who is still identified with the daemon of sexuality is able to live his sexuality only on an auto-erotic level. This is true whether the impulse finds its outlet in masturbation or whether it leads him to sexual relations with another person of either his own or the opposite sex. For as the interest and desires of the individual in this stage of development are concerned solely with his own sensations and bodily needs, his sexual instinct still lacks that degree of psychic modification which necessarily precedes any real concern with the object. Therefore almost any partner will serve for satisfaction on this level, provided the necessary stimulus is present to set off the physical mechanism of detumescence.

Consequently, persons in this stage of development are usually promiscuous and fickle, and at times may be driven by a veritable daemon of desirousness, seemingly without regard for either the requirements of relationship or the fundamental decencies. To a man on this level, a woman is nothing but a sexual object, and one woman can be substituted for another with the greatest ease. A woman in a similar stage of psychological development may long simply for a man, any man, provided he wants her sexually, for to her the man is merely a phallus bearer. The appeal of many lewd jokes and of pornographic literature in general is based on the persistence of this aspect of sexuality.

A predominantly auto-erotic aspect of sexuality is manifested in the type of woman who wants a man not primarily to satisfy her sexual hunger but rather to give her children. The woman herself may consider her instinctive longing for babies a valid excuse for seeking sexual contact with a man, even though there is no real relationship between them. She may even think that her impulse is "quite nice"—that it is a commendable evidence of love for children—for the maternal instinct in our society is heavily tinged with sentimentality. Such a woman does not seem to realize that she proposes to exploit the man's feelings in using him to fulfill her desire for offspring. Her desire is an instinctive drive no more commendable and no more reprehensible than an urge to gratification of any other primary instinct; but where the fulfillment requires the co-operation of another human being, the demand should be recognized for what it is. The self-love on which it is based should not masquerade under the guise of love for the object.

Among primitive peoples, the auto-erotic aspect of sexuality may be the only one operative in the community. Among the polygamous tribes of the west coast of Africa, for instance, the men marry as many wives as possible and live among them as lords. In reality, the men are the sexual prisoners of their harems, though they would be the last to recognize this fact. They are obliged to divide their favours among their many wives under rules the women themselves make, imposing very severe penalties for infringements. It is true that the wives do all the work and support the husband in idleness, if not in luxury; but if he does not satisfy his wives, they can leave him, taking their children with them. Thus his dominance is more seeming than real. Such a man is the slave not only of his own sexual urge but also of the women who give him the satisfaction he craves.

At this stage, the psychic counterpart or image of the sexual instinct, which Jung calls the archetype, is represented in art forms by the phallus and the yoni or the uterus. In such figures as the Greek herm or the *Sheela-na-Gig*, the strange Celtic sculptures of female creatures displaying their genitals, the sexual organ is used to represent the entire human being, the remainder of the body being either depreciated or entirely suppressed. In plate III a similar figure, known as the "Mistress of Animals," is shown clutching two beasts by the throat. This example is of Etruscan origin, but figures of a corresponding character have been found in Greece and Crete, in Central Asia, and also in China, representing the relation of a deity to her animal nature. In these cases the sexual organs of the human figure are usually greatly emphasized, as in the present example. Similar distortions are a commonplace in pornographic art.

They also figure largely in the obscene scribblings of adolescents, whose concern with the biological aspect of sex is natural enough, since they have not yet become aware of the emotional potentialities of the instinctive drive.

In the next stage of development, sexuality is definitely linked with emotion. The mutual attraction felt by the man and woman is no longer limited to the physical sphere: it is accompanied by an emotional element that becomes increasingly important as the development of the instinct progresses. This emotion must be called love, though its nature varies enormously according to the degree of psychological development that the individual has reached. Indeed, it is possible to form a fairly accurate picture of an individual's psychological development from a study of the kind of emotional involvement of which he is capable.

In the more primitive stages, the partner's qualities of either body or mind are immaterial, provided he or she is able to arouse and satisfy the physical need. But when the sexual involvement is accompanied by an emotional factor, the object of attraction is no longer merely the bearer of a sexual organ but is seen to possess the characteristics of a human being. In art, for instance, the sexual object is no longer represented by the yoni or the phallus but by the figure of a beautiful maiden or of a virile young man. The cult of the nude in art relates to this phase.[6] Even so, the attracting object still lacks any individual differentiation: it is still only *a* beautiful maiden, *an* attractive man. To the lover, it is not the one particular person, and none other, who is desirable; there is still no real love of the object as a personality. This attitude is betrayed by men in such comments as, "I love girls," or "The sex is very attractive to me," and by women in such expressions as, "I want a man to go out with," or "Men are dear things." The exact similarity of the masculine and feminine versions of this condition is illustrated to perfection in the "cock" scene in *The Beggar's Opera*, in which the hero struts possessively amongst

6. In a more advanced stage of psychological development, nakedness is often used with a symbolic significance. The implications noted above do not apply in such circumstances.

his many ladies, singing, "I've sipped ev'ry flower"; and in the chorus in *Patience*, "There's more fish in the sea, no doubt of it, than ever, than ever, came out of it," in which the rejected girls assert their readiness to accept another man, any other man, if the one they have been professing to love should depart.

Legends and myths dealing with this psychological attitude in the male represent him as surrounded by a multiplicity of alluring feminine forms, like the Flower Maidens in the scene of Parsifal's temptation. The beautiful damsels represent his own vagrant erotic impulses. They are quite indistinguishable one from another, and he has no possible means of knowing what they are really like. They are not women but only personified longings. They are "part souls"—his souls. The classical example is found in the episode of the sirens besetting Ulysses on his homeward journey, tempting him and his men to delay their return and luring them down into the ocean depths in search of an undreamed-of bliss. These temptresses try to deflect the wanderers from resuming their responsibilities to wife and child and to hold them dallying with sensual satisfactions. Psychologically this means that if they responded to the temptation they would be engulfed once more in the unconscious, for it would represent a regression to a stage of identification with the sexual instinct from which they had been at least partially released. Ulysses very wisely commanded his sailors to stop up their ears, so that they would not hear the enchanting music and follow the sirens to death.

In another version of the legend Ulysses (or Odysseus, as he was earlier called) had his sailors bind him to the mast, as he did not trust his resolution to resist the tempters. The scene is portrayed in figure 5, where we see him assailed by the apparently not very welcome attentions of three winged sirens. The siren represented in figure 6, from a twelfth-century Bestiary, is also shown as winged and having bird's feet, but her fish's tail seems to suggest that she has some relation to a mermaid, a being who is also reputed to lure sailors to their doom.

To these legendary voyagers the enchantment of such phantom beings as the sirens and mermaids represented a very real danger. For they embody the anima image, in a collective and undifferentiated form, and represent the wish-dream of a man whose eros development has not progressed beyond the auto-erotic stage. For the dream of such a person is of a situa-

Fig. 5. Odysseus Bound to the Mast and Assailed by Three Winged Sirens

tion of paradisal delight, like the harem of an oriental ruler, where he will be attracted and stirred by sensuous female dancing and ravished by the partly hidden and partly revealed beauty of maidens whose only thought is to please him. It is another phase of auto-erotism, of self-love, even though it is a more developed phase than the purely somatic one that it replaces.

The corresponding condition in woman is represented in myth by scenes of rape and abduction, by satyrs, centaurs, and primitive half-men. The rape of the Sabine women is a good example. The phantasies of a woman in a corresponding stage of development may be concerned with a "cave-man," whose so-called love-making seems in the phantasy to be so

desirable. Such a woman may indulge in phantasies of a man
of power and muscle who is completely absorbed in the desire
to capture her. His attraction lies in his brute strength con-
trasting with her helplessness and in his exclusive concern with

Fig. 6. A Siren

her. Her longing is to be carried away by this cave man and
to be overcome, so that while seeming to be indifferent or even
to resist, she can yield herself in an orgy of conflicting emotions. In the frieze from the Temple of Zeus at Olympia, representing the fight between the centaurs and the Lapiths at

the wedding feast, two women are being seized and carried off by centaurs. (See detail reproduced in plate IV.) In many parts of the world "marriage by capture," such as we see here, was formerly the custom. A young man, who sought a wife, crept into the village of a clan different from his own, and seized and carried off a maiden for his bride. It is possible that sometimes the youth and the girl were already well acquainted, or they might be complete strangers, but in either case it is quite likely that she did not resist, though her brothers and uncles pursued the fleeing couple in outrage at losing one of their women.

Even to this day, at a modern wedding, this long discarded "marriage by capture" is often mimed in the custom of chasing the bridal pair as though the groom were abducting the bride. The couple flee as if guilty and the friends who pursue them enact the part of the bride's outraged relatives hastening to rescue her and punish him.

At this level, the feminine instinct expresses itself in a well-nigh insatiable desire to be used by another being. Such a woman feels herself to be nothing, to be empty; she longs not to do or to act but to be acted upon—not to create but to be filled. This is not unselfishness or self-abnegation, as it may seem to a superficial observer; for it may be that her actions and attitudes are dictated by a very active selfishness and egotism, even though these motivations remain hidden from herself. This condition usually represents an unconscious rather than a conscious auto-erotism and frequently deceives the sexual partner. Or he may actually desire such a woman, for her instinctive attitude is really the counterpart of his own physical urge.

This aspect of feminine sexuality is today usually concealed under a conventional mask, and the modern woman rarely recognizes it as what it is. It can often be glimpsed, however, when the woman is unaware of what she is doing. The most marked examples of such unconscious behaviour occur during hysterical attacks, when a woman's attitudes and gestures may be grossly sexual, even though she may be quite unaware of a sexual motive in her illness. A similar attitude of complete self-abnegation, of an abandonment that cries aloud for a strong man to fill the emptiness, is obvious in the state of mind portrayed in the following poem by Laurence Hope:

> Less than the dust beneath thy Chariot wheel,
> Less than the rust that never stained thy Sword,
> Less than the trust thou hast in me, O Lord,
> > Even less than these!
>
> . . . .
>
> See here thy Sword, I make it keen and bright,
> Love's last reward, Death, comes to me to-night,
> > Farewell, Zahir-u-din.[7]

The attitude is also pictured in novels of a type most popular with adolescents, in the recurrent theme of the young girl who suffers some minor accident under circumstances that leave her helpless in the hands of a stalwart hero, preferably just as night is falling.

The longing for assuagement of the yearning emptiness that is the expression of feminine receptivity on this level, is often the theme of dreams and other products of the unconscious. Phantasies and free drawings, as well as dreams, may depict it with an astounding frankness, making it clearly recognizable to those who have eyes to see. Yet it may be completely hidden from the understanding of the woman who produces such a revealing image.

In speaking of the physical side of the sexual urge, I do not mean to suggest that there is something wrong or even undesirable in the physical aspect as such. Not only is it the essential factor in reproduction, but it is also a most important, perhaps even *the* most important, foundation of the love relationship between partners. However, it cannot alone carry the value of psychological relationship, and under certain circumstances the physical relation cannot be achieved satisfactorily unless the psychological relation between the partners is right, so that love can flow freely between them.[8] Then and then only can the sexual union be really satisfying. Or, to put it the

---

7. *India's Love Lyrics, including The Garden of Kama,* p. 1.
8. See Jung, "Marriage as a Psychological Relationship," in *The Development of Personality* (C.W. 17).

other way round, unless a psychological structure is reared on the foundation of the physical sexuality, there will be no permanent abode for the relationship. Bodily desire and bodily satisfaction play an essential part in all psychic activities based on instinct. Just as eating plays a part in friendship and even in religious rituals, so the sexual embrace can be the vehicle of an emotional or psychic experience transcending the physical one.

When the purely physical aspects of sexuality no longer serve to satisfy the needs of an individual whose being comprises not only animal functions but also psychological, that is, spiritual and emotional longings, a change takes place in regard to the nature of the sexual object that attracts him. This change can be readily observed in the attitudes of adolescents as they emerge from their exclusive concern with physical sexuality and discover romance. Their development parallels the cultural change of the Middle Ages through which romantic love first appeared in Western man and then rose to great importance, at the very time when man was emerging from the developmental stage characterized by emphasis on physical prowess and brute force.

In this new stage of the psychic transformation of sexuality, the object of desire is differentiated from all others as the loved one; however, the individual's love is here concerned not with the object itself but rather with the values projected upon the object from his own unconscious.[9] This is clearly demonstrated in the frequency with which romantic love arises fully formed—"at first sight," as we say—and may likewise terminate just as suddenly and inexplicably. Obviously, the love object—the woman, for instance, who so fascinates and attracts—is not loved for herself, for the lover can have no knowledge of her real qualities; rather, the sexual and romantic love of the beholder is attracted by values reflected in or symbolized by her. Perhaps it would be more accurate to say that the love object causes certain vibrations deep within the un-

9. This subject is discussed at length in Harding, *The Way of All Women*, chaps. I and II. Cf. also Jung, "Anima and Animus," in *Two Essays on Analytical Psychology* (C.W. 7), and "Mind and Earth," in *Contributions to Analytical Psychology*, pp. 128-32.

conscious of the lover, and that these produce an illusion of definite attributes in the object, much as certain stimuli can produce an illusion of visual phenomena. For example, a blow on the head makes one "see stars," and certain poisons produce hallucinations that seem to the sufferer to have objective reality: in both instances the seeming visual percept is obviously an allusion originating within the subject.

When a man falls in love with a woman at first sight, she seems to possess all the qualities that are most desirable in his eyes. In addition he feels that he has a curious, almost miraculous power of perception in regard to her. He will declare that he knows what she is like, what she thinks, and how she feels, even though he may never have heard her utter a word and obviously does not know her at all. The same can occur in the case of a woman. It is amazing how much blindness and real insensitivity a woman may show in regard to the feelings of a man who has caught her imagination and her desire. She is as if under a spell, and she feels convinced that he is in love with her. Nothing that he can do will avail to disabuse her. For her conviction arises from her unconscious instinct, not from the objective reality of the situation. Where the projection is mutual, the man and woman feel themselves to have an extraordinary kinship, a mysterious mutual knowledge and harmony. They naturally find it a marvel, a special blessing, a gift of the gods, an experience in which they are singled out for the favour of heaven. And perhaps they are right—if it lasts. Herein lies the weakness of the situation: for their sense of oneness is obviously based on an illusion that may disappear at the first touch of reality.

The phenomenon is comprehensible when we realize that the attraction proceeds from the fact that it is the other side of himself that the man sees reflected in the woman, while a similar mechanism functions in the woman. These qualities within the individual are unconscious, unknown to himself; they are not his own qualities. For he has never made them his own by consciously accepting and working on them; he has probably even repressed their germinal existence because they are inimical to those factors out of which he has chosen to build his conscious personality. Nonetheless, they represent the latent potentialities of his own nature. They are the psychic factors omitted from his conscious adaptation, and their absence means that he is one-sided and unwhole. The very fact that he has such a strange knowledge of what these qualities are when he meets a woman who can represent them, is evidence that they belong to his own psyche.

Every human being is constituted of elements derived from ancestors of both sexes. In a man the male elements are dominant and the female elements recessive, while the reverse holds in the case of a woman. This duality obtains both in the biological and in the psychological sphere. Thus a complete man must be both masculine and feminine. The totality of the elements of opposite sex residing in an individual (of the feminine in man and of the masculine in woman) makes up the soul.[10] Jung, following the classical formulation, has given the name anima to this soul complex in the man, and the name animus to the complex of unconscious male elements in the woman's psyche. He points out that the recessive aspects of the psyche, masculine or feminine as the case may be, are directed towards the unconscious and form an autonomous complex. Like all such complexes, it tends to become personified and to function as though it were a separate personality or a part soul, as it is called among primitive peoples.

The individual from whom such a personification emanates does not, as a rule, recognize it to be a factor within his own psyche. But many a person is at times aware of a voice other than his own speaking in him, or of another personality taking possession of him and bringing moods and affects that he cannot reconcile with the more accepted and more conscious part of himself. More frequently, this autonomous soul complex reveals itself by being projected upon a suitable ob-

10. *Soul* is here used in a psychological, not a theological, sense. According to Jung, the term *soul* "is really a psychological recognition of a semiconscious psychic complex that has achieved a partial autonomy of function. . . . The autonomy of the soul-complex naturally supports the idea of an invisible personal being who apparently lives in a world very different from ours" (*Two Essays on Analytical Psychology* [C.W. 7], pp. 215, 216). See also the definitions of "soul" and "soul-image" in *Psychological Types;* and chaps. 1 and 2 in Harding, *The Way of All Women.*

ject in the environment. In this case the feminine elements in a man will find their vehicle in a projection upon a woman, while the masculine elements in a woman will seek a man through whom they can be expressed.

The attraction between the sexes always contains an element of this projection of anima or animus—an element that increases in proportion to the lack of development in the individual. For if he has failed to develop a psychic function to replace the soul complex, then the archetype of the being of opposite sex—of woman in the case of a man, of man in the case of a woman—rules supreme, blinding the individual to the real lineaments and characteristics of the actual person confronting him. A man, for instance, will find himself attracted to a woman who more or less accurately reflects the condition of his own soul, and for the rest he will labour under the illusion that she completely embodies its characteristics, and will react to her as though she wielded over him and his destiny the powers actually possessed by his own soul. For as his soul is an essential part of his total psyche, he will be unconditionally bound to the woman who bears his soul image.

The concept of anima and animus is a complex one.[11] It has been gradually evolved and elaborated by Jung as corresponding to the actual manifestations of the human psyche as these have unfolded themselves to his observation throughout the years of his professional study. He defines the anima as a psychic function whose purpose is to relate the human being in a meaningful way to the contents of the collective unconscious—the archetypes, the psychic patterns or aptitudes for

11. I would refer the reader to Jung's *Two Essays on Analytical Psychology* (C.W. 7), and to *Aion* (C.W. 9, ii). In the early chapters of the latter book Jung discusses in systematic form his ideas about the layers of the psyche. First we find the *ego* and *persona*, which are more or less conscious factors of the psyche; behind the conscious *ego* is the *shadow*, an unconscious or semi-unconscious figure that personifies the personal unconscious, and behind that the *anima*, in the case of a man, or the *animus*, in the case of a woman. This figure relates the personal part of the psyche to the not-personal part dominated by the archetypes. Because the shadow and the anima (animus) are unconscious components of the psyche they are usually projected into the outer world where they become personified in some suitable person who acts as carrier for the values they represent.

functioning that are the psychological counterpart of physiological instinctual mechanisms.

When the anima or animus has not evolved to the status of a psychic function, it remains autonomous and manifests itself in dreams in personified form—as the figure of a woman in men, and as a male figure in women—and in actual life in projections to other persons. Because the soul complex in a man represents the feminine elements in his psyche, the projection of his anima will fall on a woman, who will seem to him on account of this projection to embody all of his own unrecognized potentialities, valuable or destructive, while in the case of a woman the man who catches her animus projection will in the same way be possessed of the fascination and compelling attraction of her own unrealized masculine capacities.

Thus the quality of an individual's sexual projection reflects the condition of his anima, that is, of the unknown part of his own psyche, his soul complex. If it is primitive and undifferentiated, it cannot effectively perform its intrapsychic function as mediator between the conscious personality and the collective unconscious. The tides of this vast inner ocean will meet with no effective barrier, but will impinge directly on the psyche, with the result that such a man will be subject to unaccountable moods and to the compulsive drives characteristic of instinctual behaviour. Whenever the projection of anima occurs, such an individual will act almost automatically, being completely dominated by the passion arising within him and by the inescapable urgency through which nature constrains her creatures to fulfill her purposes. A man under the spell of such a projection is hardly responsible for his actions. When an instinctive desire takes possession of him, nothing can prevent him from obeying its behest. He is like a driven beast, and only after the instinct has had its way with him does he come to his senses and become human again. This type of projection is obviously not concerned with an individual woman, but only with woman in her biological role—the least common denominator of femaleness.

The projection of the soul complex is the psychological event that underlies a sexual attraction. For it is not only on the physical plane that man and woman complement each other and are drawn towards each other, seeking physical union and biological completeness. A similar yearning towards a similar goal functions—most powerfully—on the psychological level.

In the long story of the cultural development of mankind, and correspondingly in the story of the personal development of the individual in modern times, we observe a gradual change in the character of the satisfaction demanded by the sexual instinct. The *libido sexualis*, no longer content with one goal, physical detumescence, begins to demand a further satisfaction on an entirely different plane. Physical pleasure, although it remains important, is no longer sufficient. Its primacy is challenged by the urgent desire for emotional satisfaction. The physical aspect of the sexual act itself becomes in increasing measure dependent on the emotional factor. Unless a satisfactory channel for the emotion can be established, and unless there is an emotional response from the partner, the physical contact will fail to satisfy the urgent longing of the man or woman; indeed, the sexual mechanism itself may even be inhibited to such an extent that a temporary or permanent frigidity results in the woman, or functional impotence in the man. But if in addition to the physical attraction there is also an emotional rapport between the lovers, the whole experience is intensified and deepened not only through its emotional or spiritual significance, but also because the quality of physical satisfaction in the act itself is enhanced.

BY THE TIME the sexual instinct has reached this stage of psychic modification, its expression is obviously no longer directed to the one goal of reproduction of the species. The intervention of consciousness has caused a split in the singleness of nature's primary aim. The creation of a new generation will always remain the paramount goal towards which nature lures her unsuspecting children, through the mutual attraction of the sexes and the pleasures of physical union. But as the sexual instinct is gradually modified through its relation to the psyche and so becomes more closely related to consciousness, another aim emerges from the unconscious, namely, an emotional or spiritual one. The psychological energy or libido inherent in this secondary aim also divides into an outer and an inner branch, the first having an objective goal and the second a subjective one. The outward-going stream of the libido is directed towards building a permanent relationship with the loved object and founding a family—that is, it has a social goal. The chief concern of the inner or subjective branch is the emotional experience made available through sexual love, and the inner or psychological realm into which it leads; consequently it now has a psychological goal.

The social trend of the libido, which led to the formation of the family unit, the very basis of society, has throughout the ages of civilization exerted the most profound and significant influence in curbing and disciplining the auto-erotism of the sexual urge. In addition, the stable emotional background provided for the younger generation by a permanent family life, and the prolongation of the period of education that this has made possible, have proved to be cultural factors of the greatest importance.

Thus the reproductive instinct, which originally functioned solely as a physical urge, led in time to the evolution of love and human relationship. For when the sexual partner becomes a permanent mate, the interaction between the two personalities makes the development of a further relationship essential. The formation of a home and the rearing of children lead a part of the sexual libido over into the parental phase of expression of the reproductive instinct, where the personal and auto-erotic wishes of the parents are challenged and disciplined by the needs and demands of the young.

The family unit in turn is connected with other similar units, and its members learn to take their place in the community. Thus, as a result of carrying out what seemed a most personal physical and emotional urge, men and women are led to fulfill a social obligation of an impersonal or, as it is better called, a nonpersonal nature. The discipline of this path, with the gradual change in objective that it presents, will ensure the further development of the instinct itself, in so far as it is drawn into life and really involved in the situation; in addition, the character and personality of the individuals concerned will develop and mature. They will no longer be interested solely in their own satisfactions, but will be released from the exclusive domination of the auto-erotic principle, and a wider objective will become operative in consciousness. Thus the ego will replace the autos.

The emergence of the ego as director of the conscious personality opened up a long road of progressive development. For it alone had sufficient clarity to be able to make an effective stand vis-à-vis the primitive and instinctive demands of a purely physical or auto-erotic character. In a state of nature the individual lives in the moment, reacting to whatever impulses are set in motion by the actual situation confronting him, without consciousness of other situations or interests that may be jeopardized by this single-aimed reaction. But with the emergence of an ego—a centre of consciousness—continuity of memory becomes possible. This leads to conflict between the various impulses and desires that pass through the individual in an unending stream, and he must choose between them according to some scale of values. The choice may be determined on the basis of selfish and egotistic desires reflecting a low level of development; or it may be determined by more important aims that are still, however, expressions of the ego, though they are no longer grossly selfish objectives.

In a more advanced stage of development the choice may fall on a value that is felt to surpass even the higher aims of the ego. If for example a man and woman really love each other and respect each other's personalities, a true psychological relationship may be established between them through the years.[12] In such a case, the relationship itself may be felt to have a value of such importance that it transcends all the usual satisfactions of the ego—such as the desire to have one's own way, or to prove oneself always in the right. In other cases,

12. See Jung, "Marriage as a Psychological Relationship," in *The Development of Personality* (C.W. 17); Bertine, *Human Relationships*.

activities undertaken as a means of supporting the family, which therefore indirectly depend on the sexual instinct for their energy content, come to have a value of their own quite apart from the ego satisfactions they bring in terms of monetary return or prestige. Such values may be found for instance in patriotic service, in concern for the rights of man, in devotion to scientific research, in the care for human beings through education, medicine, and the social services, or in the almost religious attitude of the artist or craftsman towards his creative ideal.

In each of these typical situations, in which the personal objective has been replaced at least in part by a nonpersonal one, the psychological evolution of the individual can proceed a step farther. For a new factor has begun to replace the ego as of central importance in the psyche.

The establishment of marriage and family life as a social institution played a part in the psychological and cultural evolution of man the importance of which cannot be overestimated. Indeed, modern man owes more perhaps than he realizes to this particular social form, which has done so much to control and harness the energy of primitive sexuality and to permit creative use of it in spheres not directly sexual. Thus through the discipline of marriage the sexual instinct has undergone a significant measure of psychic modification. However, while the taboos and regulations devised to curb this powerful instinct have assured an effective control and transformation of a part of its energy, the full force and potentiality of a primary instinct could not be so dealt with, and a large portion—how large it is impossible to ascertain, for the resources of the instincts are seemingly limitless—was necessarily repressed and lost in the unconscious.

This repression increased as the centuries passed, finally becoming so excessive as to foreshadow a danger that modern man might be cut off almost entirely from this source of energy. In puritanical countries the repression became so great, and the individual consequently suffered from so serious a split within himself, that in the beginning of the present century his condition resembled the state that overtook the world, according to the Babylonian myth, when Ishtar, goddess of fertility and of sexual love, journeyed to the underworld to search for her son Tammuz, the god of spring. While she was absent, everything fell into a condition of stagnation, depression, and inertia; nothing happened, nothing could be accomplished, everything languished, until she returned to the earth.

The fear and resistance that greeted Freud's discovery of a way of re-establishing contact between conscious man and the sexual roots of instinct below the threshold of his consciousness, as well as the avidity with which it was later taken up, reveal the extent to which modern man had been separated from the source of life within himself, and how important this re-establishment of contact was felt to be.

One of the earliest taboos placed on the sexual instinct, and one that is still almost universally observed, is the taboo on incest. Exogamy has been the rule in the majority of human societies, not because of any natural lack of sexual inclination towards related persons near at hand, but under constraint of a cultural form prohibiting sexual relations and marriage between close relatives. In addition to its biological results, this regulation had very important psychological effects. In early societies, as soon as the young man came to maturity and began to be aware of sexual urgency, he was compelled to leave the intimacy of his group to explore the world outside the village limits in search of a sexual partner. To do this he had to overcome his childish fears and learn to rely on himself. The girl for her part had to summon courage to receive a visitor from a strange clan, who for just this reason might be unwelcome to her village. Or, as is common in some primitive marriage ceremonies, she might have to allow herself to be abducted in face of the ferocious opposition of her brothers and uncles. By this adventure in search of a sexual partner, the young people widened their experience of the world and increased consciousness in themselves. This was a psychological advance for them individually and thereby for the culture of the group, as important perhaps as the physical gain resulting from cross-breeding.

As the family became more stable and children came to

be loved and cared for not solely during the helplessness of infancy but also in maturing stages as individuals, the life that could be found within the limits of the family became more satisfying emotionally, and consequently the impulse to leave it in search of a mate became less urgent. A child in such a home tends to remain attached to one of the parents or to a brother or sister in such a way that its further emotional development is hampered. The more congenial and cultured the home life, the greater is the danger of family fixation, whereby the young people are deprived of the most powerful incentive to break free from the home—namely, consciousness of unsatisfied sexual longings, which ordinarily releases the new generation to launch out into the world on their own.

This once again demonstrates how a cultural achievement, while it makes some of the energy of a primitive instinct available for the enrichment of conscious life, may at the same time cause a splitting of the primitive libido into positive and negative forms functioning in close juxtaposition. As the author of *The Book of Lambspring* puts it:

> The Sages will tell you
> That two fishes are in our sea
> Without any flesh or bones.
>
> . . . .
>
> Moreover the Sages say
> That the two fishes are only one, not two;
> They are two, and nevertheless they are one.[13]

In the sea—that is, in the unconscious—the positive and negative aspects are not sharply divided. In the case of the instinct of self-preservation, for instance, the assurance of plenty, resulting from industry, and the fear of want, resulting from greed, were brought into conscious focus through the discipline that enabled man to produce a harvest. In the case of the sexual instinct an analogous situation arises: no sooner is a part of the drive domesticated, so that out of its urges marriage and home are created, than we find these very values acting in an opposite way on the succeeding generation. A

13. Nicholas Barnaud Delphinas, *The Book of Lambspring*, in Waite (tr.), *The Hermetic Museum*, vol. I, p. 276. See also frontispiece.

family life that is too protective and too engrossing can handicap the children, keeping them immature. The urge that should launch the young people into the world is not strong enough to break the ties to home. They do not suffer from sufficient emotional hunger to be forced to go in quest of a satisfying love relationship outside the family. Their affections are satisfied with the response of parents or of brothers and sisters. Even the daemon of sexuality can remain quiescent, almost indefinitely, if the nature of the love between members of a family is not too closely scrutinized. But if it is investigated more thoroughly—as Freud showed through the analysis of the unconscious roots of such situations—an incestuous bond with the family may well be found to be hidden below the surface.

The idea that such a condition of affairs could exist was exceedingly shocking to most "respectable" people when the facts were first made public. A very common misunderstanding accounts in part for this natural reaction, for there is a tendency to take Freud's use of the term incest too literally. This has led to a rather widespread misapprehension. For the concept of an unconscious, psychological incest does not postulate overt sexuality, nor a conscious wish for sexual intimacies with a closely related person, but rather a fixation of psychological energy or libido within the family group, preventing the individual so bound from seeking a suitable sexual and emotional relationship outside the family. Unconscious sexual wishes centring on persons of the home circle may of course exist, but much more frequently the sexual material that comes to light during an analysis is to be taken as symbolic of the psychological tie to the family rather than as evidence of actual sexual desires.

Freud's researches brought these hidden tendencies into full view; but the basis of family fixation has been apparent to astute observers of mankind from the time of the Greek tragedians on. Once the correctness of Freud's conclusions was recognized, however, they were seen to be so manifestly true that we have all grown accustomed to the idea, and unconscious incestuous fixation is referred to quite openly today in fiction, biography, and drama. It is accepted as one of the most important among motives that can prevent men and women from marrying or from freeing themselves from childish bondage to family and parents.

In the past, incestuous relationships were not considered to be harmful in every instance. The social rules and customs enforcing sexual taboos were sometimes set aside, while endogenous marriages were even the rule under certain circumstances. For instance, where inheritance through the female line still prevailed, though other practices of an earlier matriarchal society might have been superseded, marriages of close relatives were sometimes actually prescribed in order to conserve the family property. In other cases cross-cousin mating was the usual cultural form. Layard [14] suggests that it is the natural one. In certain cases marriage of close relatives was obligatory for religious reasons. This rule was especially maintained in royal families (it is still held that a king's consort must be of the blood royal) and in priestly ones. The members of such families were believed to be incarnations of gods or at least representatives of divinities; hence these marriages of closely related members of the human family re-enacted, as it were, the marriages of the gods recorded in the myths. In this way the union of the two aspects of the deity, male and female, was consummated once again upon earth; and since in the myth this marriage of the gods always inaugurated a period of well-being and of fruitfulness, it was believed that the union of the royal pair would similarly produce prosperity for the realm and all within it.[15] The family of the Pharaohs presents the outstanding example of brother-sister incest continued from generation to generation. For the Pharaohs were believed to be incarnations of Isis and Osiris, the divine twins, whose union had been of such supreme importance in the found-

14. "The Incest Taboo and the Virgin Archetype," *Eranos-Jahrbuch* XII, 254-307.
15. See Jung, *Mysterium Coniunctionis* (C.W. 14), § 108-9: "The psychopathological problem of incest is the aberrant, natural form of the union of opposites, a union which has either never been made conscious at all as a psychic task or, if it was conscious, has once more disappeared from view. The persons who enact the drama of this problem are man and woman, in alchemy King and Queen, Sol and Luna."

ing of the kingdom of Egypt and in the initiation of the spiritual culture for which the Egyptians have deservedly been famous.[16]

An entirely different condition is produced in the children when the home life is not happy. If the parents have not been able to create a satisfactory relationship between themselves, but are restless and insecure, the children too will lack emotional stability. It is unlikely that they will be able to create satisfying marriages themselves, as they have never had the example of conjugal happiness before them. More probably a youth in such a family will find that an impassable gulf separates his love and his sexuality, and this leads either to promiscuity, or, because sexuality presents itself only in unacceptable forms, to complete repression.

In either case, whether the home life is too secure or too unsatisfactory, it is probable that the daemonic aspect of the sexual instinct will remain in a primitive and undeveloped condition. In the first case, it will be lulled to sleep by the surface contentment, thus remaining buried in unconsciousness; in the second it will either be forcibly repressed in an attempt to live according to conventional standards, or it will break forth in asocial ways that may well be both undisciplined and destructive.

IT IS THIS DAEMONIC ASPECT of sexuality that is involved in the second motivation of the libido. While marriage and children represent the cultural values to be achieved by the outward-going stream of the sexual instinct, the inner aspect, which is at first concerned only with physical and auto-erotic satisfaction, has for its part also a cultural goal. This is manifested in subjective experiences and in creations of no less significance than the objective achievements of marriage and the forms of social advancement related to it.

The inner or subjective aspect of sexuality has always had great importance. In the primitive, auto-erotic stage of development, the greatest satisfaction is gained when the physical

16. Cf. C. G. Jung, "Psychology of the Transference," in *The Practice of Psychotherapy* (C.W. 16), p. 229.

tension is raised to the highest possible pitch. In the romantic age in history (and this is true also of the corresponding psychological stage in modern individuals) the very intensity of the emotional experience becomes an end in itself. The segregation of the sexes, the seclusion of young girls, the form of dress, and the whole array of conventions and customs controlling the social relations of men and women were designed (though probably more than half unconsciously) to heighten the mystery and charm of femininity and so to increase the emotional and physical tension between the sexes.

This new attitude found its expression in the impulse to go in search of and rescue the maiden in distress or to abandon wife and home for the sake of some Helen of Troy. It did not arise from the domesticated side of the sexual drive, which would have found its fulfillment in a conventional marriage, but came from an untamed streak in the nature of both man and woman, which was captivated by the unconventional, the hard to attain. This fact accounts for the special allure of the lover as over against the marriage partner. The compelling power of the impulse was an expression of the unredeemed part of the sexual instinct, which was not as yet harnessed to the conscious personality through ego development. It was a nonpersonal factor that, like a daemon, can drive a human being on to seek experience beyond the range of the safe and the known, in a realm where he may be plunged into emotional situations far beyond his personal control.

In everyday life the actual situation between any man and woman is intensified or even distorted if a projection of the soul image occurs. The being who carries this image and so impersonates the lover's soul is alluring beyond compare, or, conversely, may seem threatening. The beloved thus wields an uncanny influence and attraction arising not from his actual character or personality but from that which he reflects, namely, the unknown, unrealized other half of the lover. Union with one's own lost soul is of such vital importance that whenever an opportunity for drawing near to it is offered by life, psychic forces belonging to the very depths of one's being are stirred. The urgent longing actually experienced by the individual when he falls in love does not present itself to his consciousness in any such psychological language, however. To him it is just that the object of his love appears desirable beyond measure. She draws him with a power and fascination he cannot evade or escape. Through the urgency of his love he is enabled to rise above himself, to overcome all obstacles between himself and his beloved, and if fortune favours him, even to achieve union with her. This union is simultaneously the means of satisfaction of his human love and a symbolic drama, played on the stage of real life; its deeper meaning, however, lies hidden within the psyche. For it is a ritual representation of the marriage between the individual and his own soul.

For this reason a man who falls profoundly in love (and this applies equally in the case of a woman) finds himself able, even compelled, to transcend his own limitations. During the courtship his character and psychological attitude usually appear to be deeply affected, and it seems as though a radical change had taken place. In some persons this is but a reflection of the "in love" period, as fleeting as the emotions from which it springs. But in others the experience may initiate a permanent change of character that persists even after the first intensity has subsided—showing that the soul drama has been consummated, at least in part, through the living out of the external event in the actual life situation.

For the union of the lovers is more than a simple act of physical sexuality whereby release from tension is achieved and the biological aim of reproduction is satisfied. More profound instinctual depths are touched by it—realms beyond the scope of the conscious personality. For the satisfaction of a sexual desire for union with the beloved, intensified by the projection of the soul image, demands that the lover renounce himself and his limited personal ego and receive into himself another. This means a sort of spiritual death, in which he feels himself to be lost to himself, through union with something other than himself that is at once within him and beyond him.

Thus the supreme satisfaction is sought in the act of union with the loved one; but even in the moment of closest physical embrace, final possession of the beloved seems to the lover to elude him because of the very intensity of the experience itself. For the highest bliss is an ecstasy, a going out from oneself. Ecstasis involves a loss of oneself in something beyond oneself. When ecstasis is reached through sexual expression (there are other ways in which it may be experienced), the lover's complete intensity must be concentrated upon the partner. Nevertheless, the experience itself is not of union with the beloved, but a completely separate and separating absorption in an inner happening of the greatest significance. To the lover it is as though his personality were dissolved and merged in a greater being, or as though he were being united with a nonpersonal other within himself—a happening that makes him at once smaller than his ego and very much larger.

Mystics of many religions and of many different epochs have used the imagery of this archetypal sexual consummation to describe their subjective experiences of ecstasy, which they attributed to an actual experience of union between the soul and God. When St. John of the Cross wrote the verses following, he was describing the inner experience of the love of God and an intimate communion between God and the soul, but his words might apply equally to a human relationship:

> Into the happy night
> In secret, seen of none,
> Nor saw I ought,
> Without, or other light or guide,
> Save that which in my heart did burn.
>
> This fire it was that guided me
> More certainly than midday sun,
> Where he did wait,
> He that I knew imprinted on my heart
> In place, where none appeared.
>
> Oh Night, that led me, guiding Night,
> Oh Night far sweeter than the Dawn;
> Oh Night, that did so then unite
> The Lover with his Belovèd,
> Transforming Lover in Beloved.

. . . .

I lay quite still, all mem'ry lost,
I leaned my face upon my Loved One's breast;
I knew no more, in sweet abandonment
I cast away my care,
And left it all forgot amidst the lilies fair.[17]

The Song of Songs likewise undoubtedly expresses a mystical experience of union of the soul with God, although its form is that of an erotic poem. Rabi'a, an initiate of the Sufi sect of Mohammedan mystics, speaks constantly of God as her lover, and many others, Christian saints among them, have written of their deepest and most sacred experiences in terms that would be applicable to sexual love.

This does not by any means imply that the experience is "nothing but" displaced sexuality. In some cases the phenomenon might be so explained; in others it is certainly referable to an inner experience that takes place not in the physical but in a psychological sphere. The religious mystics felt themselves to be renewed or transformed through such experiences; the transformation was often spoken of as due to a rebirth of the soul and was sometimes termed the birth of the divine child within.

The desire for ecstasis, though it is not felt by everyone, bespeaks a widespread and deep-felt need among human beings, albeit expressed in many different forms with widely differing significances. I have just been discussing it in a very positive aspect. But it must not be forgotten that the desire to plunge into the unconscious—even a passionate yearning of this kind —may have a very different meaning and outcome. Sometimes it is *au fond* a regressive or renegade tendency, a desire to "get away from oneself." Then it is really a wish to lose oneself for a time or to forget oneself, with an obvious emphasis on escape from the responsibilities or the difficulties of reality. One who seeks this kind of forgetfulness hopes perhaps that his sense of personal inadequacy may be assuaged for a time, if only consciousness with its critical attitude can be lulled to sleep. For then the unconscious instinctive personality can

17. *The Dark Night of the Soul of San Juan of the Cross* (tr. G. C. Graham), p. 29.

come to the fore and take charge of the situation, while personal responsibility ceases for the time being. Another than oneself will be acting through one, and so one cannot be held responsible for the consequences. Such might be the argument of the renegade. But he never voices it aloud, even to himself; for then he could not remain innocent of the realization that he has deserted the cause of human freedom.

An escape from the nagging of conscience and the sense of duty can be achieved through a sexual embrace, in which the individual loses himself in the ocean of instinct. Or it can be found through indulgence in alcohol or one of the drugs that produce forgetfulness and euphoria. Neurotic drowsiness and the extreme fatigue of neurasthenia may have a similar etiology. In the most serious cases of all, when the conflict produced by life and temperament has proved insoluble, so deep a plunge may be made into the maternal depths of the unconscious that the conscious psyche may be completely swamped by archetypal materials, and a psychotic interlude may result.

However, the desire for ecstasis is by no means always a renegade tendency. As already pointed out, it is part of the experience of union between the separated parts of the psyche and is felt by many to be a means of gaining, for a time, freedom from the littleness of the personal ego, through being dissolved into or being united with a force greater than oneself. If this is the nature and meaning of the experience, it does not prevent one from fulfilling one's task in life; rather, it supplies the inspiration by force of which tasks that formerly seemed impossible can at last be accomplished.

To the creative artist, his art (or his genius) is like a nonpersonal creative spirit, almost a divine being, that lives and creates quite apart from his ego consciousness. While the creative urge is on him he feels lifted out of himself; he is exalted, inspired by a spirit breathing through him. What he portrays is not invented by himself; it comes to him he knows not whence. This is a very different kind of creation from that of the rational thinker. For it is just exactly not conceived by thought. It is envisioned, or heard, or given. For instance,

Nietzsche tells us that he heard practically the whole of *Thus Spake Zarathustra* shouted in his ears as he marched over the mountains, chanting the words to himself in a mood of ecstasy. The whole work came to him of itself, practically complete. In such experiences of inspiration and rapture, the poets of all time have felt themselves to be filled with a divine influx; and through the experience they have been purified of the taint of mortality, which is division within oneself. For a short space of time such an individual feels himself to be made whole through submitting to possession of his being by a power greater than himself.

In the orgiastic religions, in which awe of the god and inspiration by him were experienced as part of the ritual, the goal of the religious practices was the attainment of an ecstasy in which the worshipper felt himself to be possessed by his god.[18] In many periods of human history this condition has been deliberately sought, with resort to various means to bring it about. The wild and prolonged dancing of the dervishes of Mohammedan countries produces an ecstatic, trancelike condition. Ascetic practices are also undertaken for the same purpose, as among the medicine men of some of the American Indian tribes, and also among the Eskimos, who become nearly crazed from fasting, loneliness, and self-inflicted pain. The latter practice played a part also in the ritually produced ecstasy of the *flagellantes* of mediaeval times, whose cult has survived even to the present day. The reports that Christian martyrs often gave no evidence of pain while undergoing torture or even death at the stake, but instead wore expressions of rapture, can probably be similarly explained. In India, the yogin seeks this ecstatic state, called samadhi, through meditation and other yogic practices, of which exercises for control of the breath, or prana, are perhaps the best known in the West. Drugs such as hashish, soma, marijuana, or peyote, in addition to alcohol, have been used in widely separated parts of the globe in connection with religious rituals to induce states of trance or of excitement.

---

18. Cf. Harding, *Woman's Mysteries, Ancient and Modern*, chap. xv, "Rebirth and Immortality."

In the worship of Dionysos, orgiastic rites were of particular importance. For this deity was not only a phallic god and the god of fertility, but also the god of wine, of poesy, of ecstasy, and of illumination. His festival was celebrated by maenads, women who became drunk on the wine that was believed to be the spirit of the god himself. In this condition they held orgies in the forests, killing deer, which symbolized Dionysos himself, and eating the flesh raw. As Harrison says:

> The Maenads are the frenzied sanctified women who are devoted to the worship of Dionysos. But they are something more, they tend the god as well as *suffer his inspiration* [italics mine].[19]

She quotes from the *Bacchae* of Euripides as follows:

> I have seen the wild white women there, O King,
> Whose fleet limbs darted arrow-like but now
> From Thebes away, and come to tell thee how
> They work strange deeds.[20]

The same writer says:

> Maenad is the Mad One, Thyiad [another of the worshippers of Dionysos] the Rushing Distraught One, or something of the kind. . . . Mad One, Distraught One, Pure One are simply ways of describing a woman under the influence of a god, of Dionysos. . . . When a people becomes highly civilized madness is apt not to seem, save to poets and philosophers, the divine thing it really is.[21]

It is this desire to achieve divine madness, to be raised to a state of consciousness so far exceeding the normal that it can be explained only as an experience of being beyond oneself, or lifted out of oneself into a state of divine consciousness, that underlies many religious practices of emotional or even orgiastic character. These manifestations of excitement, these excesses practised in the name of religion seem, when viewed from the standpoint of the rational or conventional person, to partake more of debauchery than of religion. But to those who undergo them these experiences have a value that cannot be explained in rational terms nor accounted for in accordance with conventional ways of thinking. For through them the individual is put in touch with the powerful and compelling energy of instinct that lies deep within the human psyche. He is reunited with the nonpersonal source of life; he achieves an inner marriage with his soul. Through such a union with the inner spirit, the primal flow of life is restored in him.

What then of the other aspect of such experiences—the debauchery, the frenzy, the abrogation of self-control, the debasement of culture and disregard of decency? These too may be the results of union with the forces of the unconscious; for the energies thus released can be destructive as well as creative. The dynamism that has erupted in Europe in our own times is an example of this aspect of reunion with the collective and instinctive forces of the unconscious. Those who gave themselves up to this dynamism experienced a release not unlike the ecstasy of the maenads, which perhaps accounts for its widespread and profound influence.

If a study of the religious experience of ecstasis could yield any information as to how men can establish a positive relation to such a dynamism, instead of falling helplessly under its spell, it would be most helpful. There is no doubt that life is renewed through contact with these instinctive depths, dangerous though such a contact is to the structure of conscious values so laboriously erected. Moreover, when the ecstasy is experienced in what may be called, for want of a better phrase, the right way, it is not destructive but life-giving. Individuals who have had such experiences assert that they attained a sense of redemption or of wholeness through such a consummation of union with the daemonic force, which they conceived of as God.

Even so, the new realization may be seriously at variance with the conscious attitudes formerly considered moral and right. For this reason, a direct experience of the nonpersonal forces within is never an easy matter to one who is aware of the moral obligation to seek wholeness. For it will surely bring with it the necessity of re-evaluating much that has previously been taken for granted. It will raise problems that it may take years of conscious effort to solve. The saying of Christ, "I came not to send peace but a sword," is true today as of old.

THOSE WHO ATTEMPT to describe the experience of ecstasis commonly use the language of erotic love. The essence of the experience seems to be that in the ecstasy the individual loses his personal self and merges into something beyond himself. He does not feel this to be a loss, but rather a gain, as though he were thereby renewed, or transformed, or made whole. Something, some other, of greater power and dignity and of greater authority than his ego, takes possession of his house, which is willingly resigned. This other may be a good daemon or an evil one. At the moment of ecstasis, the individual is in no condition to determine which it is, for his whole being is centred on the inner union that is being consummated. The ego is cured of its littleness and its separateness, and is made whole through union with the nonpersonal daemon of instinctive life.

Although at the moment of this inner surrender the individual may not be able to concern himself with the nature of the other in whom he is allowing himself to be merged, the effect upon his whole being will depend very much on whether it is demonic or divine. John, it will be recalled, warned his disciples to "prove the spirits whether they be of God" or of the devil. He is not alone in warning those who follow the ecstatic road of the dangers it involves, in that false or evil spirits may usurp the place of the god whose presence is being invoked. It was probably on account of the very dubious effects of these ecstatic experiences that the restraints and repressions by which man has tried to control the nonpersonal powers within the psyche were developed. These repressions, long practised by the Roman church, reached their apogee under the Puritans, who sought to repress all spontaneous or original promptings of the inner spirit by an overdevelopment of control by the conscious ego.

When the instinctive expression of life is denied too drastically, it must sooner or later burst forth from its confinement. Its manifestation will then not be adapted but will probably take an atavistic or destructive form. For instance, during the height of the Puritan repressions, an archaic and debased form of phallic worship appeared in western Europe and in America, in the form of witchcraft.[22] The central rituals of the witches' sabbats were sexual. The leader, a man, impersonated the devil; he was worshipped as a phallic god by women, with whom he performed sexual rites, often of a perverted character. This cult was stamped out only with the greatest difficulty and with a fantastic cruelty that surely had its origin not in heaven but in hell. Hundreds of persons suffered torture and burning in preference to recanting. For the ecstasis they had experienced in their orgiastic rites was of such reality and significance that they were willing to face death rather than to renounce or to deny it. This historical fact attests the value and importance that such an experience holds, even when it occurs in a debased form. How much more then must the experience of union with God mean to those who achieve it. Yet it is not without danger. For unless the psychic structure is made firm through having attained wholeness—the one-sidedness of the conscious attitude being balanced by a recognition and acceptance of the other side—the individual will be unable to withstand the influx of unconscious, primitive forces, and will lose his human value in a torrent of instinctive compulsions. But if he has achieved a sufficient inner stability to stand the impact, he will be regenerated by the new energies released in him.

Sparkenbroke, a novel by Charles Morgan, presents a very interesting discussion of the quest for ecstasy and the release it may give from the bondage of self. The hero of the story longs for the experience, feeling that it could bring him illumination or even transformation. Morgan describes it under three aspects or modes: the ecstasy of consummated sexual love achieved through union with the beloved woman, who in the novel is obviously an anima figure; the ecstasy of the act of artistic creation, which is a union of the artist with his genius; and the ecstasy of death, a union with the world spirit—with God.

22. Cf. M. A. Murray, *The Witch-Cult in Western Europe.*

The Buddhists [23] describe four stages or aspects of samadhi, or illumination, in the highest of which the finite mind of the seeker attains at-one-ment with its source, the dharma-kaya, the divine body (or state) of perfect enlightenment. During this condition of ecstasy, the mind of the seeker ceases to exist as finite mind, being absorbed into the infinite mind.

Such descriptions obviously refer to subjective experiences that must be accepted by the psychologist as valid, even though he may not be able to subscribe to the theological or other hypothesis invoked to explain them. In the ecstasis there is without question a sense of enlargement of consciousness, in which the finite mind, to use the Buddhist phrase, or the personal ego, in the terms of Western psychology, is replaced by an all-mind, an infinite mind, or, in psychological terms, by a nonpersonal psychic factor transcending the conscious ego in both scope and power. The experience of being given over to something beyond the ego brings with it a sense of wholeness that persists after the ecstatic state has passed, and may result in an enlargement and unification of the personality. He becomes more truly an individual, less divided, more whole. These effects can be observed by an onlooker. To the individual who has undergone the experience, it seems that the whole world has changed. This is because the very structure of his psyche has been altered, so that his moods, his reactions, his thoughts—his whole experience of himself—are no longer as they were. His perception of the world about him has changed too, with the result that conflicts previously insoluble are seen as it were from a different angle. His reactions become unified instead of being partial and therefore inconsistent, for they now come from a deeper, a more fundamental level.

Perhaps it is because Western religious mystics are concerned with the aspect of the search for wholeness symbolized by union with the soul figure, the anima or animus, that their experiences are so often expressed in sexual terms. It may be that where the experience is concerned with a further exploration of the unconscious, and where the figure involved in the union is of the same sex as the conscious ego (the Wise Man

23. W. Y. Evans-Wentz, *Tibetan Yoga and Secret Doctrines*, pp. 90, 99 ff.

in the case of a man, the Magna Mater in the case of a woman), the ecstasy has a different form.

For the Western man to seek ecstasis as an end in itself, or to follow the road travelled by the Oriental yogin or the mediaeval religious mystic, would obviously be quite false and even dangerous. For in the West we have committed ourselves to the search for truth by the scientific road, and we throw away the consciousness that has been achieved on this path only at our peril. If we are to experience the enlargement of personality that comes from an acceptance of the nonpersonal forces beyond our limited consciousness, it must be accomplished not by a denial of all that our fathers have built up but rather through an extension of their conquest. The aspects of experience they disregarded must in their turn be included in our *Weltanschauung*. In other words, it is through a psychology based on scientific observation that we must approach these strange and unknown regions of the psyche. While permitting ourselves to experience the nonpersonal or archetypal realities within, we must also seek to understand them and weld them into the totality of our psychic structure.

If an individual throws himself into the ecstatic experience without restraint and allows himself to be swallowed up by the nonpersonal forces of the psyche, through temporary sacrifice of his individual and conscious standpoint, he achieves a sense of wholeness, it is true; but when he comes to himself again, he may return to his former condition of limited consciousness dominated by the rational ego, while that aspect of the personality which lived during the ecstasy will fall back into the unconscious. Thus his consciousness is split and he lives as two distinct personalities.

In other cases the man who has such an experience may remain in the ecstatic state, going over completely to the condition of "superior" consciousness. If this happens he will lose his contact with everyday reality: he may become a fanatic, or even a psychotic, being alienated from himself, while what was formerly his conscious personality drops into the depths of the unconscious and is lost to sight. This man will escape the experience of conflict, just as does the one who identifies completely with his rational and conscious personality and represses the irrational experience.

But if a man who has had an ecstatic experience succeeds in holding to his conscious standpoint and its values, and also retains the new influx that has come to him from the very depths of the psyche, he will be obliged to endure the conflict that two such widely different components will necessarily create, and will be compelled to seek for a means of reconciling them. This attitude is the only safeguard against falling under the spell of the nonpersonal, daemonic powers of the unconscious; it is the modern way of following John's advice to "prove the spirits." [24] If the effort is successful, an inner marriage will be consummated, the split between the personal and the nonpersonal part of the psyche will be healed, and the individual will become a whole, a complete being.

THIS BRIEF DISCUSSION of the instinctive forces manifested in sexuality has merely indicated the many aspects of life that spring from the *libido sexualis*. Not only are the urge to physical satisfaction and the biological aim of reproduction served by it, but many other trends, cultural and religious, stem from the same source. Much that is most characteristically human has been achieved because man has been compelled to strive for release from the domination of this strange and mighty instinct whose potentialities have been so little understood. Well may the Buddhist aver that the cock, embodiment of sexuality, is one of the three creatures whose insatiable desirousness keeps the wheel of life forever revolving. [25]

24. Cf. the discussions in Jung's writings on the following topics: the inflation of personality resulting from the inclusion of nonpersonal factors, as it happened to Christina Alberta's father ("The Mana Personality," in *Two Essays on Analytical Psychology* [C.W. 7]); the attitude of the modern psychologist towards religious experience ("Psychology and Religion," in *Psychology and Religion: West and East* [C.W. 11]); the Western scientific attitude and Eastern yoga (*The Secret of the Golden Flower*).

25. For a discussion of the part sexuality may play in psychological development, see below, "Coniunctio" in chap. 12; and see also Jung, "Psychology of the Transference," in *The Practice of Psychotherapy* (C.W. 16), and *Mysterium Coniunctionis* (C.W. 14).

7

Reproduction

II. MATERNITY: *The Nourishing and the Devouring*

THE INSTINCT that assures the preservation of the race fulfills only a part of its aim in the satisfaction of sexuality. By means of this gratification, it is true, the individual is lured into playing an active part in the fertilization of the ovum. But the end result of this action is, so far as the sexual urge itself is concerned, an epiphenomenon—a fortuitous occurrence that neither adds to nor detracts from the experience of the sexual act per se.

In all animals except man, awareness of the connection between sexual intercourse and pregnancy is absent. Even in human beings who are fully aware of the connection, the knowledge may be only intellectual; it is not usually an integral part of the desire for sexual contact nor of the actual experience of union. This is particularly true in the case of men. It does not hold true to the same extent in the case of women. For so important is the maternal instinct that the reproductive urge may appear in a woman's consciousness in the form of a desire for babies, with no physical or psychological realization within herself of a corresponding desire for intercourse. In such women the sexual aspect of the reproductive instinct is repressed or inadequately developed. Some women who are frigid, or completely anaesthetic sexually, nevertheless long to bear children—a strange phenomenon that probably occurs only under the conditions of modern civilization.

This situation has its psychological counterpart in the curious way in which the development of love may skip the stage in which the focal emphasis is on love of mate, and which should occupy the middle position between the childhood stage of love for the parent and the parental stage of love for the child. Many young people pass directly or almost directly from childhood to parenthood not only outwardly but also in the character of the love relationships they are able to establish. A young woman, for instance, centres her love in childhood and adolescence upon someone older and wiser than herself, who is able to guide and protect her—in other words, a parent or parent surrogate. Then she marries. Almost immediately she either makes her husband into a father or thinks of him and acts towards him as if he were her child. A similar type of transition can occur in a man; because of the greater urgency of the sexual impulse in the male, however, it is not found quite so commonly in men as in women, except where the relation to the mother has been a particularly important element in the man's emotional development.

The sexual impulse itself is satisfied in the union of the partners, and this apparently marks the end of the cycle. But if fertilization occurs and an embryo begins to develop, a change is initiated in the woman's body and as a rule in her psychological condition as well. The man does not experience this psychological transformation, just as he does not undergo the physical one; he may even be ignorant of the fact that pregnancy has resulted from the act in which he participated, for once the sperm has left his body its physical fate is apart from his.

The situation of the woman, however, is entirely different. If she is sufficiently conscious and introspective to have a critique of her subjective condition, she will observe that she is reacting in a new way. Her feelings, her thoughts, and those deeper impulses which arise from unconscious levels, undergo a change characteristic of pregnancy. This psychological change is connected in some way with the physiological processes taking place in the woman's body. These processes go on below the threshold of consciousness, and she can neither

observe them directly nor control them; they manifest themselves to her only through their physical effects. The new
psychological factors related to these biological changes also
originate below the threshold of consciousness, and the woman
experiences them as inducing strange moods and altered reactions to life that are not due to any ideas she may hold in
regard to motherhood; they arise of themselves and may seem
very strange to her. They constitute a new experience of life.

A reaction on a deeper level of the unconscious may also
be observed. For pregnancy usually releases psychological
images of a mysterious and archaic type that arise from profound reservoirs of the unconscious. This phenomenon is
bound up with the fact that childbearing is a collective or
racial task, imposed by the instinct for race preservation. It
is at the same time a personal matter having an individual significance for each man and woman. But it would be a mistake
for them to consider it as solely personal; for in creating children they are obeying one of the oldest laws of nature, namely,
the law that the life of the individual must be devoted not only
to self-preservation but also to continuance of the race. For
this reason the experience of maternity puts a woman directly
in touch with the primordial female being deep within her,
who awakes from her slumber when the age-old task of reproduction is begun. This archetypal woman takes a greater share
in controlling the situation than most women realize. If this
were not so, how could a woman who has had no personal
experience or instruction about pregnancy and childbirth instinctively know, as it were, how to nourish the child in her
womb and how to bring it forth when the right time comes?

It is strange to use the word "know" in discussing unconscious and instinctive functions that every female animal can
perform unerringly. Nevertheless these constitute for each
woman who becomes a mother a new experience, part of which
at least requires conscious collaboration that she does not know
how to give until the moment arrives. Then very likely she
will have the quite irrational feeling that she has always known.
A young mother once said to me: "I felt anxious about my
delivery, for fear that in my ignorance I might do something

wrong. But when the time came I suddenly realized that I had known all about it from the beginning of the world." This unknowing "knowing" comes from the archetypal woman in the unconscious, who has experienced childbirth countless times in the long past.

Materials dealing with this archetype are at hand in great profusion. From the beginning of history, it has formed the theme of myths and legends showing how it functions in the spiritual and emotional spheres and how it has changed and developed throughout the centuries. Thus primitive cosmogonies often refer quite literally to the earth as the mother that gave birth to the human race. Further evidence is available to us in the world's inherited store of statues and pictures representing the Great Mother.

These art expressions are most helpful in exploring the significance of the maternal archetype. For the being of the mother has appealed to the artist in man in all times and places, and he has felt himself compelled to express in painting and sculpture what it has meant to him. Jung writes:

The most immediate primordial image is the mother, for she is in every way the nearest and most powerful experience; and the one, moreover, that occurs in the most impressionable period of a man's life. Since the conscious is as yet only weakly developed in childhood, one cannot speak of an "individual" experience at all. The mother, however, is an archetypal experience; she is known by the more or less unconscious child not as a definite, individual feminine personality, but as the mother, an archetype loaded with significant possibilities.[1]

Through his attempts to express these "significant possibilities" in concrete form, man sought to release himself from the inner burden of them. He could then relate himself to the value they represented through the rites he performed before the externalized image; at the same time, he could separate himself as a free individual from the nonpersonal, daemonic instinct represented in this being.

For this reason, the artist has not usually portrayed the Mother in a personal form, reproducing the likeness of his own

1. "Mind and Earth," in *Contributions to Analytical Psychology*, p. 122.

mother; rather, he has depicted the universal mother—Mother Earth, Mother Nature, the Mother Goddess, or Magna Mater. Mrs. Olga Fröbe-Kapteyn made a collection [2] of over a thousand representations of this goddess, dating from all periods of historic and prehistoric time and culled from all parts of the earth. This collection, considerably enlarged, was used by Erich Neumann as the basis for his classic interpretation of the meaning of this fundamental archetype.[3] One cannot but be impressed by the universality of the image. And, indeed, that so many representations of woman as mother should have been created throughout the ages is evidence of man's passionate concern with the experience of woman as bearer and nurturer of life. Whether we think of her as the mother, or designate her merely as a fertility figure, the fact remains that woman as creator and nurturer of life has been of overwhelming importance to mankind. Artists have sought to create a general, even a universal image of woman that should embody a sense of the power or influence she carries: that is to say, each has tried to portray his inner image of this aspect of womanhood.

This inner image has been depicted countless times. Often, in order that it might persist as a permanent record, it has been carved in the hardest and most refractory of materials. For instance, many of the statues are of stone, carved at a time when only the crudest of stone implements were available. We are left with amazement at the extraordinary power and persistence of the impulse that drove even primitive man, whose attention was notoriously fickle, to the concentrated effort necessary for such achievement.

Man has been impelled—by a deep instinct, it would seem —to represent in permanent form the images of his most significant experiences. The images most frequently portrayed will obviously be those embodying human experiences of the most general or universal character, the so-called archetypal images. For the archetypes are built up out of the accumula-

2. Also see *Eranos-Jahrbuch 1938*, which is devoted to the theme of the "Great Mother."
3. Neumann, *The Great Mother*. See also M. E. Harding, *Woman's Mysteries, Ancient and Modern*.

tion of countless actual experiences embedded in the whole of the history of the race. They are the psychological counterpart of the instincts, being, as it were, instinctual patterns. One of the most fundamental of the archetypes is the mother image. The experience of mother is universal, reaching back into each individual's earliest memories. Long before the father held any great importance for the child, the mother was present, the most significant, the most inescapable fact in his life. The experience of mother also reaches back into the most remote memories of the race. In early societies the family consisted of a woman and her children; the father was merely a visitor. Thus, for the race as for the child, the mother is "the one who was always there." She is the eternal, the unborn, the primal cause.

Accordingly, the mother or the old woman is a universal figure in nearly all mythologies. This woman has a child but no husband. Sometimes a mother and daughter are venerated, as in the Greek worship of Demeter and Persephone; sometimes it is a mother and son—Ishtar and Tammuz, Aphrodite and Adonis; or occasionally it is a grandmother and her hero grandson, as in some of the American Indian myths. The earliest religious practices of mankind relate in no small measure to this Magna Mater, her deeds, her attributes, her relations to men. The biological fact of the mother as the source of life on the physical plane is perhaps the earliest form of the archetypal image entering into religious ritual, but religious symbols are not static and fixed for all time. Through the long stages of history they undergo a very slow change that is closely related to the evolution of culture. The transformation of the symbols corresponds with the psychological development taking place in men as their instincts are modified through the centuries in the process described by Jung as psychization. The evolution of the Greek gods from the swashbuckling adventurers of the *Iliad* to the serene Olympians of the later Greek poets and philosophers, is a well-recognized example of the change that takes place in the character of a nation's gods as the people emerge from barbarism to civilization.

A similar change takes place in the symbols arising in the

dreams of modern individuals. During a period of transition, such as occurs during a psychological analysis, archetypal images appear in the dreams and phantasies, often in very archaic forms, indicating that problems or themes of ancient date, or deep-rooted in the psychic structure, have been activated and need attention.

When for instance the relation to the parents has not developed in an orderly way, and the individual becomes aware that his road is obstructed so that he can go no farther, the parent archetypes will begin to arise in his dreams. At first they may appear in modern guise; but if the problem cannot be solved on this cultural level, the images encountered in the dreams and phantasies will take on more and more remote and archaic forms. The dream content may present first the actual mother, then the grandmother, then a generalized old woman. It may be an old woman of bygone times—in the case of a European possibly an oldtime peasant or a mediaeval figure, in the case of an American an old Negro nurse or an Indian squaw. Sometimes the figure is a mythological old crone who seems hardly human and acts in an archaic or barbaric fashion.

In these circumstances, the problem obviously must be solved in more fundamental terms. This individual apparently is unable to accept the psychological outlook of his generation, taking it for granted as his contemporaries do, but must return to his psychic origins and recapitulate in his own experience the history of the race. This process may take place unconsciously, in dreams or phantasies not understood by the individual himself. But the full value of the process cannot be realized unless the recapitulation is experienced consciously, for only through conscious understanding can the lessons of the past be made available for effecting a present-day adaptation to life.

An individual who, for whatever reason, is unable to base himself unquestioningly on the stage of achievement of his generation, is obliged to live for himself the long history of the development of mankind and to come by a conscious process to a state of psychic civilization. As he does not participate in the cultural development of his era, which comes to many persons naturally as the gift of their inheritance, he must win his culture by his own effort. Development for him must be an individual attainment. This process corresponds to the psychic evolution that religious initiations are designed to produce. In some religious systems, this educational process is only roughly worked out; in others, however, especially in the Orient, a very high degree of differentiation has become established. The levels of consciousness these systems define are found, in actual practice, to correspond with the stages of development that an individual experiences while undergoing psychological analysis. In addition, the symbols used in the religious rituals often correspond in an extraordinary way with those appearing in a progressive sequence in dreams and phantasies that arise from the unconscious during analysis. Individuals initiated into ritual practices of ancient religious systems were believed to be thereby released from the bondage of their animal or instinctive natures. Thus they were endowed with souls and became men instead of remaining mere animals: as we should say, they became conscious individuals.

The relation of the individual to the mother is one of the crucial factors in psychological development, both because the early relation to the mother spells dependence, and because for the child she represents the feminine side of life. And, as Jung remarks:

In the unconscious the mother always remains a powerful primordial image, determining and colouring in the individual conscious life our relation to woman, to society, and to the world of feeling and fact, yet in so subtle a way that, as a rule, there is no conscious perception of the process.[4]

Thus the mother represents the principle of relatedness, of the feeling values, and of love, called by Jung the principle of eros.[5]

4. "Mind and Earth," in *Contributions to Analytical Psychology,* p. 123.
5. "Woman in Europe," ibid., pp. 175 f.: "Before this latter question [i.e., the psychic or human relationship between the sexes], the sexual problem pales in significance, and with it we enter the real domain of woman. Her psychology is founded on the principle of eros, the great binder and deliverer; in modern speech we could express the concept of eros as psychic relationship." Cf. also Harding, *Woman's Mysteries, Arcient and Modern,* pp. 34 ff.

So long as the eros remains under the influence of the mother, symbolized by her image, it must continue undeveloped. For when the feeling values are vested in the mother, she is necessarily the one who takes the initiative. The child is only the recipient of feeling, not the initiator, and so does not explore nor develop the potentialities of his own nature. To a person whose relation to the mother has remained unchallenged and unbroken, love means not "I love" but "I am loved." The ability to love as an adult can be gained only after the individual has made good his escape from his childish bondage to the mother. So long as he continues to be under the necessity of receiving mother love, he remains the conditioned one. If he cannot give love and himself create warmth of feeling, he has acquired no personal initiative in the realm of love. His position may seem to be dominant, for he is the demanding recipient—"King Baby"—with mother always at his beck and call. But he is really conditioned in his love life by an a priori presence, the mother—who, because she is the one who was there first, has made or seems to have made the conditions that rule her child's whole world.

When such a child grows up, he may achieve a satisfactory work adaptation to the world outside the family circle and may even develop a highly differentiated relation to the intellectual and masculine side of life, in which he is quite competent. Yet he may remain very childish in his emotions because he has failed to release himself from the mother. So common is this condition that many people in the modern world are hardly aware of its existence. It might almost be called normal for adult men and women to consider the bond between child and mother as the ideal of love. But although this relationship is entirely suitable for children, it is hardly adapted to the emotional needs of adults. So long as the eros remains under the sway of the personal mother, however, it is not possible for men and women to envisage a new ideal of relationship, let alone create it in reality.

It is necessary to bear in mind that the precursor of the emotion we call love is to be found not in the sex instinct and the relation between sexual partners but in the maternal instinct and the relation of the mother to her child. Therefore, unless this relationship is a positive one and unless it develops favourably, the adult will be hampered all his life for want of a satisfactory foundation on which his later relationships can be based. Long before the evolution of any relationship between adults of opposite sex—other than the most transitory coming together for sexual purposes—the mother's concern for her young, even among animals, contained the germs of love. This concern, being hardly more than a biological prompting, was based, it is true, on identification with the offspring; nevertheless, it gives unmistakable evidences of having been the forerunner of love.

In archaic times, and in certain primitive tribes today, sexual contact is marked not by affection but by combat. In the sexual play of more sophisticated lovers, the element of combat is often present as an instinctive feature, appearing usually as play because of the psychic modification of the instinct, but still carrying a reminder of a more primitive and brutal past. Indeed, even modern, so-called civilized persons may discover elements of sadism or masochism latent in themselves, or repressed into the unconscious, and only awaiting a sexual involvement to raise their ugly heads. When—relatively late in human evolution—true mating, as distinct from mere sexual congress, made its appearance, a certain loyalty towards the partner was developed, although at first the alliance was usually made for the protection of the young rather than on account of any emotional bond between the mates. Even in present times, in a marriage where love has died, the husband and wife may decide the problem of the family by giving precedence to the needs of the children as against their own wishes or the demands of the situation in terms of their mutual relationship. For love as we know it today grew out of the relation of mother to child, and in its beginnings it was love of mother for child and not love of child for mother.

On its most primitive level, however—among the uneducated natives of some backward country or among would-be civilized and developed Western people—the love of a mother for her child is an unconscious and instinctive reaction. It is still not a real concern for the offspring as a separate entity; rather, it is based on identification. The mother reacts to her baby as if it were still a part of her own body as it was throughout the period of gestation. The child is a part of herself, to be loved as she loves herself, and to be disposed of as she sees fit. This instinctive identification forms the root and source of mother love, however much it may be modified. Among animals and primitives, no law protects the persons of the young, who are fed and tended or neglected and ill-treated as the unconscious instinct of the mother may dictate. If the infant seems superfluous to her, she will kill or desert it, just as in other circumstances she will sacrifice her own well-being or even her life to protect it.

For this reason the archetypal figure of the mother [6] appears in the most primitive myths and sculptures as huge, all-powerful, and overwhelming. Correspondingly, the rituals practised in relation to her were concerned not with seeking her love but rather with placating her. The mother of these myths is represented in a barbarous or bestial aspect most repugnant to civilized people. On the other hand, it is not uncommon to hear of unwanted infants being destroyed or deserted by desperate mothers today even in Christian countries; and an acquaintance with the seamy side of family histories reveals that the so-called rejected child is by no means rare, even in situations in which the physical and material welfare of the child has always had scrupulous attention. In the dreams of such children, or of the men and women they become, there can be found traces of the archetypal, barbaric mother. For she has exerted a far greater influence upon their psychological development than has the outward, conscious attitude of the actual mother, whose solicitude for their health and happiness has been only skin deep.

This situation is illustrated by the history of an artist of great sensitivity, whose whole life had been warped by fear and bitterness. These negative feelings were directed to his dead mother and his older sister, and in particular to the Catho-

---

6. For a most valuable discussion of the subject, see C. G. Jung, *Symbols of Transformation* (C.W. 5), chap. VII, "The Dual Mother."

lic church. He felt that his sister and the church (*Mater Ec-clesia*) both sought to dominate him, to strangle and destroy him. During the course of his analysis he recalled with great emotion an episode that had occurred when he was six or seven years old. He was playing in a vacant lot near his home, where he had been forbidden to go, as it was frequented by tramps and the riffraff of the city; boylike, however, he was lured to it mainly because of its atmosphere of strangeness and adventure. On this occasion he had just crawled through a hole in the fence when he saw two policemen coming across the lot to meet each other. One of them carried a bundle. The boy dodged down behind a bush and remained hidden. The men met opposite the bush and opened the bundle, and the child saw to his horror that it contained the body of a dead baby. Intuitively he realized that this infant had been "thrown away" by its mother. Here the unconscious came into play, and he felt that his own mother had likewise wanted to throw him away, but had been prevented from doing so—a frustration that accounted for her habitual faultfinding. In addition, he felt that his sister, who knew of this secret wish on the part of the mother, was only waiting for an opportunity to put it into effect. Needless to say, he did not dare to tell his mother what he had seen; and although in time it faded from his mind, the vision of the inhuman mother remained with him, a predominating influence in his life, till at the age of forty-eight he came to me for help. This problem, as one would expect, formed the focal point of his analysis, and just before his death a new feeling was born in him and he became able, for the first time in his life, to love and to trust. This experience was like a rebirth to him and he represented it in a drawing in which the eyes of a little boy are being opened by a beautiful nude woman obviously representing both anima and mother in her divine aspect.[7] For, indeed, his eyes had been opened to see an entirely new world. He was reborn as a little child, but, strange to relate, within a week he died in an accident.

In this case there had been actual and very traumatic experiences that would amply account for the negative aspect

7. See plate V.

of the mother image he experienced, which persisted for a good part of his analysis. These had been so severe that, in spite of the insight and renewal that came to him at the end, this man was not able to create a new life for himself. But there are other cases where, although there has been no such actual experience in childhood to focus the negative aspect of the archetypal image in the unconscious, it may, nevertheless, appear in a negative form in dreams,[8] especially at those times when the individual should be venturing upon some new enterprise and is held back by a childish need for encouragement or support. At such times he may dream of an old witchlike woman who kills and eats small animals that in the moment turn into human infants. For his own life effort is being devoured by the archetypal mother, who represents the unconscious source from which he has failed to free himself.

THROUGHOUT THE AGES man has sought to make some representation of this source—the dark abyss from which he emerges as a separate being. The cavern of the womb whence the child is extruded, laved in the natal, the primal waters, has fascinated him. The mystery of birth has seemed to hold the secret of life itself, the life of the spirit as well as of the body. The mother great with child embodies this mystery, as does also the womb. And so a great rounded stone [9] was often worshipped as representing the mother, and a dark cave or round building could serve as a womb in which the mystery of second birth might be enacted.

The stone representing the Mother Goddess appears in many forms. Sometimes it is simply a rounded cone; or there may be a knob at the top and extensions or crossbars at the sides, so that it resembles a crude human figure and suggests a stone woman. Long ago, sacrifices of human infants were made to stone mothers such as these. The Mother Goddess, giver of life and fertility, guardian of childbirth, is also the Terrible One, Death, the Devourer. She represents the invol-

8. See J. Jacobi, *Complex/Archetype/Symbol in the Psychology of C. G. Jung,* for an analysis of dream material of this type in a child.
9. Cf. Harding, *Woman's Mysteries, Ancient and Modern,* pp. 39 ff.

untary, compulsive urge to bring forth life, which functions quite blindly in the female. After the young have left her womb, she suckles and cherishes them as long as her biological urges impel her to do so; beyond that, she has no concern for them or for their welfare. They exist for her only as the means of fulfillment of her own instincts.

In the Celtic countries the Mother Goddess was represented by a great stone cauldron [10] over which human sacrifices were made. The "Cauldron of Gundestrup" (see plate VI) shows a sacrificial scene, embossed on the inside of this silver vessel. The chief priestess, we are told, was charged with the slaying of the victims, who were generally prisoners of war rather than infants offered in sacrifice by their parents as in the Phrygian ritual. Where infants were sacrificed, it was believed that the goddess drank their blood, which renewed her own powers of fertility. In the Celtic sacrifices, the blood of the victims slaughtered over the cauldron that represented the womb of the Great Mother served a further purpose, for the cauldron became a kind of baptismal font. Persons bathed in it were believed to be endowed with eternal life, while those who drank of the blood it contained were granted the grace of inspiration.

This ritual is obviously connected with the legends of a magic cauldron that recur frequently in the romantic literature of the twelfth and thirteenth centuries. These themes date from a much earlier time: many of them are pre-Christian, even prehistoric. Such is the story of Branwen, daughter of Llyr, which tells of a cauldron that had power to bring the dead to life:

And Bendigeid Vran began to discourse, and said: "I will give unto thee a cauldron, the property of which is, that if one of thy men be slain to-day, and be cast therein, tomorrow he will be as well as ever he was at the best, except that he will not regain his speech." [11]

10. J. A. MacCulloch, *The Religion of the Ancient Celts*, p. 383; idem, "The Abode of the Blest," in J. Hastings, *Encyclopaedia of Religion and Ethics*, II, 694.
11. C. Guest (tr.), *The Mabinogion*, p. 37. Cf. also J. A. MacCulloch, *Celtic Mythology*, in L. H. Gray (ed.), *Mythology of All Races*, III, 112.

Later Bendigeid Vran related how he had got the cauldron from Ireland. This is probably the same cauldron that was possessed by the Tuatha De Danann, gods of ancient Ireland, whose name means "the folk of the goddess Anu" (Anu was a moon mother goddess). One legend relates that at a time when the Tuatha were residing in Asia, and were at war with the Syrians, they were enabled to triumph because they had the art of resuscitating those killed in battle. It is also said that the Tuatha owned a well in Ireland whose waters healed the mortally wounded.[12]

MacCulloch [13] relates another Celtic myth, centring about a cauldron that supplied abundance and gave life to the dead. It had been "fetched" from the Land beneath the Waves, and was owned by Cerridwen, who dwelt by the Lake of Bala in Wales. She was a goddess of plenty and of inspiration, for her father Ogywen was god of language, poetry, and the alphabet, that is, he was god of the magic runes. This cauldron is connected with the "grail," also called a cauldron, that Arthur caused to be fetched—or stolen—from Annwfn, the underworld. This cauldron too had life-giving powers, and after boiling for a year, gave inspiration and knowledge of all things to those who tasted its elixir.

This symbolism is familiar to us in the Christian sacrament of baptism. The font, or fountain of life-giving water, is known as the *uterus ecclesiae*. In old churches, especially those of Norman architecture, it has the form of a hollowed-out stone. It is taught that immersion in this font endows the recipient of the sacrament with an immortal soul, just as immersion in the Celtic cauldron was thought to bring life to the dead or to bestow immortality. The idea of the mother, source of the life of the body, is here expanded into the idea of a divine mother giving birth to an immortal spirit in the mortal being, who is born a second time through immersion in the living waters of the font.

The symbol representing the mother underwent a similar development in Egypt. Mother Isis, whose emblem is an amulet

12. Guest, *The Mabinogion*, p. 295.
13. *Celtic Mythology*, in Gray, *Mythology of All Races*, III, 109 ff.

possibly representing a knot of flax tied so that it closely resembles the Great Mother stone at Paphos, came to be symbolized by a vase of water. In the festival called Phallephoria,[14]
this vase of water was carried before the colossal image of the
phallus of Osiris. It symbolized the female creative principle,
the womb, and the water it contained represented the moisture
that brings fruitfulness to the desert. In figure 7 we see Nut,
a variant of Isis, represented as a tree numen. The figure comes
from a vignette in the *Book of the Dead*, where the text reads:
" 'Hail, thou sycamore of the goddess Nut! Grant thou to me
of the water and of the air which dwell in thee.' The goddess
is seen standing in a tree. . . . She sprinkles water upon [the
deceased] as he kneels at the foot of a tree." [15]

But Isis was not only the mother who gives life. In certain
elements of her story [16] the negative aspect of the mother appears. For instance, twice in her life she nursed with great
tenderness the victims of a serpent that she herself had created
to wound them. This bespeaks the maternal instinct that must
at all cost have something to mother. It is a primitive instinct
that can even injure the loved object if it is thereby handed
over to the mother like a helpless infant. The compulsion of
the mother to tend and nurture someone may lead her to create
the need in the filling of which her own instinct and craving
are satisfied.

In the Isis story these incidents are told with primitive sim-
plicity. There is no attempt to conceal the expressions of the
instinct under a mask of good feeling. Mother Isis lived her
impulses uncensored: the juxtaposition of the negative and
positive aspects caused her no conflict, and apparently her
worshippers felt none either. The contradiction in her character may have caused some difficulty to the devotees of later
centuries, but they probably accounted for it as a divine mystery. For as man developed a conscious standpoint and ethic,
the opposition of yea and nay in the primitive instinct was

14. Plutarch, "Isis and Osiris," tr. in G. R. S. Mead, *Thrice Greatest
Hermes*, I, 279, 312.
15. E. A. W. Budge, *The Gods of the Egyptians*, I, 107.
16. Frazer, *The Golden Bough*, p. 260.

Fig. 7. The Goddess Nut as a Tree Numen Bringing Water

pushed farther and farther into the background. The gods continued to evince a duality from which man has sought to free himself partly through psychic modification of the instincts and partly through repression. Thus the story of Isis and her poisonous worm, and of the magic with which she exorcised its venom, became a formula recited to cure snake bite. For surely if Isis made the poison, Isis was able also to nullify its effects.

THE MOTHER who was represented in the most archaic period by a cold, hard stone is symbolized in more civilized times by the life-giving water. This change corresponds with the evolution of the maternal impulse. In the most remote period maternity was no more than biological fact. The child was protected merely as a part of the mother. Love, tenderness, and gentleness were not recognized as virtues; if such feelings existed at all, they were probably treated as weaknesses. The savagery, the callousness, the hardness of unconscious functioning dominated. Little by little, however, through a gradual modification of the maternal instinct, kindness developed. The mother began to care for her child and its welfare as independent of her own. She came to recognize it as a being apart from herself: the child acquired certain individual rights and was no longer sacrificed completely to the mother's instinctive demands. Mother Isis, memorable for her love and longing for the dead Osiris, was represented not by a stone—although her personal emblem resembled many of the sacred stones of the mother worship of more primitive cultures—but by a vase of water.

In the next phase, the vessel becomes the chalice containing the spiritual draught. The mother, originally the giver of physical life, is now the life-giver on the spiritual plane. This transition was already hinted at in the symbolism of the Celtic cauldron, which was the forerunner of the Holy Grail [17] of the Arthurian cycle. The form of the grail itself varies. We

17. MacCulloch, *The Religion of the Ancient Celts*, p. 383; idem, "The Abode of the Blest," in Hastings, *Encyclopaedia of Religion and Ethics*, II, 694; idem, *Celtic Mythology*, in Gray, *Mythology of All Races*, III, 202.

are never told precisely and finally just what it was. Often it was a stone having magic powers, or a dish that gave to each the food he liked best; sometimes it was a cup containing the nectar of the gods, or a cauldron with power to restore the dead to life. In mediaeval versions of these stories, it takes on Christian symbolism. Thus it is the cup used at the Last Supper, and contains the lance, still dripping blood, with which Longinus pierced the side of Christ. From it shines an unearthly light. It is the chalice transformed into a spiritual vessel containing the draught of immortality, the treasure above all treasures.

The idea of immortality itself underwent a gradual change during the centuries. It began as a concrete and materialistic wish to escape physical death, while the afterlife was pictured as exactly similar to earthly existence. In Egypt, for instance, models of common domestic objects were placed in the grave so that the ka or soul might not be without the things it would need in the Egypt above. The American Indians, with a slightly different conception, hope to reach the happy hunting grounds when they leave the familiar ones of earth. But these hunting grounds are always "happy"; that is, they are in some way better than those on earth. This is an attempt to transcend physical life by glorifying its qualities in the hereafter. It is a process with which we are familiar in the concept of heaven as a city of golden streets and white robes and perpetual music. This endeavour to reach the spiritual by transcending the physical was reflected in the thought of mediaeval philosophers, who tried to grasp the character of the nonmaterial by imagining things of smaller and smaller size and of more and more subtle substance. But for mediaeval man the material substance still remained, however much he refined it. This attempt to grasp the essence of the inner reality by freeing it from its materiality led to a preoccupation with many strange speculations, such as the question as to how many angels could stand at one time on the point of a pin.

Gradually the longing for a life after death became the hope for immortality in a nonmaterial, a spirit body. Finally it became the desire to create within the psyche a nonpersonal, an immortal spark that should represent the total or complete individuality. This immortal spark cannot be created by conscious effort or by will, for it resembles the life of the physical child, which must be born. Thus man returns again to the mother, the life-giver, the source of spiritual as of earthly birth, the Magna Mater. The earthly mother is transformed into the heavenly mother—the *mater coelestis*, Sophia, the divine wisdom.

An evolution similar to this may be perceived in the personifications of the Magna Mater. In the dim ages of the past the Mother Goddess was represented as an animal—a recognition of the fact that the mother impulse in human beings is motivated by animal instinct. The farther back we trace the mother image, the nearer do we come to the animal concept. Artemis was once a bear; Cybele was a lioness, as was also Atargatis; Hecate was the three-headed hound of the moon, and Isis was identified with Hathor, the cow goddess. In later centuries, when the Hellenized form of the Egyptian mysteries became popular, Osiris, the moon god and consort of Isis, was worshipped in the Serapeum under the guise of Apis, the sacred bull. In explaining this animal worship, which must have seemed strangely barbaric to the cultured Greeks, Plutarch states that the bull Apis is not Osiris himself but the spirit of Osiris. This gives us a clue to the evolution of religious thought.

First the god is an animal. Later he is attended by animals, as shown in plate III, and in numerous other representations to be found all over the world. Still later the animal nature of the god is represented by the mask he wears, just as even today the American Indians wear animal masks when representing gods in their ritual dances. Plate VII shows a stone statue wearing a lion's mask. It represents Sekhmet, an Egyptian goddess who was the counterpart, or consort, of Ptah. She was the protector of souls, but also the personification of the fierce, scorching, and destroying heat of the sun's rays.[18]

18. Budge, *The Gods of the Egyptians*, I, 515.

It is these qualities that are represented by the lion's mask in our illustration. But the spirit of the god is still an animal, and the animal attendants of the Magna Mater must constantly have reminded the latter-day worshippers of the wilder and more brutal aspects of her nature, now in part sloughed off by evolution. Her animals still accompanied her, however, for she could not be comprehended except in the light of her past.

The psychological meaning of this gradual change is clear. In the remote past the maternal instinct was entirely animal in character. The mother, whether animal or human, would under certain circumstances give her own life to protect her young; under others she would with the same readiness kill and eat them. This brutality was entirely instinctive and unconscious; there was no egotism or self-concern about it. As civilization progressed, however, the emotion she experienced in regard to the child grew into something nearer to what we call love.

At the same time the Mother Goddess gradually rose above her animal nature. Starting with a crudely animal conception, the representations of her finally attain a sublimely spiritual expression. There is for example a rough little Babylonian stone image of Artemis, or Ishtar, in which the goddess is depicted as hardly human; her figure is little more than a pillar adorned with many breasts, and with the tongue protruding from the mouth. In a statue of later period this same Artemis is to be seen standing in the same ritual position, still many-breasted, and with her animal children grouped about her. A great change has taken place, however. The grace and beauty of the workmanship reflect a refinement of feeling far removed from the experience of the men who made the crude, hardly human figures that represented the Great Mother in earlier centuries.[19]

The Magna Mater is an almost universal religious symbol, a fact that reflects the universality of the problem inhering in man's relation to his personal mother and also in his dependence on the impersonal or archetypal mother, source of life

19. See Neumann, *The Great Mother* and *The Archetypal World of Henry Moore.*

itself. For unless his life is renewed ever and anon by contact with its instinctive sources, it will wither away. His body must be renewed in sleep, and his spirit by immersion in the dark tides that flow beyond the comprehension of his conscious intellect. His longing for the maternal depths is the expression of his need for renewal; but it is also a menace, a danger in his path. For in these depths he can lose himself, together with his conscious problems and conflicts; he can find eternal rest by dissolving in the primal waters of being. But this means death for the conscious personality. As Jung writes:

> In the morning of life the son tears himself loose from the mother, from the domestic hearth, to rise through battle to his destined heights. Always he imagines his worst enemy in front of him, yet he carries the enemy within himself—a deadly longing for the abyss, a longing to drown in his own source, to be sucked down to the realm of the Mothers. His life is a constant struggle against extinction, a violent yet fleeting deliverance from ever-lurking night. This death is no external enemy, it is his own inner longing for the stillness and profound peace of all-knowing non-existence, for all-seeing sleep in the ocean of coming-to-be and passing away. Even in his highest strivings for harmony and balance, for the profundities of philosophy and the raptures of the artist, he seeks death, immobility, satiety, rest.[20]

The part of the problem relating to this nonpersonal source of life remains. But the childish relation to the personal mother should be resolved, giving place to the problems and reactions of adult life. Childhood is only a transitory phase. The child grows up and becomes a parent in his turn. Thus the parent-child problem is gradually reversed. On the physical plane this change is accomplished in the majority of cases without too much difficulty; the corresponding psychological transformation often lags behind. In spite of this, the young woman in her early twenties, whether she has children or not, begins to develop the mother in herself. Womanhood begins to express itself psychologically within her, not only through the appearance of the archetype of the mate, but also through the po-

20. *Symbols of Transformation* (C.W. 5), pp. 355-56.

tency of the mother image—in growing up she has to become the mother in her own person.[21]

The problem of the child and its struggle to release itself from the mother has been very fully discussed by modern psychologists. The problem of the woman and her relation to her own maternal instinct has not received as much attention, in spite of its great importance.

When the mother archetype, representing feminine nature, manifests itself in a modern woman only in its least developed form, that is, simply in the biological function of bringing forth and tending young, her relation to her sexual partner is likely to be dominated by the instinctual need for maternity and not by a sexual urge. Her actions and emotions will be controlled by her desire for children, whether this is realized as a conscious wish or experienced merely as an instinctive impulse. If she allows this unredeemed maternal impulse to dominate her, she may be impelled to seek sexual relations with a man even though she does not love him and the mating is in no way suitable except as a means to pregnancy. She may even make love to him for the sole purpose of using him to give her a child.

Strangely enough, this strategy is by no means always recognized by the man for what it is—a cold-blooded exploitation of his feelings for the gratification of a nonpersonal instinct. Instead of feeling himself exploited by the woman's attitude, he may be attracted by it: he may think her desire very sweet and noble, and may even idealize the lack of natural sexuality that often accompanies such an uncompensated domination of the maternal instinct, believing it to be an evidence of spirituality or of unselfishness. In reality her relation to him is seriously lacking in true feeling, and it is quite likely that her attitude towards the child resulting from such a union will also be selfish and egocentric. For the desire for children may be but the expression of an instinct whose sole purpose is the satisfaction of a biological need, and unless it is brought into a mean-

21. Cf. the relation of Kore and Demeter. Demeter as mother contains her own youthful side, Kore, within her, while Kore becomes Demeter in her turn. See Jung and Kerényi, *Essays on a Science of Mythology*, pp. 168 ff.

ingful and conscious relation to the woman's total personality it will remain without psychological or emotional value. Such a woman is in danger of falling under the daemonic power of the maternal instinct that impels her to bear children, whom she will then regard as merely adjuncts to herself, possessions without individual or human rights.

A woman still in this earliest phase of development devours her children, metaphorically speaking; she is compelled by a force beyond her control to nourish herself emotionally by consuming those on whom she centres her maternal care and solicitude. She seems most kind and motherly, but there is always a doubt whether she is not in reality seeking an emotional meal. She flourishes on her "self-sacrifice," while the recipients of her benefactions often grow pale and wan. In such a case the maternal impulse functions like the stone-mother of old.

Needless to say, the woman of this so-called "very maternal" type is not herself aware of the real nature of her impulses. She is probably convinced that her motives are entirely kind and altruistic. The true nature of her involvement is likely to be revealed, however, if the object of her solicitude should become independent and no longer need her care, or transfer his dependence to someone else. If her "love" is real affection for the child himself, she will continue to love him while relinquishing her claim upon him. If, however, she becomes hostile and resentful towards him because he has cut himself away from her apron strings, we must question the basis of her attachment.

Solomon of old recognized this touchstone of the mother relation in judging between the women who came before him with two babies, one living and one dead. Each claimed to be the mother of the living child.

Then said the king, The one saith, This is my son that liveth, and thy son is the dead: and the other saith, Nay; but thy son is the dead and my son is the living. And the king said, Bring me a sword. And they brought a sword before the king. And the king said, Divide the living child in two, and give half to the one and half to the other. Then spake the woman whose the living child was unto the king, for her bowels yearned upon her son, and she said, O my lord, give her the living child, and in no wise slay it. But the other said, Let it be neither mine nor thine, but divide it. Then the king answered and said, Give her the living child and in no wise slay it: she is the mother thereof.[22]

The real mother would rather lose her child than see him killed. But where a woman cannot bear to give up her child even though the time has manifestly come for him to lead his own life, she will try desperately to keep him with her, perhaps by raising apparently reasonable objections to his departure, or by pleading her own need, or as a last resort by invoking the traditional plaint that he will bring down her gray hairs with sorrow to the grave.

Where the child succeeds in breaking away—either in response to a real external necessity or by going over into a negative and rebellious attitude—the mother, unable to reconcile her natural grief at parting from him with her equally natural desire for his psychological growth and development, violently resists her fate. Her emotional disturbance over the child's defection may precipitate a serious psychological crisis; she who has till then seemed to be the strong one, the giver, may break down emotionally or may fall into neurosis, thus making it quite clear that her so-called love was concerned not with the real welfare of the child but rather with her own emotional satisfaction. On this basis, her determination to prevent the separation is understandable. Her motherhood could be satisfied only by receiving and responding to the emotional dependence of the child: she was as much bound as he was. Such a "bereaved" mother may be heard to lament, "I have no reason for living any more. Nobody needs me."

WE HAVE SEEN that in the earliest and most archaic symbolizations the Mother Goddess demanded the lives of children, for only by devouring them could her own life be maintained. The ritual of the sacrifice of the son in the much later mystery cults of antiquity was based on the myth of the sacrifice per-

22. I Kings 3:23-27.

formed by the Mother Goddess herself, but it now had an entirely different significance, for it had as its purpose the release of the human mother from the compulsive power of her instinctual bondage to the child. The experience or initiation [23] by means of which the modern woman can be released from the barbarous aspect of her instinct corresponds to this later ritual in which the goddess sacrificed her own son, allowing him, or, in a still later form, even compelling him to go free: that is, she voluntarily renounced both the child and his dependence and was left alone with her grief.

In Indian mythology this dual aspect of the mother is especially clearly depicted. Heinrich Zimmer in an article on the Indian World Mother writes: "She remains what she is: the totality maintaining its balance by contradictions: sheltering maternal womb, silently nurturing, generous breast and hand—and devouring jaws of death, grinding everything to bits." [24]

The ritual sacrifice of the son that formed a central theme in the mystery teachings regarding the Great Mother throughout the Near East took a different form. The outstanding legends exemplifying it demonstrate once again the evolution of the maternal instinct and its gradual modification through the centuries.

The earliest of these legends is that of the Phrygian goddess Cybele, who fell in love with her son Attis.[25] He, however, loved the king's daughter, and his mother, raging with jealousy, struck him with madness. He forthwith castrated himself under a pine tree—a symbol of the Great Mother—and bled to death. Another version of the myth, however, relates that he was killed by a boar—the animal form of Cybele herself. Adonis too, the youthful lover of Aphrodite, whom the goddess had reared from infancy as her son, was killed by a bear—once the embodiment of herself—while she sat passively by. An allusion to the myth may still be seen at Ghineh, where the figures of Adonis and Aphrodite are carved on the face

23. Harding, *Woman's Mysteries, Ancient and Modern*, chap. xiv.
24. "The Indian World Mother," *Spring*, 1960.
25. Jung, *Symbols of Transformation* (C.W. 5), pp. 204, 423; Harding, *Woman's Mysteries, Ancient and Modern*, pp. 141-42.

of a great rock.²⁶ Adonis is portrayed with spear in rest, await-ing the attack of a bear, while Aphrodite is seated in an attitude of sorrow.

In these legends the mother loves her child but wants him for herself alone. She will not permit him to leave her and would rather kill him in her jealous rage than lose him. In similar vein Ishtar condemned her own son, Tammuz, to a yearly death, while Isis refused to allow her enemy, Set, to be executed, although he had killed her husband Osiris and wounded Horus, her son; in consequence, he lived to repeat his treacherous attack. In each case the mother is shown as permitting the death of her son or youthful lover, or even directly causing it and then grieving over her loss.

In the most barbaric days, the Mother Goddess devoured the human infants sacrificed to her, and there is no indication that she experienced any emotion other than satisfaction over her ghastly meal. These later goddesses do not demand the death of the children of worshippers, but instead sacrifice their own sons. Apparently the archaic maternal instinct still func-tions in them autonomously, since they cannot help killing their sons—as is clearly indicated where the sacrifice is carried out by the animal counterpart of the goddess—but having done so, they grieve over their lost beloved. Yet when the condi-tions that set off the instinctive reaction occur again, they repeat the murderous act. These myths depict the tragic dilemma in which mankind finds itself. As Paul says, "That which I would not, that I do." It seems as if these poor god-desses simply could not learn—just as mankind, for all its horror of killing, cannot find a way of avoiding wars and their endless slaughter.

Turning the pages of history, we come to a later record that in its setting closely resembles the myths of Cybele and Aphrodite. This story too takes place on the eastern shores of the Mediterranean. Again there is a virgin mother of a dearly beloved son. He must leave her to undertake the teaching of mankind. She tries more than once to hold him back, but he tells her that he must be about his Father's business, and

26. Frazer, _The Golden Bough_, p. 329.

she desists. Then, when he falls under the displeasure of the ruling powers and is impaled on a tree, like his predecessor Attis, she and the other women who loved him stand by the cross and lament his death. Mary in her turn came to be known as the Great Mother; but she is unlike her precursors in that her relation to her divine son is one of yearning tenderness and of willing co-operation in his mission.

In each of these instances the son goes to another realm, to fulfill a destiny in which the mother has no part. He is her child, but he must go beyond her and she dare not hold him back. In this way she frees herself from her bondage to her child. Or, to put it a little differently, she frees herself from her identification with the mother role.

In the myth, this identification between mother and child must be resolved by the removal of the son through actual death. In modern times many women literally make this sacrifice in giving up their sons to fight for something more precious than life itself. It must be made on the psychological plane by all women if they are not to remain under the domination of a blind instinct. Instead of killing her child, the modern woman must "kill" or renounce her claims upon him, give up her demand that he remain her child, oriented to her alone, and allow him to set forth on his own life adventure. This is the way in which a woman must relinquish that aspect of the maternal instinct under which she regards her offspring as her personal property, which she has a right to use in whatever way she wishes for the satisfaction of her own desires. It is a psychological sacrifice that often seems as high a price to pay as would the son's actual death. Through it the stone-mother, the compulsive, nonhuman aspect of the maternal instinct, is overcome: by this sacrifice a woman learns to give without demanding any return, and to find her satisfaction in the giving. Thus a new step in the psychic modification of the instinct has been achieved, corresponding to the progression of the symbols of the Great Mother by which the stone is hollowed out and becomes the vase, container of the living water.

A woman who has reached this stage of inner development has done much to solve the problem of the mother-child relation. In the average woman of today, however, the maternal instinct has not as a rule reached this level. The conventional mode of behaviour seemingly corresponds with this ideal, but the disidentification represented by the sacrifice of the son has usually not been attained.

Most modern women strive to live up to this ideal through a refinement of the instinctive maternal feeling brought about by ego consciousness, while its unacceptable elements are repressed. This condition represents the highest stage of culture to which they personally can attain. There are many women, however, who are not content with this solution of the problem, for they realize that the compulsion to act the part of mother may interfere with their desire to become whole individuals. They realize that the maternal instinct must take its place as one, and only one, of the fundamental motives on which the complete human personality is based. This realization can lead to the most painful psychological conflict or become a cause of ill-health or other neurotic symptoms. In such cases, the images arising from the unconscious in dreams and phantasies may bring to a cultured woman the knowledge that impulses and emotions characteristic of the stone-mother slumber deep within her beneath the surface appearance of benevolence, and that these may even be motivating her apparently self-sacrificing actions. It is these unacceptable impulses that are the cause of her unhappiness or neurosis.

So long as she thought of her mothering instinct as kind, she was not concerned to be released from the compulsion it put upon her. For her kindness and generosity raised her in her own esteem as well as in that of her circle. But when a realization of its underlying nature has been forced upon her, she can no longer take pride in her so-called goodness. The real love of the object, the desire to love the child for himself that is also present—at least in most women—comes into direct conflict with the desire to possess and dominate him. That is to say, her need to be herself, to become whole, is opposed to her subservience to the mother instinct. For these impulses are contradictory; if the woman cannot release herself from her identification with her child, that is, from her identification with the function or role of mother, they will neutralize each other or else create an irreconcilable conflict. For this mother role is the archetype—the ancient stone-mother within.

When a woman is identified with her child in this way, she denies him the right to be a separate person with an individuality of his own. At the same time her own individuality will be as constrained and unfree as his. She has a fate and a task transcending her maternal function, as well as duties and experiences that, in the nature of the case, her children cannot share. In denying her child the right to be himself, she is depriving herself of the same privilege. There comes a time, therefore, when she must sacrifice her son—not only externally, by letting him go out on his own path, but also on a deeper, a more spiritual level.

This sacrifice can be accomplished by the modern woman through a refusal to continue to be identified with the role of mother. When she reacts to her grown child as one adult to another, compelling him to take responsibility for himself, she is "sacrificing the son"—an act that seems, in the eyes of many mothers, most reprehensible. For not infrequently a woman is under the illusion that it is highly meritorious to deprive herself quite unnecessarily, if thereby she can give more to her children. It requires considerable insight to realize that this would only chain the children to her and deny them their individuality, and would also mean that she would be eaten up —not by the children, but by the mother archetype within her, by her own undisciplined maternal instinct.

If she refuses to succumb to her primitive impulses and, in order to release herself from such dominance, sets her ego against the unqualified demands of the maternal instinct, a new problem arises. If the ego usurps the place of the maternal instinct and takes over its energy unchanged, the woman will become a domineering mother; for the maternal instinct now amalgamates with the power instinct. This reaction may represent an instinctive attempt on the woman's part to free herself from the maternal archetype, much as certain women clutch at maternity and the maternal role as a means of escape from the claims of sex. But just as the woman is more than a sexual object for the man, so is she also more than mother to her children. As a whole being she is moved by both of these instinctual impulses, but she must develop a relation to them instead of falling helplessly under their dominance. It is only when instinctual energy is transformed that it can become available for the enhancement of the conscious values of the personality.

In our present-day culture, the aspect of maternal instinct symbolized by the stone-mother slumbers unrecognized. Mothers are usually kind and loving to their children, and their attitude of self-sacrifice is proverbial. It is our mode to be quite sentimental and uncritical about this relationship. We speak of "sacred motherhood," and we even have a Mother's Day, on which in some circles every son and every daughter is expected to send a gift to his or her mother. The attitude seems to be that beyond the demands of personal relationship— fitly honored by a gift on the birthday of the particular mother —there is need for a general recognition, requiring, so to speak, a collective push, a united effort to remember not my mother or your mother but just "Mother." It is a generalization of the personal feeling that results in a deterioration of the filial emotion to sentimentality. A woman who accepts the homage and the gifts offered to her on Mother's Day, and takes to herself the prestige and honour that really belong to the maternal role she has filled, has identified herself with the archetype. Although her individuality seems to be enhanced, this conscious superiority is compensated and nullified in the unconscious. For she has become *nothing but* mother, and her personality is sacrificed to the archetypal image that usurps the place of her individuality.

If this homage were rendered quite frankly to "the mother" in a religious spirit, it would have quite a different significance. It would then be a ritual whose aim and effect would be to cut the tie to the personal mother and to strengthen in its place the relation to the nonpersonal mother, the Magna Mater, source of all life.

The mother may have reached a personal development that would allow her to give up her bondage to her child, but unless the son or daughter undergoes a corresponding development he, or she, will not be able to relinquish his childish clinging to the mother, for it is far easier to remain a child than to launch out into all the perils that independence involves. And so it is necessary for the child, also, to undergo an initiation involving a ritual of sacrificial death. By this he dies so far as the personal mother is concerned, and is thus released from his childish dependence on her, and is reborn as child of the universal mother, who is earth mother, the mother of his physical body, and becomes by this act the mother of his spirit, for she is also the heavenly mother. The ancients conceived of this rebirth in a quite concrete fashion, as evidenced by the pictures of the Pharaoh as an adult man being suckled by the Mother Goddess [27]—by Hathor as the heavenly cow, or by Isis, the Great Mother in her human form.

The Magna Mater is not only the mother of one son, she is also the universal mother; that is to say, she is the mother power in all female beings that give birth, animal as well as human. She is source of all generation and carries the seed of all beings. She is therefore represented as bearing the god within herself. This theme is beautifully portrayed in Christian as well as in pagan art. St. Anne, the human mother of the Virgin Mary, is shown with her daughter in her arms; but the Virgin also holds her own child, the infant Jesus. If we go back into antiquity we shall find many other representations of the same archetype of mother, daughter, and child. For instance, the little ivory group which was found in one of the Mycenean rooms of the Bronze Age Palace, below the foundations of the Greek Temple of Mycenae, shows three linked figures, mother, daughter, and boy, and, as Wace reports, this "may well represent the two goddesses, the Great Mother and her younger associate, and their young male companion." [28] He continues: this "representation of two women and a boy, recalls . . . the Eleusinian trinity. . . . In any case the group may be taken to represent the goddesses who had many names,

27. See plate VIII.
28. Wace, *Mycenae*, p. 115. See plate IX.

Demeter and Persephone, Demia and Auxesia, or simply the Mistresses. The boy is naturally both Iakchos and the young male god of the Minoan-Mycenean religion . . . terra-cotta figurines of Demeter and Kore found in Rhodes and Cyprus [show] the two goddesses represented as wrapped in one mantle. Thus it might be possible to interpret the shawl that covers the backs of the two women in the ivory group as an analogous garment and as a confirmatory indication that they are the Mycenean forerunners of the Eleusinian goddesses." [29] This group seems to embody the idea of the universal maternal quality of the feminine: woman as source of the life power, represented by a child. This child may indeed be conceived of as a god, so Horus is shown seated within the womb of the universal mother. This conception is carried over into Christian symbols, too. There are, for instance, representations of the Virgin in the form of a shrine, with a little door in the abdomen of the statue opening to reveal the Christ within, sometimes as a babe, sometimes as the grown man on the cross. In other instances, the figures within the abdomen represent God the Father with the Son in his arms. The Virgin is also portrayed as bending down from heaven after her assumption and spreading her starry robe over the whole congregation of the faithful—that is, she is the mother of all who have been reborn through baptism.

In Buddhist pictures we see Maya in her terrible aspect, bearing in her abdomen all the worlds—the heaven worlds and the hell worlds. In this she differs from the Virgin, who accepts only the faithful; for Maya receives all, good or bad. It is perhaps for this reason that she is represented as the devouring mother. For this mother (Mother Nature, as we should call her) is not only the giver of life; she is also the destroyer. She is fecund and cruel. Her law works for the continuation of the race. The young are important as such, for they represent the next generation. Yet if many die, there are always more to replace them. As individuals they are of very little importance in the eyes of Mother Nature, who creates living crea-

29. Ibid., pp. 84, 86.

tures in great abundance and then destroys them all. For this is nature's way.

In the cults of the Magna Mater, this dual quality of Mother Nature was invariably recognized. She was black as well as white, destructive as well as creative. In our culture, we disregard the dark or under side of the maternal instinct and pay conscious attention only to the kind, nurturing, unselfish aspect. This accounts for our sentimentality in regard to motherhood. If, however, a woman's kindness is due to identification with the upper side of the maternal instinct, its dark and cruel aspects being repressed, she will act at times in such a way as to produce an effect of cruelty, even though she is motivated, so far as she herself knows, only by the most genuine altruism.

The point that should be realized is that it is not the instinct that is good or bad, virtuous or evil, but the human being. The instinct is daemonic and transcends the limits of the conscious personality. It functions in and through the woman, and it is her task to detach herself from its compulsions and to relate herself to it in a meaningful way. Then she will voluntarily serve life through submission to its demands and with conscious co-operation in its purposes; then life, not death, will flow in her through the working of the transformed instinct. The desire to bear children and to protect them will no longer function in her as a purely biological urge that can override all decent human feeling and depotentiate all other aims; it will instead be given a relative place in the completeness of her personality.

But profound transformation of an instinct can be achieved only through discipline and at the cost of much conflict and suffering. The maternal instinct is no exception to the rule. For just as greed must be checked if men are not to starve, just as the carnal man must be controlled if the spiritual man is not to go hungry, and just as the lust of the body must be curbed if love between the sexes is to develop, so too the mother's instinctive identification with the "fruit of her womb" must be broken if she is not to destroy her son's right to his own life. The transformation of the maternal instinct, as we have seen, involves the "sacrifice of the son." [30] It is a sacrifice that has always been demanded of the mother. It must be made in progressive stages from the moment of the child's birth up to the time when he reaches manhood. Unless she performs this sacrifice faithfully, step by step, she will be unable to release him from their mutual bond. During the war, the sacrifice was demanded with a new and heart-rending reality. The mother had to release her son to fulfill a destiny—perhaps a tragic one—beyond the reach of her help; she could not protect him from harm, nor comfort him in distress, nor even know where he was nor how he was faring.

An interesting custom related to this aspect of the mother's experience prevails in many parts of India.[31] On her birthday the mother, instead of being congratulated and receiving gifts, is required to give the priest her dearest possession—in token, as it were, of the fact that one day she will have to give up her child. She is reminded that in her role of mother she does not possess her little one, and that she may not demand gratification for herself. In other words, it is by no virtue of her own that she has the blessing of sons while other women perhaps are childless. She is only an instrument for the fulfillment of the will of the gods, who ordained that man should be fruitful and multiply. She is to be grateful that she was chosen for the role, which brings with it sorrow and joy, pain and delight—as significant perhaps as any that can fall to the lot of woman. But as she did not herself create the child, so she cannot claim possession of him. He and she are bound together through that closest of biological ties, which should be and usually is the basis of a unique spiritual bond; but both mother and son must release themselves from this unconscious, instinctive tie by differentiating between the human mother and the archetypal image that she carries.

The woman who realizes that a "natural" or instinctive attitude towards her maternal function is not sufficient, and who cannot be satisfied with a conventional way of acting be-

---

30. This subject is discussed in greater detail in Harding, *Woman's Mysteries, Ancient and Modern*, chap. xiv.

31. H. Zimmer, "The Guidance of the Soul in Hindooism," *Spring*, 1942.

cause of her more sensitive awareness of the undercurrents within, may come to doubt the quality of her own feelings. The moral conflict resulting from this suspicion may compel her to go back to the past and experience for herself the power of ancient attitudes that have long been repressed or discarded. She seems in some strange way to be set apart by her conflict in order to bring the past into the present. She is obliged to relive consciously, and in condensed form, the emotional history of the race. By her personal assimilation of the old and brutal aspects of the maternal instinct she is performing a cultural task of real value: by her act she is making it possible for a new attitude to be evolved. Each individual who can hold the ancient cold-blooded aspect of the maternal instinct in consciousness together with the gentle and kindly aspect, and can reconcile the one with the other not only in thought but in actual reality, has stepped beyond the culture of her contemporaries. She has performed a creative act; for she has transcended the consciousness of the generation into which she was born. She is a pioneer of a new and more cultured attitude, in which the individual is released from the compulsive domination of the blind maternal instinct and becomes capable of real love of the object.

8

The Ego and the Power Problem
SELF-RESPECT AND THE WILL TO DOMINATE

IN THE PRECEDING chapters we have been considering the psychic forces underlying the life and experience of man. Surging waves of desirousness, rising and falling like the tides in some great psychic ocean, beat upon him; they pulse through him and carry him along regardless of his personal wishes or intent. While he is possessed by such an instinctive urge, the individual loses all consciousness of his personal wishes and permits himself to be completely dominated by the aims of the compulsive force that has him in its grip. That which is in reality least personal, least individual, seems to the victim of a collective nonpersonal power to be most his own, most closely connected with his sense of I-ness. It is only when the intoxication passes that he sees, even dimly, how far he was "carried away," how seriously he lost touch with those values which mark the human being as more developed than his animal brothers.

From time to time while discussing the basic instincts and that nonpersonal part of the psyche of which they are the manifestation, I have had occasion to speak of something within man himself that strives to set itself up over against the blind compulsion of the instincts—something that is associated with desires and interests other than those of nature, even of nature as he experiences it within himself.[1]

1. Cf. the antithesis of the natural man versus the civilized man, or of the carnal man versus the spiritual man.

Now this is a very strange phenomenon, but we are so accustomed to it that we usually accept it without stopping to consider its strangeness. What we call nature is not, so far as we know, a force, still less a person, apart from the natural phenomena of the world. The rocks, the trees, the animals are expressions of nature: only through them, their structure and their functioning, do we know nature at all. On the face of it, it would be expected that man for his part would express nature in a similar way, and nothing but nature—that his being would be subject to the same laws that govern all other phenomena. But when we observe ourselves and consider the history of mankind, it is obvious that a force other than blind instinct is at work within man.

In the early beginnings of the life of the race, as in the life of any infant, the forces of instinct alone dominated the scene. But at some time there arose another power setting bounds upon the untrammelled desirousness of instinct, and this power is found to be at work, in some measure at least, in all peoples, even the most primitive. This power we call will. Its energy is recruited from the instincts and is used by the ego, which arose *pari passu* as the instincts were tamed.

Obviously we do not know how the ego arose in man. We have certain myths showing how ancient man thought about this problem, and we can observe the phenomenon in very young children today. Just as the individual child must undergo training and discipline, so too the primitive nature of man had to be housebroken and domesticated, restrained and adapted, if he was to advance in culture and in ability to control his environment.

The self-restraint and discipline demanded of the infant and young child are difficult enough to acquire, even though he finds himself in an environment where the standards of behaviour are fixed, and accepted without question by everyone about him, so that all he has to do is to reach the level of self-control that his elders have already attained. How much harder must it have been for corresponding disciplines to come into being in communities in which the civilized condition had not yet been achieved nor even envisaged, except dimly by one or two individuals. Yet consciousness and the ego must have arisen somewhere as a spontaneous growth. That there could arise in man a function capable of standing over against the blind urgency of instinct, is cause for continual amazement. Man alone among the animals, so far as we know, has developed this function, which we call the ego. He alone stole from the gods something of their divine prerogative of power, the power to do something on his own initiative, to create something new. He alone learned to know, to remember, to foresee, and to judge all things as relative to himself and to his own well-being.

For man, the coming of consciousness meant that everything became oriented to himself. No longer was every happening, every condition, regarded as just existing: from that time on it was seen through the spectacles of his ego. It was good—for *him;* or it was bad—for *him.* For him, all things that in their own being are one were split into two. For him, consciousness divided the primary oneness of nature into pairs of opposites. As the alchemists, the psychologists of the Middle Ages, put it, "two fishes are swimming in our sea"—that is to say, in the ocean of the unconscious the pairs of opposites swim side by side, undifferentiated, but the conscious ego knows them as two.[2]

As the world has been split into pairs of opposites for man, so man likewise has become split within himself. For a part of his psyche, namely, his ego consciousness, has set itself up against the dominance of nature within him. He no longer acts just as his nature dictates, but weighs, considers, judges, chooses; in some degree he is able to act as his ego wishes, although nature through his instincts may impel him at times to act differently. This division within himself, this rebellion against nature, was the sin of Lucifer, as it was also the sin of Adam and Eve, who acquired power to choose for themselves through eating the fruit that gave knowledge of good and evil, that is, knowledge of the pairs of opposites. Thus, instead of remaining blindly obedient to the laws that govern all other natural phenomena, the parents of mankind pro-

2. See above, p. 143.

claimed themselves to be free individuals. But God, we are told, was angry and said in effect: "Very well. Take your freedom and see what you can make of it. But nature will no longer be a kind mother to you"—in the scriptural wording, "thorns and thistles will it [the earth] bring forth unto you."

From one point of view this way of looking at the beginnings of consciousness is a valid one; it is the angle taken by the myths, which assume that consciousness was stolen from the gods and is therefore not a natural product of life on earth. But as psychologists we can hardly consider the ego as belonging to a separate system, or as a principle differing from all others. We are obliged to predicate that the ego arose in the course of the natural development of life on the earth: that is, consciousness arose out of unconsciousness, by a natural or evolutionary process. So it is probably nearer the truth to say that there are within man two natures at variance with each other, than it is to say that man is in conflict with nature. For if the latter statement were true, it would be equivalent to saying that man created his own ego. When in Egypt the question arose as to how the first god, the creator, Khepera, had come into existence, the answer given was that in the beginning Khepera created himself, by calling his own name. Every child who for the first time calls himself "I" repeats that creative act. Up to that moment he has spoken of himself only in the third person: "Baby will do"; "Baby will go." Then there comes a day when he says, "I will do," and a new individuality, a new ego, has come into being.

So much is true, but we are still left with the problem of what or who it is that calls the name. Perhaps the history of culture can throw some light on the problem. The power that man has developed over against the compulsoriness of his instinctive drives, evolved as the result of an educational process that began with magic or religious practices on the one hand and social pressures on the other. As far back as we can see in time, all those things in the world which happen without man's personal intervention have been regarded as the doings of gods or daemons or of magic powers inherent in natural objects and natural phenomena. To the primitive mind the forces of nature, and the instinctual forces in man as well, were the possession of the gods, by natural right, and man's desirousness in regard to them was curbed by prohibitions and taboos imposed by the gods. Through his compliance with these divinely instituted restrictions and through the superstitious fears that hedged them about, man developed an ability to say no to himself.

Viewing the situation from this angle, we are obliged to say that man was compelled to make a distinction between himself and the drive of natural desire within him because of the possessiveness of the gods. But this does not really answer the question. The problem is only shifted; for it took a man, the medicine man or priest, to translate the wishes of the gods and institute the taboos. But how did this man know what taboo the gods decreed, and whence did he acquire the authority by which his fellow man was induced to obey laws that went against his nature, in just those spheres where the natural impulses are most tyrannical in their demands? The only possible answer is that those taboos which were effective arose from reactions to archetypal images, which the priest or medicine man was able to discern on account of his unusual intuitive faculty: these prohibitions expressed something that lay unrecognized in the unconscious of the whole tribe. The taboos really represented man's own religious instinct, which was directed to a goal different from that of the so-called natural drives. That is to say, the potentiality for an ego consciousness exists in the unconscious itself. This is the meaning of the light sparks in the ocean that the alchemists speak of,[3] and that occasionally appear in the dreams of modern persons.

In the group life not only were religious taboos actively fostering the restraint of natural instinct, but social restraints were simultaneously exerting a corresponding pressure. For contact between human beings and their interaction upon one another, also served to develop in man a capacity to withstand the pressure of his inherent impulses. The individual man accepted this social discipline and submitted to it partly because of the necessity of developing group activity if he was

3. See C. G. Jung, *Aion* (C.W. 9, ii), p. 220.

to survive under the conditions of the world in which he found himself, and partly from natural gregariousness.

Thus one instinct was set over against another, one instinct withstood and curbed another, and this produced a conflict of aims and desires. Through this conflict consciousness arose, for man had to make a choice, lest he be completely bogged down in an indecision that could only result in extinction. As has been truly said, consciousness arises only at the point of discomfort. Just as, in common parlance, "necessity is the mother of invention," so conflict might be called the mother of awareness. When all goes well for us, we swim with the current; it is only when things do not go well that we become aware of the conditions of our lives and arouse ourselves to play an active role in regard to our own fate. This is one reason why war produces such a rapid advance in many spheres of activity, as for instance in scientific research; human life as a whole seems to be speeded up by the threats and dangers of war. When there is enough of everything for the majority to have comfort, life drifts along. When, however, life itself is threatened, and shortages appear in all sorts of unexpected places, the situation becomes a summons to the creative genius that slumbers or at least dozes in the halcyon days of peace, and men begin to live creatively again. Consciousness awakens —consciousness of the outer world at all events. Would that we might hope for a corresponding psychological awakening to occur at the same time.

If the gods possess the nonpersonal powers, if it is they who give abundance, rain and sunshine, fertility and health, and power to overcome the enemy, then man must obey the commandments of the gods. How else can he hope to escape the hazards and misfortunes that loom so large in the life of primitive peoples? The divine commandments are always expressed first under the imperative, "Thou shalt not!" They are prohibitions or taboos. Man feels that he must refrain from certain acts—usually acts that would seem to be quite natural —in order to propitiate the gods. Or he must please them with gifts or sacrifices—often of those things which are dearest to him—or practise abstentions, which are a sort of sacrifice of himself, a mitigated sacrifice of his own life. He feels that these things are pleasing to the gods and does not realize that the discipline, the austerity, the self-control he thereby imposes on himself are the real cause of his increased prosperity. For introspection is a late-comer among the powers that man gradually acquired through the thousands of years during which the first glimmering light of consciousness was being evolved. This consciousness was first developed in relation to the external world; consequently all those phenomena which make up the inner world were projected and so appeared to man to emanate from beings outside himself, from gods and daemons, from principalities and powers of an unseen but very real world.

The animals follow the natural law only. It speaks to them and guides them by force of their own instincts. They give unquestioning obedience to this law and are at peace with themselves; they are truly pious, truly devoted, for the voice of the natural instincts fully expresses their own natures, and nothing in them rebels against it. With man things are very different. He is not at one with himself. He is subject to two laws that do not by any means always coincide. Consequently he is inwardly divided.

Whether we consider the split in man as due to a conflict between man and nature (or man and the gods), or recognize it as a cleavage between two natural lines of development within him, depends on whether we consider the nonpersonal, instinctive forces as inherent in man's psyche or subscribe to the theological hypothesis and regard these forces as emanating from a being or beings existing apart from man, that is, from gods or daemons. Up to the time of the rise of modern materialistic thought, this problem was barely recognized, so universal was the acceptance of the hypothesis of divine beings. But with the ascendancy of the intellect, the gods were overthrown and the laws of natural science put in their place. Whatever could not be explained by these laws was as far as possible disregarded. The hypothesis that rational thinking could solve all the problems of the world was very widely accepted. But there remained the irrationality of man himself. If only man would act rationally, perhaps wars and depressions and insanity could be avoided; but unfortunately man does not seem to be any more capable of acting sanely now than he was a thousand years ago. We are still confronted with man's own irrational behaviour and the untamed forces within his psyche.

In this twentieth century we are living in a transitional period. The rational scientific mind in us, which refers every fact, at least theoretically, to known or knowable causes, revolts from the hypothesis of divine beings; the primitive in us continues to create gods and daemons to account for certain experiences that have the quality of irrational compulsiveness about them, and the religious being in us bows in awe before mysteries of life that our science is impotent either to explain or to explain away.

The psychologist takes a middle position. He does not have to give an answer to the riddles of the universe; his field is the study of man. He observes the existence of powers and forces arising from the unconscious and acting as if they were autonomous beings. This *as if* is a very valuable formulation, for by it we are enabled to observe, in a truly scientific fashion, the laws governing these forces, and the effect that the conscious attitude has upon them, without committing ourselves to dogmatic assertions as to their nature or origin. Under certain circumstances these autonomous factors can acquire so much energy that they actually usurp the whole field of consciousness and reduce all other factors to a relative position. They may destroy all that has been built up through a lifetime. On the other hand, when the conscious attitude towards them is modified, they may lose their threatening aspect and instead of causing death or insanity, may produce a renewal of the life current, a veritable renaissance.

WE ARE THEREFORE on safe ground when we speak of a personal part of the psyche consisting of the conscious and controllable elements, and a nonpersonal part consisting of those elements not controlled by the conscious I but superordinated to and acting independently of it, often dominating it and forcing it to act contrary to its desires. When consciousness is still only a very small part of the psyche, being restricted to awareness of the body and its needs, the centre of consciousness is the autos. When consciousness grows by taking up a part of the energy inherent in the instincts and directing it to a different aim, a new centre of consciousness develops: this we call the ego. The ego has the capacity of seeing itself, at least in some measure, in relation to the rest of the world, a power that the autos does not have. It also becomes aware that others likewise possess ego consciousness and the power of criticism. Thus it is aware of what others think and say, and aware also of what it for its own part thinks and speaks. It can say, "I am the one, I am the thinker, the doer."

But beyond this it does not go. For instance, a man in this stage of self-consciousness does not realize as a rule that ideas occur to him without his willing them, that actions are performed through him—that he is being used by thoughts and impulses arising from something other than his I. It is not until he takes a further step in freeing himself from the instinctive drives that he becomes conscious of others and of himself as separate entities, that is, as entities not oriented to nor dependent on himself—conscious even that his ego is not identical with the new self in him that now in turn says "I." This parallels the development of the earlier stage, when he came to realize that his ego was not identical with his autos, for the ego could want and work for objectives that his auto-erotic self did not want and did not subscribe to.

It was recognized long ago (certainly before the seventh century B.C.) by the profound thinkers of ancient India that there is more than one factor in the psyche that can call itself "I," and that it is of great importance to distinguish these factors one from another, so that one may know which it is that is speaking when a man says "I want," or "I will do this or that," and that it is even more important for each man to discover for himself which I is speaking in himself. This problem is elucidated by a very instructive story recounted in the Chhāndogya Upanishad.[4] It relates that the gods and the de-

---

4. Chhāndogya Upanishad, eighth prapāthaka, seventh and eighth khandas, in F. Max Müller (tr.), *The Upanishads* (in *The Sacred Books of the East*), I, 134 ff.

mons (devas and asuras), who were the children of Prajapati, the Father God, had heard him speak of the Atman, the Self that is free from sorrow, from age, and from death: "He who has searched out that Self and understands it, obtains all worlds and all desires." Wishing to obtain the blessings of the Self, they each sent one of their number to ask the great god more about it. Virochana was sent by the asuras and Indra by the devas, and the two came to Prajapati, and at his command served thirty-two years as his pupils. Then he asked them what they had come to seek. They told him, and he instructed them to look into a pan of water and tell him what they saw. They reported that they saw themselves. The story records his further words with them:

After you have adorned yourselves, have put on your best clothes and cleaned yourselves, look again into the water-pan. . . . What do you see? They said: Just as we are, well adorned, with our best clothes and clean, thus we are both there. Prajapati said: That is the Self, this is the immortal, the fearless, this is Brahman. Then both went away satisfied in their hearts. And Prajapati, looking after them, said: They both go away without having perceived and without having known the Self, and whoever of these two, whether Devas or Asuras, will follow this doctrine, will perish.

Now Virochana, satisfied in his heart, went to the Asuras and preached that doctrine to them, that the self (the body) alone is to be worshipped, that the self (the body) alone is to be served, and that he who worships the self and serves the self, gains both worlds, this and the next.

But Indra, before he had returned to the Devas, saw this difficulty. As this self (the shadow in the water) is well adorned, when the body is well adorned, well dressed, when the body is well dressed . . . that self will also be blind, if the body is blind, lame, if the body is lame, crippled, if the body is crippled, and will perish in fact as soon as the body perishes. Therefore I see no good in this doctrine.

So he returned to Prajapati, who agreed that the solution was not satisfactory and promised, if he would serve another thirty-two years, to give him further instruction and enlightenment on the problem.

If the instinctive drives arising from the nonpersonal part of the psyche are considered to manifest the immutable laws of a deity, then man's development of an ego that can stand against their demands and go its own way is equivalent to the crime of Lucifer, who defied God and was cast out of heaven. Lucifer acted on his own initiative. He claimed to be himself, to own himself. In reality he was claiming to be his own creator and undertaking sole responsibility for himself, for his acts and their consequences. If we translate the myth into psychological language, it states that the ego, the rebellious one, the Lucifer in man, created human consciousness—that it did not evolve in the same way as other natural phenomena.

Obviously this is an absurd position to take, and when it is put in these terms no one would seriously uphold it. Yet when we come to analyse some of our own attitudes and reactions, we cannot help but suspect that some such assumption lies behind them. It is as though we unconsciously assume that man is responsible for his own being and his own doing: we seem in truth to assume that man has made himself. Is not such an attitude, unconscious though it undoubtedly is, a repetition of the Luciferian crime? And just as Lucifer was cast down to hell in punishment of his overweening pride, so the arrogant assumption that man creates his own consciousness has brought untold misery on the world, and this in spite of the fact that ego consciousness represents in itself one of the greatest forward steps in psychological evolution that the world has yet witnessed.

When the ego arose in man, he obviously assumed responsibility both for himself and for his fate. Yet, as his rebellion against the gods did not succeed in producing an ideal situation, and he could no longer blame God and the Fates for his misfortunes, he began to suffer from a sense of inferiority and guilt. Modern man in particular is hampered by guilt and inferiority feelings that surely arise from this unconscious assumption. Why should a man feel inferior about a physical defect, unless it is that he considers the imperfection to be his own fault, or at least his own responsibility? Or does he perhaps assume that he has a right to be as agile or as powerful as his neighbour? In either case the feeling of inferiority that oppresses him consciously is just one side of the problem, for it rests on an unconscious assumption of superiority, an arrogant insistence that he ought to be perfect, thus preventing him from taking his handicap in a simple and matter-of-fact way, as animals and more unsophisticated human beings do.

This hampering sense of inferiority is associated with moral and character defects as well. But here we are not on equally secure ground, for unless man asserts himself as a free agent over against the blind drives of his instinctive nature, he remains the puppet of the nonpersonal forces within the psyche. From this point of view the Luciferian rebellion is seen to be a moral act. For when man became responsible for himself he could no longer say that all that happened to him was the doing of the gods and that the responsibility was theirs. He could no longer project his unconscious drives into invisible but all-powerful beings external to himself. He was obliged to observe the effects of his actions and learn how to influence his fate by applying the results of his observations. He began to recognize the law of cause and effect, which, as the Tibetan text declares,[5] is the great teacher of those of "little intellect," or of slight psychological development. Furthermore, he began to develop a moral sense, a conscience, a voice within replacing the fiat of the gods. The moral law came to be administered from somewhere deep within himself, instead of by arbitrary edict of an unaccountable deity residing in the external universe. Some part of the god's prerogative was taken over by man himself.

Thus with the evolution of the ego, the centre of consciousness shifted. Formerly there was only the dim consciousness in the body, a sentience of needs, of well- or of ill-being: this is the dim light we have called the autos. It is, so to speak, a somatic awareness that can be observed in young children long before a definite I has evolved and that continues to function throughout life. Quite serious consequences result when consciousness is too much isolated from it. In myths and dreams this body consciousness is frequently represented by an animal.

5. See above, p. 35.

This is the meaning of the helpful animal that in fairy tales appears at the critical moment—when, for instance, the ego consciousness is inadequate to the situation—and tells the hero what to do, just as in actual fact a horse will take his rider home even though the latter himself is completely disoriented by fog or darkness. In the same way a dim consciousness in the body may react to danger and initiate the steps necessary for safety before the ego consciousness awakens to the situation.

When the ego is inadequately organized, or when, for any reason, instead of becoming a conscious principle, accepted as the governor of conscious life, it remains no more than potential in the unconscious, the autos continues as the ruling principle, even in the adult. For such persons the subjects of paramount interest are matters of bodily comfort and well-being. Food, comfortable beds, the weather as it affects their comfort and convenience, form the staples of conversation; any situation that arises will be considered exclusively from the perspective of its effects on themselves, under the criterion of whether it brings pleasure or pain. This self-centredness is not the result of a deliberate ignoring of the rights or convenience of others; it comes about simply through lack of awareness that the situation could possibly be different when viewed from another angle.

A person whose consciousness has not grown beyond the stage of the autos can nevertheless undergo a process of development and refinement. The focus of his interest may shift from the more grossly physical to the aesthetic, and he may acquire all the subtleties of cultured appreciation; nevertheless, if his consciousness is oriented to the effects on himself only, he is still in the auto-erotic stage of development. His consciousness may even expand to take in others, but if he seeks for them likewise only auto-erotic satisfactions, he is still under the domination of the autos.

Such a person will give the impression of being an egotist, but his egotism is not the result of a conscious determination to have his own way, of a will to power; rather, it is due to his complete ignorance and unawareness of any aspects of the situation except such as affect him, or those with whom he is identified. That is to say, it is unconscious egotism, and the will to power that accompanies it is also unconscious. Such a person does not realize that he is dominating his environment or demanding more than his share, and he would be amazed if he were to be made aware of the true nature of his attitude.

MAN, LIKE THE OTHER ANIMALS, is originally simply the puppet of instinct, just as the infant is. Unless he is moved by instinct, he remains passive, even asleep. When instinct is aroused he reacts precipitately, with a characteristic all-or-none type of reaction. He is aware, it is true, of what he does and of what happens around him. But he has no self-awareness: psychic images flit past in his consciousness, leaving little or no trace, no residue as it were, much as a moving picture flits over the screen. As long as the picture is being thrown upon the screen, it dominates the space; when the light goes out the picture disappears from the screen and leaves no trace upon it. Such is man's consciousness before the ego develops.

In an infant or young animal we observe next the formation of the so-called conditioned reflexes. Certain repeated stimuli come to be remembered, not as memory images in the mind, but either as somatic responses, memories in the body, as it were, or perhaps as psychic images that remain in the unconscious, inaccessible to consciousness unless they are activated by appropriate stimuli.

For instance, certain dim images cannot, even in the adult, be recalled voluntarily, but arise spontaneously when stirred by some association, frequently of a sensory variety. Certain smells may reactivate long-past and long-forgotten experiences, or one goes to a place one has not seen since early childhood, and as the road unfolds to view, it recalls past happenings. The place seems strangely familiar, and once again one is the small child of many years ago, plodding on little short legs along a dusty road innocent of cars; once more one views the fences and the houses from the three-foot vantage of the little child of years ago. Or one comes to a turn in the road, and a long-forgotten conversation, about something quite trivial perhaps, repeats itself in one's ears. Walt Whitman refers to this dim, unconscious memory when he writes of the live oaks under which he thinks certain thoughts that he cannot remember elsewhere: "Sometimes I think they hang there waiting."

Then there are other "memories"—memories of things that have never happened to the particular individual—which slumber in the unconscious, in the form of archetypal images whose effect is to guide and condition experience while remaining entirely unknown and unrecognized, unless the consciousness of the individual has developed to a stage at which it is possible for him to find an Archimedean point from which he can observe what goes on within himself.

Those dim memories, whether of a personal or an archetypal nature, which need external stimuli to set them off, are experiences that have not been attached to the ego in a way that makes them accessible to willed recall. Consciousness initially consists of isolated flashes of awareness, but as a centre of consciousness gradually develops, these islands coalesce and the individual's experiences of life become attached to the ego and so come under control of the will. Thus consciousness gains a much greater degree of continuity than it formerly had. The power of the ego is strengthened by each additional area of psychic experience it conquers, for the energy inhering in the experience is added to the common pool and made available to the centre of the new consciousness, namely, the ego.

From the very beginnings of community life, the man who had memory had power, a different kind of power from that wielded by the man of brawn; it was a power destined to dispute that of the "strong" man and thus increasingly to win mastery. The man who had memory gained power over himself and also over his neighbours. He could predict what would happen and take steps accordingly. This is largely the basis of the prestige of the "old men," the elders.

Individuals who could remember that crops did well when treated in a given way, and would fail if treated differently, were obviously in an advantageous position. And, as has been pointed out earlier,[6] those who had learned to control their

6. In chap. 4.

instincts had an advantage over those who could not do so. For instance, the man who first learned to control his appetite in order to save sufficient seed corn, had a better harvest in the following year than his neighbours. But it takes a strenuous effort of memory for primitives to remember from the winter that is past to the harvest at hand and to curb their appetites accordingly. One may see such power awakening in a young child. I recall an instructive incident that came under my own observation. I was having tea in the house of a friend when her little boy, a child of four years, came into the room to meet the visitors. He was told that he might take a piece of cake for his nursery tea. He went immediately to the rich chocolate-iced cake, but his mother said to him: "Do you remember what happened the other day when you ate chocolate cake?"

The child thought for a minute, then nodded solemnly.

His mother added: "Then don't you think you had better choose this plain cake instead?"

The child took it and went soberly off to the nursery.

This little boy gained power over himself by choosing not to follow his instinctive desire for the sweet cake, because he realized that present pleasure may lead to future pain.

In the early community, the man who had learned to bide his time, for either revenge, barter, or any other objective, also had the advantage over the one who was compelled to act when the stimulus arose, without consideration of the consequences. Through having disciplined his own instincts such a man gained power over his more instinctively acting neighbours. The power of the medicine man rested largely on such self-control.

Religious practices such as taboos and rituals originally devised to placate the gods, and to persuade them to use their divine or daemonic powers in man's behalf, invariably meant discipline for the man who carried them out and so increased the power of his ego. Later it was felt that asceticism was pleasing to the god for its own sake and that he would bestow blessings and favours upon those who undertook to practise self-restraints, disciplines, and austerities. Then sacrifices were offered to the god to compel him to bestow boons, or ascetic practices were undertaken with the same aim, and it was believed that he could not refuse. In this belief we see a dim foreshadowing of the recognition that the gods are not beings having an existence entirely separate from and independent of man's, but instead are relative to him, subject to conditioning by his actions and attitudes. It would seem that it could not be a very long step from this point to a recognition of the gods as personifications of unconscious factors within man's psyche; but something like three thousand years have passed since the Egyptians told of the gods being compelled to come when man invoked them, and almost as many since the Hindu wise men told the story of Golden Garment.

The Egyptian hymns relate that the gods were attracted by the smoke of the sacrifices and were unable to keep away: "they swarmed over the sacrifice like flies." The Hindu myths are full of stories of individuals who practised austerities in order to gain power to compel the gods to grant boons that they would be simply unable to refuse. Golden Garment was such a one.[7] He was one of the asuras, the demons, who, it will be recalled, learned from Virochana's teaching that the highest good is to be found through adornment and care of the ego. Golden Garment aspired to obtain power over the whole world. Therefore he practised asceticism, fasting, and celibacy, together with yogic disciplines of the greatest severity. He persisted thus for many years, until he had heaped up much merit. Then he went to Brahma and demanded of him the reward of his self-discipline. Brahma agreed to grant him a boon. Golden Garment's desire was that he might not be killed by any man or animal, nor by any weapon, nor in any house, nor in the open.

This was granted him. Then, feeling entirely secure, Golden Garment proceeded to oppress the people, who were of course vulnerable to his assaults while he could not be harmed. Gradually he subdued and enslaved the whole world, and built himself a castle on the top of the highest mountain. There he

7. H. Zimmer, *Myths and Symbols in Indian Art and Civilization*, p. 180, n.; A. B. Keith, *Indian Mythology*, in Gray, *Mythology of All Races*, VI, 123.

lived in great splendour while all the rest of mankind groaned under his yoke. The groaning of the people in their sufferings arose as a smell to the place of the gods, who called a council to discuss what could be done to rid the world of the tyrant. None of the gods could find a way of overcoming him, protected as he was by the word of Brahma. Then Vishnu arose and offered to make the attempt. He changed himself into a monster, half man and half lion, and hid in the pillar of the banquet hall where Golden Garment was accustomed to feast. When the feast was in full swing he burst the pillar asunder, seized the tyrant, and tore him in pieces with his claws. Thus was Golden Garment overcome by neither man nor beast, by no weapon, and neither in a house nor in the open. (See figure 8.)

If a man puts himself under discipline in order to gain power over himself and to dominate or enslave his neighbours, he will become a menace to society, for he arrogates to himself the position of a god. The modern dictator is a very apposite example. And just as Golden Garment eventually aroused against himself not only the hatred of mankind but also the power and ingenuity of the gods, so of a certainty a saviour will appear in the case of every tyrant to devise some entirely new way of tackling the problem resulting from the hybris of the ego. This saviour, be he god or man, will owe his power to his disinterestedness—that is, he will be fighting not for himself and his own prestige but for the good of mankind or for some other nonpersonal objective. Thus the ego is supplanted by a new supreme value.

It is obvious from all that has been said that the subject of the ego and its place in human development is by no means a simple one, and it might be well to summarize our findings about it. For the ego is the pivotal element in the problem we have undertaken to explore, namely, the relation of the personal to the nonpersonal part of the psyche. The ego represents the highest stage of development of consciousness achieved in a given culture. Some members of the group lag below this level; others, the pioneers, have already surpassed it; but the general level of a culture can be estimated by the degree of development of the ego that prevails in general. What the ego has not yet learned can be attained only by a heroic deed on the part of one who transcends this ego level—as by the

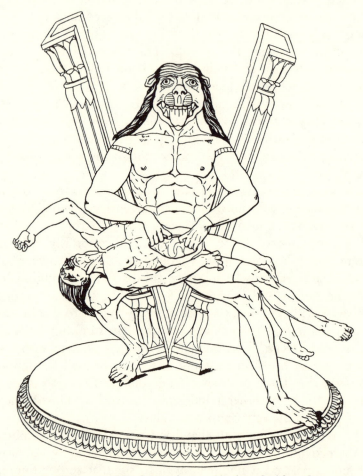

Fig. 8. Vishnu in His Lion Avatar Slaying Golden Garment

knight who gives up all to follow his quest, or by the mystic who renounces the world to seek for something beyond the world.

But these are necessarily the few. They are not representative of the general level of their generation. They live a solitary life and are frequently misunderstood; indeed, they are rarely adapted to the world as it exists, for they are concerned with precisely that which has not yet been made part of the culture of the day. If their quest is successful, however —if their conflict results in the overcoming of the dragon of the unconscious depths—what they achieve in solitude in their day will become the basis of a new culture, possibly even of a new world order, in years to come. Always, that supreme value which has power to redeem either the individual or the world appears first in humble and despised form. The new is always the enemy of the old, for the new will surpass the old. The birth of the new spells the death of the old. Consequently the pioneers of a new age are rarely accepted or acclaimed in their own time and place. Yet the new must evolve out of the old. The new self or centre of consciousness can be found only when the ego consciousness is pushed to its limits.

AS THE EGO AROSE spontaneously, appearing out of the unconscious part of the psyche, through the coming together of scattered elements, such as memory images and the like, we are obliged to speak of an ego complex as preceding the formation of a conscious ego.[8] Where the ego is inadequately developed in modern adults and is not made conscious, we find that the ego complex remains in the unconscious and functions from there. In consciousness an individual representing this level of development may be conspicuously lacking in that concentration or centredness which is characteristic of the person with more conscious ego development; yet egotism and will to power, of which the unevolved person is himself unaware, may function nonetheless and produce their inevitable effects on all with whom he comes in contact.

A typical example of this situation is to be found in the gentle, rather vague woman who appears to be entirely soft and pliable and yet manages to dominate her whole household, not by assertion of her will nor through aggressive demands,

8. See Jung, "Spirit and Life," in *The Structure and Dynamics of the Psyche* (C.W. 8), pp. 323-34.

but through her very helplessness. No one can bear to cross her, and indeed if they do not do exactly as she wishes, she may well react with neurotic symptoms—a sick headache, an attack of palpitation, or some other negative reaction of the body that compels her family to care for her and makes them feel remorseful into the bargain. In her, egotism and self-will are in the unconscious, and as they are not subject to any critique on her part, as they would be if she were conscious of them, they manifest themselves in somatic, that is, in pre-psychological form.

When the ego comes to consciousness and the individual becomes aware of himself as I, the reaction to difficulties or obstructions will no longer appear in physical form as symptoms but will be recognized in consciousness as emotions. That is to say, the reaction will be a psychological one. This is an advance of great cultural value. Having achieved it, the woman of our illustration will have to face the unpalatable fact of her unconscious domination of her household. She will discover that she is not the self-effacing person she has thought herself to be, but in reality a being of very different character.

Thus the emergence of the ego from the unconscious brings with it a new problem, the problem of the will to power. If this woman is to be freed from her neurotic symptoms, she will obviously have to renounce her old unconscious technique for getting her own way. She will thereupon have to develop a new way of reacting to life; she will be compelled to face things much more directly and will have to go to work at creating conditions satisfactory to herself, instead of permitting the egotism of which she is unaware to manipulate her environment to her own advantage. Thus she will gain in real power both over herself and over her environment.

So universal in the psychology of modern Western man is the presence of the ego, either as a conscious I or as an ego complex in the unconscious, that we are actually constrained to speak of a power "instinct." But it is probable that the power motive is not on the same level as the primary instincts we have been considering, for it seems to derive its energy from one or other of the two life instincts, those concerned with self-preservation and with reproduction. When the ego complex succeeds in wresting energy from one of these and becomes possessed of it, the ego identifies itself with this energy, and the power complex begins to appear.

I feel rather hesitant in making this distinction between the power "instinct" and the basic instincts, for the will to power certainly functions compulsively like an instinct and is associated with an all-or-none type of reaction; but it is so closely linked with the sense of being "I" that it appears preferable to regard it as a part of the ego complex. However, in the Buddhist texts already referred to, the power drive is treated as on an equality with hunger and sex as one of the three basic desires or *kleshas* whose energy keeps the wheel of life forever revolving. In this system the will to power is called anger and is symbolized by the serpent, which when disturbed or frustrated strikes automatically at friend and foe alike, which cannot be taught to love, and which hypnotizes its prey with its glassy stare and devours it alive.

As we have seen above, man began originally to overcome the compulsions of his instinctive drives in order to pursue the objectives of the instincts more effectively. For example, he learned to curb his natural voracity so that a store of grain might be accumulated for food in winter and for seed. When this had been attained, the possession of a store of provisions became a source of satisfaction in itself, a means of gaining attention, envy, admiration, prestige. The sense of power became desirable in itself, quite apart from the value the possessions had as real wealth and for use in barter, etc. The power motive came to be concerned with property.

The sense of power is also closely bound up with actual physical might. The most powerful individual in a group can obviously dominate the others, in addition to gaining prestige as a champion or a hunter. He becomes a "mighty man of valour." Among naïve peoples the expression of this power is simple. The possessor of it may strut about, he may brawl; but for the most part he uses his strength much as an animal does, and usually he manifests a similar dignity, which his fellows respect as much as they do his power. Not infrequently such an individual is made chief and holds the headship so long as he remains the most powerful member of the tribe. When his strength fails and he is surpassed by a younger man, he is replaced and may even be put to death.[9] But as the ego develops, there evolves in the individual a tendency to utilize his strength to dominate his fellows and to use them for his own advantage. Thus there emerges the tyrant, the bully, the gangster.

In the realm of sexuality a similar development can be traced. At first the instinctive process is directly related to the physical urge. It is unconditioned and simple. Then, when the compulsive drive of sexuality is so curbed that promiscuity can be renounced in favour of marriage, energy again accrues to the ego, and the demand for possession of the sexual object and the offspring makes its appearance. In its negative form the expression of this energy appears in life as jealousy, which is a power manifestation. Here also the prestige factor enters into the picture. A man who could not hold his wife was ridiculed by his fellows. Women began to keep themselves aloof, recognizing that they had power over men on account of the urgency of the sexual need of the male and that they could get what they wanted by giving or withholding their favours. Men too began to boast of their conquests. Sex and the will to power were thus welded together.

The maternal instinct also gives its quota to the power complex. The mother's sense of I-ness is enhanced through her children, either directly by reason of their number or beauty, or in relation to her power over them, or on account of their devotion to her, or, more indirectly, because of the prestige they can bring to her by their achievements in the world. Maternal pride and maternal ambition are aspects of the power complex that perhaps are looked upon more leniently today than any others.

In the majority of cases the connection of power with the primary instincts is natural. Here I am speaking not of a power complex, or of an identification with the will to power, but rather of the feeling of ability to control oneself and one's

9. See J. G. Frazer, *The Golden Bough*, p. 265.

actions, and of the power to choose a goal and to do what is necessary to achieve it. This is a positive factor leading to self-discipline and culture, and on its development civilization largely depends. Where the will to power becomes dominant, however, the resulting complex has a most unfortunate effect on the personality. Love of possessions becomes overwhelming ambition; the lust for power brings the desire, even the necessity, to domineer over other people; sexual desire expresses itself in compulsive efforts to master and control the partner, often by tyrannical methods, varying all the way from sadistic practices to the mental torture induced by unreasoning jealousies and assumption of the right to possess the so-called love object completely.

Yet, in spite of these abuses, the ego is perhaps the greatest single achievement of mankind. The ability of modern man to undertake and carry out difficult tasks, requiring months or years of concentrated and directed effort, has come about only through the development of the ego—that is, through the concentration of consciousness under a ruler we call the I. Primitive man cannot do such things. His interest and attention are too easily distracted: in face of the actualities of the moment, the remote goal cannot be envisaged with sufficient clarity to become real. Without the development of the ego and its discipline, the growth of modern thought, modern science, modern technology would have been impossible. Man's intelligence has apparently not increased—at all events, not during historical times—but his ability to govern and direct it has expanded enormously.

It was absolutely necessary that the light of consciousness, so diffuse in primitive man, should be focused, and his unstable attention controlled, if any progress was to be made at all. When we compare the modern Western man with the primitive inhabitant of some undeveloped island, we may well be impressed with the advance that has been made. Civilized man's ability to hold his aim in view, his relative freedom from the compulsion of instinct, and the large amount of libido at his disposition, all witness the progress that has been made through the development of ego consciousness. This man is able to avail himself not only of those things which his own consciousness can create but of the fruits of other men's efforts as well. He is not limited to what he himself can achieve in the short span of his own lifetime; he can utilize the inventions and devices of countless others, whose ego consciousness first created them and then disseminated information about them.

These things are indeed impressive. But when we turn and look at the area of man's lack of freedom, his bondage to his impulses, his inertia, his angers, his desirousness, we see another side of the picture, and its blackness is abysmal. The libido that modern man has wrested from the unconscious and organized under the ego has revolutionized life on earth. But this power is as nothing compared with the untamed forces of nature, which can sweep away man and his works in a night; while the power he has acquired over himself has hardly even begun to challenge the primordial forces within him. The powers of instinct, of untamed nature, do not willingly resign their claims upon the energy that man seeks to retrieve for himself; rather, they frequently take back to themselves the treasure that the ego has thought to exploit.

As has been shown above, the power "instinct" is nourished by the achievements of the ego consciousness, and not infrequently the man who has thought to segregate for himself certain powers of the unconscious instincts becomes himself the victim of the same old compulsions. He does not control those things that he thinks he controls, instead they control him: his will, his aims, whether consciously chosen or unconsciously forced upon him, compel him to labour, compel him to act, compel him to think, compel him to feel, not as he would, but as they dictate. He is still unfree. The impulses that drive him have, however, undergone a change. They are no longer naïve, with that innocence which belongs to simple instinctiveness. They are now contaminated by the ego, they are purposive, often poisoned by a self-seeking and negative quality. They constitute that which we call egotism. The ego, which has seemed the highest and most human quality of man, has lost its humanness and functions as a nonhuman driving force once more.

If further steps are to be taken in the most important psychological and cultural task of freeing man from the compulsions of the instincts and making their energies available for further development, the power and refinement of the ego will have to be greatly increased. Each generation of men, each human being in his generation, must undertake individually the discipline and development of the ego. Though the ego complex arises spontaneously, it must be brought up to consciousness through persistent and directed effort, if it is not to remain in a barbaric and rudimentary state. Without this, no further step in psychological development is possible. The ego cannot be surpassed if it has not been attained.

The first, tentative appearance of the ego can usually be observed in the child just emerging from the stage of infancy. At the age of three or four years, the child begins to recognize itself as a person. It says "I" and gradually comes to realize that it has an inner power over its own actions. The wise parent or teacher seizes upon these first manifestations of the ego and fosters them. Where the unwise parent says, "You must do it the way I say," the more discriminating one says, "You are a big boy now, go and do it for yourself." I have often been amazed at the response one can get from even tiny children by this approach. When I was doing my hospital internship work, I found that almost invariably it was possible to get the co-operation of three-year-olds by appealing to their sense of being persons. If, when giving injections, which are certainly not painless, one said to a very small child, "You are a big girl, *you* mustn't cry," she would usually summon up enough courage to bear the pain bravely.

Throughout childhood this evocation and education of the ego has to go on. The child must be given the assurance that his developing ego is welcomed, while at the same time being taught to curb excesses of his will that would infringe on the rights of others. In this way the worst problems of self-will are circumvented, and the child is encouraged to venture out into real life, where the law of cause and effect takes over the lion's share of discipline.

As adolescence approaches, the ego impulse begins to split

into two streams. One continues in the direction of enhancing the power and prestige of the individual: usually the impulse to dominate others becomes much more marked at this time, while the sense of being a person is definitely linked with a will to power. The second current now makes itself felt. This stream takes the direction of depotentiating the personal ego in favour of the group. Quite naturally at this age children begin to ally themselves under a leader, to form gangs or teams or clubs.

The prestige of the group brings prestige to each one personally, while the individual ego-needs seem to find their satisfaction in the prestige of the leader. The period of this spontaneous development in modern youth corresponds to the time of the puberty initiations among primitive peoples. Through it a further discipline and refinement of the ego impulse are brought about. This is the moment when the developing child is susceptible to group culture, and it is deplorable if the opportunity for this type of education is missed, and the young people are left to develop it as best they can, often in asocial ways, when, rightly guided, it could give the impetus needed for carrying the generation over from a purely egocentric orientation to concern for the social group.[10]

As the end of adolescence approaches, a further development of interest is usually seen. In the latter part of the teens and the beginning of the twenties, boys and girls usually manifest a concern over nonpersonal values. This may show itself in desire for public reforms, in a longing to devote themselves to some altruistic work for the good of mankind, such as social service or scientific research; or it may appear as a preoccupation with romantic love of an ideal type, or love of poetry, or absorption in religious experiences. It is as though at the moment of culmination of physical growth, the ego were about to be replaced by a nonpersonal principle. Shortly, however, the claims of adult life recall the young man or woman

10. It must be noted that these immature strivings towards group identification make the young people peculiarly susceptible to the influence of any leader who appeals to their imaginations. This may be turned to valuable ends, or it may be ruthlessly exploited. Cf. the Boy Scouts and, on the other hand, the Hitler Youth.

to the necessity of earning a living and founding a family, objectives that require further striving on the part of the ego and further discipline and development of it. And it is generally not until the zenith of life has been passed, and man begins the descent towards old age and death, that the impulse to supplant the ego goals with a suprapersonal objective returns.

By this time it should have become apparent to the individual that there are definite limits to the achievement possible under the sway of the ego. Signs of dissatisfaction with its powers are usually beginning to make themselves felt. Then the unconscious begins to point towards a new field of endeavour. The man who still seeks to satisfy his craving through the ego and its achievements will remain as dissatisfied and unhappy as the youth who clings to the auto-erotic satisfactions appropriate to infancy. But if he can find a way to sacrifice his identification with his ego point of view, a new centre for his life will develop; in its service he will be able to explore new realms of greater meaning and value than those accessible to the ego.

THE DEVELOPMENT OF THE EGO brings with it certain positive values of great significance both for the maturing of the individual and for the accomplishment of the world's work. Among these, self-respect is one of the most important. With it can be reckoned ambition of the positive sort, expressed in the desire to do a good job, get on in the world, and fill one's role adequately, not only because of the prestige it will bring but also because of one's own inner standards. These qualities are connected with the sense of being a person, an I, someone with rights and dignity—someone, moreover, who is able to take his place in the community, yet also able to maintain himself even if cut off from the support of the community. The individual with adequately developed ego is competent not only to overcome obstacles in the outer world and so to make a satisfactory work and social adjustment, but also to rouse himself from the inertia that saps his energy even before he makes the attempt to tackle the external problem. For the ego is the function that man has developed to deal with this primary inertia.

When the individual has succeeded in making a satisfactory adjustment on the ego level, he is rewarded, as a rule, not only by attainment of his objective goals but also by acquisition of a certain prestige. This prestige, which comes from the approval of his fellows, becomes in turn the motive for further efforts to overcome himself and to control his environment. It would seem as though such a man were well on the way to the attainment of a satisfying life. But usually he finds that the objects of desire that looked so glamorous when they gleamed far above, lose their charm to a great extent when they are within his grasp. At first he takes them in his stride and passes immediately to the struggle for another objective a little farther ahead. Perhaps he fails to gain his objective, and his ambition is frustrated over and over again. In any case the time will come when any man with capacity for introspection will begin to ask himself: "What's the use of this? What am I doing it for?" The prizes of effort do not satisfy the urge of ambition. Some resign themselves with a cynical gibe to the effect that all is vanity. Others, however, begin to question whether their efforts have not perhaps been directed to the wrong goal. Is it possible that the prize they sought was like the carrot tied in front of the donkey's nose, and that the real objective lay, as the Hindus say, in the striving, not in the "fruits of action"? Through the action an effect was being produced in themselves, an inner change was taking place. The sense of being a person was becoming stronger and more definite.

In primitive communities the being of the tribe or of the group is felt to surpass in importance the being of the individual, who hardly appears to himself to be a separate person with a distinct life of his own, as is evidenced by the fatalistic attitude with which he accepts death. In the evolution of consciousness men became aware of the group, as an entity, long before they became aware of themselves as separate egos. In primitive tribes the puberty initiations are designed to make the boy or girl a member of the tribe; the religious mysteries of more developed communities, on the other hand, confer on the youth a separate soul, or, as they say, change him from an animal into a man.

The intense concern with the personal life that is so characteristic of Western civilization is unknown among primitives. Orientals too have it in strikingly less marked degree than do Occidentals. In India, for instance, the dominant religious teaching is that the goal of life consists in loss of the personal ego through union with or mergence into the All-Consciousness, the Atman. This doctrine is in contrast to the Western concept of the importance of the personal soul. Does it perhaps give a clue concerning the stage of consciousness that must follow on the disillusion so frequently encountered in middle life? Must the ego be replaced by a new centre of consciousness, much as the ego itself replaced the autos at a lower level? Certainly the Hindus have explored the inner realm of the human psyche far more deeply than we have, for while we have been concerned with the problems of the outer world, they have been profoundly occupied with those of the soul. We cannot, of course, take over their teachings and accept them on faith: that would represent a regression from our own conscious achievement. But it is possible that if we follow our own path of development in our Western way, and explore the hidden depths of the psyche with the help of psychological analysis, we may find that some of their conclusions are really faithful to fact.

THE EMERGENCE OF THE EGO brings with it the problem of the will to power. For as man gradually emerges from unconsciousness and learns to subdue his instinctive nature, making it serve him and his needs, he possesses himself of the energy that formerly resided in the natural process. This progressive transference of energy takes place wherever man struggles to know and to understand. In the larger realm of the relation of mankind to the world, and also in the smaller where the development of each individual is concerned, this process continues. Through his conquest of the world and through his increasing understanding of the laws of nature, man has become master of untold resources and power. Compared to the naked savage of the jungle, modern man is a king.

But he is in danger of forgetting that, impressive as his achievements are, the secrets of nature and her store of energy are hardly touched. Man is still at the mercy of natural forces he cannot control. Furthermore, this conquest of the outer world has been made possible through a conquest of the natural forces within himself; and today, unfortunately, Western man is not much interested in the problem of self-mastery. These facts have been brought out in detail in the preceding chapters, where it has been shown that the struggle to overcome sloth and greed and primitive sexuality has been at least half of the problem that man has faced in his battle for survival. Here we are concerned with the use that has been made of the new powers achieved through man's struggle with nature on the one hand, and against the compelling power of his instincts on the other.

Unfortunately for mankind, these two processes have not gone on at equal pace; no balance has been kept between them. In the Orient, especially in India, the ideal of culture has been related to the conquest of the forces of nature within the human being, with the idea of freeing him from the power of his instincts and from the conflict of the opposites. Religious training such as the yogic disciplines of India and Tibet, and the Zen training of China and Japan, seeks to make conscious the psychological happenings that normally go on below the threshold of consciousness. Through these disciplines the adept acquires conscious control of energies that usually function autonomously. This is accompanied by certain psychic experiences described in the texts as being of the nature of an expansion of consciousness beyond the ego state, with a consequent freeing from the passions and desirousness that bind men unconditionally to the world.

To the Occidental there is something extremely strange in the idea that culture and education can rest on such a basis, for Western man has taken the opposite road in his cultural development. While the Oriental turned inwards, seeking to gain mastery of the inner realm, Western man turned his eyes outwards and developed a technique for controlling the external world. These are respectively the introverted and extraverted way. Each has given man control of energy redeemed from the unknown in nature, in life itself. But because development has been one-sided, the extraverted nations knowing little of the introverted way, and the introverted nations caring nothing for extraverted achievements, the progress of mankind as a whole has been seriously handicapped, and the individuals of both cultures have remained immature in one respect or the other.

In the case of Western culture, the work that has been done on the forces of nature has released energy for the use of the ego. However, the ego identified itself with the powers it had acquired and became inflated by them—or perhaps it would be truer to say that when the ego emerged it failed to disentangle itself completely from the other contents of the unconscious and so remained identified with them. Man's inflation increased as his control over nature advanced. He felt as if he were the creator of the life within himself, or at least its master. Unfortunately, however, this left the ego in a very precarious position, for if it was master and took all the credit when things went well, then it had also to take the blame when things went badly. And since even at the present time, with all the experience of centuries behind him, man is still by no means able to control nature, he is left with an overwhelming sense of guilt and inferiority that is the under side of his assumption of power.

When some event in the outer world makes it evident that his power and understanding of nature are inadequate to prevent disaster, modern man feels guilty. We not infrequently hear someone say it is "awful" that a famine or some other disaster should occur, for with all our technical knowledge we ought to be able to prevent that kind of thing. Here the speaker is putting the responsibility and blame on someone else but is nonetheless assuming that mankind as a whole ought to be able to control natural forces and is guilty if it fails to do so. The sense of guilt is even greater when the disaster is due to lack of understanding of psychological conditions.

There is an example in contemporary history that touches us all very closely. The pacific attitude of the democracies in the years following the first world war was due to a genuine desire for peace and fair play all round. The fact that it failed, and that a destructive dynamism erupted from the unconscious into the world—owing its initial success in no small measure to this very attitude of pacifism—has profoundly shocked very many people, who feel baffled and guilty at the thought that while they sought only peace and good will, their generation has actually bred hatred and war.

This is in truth a very sobering thought. But surely the sin has lain not so much in the inability to produce utopian conditions as in that unconscious "God-almightiness" which assumes that mankind could produce a utopia if only it would. This preconception depends on an inflation of the ego by forces that come from the very source of life itself. Thus the ego sets itself up as master over powers that are obviously beyond it. Actually the ego is only a puppet in the hands of these forces, and the arrogant assumption of such impossible authority puts it into an entirely false relation to life.

The man who is overwhelmed by a sense of guilt at the failure of mankind also suffers from an inflation, but as his identification with the nonpersonal powers is a negative one, the resulting inflation is likewise a negative one. This condition is met with in persons who claim to be the worst who ever lived, or the most inferior. It is a state of mind that paralyses all effort and seems to justify complete inertia. "Why should I try to do this?" such an individual says. "I shall only make a failure of it. Someone else, anyone else, can do it better than I." A negative inflation of this kind is against life. The ego sits secure on its stool of negation, and as it never attempts anything difficult, so it never learns, never develops, and the individual remains isolated from life.

Just as a negative inflation brings life to a standstill, so a positive inflation, causing the ego to feel itself powerful, dominant, and "always right," is likewise against life. For a person whose ego suffers from such an invasion of nonpersonal powers does not contact life directly either. Instead of facing life and its tasks realistically on the level of his actual attainments, he approaches them with the assumption that he is master. He identifies himself unconsciously with some great figure, Napoleon or Beethoven or Christ. Such an image is technically called the archetype of the "mana personality." [11] Perhaps the man's assumption of superiority works; then those around him will pay him the deference his attitude demands and follow his leadership. If this happens, he may succeed, for as long as the identification continues to be effective. But he will remain undeveloped as a human being, as a man, for instead of living his own life, he is living the life of an archetypal figure endowed with nonpersonal powers. While the identification holds, he feels himself to be in control; actually, however, his psyche has been invaded and he himself has very little to say about his own acts and thoughts. If the inflation leaves him he will be empty, deflated and helpless; if the identification with the powerful archetype becomes complete, he will have lost his humanity, that is to say, he will be insane.

If such an assumption of power is very far from the reality of the man's actual capabilities, it will arouse ridicule or hostility instead of acclaim. This reaction from the people around him may bring him to his senses and enable him to correct his attitude. But if his identification with the mana personality is a profound one, it cannot be corrected by conscious effort, for the conscious ego has been overrun by the instinctive energy of the unconscious role. Then the individual so afflicted will become obsessed with the idea that he is misunderstood and persecuted. Consciously he feels himself to be a martyr—identifying himself with that figure in the unconscious which is the other side of the mana personality and compensates it. One can no longer reason with such a man; he will interpret every incident that befalls him in terms of his obsession, and judge every situation from the same distorted viewpoint.

These examples serve to show how the ego, even after it has emerged into consciousness and undergone considerable development, can be invaded and swamped by the archetypal

11. Jung, *Two Essays on Analytical Psychology* (C.W. 7), Second Essay, pt. ii, chap. iv, "The Mana Personality."

powers of the unconscious. This is one of the dangers constantly threatening the psyche. For the ego is only a small
part of the whole psyche, and it has to strive mightily to wrest
from nature even a small amount of energy for its own purposes. And no sooner does it get free than it is in danger of
being invaded and swamped once more. But now it assumes
that the power working through it is its own.

The dynamic energy of the living organism comes from
the basic instincts. In them is vested the energy of life itself.
When the ego separates itself from the rest of the psyche it
is very small; it is naked and helpless in face of the enormous
forces of life that remain inaccessible to it, and of whose nature
and extent it remains totally unaware. That is, the ego is unconscious of these forces. Or, to put it inversely: from the
point of view of the ego, the powers are in the unconscious.
And when the ego seeks to possess itself of this energy, the
tables may be turned and the forces of the unconscious may
take possession of the ego. The situation recalls the old story
of the private who called to his superior officer: "Captain, I've
taken a prisoner."

The captain called back: "Bring him here for questioning."

After a long pause the private replied in a small voice:
"Please, sir, he won't come."

In the ages before man came to know something of the
laws of nature, he conceived of all the unknown powers of
life as emanating from living beings, spirits, or gods. He personified the unknown forces of the world, and because his
own psyche was quite unknown to him, he projected its powers too and likewise personified these. It therefore appeared
to him that the world was inhabited by hosts of unseen daemons who possessed all the powers of the universe and all of
its treasures, except for that small portion which man could
succeed in wresting from them.

In order to increase its power, the ego had to redeem some
of the energy vested in the basic instincts. In this way it overcame the autos and relegated it to a subservient place. The
autos is not, indeed it should not be, entirely suppressed, for
the information it brings to the service of the ego is most

necessary for the health and well-being not only of the body
but of the whole organism. Some persons, it is true, do repress
this side of life so completely that they are seriously handicapped for lack of the knowledge that only the autos can
supply. Some, for instance, are unaware of what is wrong
when they are hungry or cold or fatigued. Instead of attending to these perfectly natural bodily needs, they will go on
demanding service from an overworked physical organism
until it finally breaks down. Many a man considers himself
noble, or at least superior to others, because he does not need
to stop his work for meals or for rest, claiming that he gains
in concentration through not paying any attention to his little
aches and pains. It is undoubtedly true that some discipline of
the auto-erotic aspect of the psyche is necessary if the ego is
to have any psychological energy at its disposal. But if the
repression is practised for the sake of enhancing the ego and
its prestige and not in the service of life, it will necessarily be
destructive.

For when the ego, in its determination to be master, re-
moves itself too far from the instincts, it loses its contact with
the life stream within. It becomes more and more shut up
within itself, restricted to its own resources, which are at best
very limited, so that in course of time the sap of life within
it dries up. A life that is lived only within the precincts of the
conscious ego becomes arid and sterile and stands in danger of
death. This point is clearly illustrated in myths and legends
from many parts of the world.

Adam and Eve were driven out from the garden of Eden,
as we are told, in order that they should not eat of the fruit
of the tree of life. For having acquired the power to distinguish good from evil, through eating of the fruit of the tree
of knowledge, they were made subject to death. That is, the
conscious ego had come to birth in them, they had set up their
wills against the edict of God as personifying the eternal law
of nature—and so had become subject to the limitations of
mortal consciousness.

Golden Garment of the Hindu myth [12] represents the ego.

12. See above, pp. 212-14.

He obtained control of the instinct powers through his ascetic practices, but used them only for his own advantage. Vishnu, who served the supreme value of life and not his personal interest, represents a factor in the psyche that transcends the ego.

The struggle between the two attitudes represented by Golden Garment and Vishnu is actually a conflict that has to be fought out within the human heart. This conflict must be faced in the life of every great leader. Moses was such a one. We are told that in their wanderings in the wilderness the Children of Israel came to the desert of Zin and were in danger of perishing from thirst. Moses prayed God to give them water:

And the glory of the Lord appeared unto them. And the Lord spake unto Moses, saying, Take the rod, and gather thou the assembly together, thou, and Aaron thy brother, and speak ye unto the rock before their eyes; and it shall give forth his water, and thou shalt bring forth to them water out of the rock; so thou shalt give the congregation and their beasts drink.

But Moses was angry with the people and addressed them with reproaches.

And he said unto them, Hear now, ye rebels; must we fetch you water out of this rock? And Moses lifted up his hand and with his rod he smote the rock twice: and the water came out abundantly, and the congregation drank, and their beasts also.[13]

The magic ritual worked, the people were saved; but Moses had claimed to be able to do something he obviously could not do by his own power; he had arrogated to himself powers that belonged only to the Lord.

If we take this story as legendary rather than as factual history, we need to interpret the symbolism underlying it. Up to the time of this incident Moses was the "hero" who had rescued the Israelites from the oppression of the Egyptians. In all his earlier exploits, being keenly aware of his human fallibility, he had made a definite distinction between him-

13. Num. 20:6-11.

self and the mission entrusted to him,[14] and so he belongs among the heroes to be discussed in the next chapter; but in this incident of the rock he regressed and fell into egotism. He had just come down, it will be recalled, from his long colloquy with God on Mount Sinai, where he had received unique evidences of God's favour. It is recorded that his face shone with so great a light that he had to veil it—that is, he had become one of the illuminati.

It is always at such moments that a man's particular devil appears to tempt him most sorely. This devil is usually Lucifer, the power devil, the hybris of the ego. So it was in the case of Moses; he identified himself with God, saying, "Must *we* fetch you water out of this rock?" To bring water out of rock means to have power over the hidden streams of life, and as if to show that he considered himself the most important part of the combine, he not only said, "Must we fetch you water?" but he also smote the rock, although his instructions were only to speak to it. The consequence was a quite natural one: he was debarred from the Promised Land. This is to say that a man whose ego is inflated by the nonpersonal powers of the psyche cannot enter paradise.

The outcome of this story of Moses is in marked contrast to that of another, the content of which is otherwise very similar. When Jesus of Nazareth came to John the Baptist to be baptized, the Spirit of God descended upon him in the form of a dove:

And lo a voice from heaven, saying, This is my beloved Son, in whom I am well pleased. Then was Jesus led up of the spirit into the wilderness to be tempted of the devil.[15]

Here, as in the case of Moses after the illumination, came the temptation to egotism, and again the tempter was the power devil. If Jesus was really the Son of God, he might prove it to himself by leaping down from the pinnacle of the Temple; then all other men would see and recognize him to be the Messiah. If he would worship the power devil, he should

14. Cf. his attitude in the story of the burning bush, Exod. 3.
15. Matt. 3:17-4:1.

receive all the kingdoms of the world and their riches. If he would make power the god he worshipped, he could rule the world, he could be another Alexander, another Caesar. But Jesus of Nazareth recognized what manner of spirit it was that tempted him and refused to be caught by the lure of personal power.

It has been pointed out above that the will to power functions like an instinct, and we must ask ourselves what the value is that this instinct serves. There exists in every individual a feeling of the sacredness of the I. When it is encroached upon, a power reaction is aroused, as if one's very life were being threatened. Obviously an essential or unconditioned value is involved. It is felt at first to belong to the body or person, that is, to the autos, the somatic I; next it is identified with the ego, the conscious I. But this supreme value belongs to the whole psyche; it cannot be pre-empted by the ego without producing the results described in the legend of Golden Garment.

Therefore whenever an individual is roused to an emotion of greater intensity than the threat of the circumstances would seem to warrant, concern for a supreme value probably lies behind the "powerish" reaction. In our condemnation of the asocial behaviour we must not overlook this hidden value. This is an important point not only in dealing with children but with regard to maturer persons as well. When for instance a child becomes frantic at being overpowered by an adult's superior strength, the power obsession of the autos conceals this value. Similarly, when a grown man is up in arms over some frustration of his will, it is because he fears that the core of his self is assailed. The power stirred in this reaction represents the fundamental life energy. This energy must be rescued from autos and ego, for it can only be adequately used for the total personality when it is vested in the Self. In the story of Golden Garment this difficult task was undertaken by Vishnu, who symbolizes a more enlightened consciousness superseding the ego consciousness represented by Golden Garment.

In order to find the Self—the centre of the total psyche— one must be freed from ego desirousness and from the conflict

The Corn Mother of the Pawnee Indians

From an ethnological report

The Slaying of the Bull

Modern drawing

The Mistress of Animals

Etruscan bronze plate, vi century B.C.

The King of the Centaurs Seizes the Bride

Fragment from the Temple of Zeus, Olympia

The Anima Opens the Eyes of a Child

Modern drawing

Human Sacrifice

Detail from panel (below) of silver cauldron, Celtic,
c. I century B.C. (found at Gundestrup, Denmark)

Mask Representing the Animal Nature of the God

Granite statue of Sekhmet, Thebes, 19th Dynasty

Isis Suckling Pharaoh

Limestone relief, Temple of Seti I, Abydos, 19th Dynasty

Two Women with a Child

Front and back views. Ivory, Mycenae, Bronze Age

IX

QUENTIN MATSYS: St. John with Chalice and Dragon

Detail of altarpiece

PIERO DI COSIMO: St. John with Chalice and Serpent

Jonah Cast Up by the Whale

Miniature painting from a Persian manuscript, *c.* 1400

The Rescue of the Black Man from the Sea

From a manuscript: Solomon Trismosin, *Splendor solis,* 1582

The Circle of the Psyche

Modern drawing

Vajra Mandala

Tibet, Lamaist sacred painting used in meditation

The Impregnation of the Centre through the Bite
of a Serpent

Modern drawing

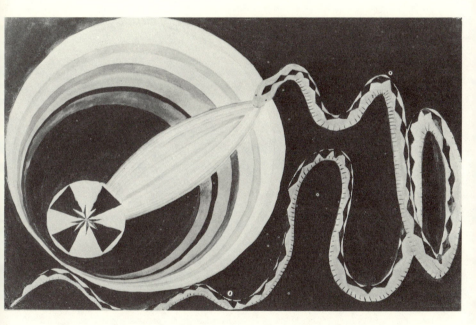

The Fertilization of the Centre by the Great Serpent

Modern drawing

The Dragon Guarding the Centre

Modern drawing

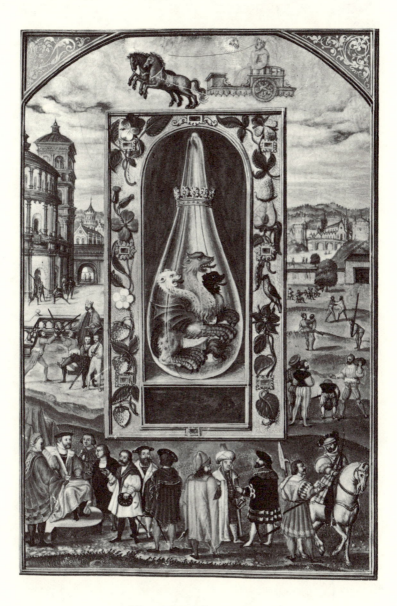

The Transformation

The hermetic vase, sealed and crowned, containing the triple
dragon. From a manuscript: Solomon Trismosin,
Splendor solis, 1582

The Consummation of the "Great Work"—
the *coniunctio*

From the *Mutus liber*, edition of 1702

XX

of the opposites. One must learn how to undertake action for the sake of action, not for the fruits of action. But this attitude cannot be achieved by refusal to enter the struggle, or by evasion of the difficulties and problems connected with the development and discipline of the ego. Unless the ego has been developed to its fullest capacity, it cannot be renounced. The possibilities of ego consciousness must be fully explored; then it will be possible perhaps to go a step beyond the accepted cultural level of the day and bring up from the depths of the unconscious a value that will produce an enlargement and transformation of consciousness itself.

Just as Indra [16] came to the conclusion that the ego with its achievements, however well cared for, however well adorned it might be, could not bring lasting satisfaction, so likewise many persons throughout the ages, having gained all that the world has to offer, have found themselves dissatisfied and disillusioned. The present age is no exception to this rule. As Indra said: "Just as that one (reflected in the water) is well cared for when this one is well cared for, so that one is ill or unhappy when this one is ill." Having reached this point in his meditation, Indra, it will be recalled, returned to Prajapati and asked for more enlightenment. Apparently he was still not qualified to receive further insight, for he had to serve another thirty-two years before initiation into the next stage was possible. Then Prajapati taught him about the self that dreams—meaning that it is possible to be disidentified from the happenings of the world and to view them dispassionately as if they were occurring in a dream, even though they affect oneself. Indra was still dissatisfied, and Prajapati told him of the self that sleeps dreamlessly—namely, that an individual can reach a condition of nonbeing in a dreamless state of samadhi. But Indra objected: "Sir, in that way he does not know himself (his Self) that he is I, nor does he know anything that exists. He is gone to utter annihilation. I see no good in this."

Then at last Prajapati agreed to give him the final initiation, if he would submit himself to the last five years of probation, which would make one hundred and one years in all. For such

16. See above, p. 205.

enlightenment is the treasure hard to attain. Now Prajapati explained that behind the ears is one who hears, for whom the ears are only the instrument of hearing; similarly there is one behind the nose and behind the eyes, for whom these are but instruments. So too behind the mind, the consciousness, is one who knows:

> He who knows, let me think this, he is the Self, the mind [consciousness] is his divine eye. He, the Self, seeing these pleasures (which to others are hidden like a buried treasure of gold) through his divine eye, i.e. the mind, rejoices. . . . He who knows that Self and understands it, obtains all worlds and all desires.[17]

The importance of this story for our discussion is obvious. In Indian philosophy the problem of the Self, the consciousness behind the ego, containing and transcending the ego, has been a subject of profound psychological research for centuries and has been the focus of the prolonged and disciplined endeavour of thinkers who have sought to fathom the mysteries behind the surface of conscious life. The descriptions of this state of consciousness clearly show that it does not consist in loss of the ego self in a vague nirvana; rather, it is a state of heightened awareness, more intense and more extensive than any that is possible under the limitations of the ego. For just as one who knows that he sees, and what it is that he sees, is more conscious than one who merely sees, so one who knows that his mind or consciousness sees or experiences, and who understands what it is that it sees, is more conscious than one in whom thoughts and impressions merely pass across the mind like shadows.

An example may make this clearer. If a layman looks through a microscope, he will see the slide and the coloured specimen within his field of vision, but he will not understand what it is that he sees. If a trained microscopist looks at the same slide, his eye will see and recognize what is before him. He will not only know the meaning of what he sees, but he will actually see much more than the untrained observer. He has acquired a consciousness that the other man does not possess.

17. Max Müller, *The Upanishads*, I, 142.

The next step in psychological development beyond the level of ego consciousness is concerned with bringing this Self, the doer or thinker behind the action or thought, up to consciousness. If this could be achieved, the split between the ego and the instinctive nature in man would surely be healed.

PART II

THE Transformation
OF PSYCHIC ENERGY

9

The Inner Conflict

THE DRAGON AND THE HERO

WHEN THE EGO BEGINS to develop and gains some autonomy—some power, over against the might of nature,
to determine and control itself and its environment—it gradually acquires a feeling of being a separate entity. The individual learns to differentiate between the I and the not-I, with
an ever increasing emphasis on the value of the I. That is, he
becomes aware of being a self. This awareness is accompanied
by an intoxicating sense of selfhood, an inner expansion of the
I. Unchecked, this will produce an inflation not unlike the
fatal swelling of the frog, that tried to puff itself up to the size
of the ox, so aptly depicted by Aesop. Herein lies the origin of
the typical power attitude discussed in the preceding chapter.

In the outer world the ego seeks to dominate its environment and to subject all things, persons, and conditions alike
to its interest. In the inner world, as many psychic contents as
possible are brought under its control, and those which cannot
be dominated are suppressed. In this way a threshold is built
up between the conscious and the unconscious part of the
psyche. The unacceptable elements may be so far repressed
into the unconscious that they actually become unavailable to
consciousness. The ego cannot reach them and they are lost
until a time comes when, having become laden with unexpressed energy, they erupt into consciousness, bringing up
from the depths archaic materials utterly unadapted, and there-

fore usually destructive, to the laboriously built-up conscious adaptation. When, however, these repressed elements are activated with unused energy but nevertheless do not break through to consciousness, either because their potential is not high enough, or because the resistance of the ego to their becoming conscious is too robust, they begin to influence the conscious personality, attracting its energy into the unconscious complex. As a consequence the conscious energy is sucked away and the individual begins to feel depleted and inert. If, by a renewed effort, the ego succeeds in overcoming this tendency and represses the intruding elements once more, it becomes inflated and takes on the arrogance, the spiritual pride, that the ancients called hybris, while the individual braces himself once more to conquer the world.

If, however, the task presented by life seems too hard, and if the inertia is too great, an alternative possibility will present itself. Why should one continue to struggle—why not give up the attempt and just drift along with the current? Baynes aptly calls this the renegade hypothesis.[1] He points out that the renegade is not merely an individual who can no longer struggle; he is actually a deserter, a traitor who by his sabotage, his alliance with all the destructive forces that lie buried in the unconscious, actively endangers the whole enterprise of consciousness. The final expression of this attitude is suicide.

In his passive form the renegade pleads: "Let us give up the struggle, let us even give up life itself rather than struggle, let us sleep the sleep of death." As Tennyson's lotos-eaters sing:

> Let us alone. What is it that will last?
> All things are taken from us, and become
> Portions and parcels of the dreadful Past.

1. *Mythology of the Soul*, pp. 40 ff. This book, a discussion of two borderline cases treated by the method of analytical psychology, is based on the whole problem of the renegade hypothesis. Baynes shows that the alternative to the progressive attitude to life is not merely a *laissez aller* course but a giving over of oneself voluntarily to the archaic and regressive elements within the psyche. According to Baynes' view, with which I heartily agree, it is this voluntary renunciation of the struggle for consciousness, the going over to the side of the archaic and irresponsible elements of the psyche, that constitutes the turning point between neurosis and psychosis in the majority of cases, perhaps even in all.

Let us alone. What pleasure can we have
To war with evil? Is there any peace
In ever climbing up the climbing wave?
All things have rest, and ripen toward the grave
In silence; ripen, fall and cease:
Give us long rest or death, dark death or dreamful ease.[2]

This attitude is illustrated also in Wagner's *Siegfried*. When Siegfried, having forged anew his father's sword, that is, his manhood's will, goes to search for the treasure, he finds the dragon Fafnir, guardian of the golden hoard, asleep in his cave. Siegfried challenges him, but Fafnir replies: *Lass mich schlafen* ("Leave me alone, I want to sleep").

Thus the first exploit of the hero is to arouse the dragon, that lurks in the unconscious, so that he will come out and fight, for only by this manoeuvre can the treasure concealed beneath his great bulk be revealed.

In his active form the renegade is perhaps even more dangerous. Baynes describes this attitude in the following passage:

There is something . . . in the schizophrenic subject's blood which seeks out and responds to the violence and dread of the daemonic unconscious forces. Something in him shouts the devil's laughter as the ship is battered and broken by the attacking sea. The renegade in the psyche is archaic and nihilistic, seeking violence involuntarily, as an insecure ruler seeks war. Men of insight can perceive the presence of this renegade voice in their own make-up.[3]

Throughout the ages the problem of man's relation to the untamed powers of the unconscious has been expressed in myths and legends depicting this eternally recurrent conflict as a struggle with dragons. Like all fabulous or mythological creatures, dragons represent the denizens of the inner world, unrecognized as such, and therefore projected into outer forms. They are personifications of the nonpersonal forces in the depths of the human psyche that nourish and aid or devour and destroy man's feeble and naked consciousness.

The myths about the dragon and man's struggle to be

2. Tennyson, *Poetical Works*, "The Lotos-Eaters," "Choric Song," p. 52.
3. *Mythology of the Soul*, p. 3.

freed from his depredations are legion. But whether they take their origin in Syria or India, in Greece or the Celtic countries, in the South Seas or among the red folk of the Americas, they have certain features in common. Here, instead of recounting specific examples, I shall attempt to give their salient features in a short composite story.

The legends tell how long ago, when the world was still young, dragons roamed the earth unchecked. They lived and fought and bred and died, following only the law of the unknown god who had created them. Their sway was absolute, unchallenged by any; but no one knew of their prowess, of their lives or their deaths, not even they themselves, for the consciousness that can "know" as well as "be" was not yet born.

But after centuries, millenniums rather, when the dragons had already disappeared from sight, though they still ruled the world and dictated its conditions, a little naked creature appeared upon the scene. He would have been entirely unimportant in the scheme of things, were it not that by some strange accident, an accident that has sometimes been called divine providence, this little creature had a spark of consciousness: he began to be aware that he did things, an experience over and above the mere doing of them. This unique quality gave him a certain superiority over the other creatures, so that he began very, very slowly to dream about making for himself conditions better fitted for his life. Gradually his spark of awareness grew; he looked at himself and saw what he had accomplished and said, "We shall be like gods." Already he had wrested from the dragons something of their power. Man had acquired the ability to do something on his own initiative, something he was not forced to do by immediate necessity; he had also learned how to refrain from some action to which his impulse, his immediate desire, might urge him. Thus sloth and instinct no longer reigned supreme.

At this the dragons, invisible to the outer eye, withdrew a little and slept, as dragons do. Man too rested, content with his achievement. But ever and anon the spark within him burned brighter, and he set about a new task in conquering the outer and the inner world. The wise men of the tribes built fences around the cleared fields and set boundaries and taboos upon the inner treasures in order to guard against the incursions of the dragons, who, at times when it was least expected, would rouse themselves from their lethargy and make forays upon the villages.

But dragons are ancient and slow. They sleep away the centuries and hate to be disturbed. So they usually said to one another: "This man has taken a tiny piece of our ancient domain and a morsel of our power, but it is so minute, compared with the vastness of our store, that the wise thing to do is to ignore it. If he becomes too presumptuous we can always go and lay waste one or two of his villages or, if need be, destroy him utterly with one puff of our fiery breath."

So long as the memory of these incursions remained vivid to them, the puny humans were cautious. They built their walls and obeyed the laws of their wise men and priests. But a younger generation, not remembering the days of the dragon incursions, rebelled against the rule of the wise men, saying: "These are just old tales. Why should we bother about such things? Let us eat and be merry. Those silly old men wanted to make the world safe for Caesar or safe for democracy— well, just to make the world safe—and now the world is safe, the dragons will never rise again, and anyway we don't believe there ever were any dragons. We have everything we want, if only our neighbour would let us enjoy it in peace. The war against the dragons was all imperialism, and the moral code was due to an outworn and stuffy puritanism. This is what made the old people so belligerent and so stern. We are more civilized and more sophisticated."

And so the young people let the walls fall into disrepair and neglected the regulations and taboos they had been taught. And then a still later generation arose that had not even been taught the law. They lived easily and loosely, and when the dragons, waxing bold in the spiritual darkness that was gradually descending upon the world, came and attacked them, they merely evacuated the outlying villages and either went to sleep again or fell to quarrelling among themselves.

Now all this happened a very long time ago, of course, when tales about the dragons were still current, and when some people actually claimed to have seen them on the outskirts of the cultivated lands, and no one as yet suspected that they were not outside man but within him. They were thought of as if they were actual beasts. Some said that they were like dinosaurs, but strangely enough the reality of the dragon is closer to us than the reality of the dinosaurs, so that it is much more natural to say that a dinosaur was like a dragon than to say that a dragon was like a dinosaur. Others said that they were huge snakes, and we still hear occasionally of a great sea serpent seen by sailors in distress; still others, especially in the Far East, said that they flew through the air. But all were agreed, when they did not pooh-pooh the whole thing as a fable, that these monsters were very terrible and very strong, that they guarded a vast treasure hoard, and that in addition their blood was potent for good as well as ill. They alone could bring the rain in its season, and in time of famine and drought it might even be necessary to approach one of these fearsome creatures in his den—or so the old people said—in order to persuade him to give, out of his hoard, enough rain to bring back fertility to the earth. At such times the dragon demanded the sacrifice of a beautiful maiden, and when he was in a particularly bad mood it might be necessary to bring him a score or so of maidens as the price of the needed rainfall.

Sometimes, however, the dragon remained sulky and refused his help. He might even become ugly and, rousing himself, might emerge from his den with a roar, set upon the suppliants who had brought him gifts, and devour them. But the people had become soft and lazy through their neglect of the laws and their love of good living, and they did not know what to do. Many thought that the best course was to appease the dragons. But such concessions only made them the more bold, until the people could stand the situation no longer. They called a council and decided to send out a band of young men to teach the dragon a lesson. They chose those who, it seemed to them, could best be spared, sturdy ruffians with plenty of brawn but not much intelligence, and sent them forth to fight. Some reached their destination, but many stopped to rest by the roadside, and the dragon breathed upon them his poisonous breath, which brings an unendurable drowsiness, and they are sleeping there yet. Others, when they saw the dragon, fled in terror, and those who actually attempted to approach him were stricken down and never heard of again.

This sort of thing went on for many centuries, as can be read in many a mediaeval legend. Some communities, and these not the most backward in culture and achievements, disappeared entirely under the assaults of the dragons; but in others a new factor came into play. There appeared a man who succeeded in overcoming the dragon and driving him back, even taking from him the victims he had recently killed and restoring them to life, so it was credibly asserted, by giving them to drink of the dragon's blood. Most important of all, the maidens who had been given in sacrifice to the dragons were also rescued. Such a man was called a hero.

But here the stories and legends diverge, for in some cases the hero is said to have been a godlike being, of divine or semi-divine birth, who came to this world solely to rescue mankind. His courage and prowess were beyond doubt, and he was armed with an invincible weapon and guarded by divine protection and miraculous armour. But there are also stories of a different kind of dragon slayer, who was not hero-like at all. He was just an ordinary human being, often a rather poor specimen at that. He did not look the part, he had no shining armour nor gleaming sword. He did not go into battle with assurance of victory; he did not see himself as a hero, and certainly his schoolmates and fellow townsmen never thought of him in that role. Often he lacked even ordinary courage and would go to any length to avoid unpleasantness; indeed, it was not unusual for him to be actually forced into the hero part just because he had run away from some task or obligation—an act that put him outside the pale of society. Then, when he found himself isolated, he was attacked by the dragon and so was compelled to do battle alone or suffer a worse fate.

But this man was no shining hero descended from above to

redeem men or release them from the power of the dragon. He was no divine or semidivine being whose powers and ultimate victory were never for a moment in doubt. He was a poor weak human, called upon to perform heroic feats seemingly beyond his power. The outcome of the struggle was frequently in the gravest doubt, not only on account of the power of the dragon, but also because it was never certain that the so-called hero might not turn tail and run away or perhaps at the critical moment sit down under a tree and start smelling the flowers, hoping that the dragon would overlook him, like Munro Leaf's Ferdinand the bull. (Ferdinand had been bred to fight in the bullring, but when the young bulls were taken out to start their training he preferred to contemplate the beauties of nature, rather than to risk the hazards of the ring.) For such heroes are weak and unsure of themselves; in fact, they are not heroes at all until after they have accomplished their tasks, and for this reason they engage our sympathy and understanding as the other type cannot, however much we may admire their shining courage and invulnerability.

The happenings related in these legends are always represented as having taken place "very long ago," which means that they refer to the archaic parts of the psyche, not to the conscious, so-to-speak modern part. The dragons, the powers of earth, sky, and the underworld, represent the instinctive life urges that sleep for the most part, held fast by a profound inertia, like that of nature. Natural man is aroused from this all-pervading sloth only by the prick of necessity.

In the legends the group frequently plays a rather important part in sending the young men out to fight the dragons. This circumstance is further reflected in war dances and hunting rituals of primitive communities. We see the same phenomenon in the organized cheering crowd at a college football game. In a similar way the enthusiasm of a leader at a mass meeting may rouse the rank and file to acts they would not undertake individually.

The legends report, however, that the young men thus mobilized do not usually succeed in overcoming the dragon; on the contrary, they frequently fall victim to its poison. This surely indicates that unconsciousness is a condition of individual persons and must be dealt with by an act of personal heroism. The enthusiasm engendered by collective activity does not express a conscious determination, nor is it under conscious control; it is rather the result of an invasion of the personal psyche by collective impulses or energies, which have the effect of drowning or swamping individual consciousness. It is therefore akin in its nature to the dragon power, as if one dragon had been aroused to combat another. Collective or group activity can never, in the nature of things, create individual consciousness. It is true that when the way has been opened by an act of individual heroism, the group can follow in the same path and so enjoy the benefits made available by the hero's act. But these followers have not gained within themselves that development or understanding which is the individual's sole guarantee against subsequent invasion by the dragon.

An example may make this clearer. In the outer world we all enjoy the benefits of scientific knowledge and understanding. The veriest child among us can use electricity by merely turning a switch. The benefits of the battle against ignorance won by the scientists are accessible to all. But that does not mean that we have each and all won this battle. If a modern city were to be invaded and all the scientists and mechanics killed, the generality of the populace would be utterly helpless and in far worse plight than a much more backward community, for they would be unable to keep going all the mechanisms of civilization on which their daily life so largely depends. Their seeming independence of nature only masks a greater ignorance than that which conditioned primitive man.

We are in a similar situation as regards the subjective side of life. We have grown up in a civilization founded on the spiritual and cultural accomplishments of our ancestors, who had a profound experience of inner truth under the form of the Christian faith. But the majority of twentieth-century individuals have had no similar experience within themselves. Thus when the day of trial comes they are more helpless in face of universal moral problems than seemingly far less civilized men. The legends are quite correct, therefore, when they relate that the dragon must be overcome by the act of a single hero.

The allegory of the attempt to appease the dragon by the gift of a beautiful maiden means that man's soul, his anima, the feminine component, is the first value to be swallowed by the aroused powers of the unconscious. This is particularly unfortunate, for the anima is the function that should relate him to the unconscious. When his anima is overwhelmed he is left defenceless in face of the untamed forces of the depths. This formulation naturally relates to the psychology of men. In women it is the animus that is engulfed, and then we have the story of the frog prince, or of the lover dwelling in a cave by the sea or perhaps under the sea, that is, the prince, the hero, the protector, is hidden—shrouded in an unacceptable form—in the unconscious.

In many of the dragon legends, when it is a question of rescuing the maiden, the sacrifice of a lamb is demanded. This means that the childish innocence within man must be voluntarily relinquished. If he is to become a conscious being, he cannot remain innocent like the animals. The maiden, the anima, represents his unconscious feeling, redeemed at the price of his childishness. In order to achieve a direct relation to his own deepest emotions, he must sacrifice his wish to be a little lamb to his own mother and to all other women.

The legends tell of two types of heroes who fight against the dragon. The divine hero obviously does not represent a human being at all; rather, he symbolizes a nonpersonal or divine factor deep within the psyche that arises ever and anon without conscious volition on the part of the individual. This hero might be said to equate with the heroic quality of the individual who is called upon to play a hero role. The second type of hero, the feeble little person who is a hero against his will, personifies the frail humanness of ordinary men. Each of us knows only too well his reluctance to take up the hero role. His excuses are our excuses, familiar to us in our fellows in all walks of life—in the patient who comes into the analyst's office announcing with an ingratiating smile, "I'm the baby type," and no less in the modest person who, confronted with a public task that cries out to be accomplished, withdraws to the ease of private life, saying, "It would take a better man than me to do that." Each of these refuses to face and do battle with his own particular dragon.

But there are others who in similar circumstances say: "There does not seem to be anyone else. I guess I've got to tackle this job, and if I make a mess of it, at least my attempt will have broken ground, someone else will take it up where I leave off." Or, even less heroically, they may say with the little boy who had a pain in his tummy: "Mama, that pain's come back! I think I'll go and try." Young as this child was, he had at least discovered that no one else could tackle his difficulty for him. This is not exactly a heroic attitude; some heroes, however, are made, not born—made by inexorable circumstance. They suffer the buffets of outrageous fortune until some obstinate streak in them rises up and they refuse to be victimized any longer; then in sheer desperation they turn, like the proverbial worm, and accomplish the task they can no longer avoid, even though the attempt costs them present suffering and may exact the final sacrifice.

Fortunately for mankind there have been many heroes of both classes. In times of distress they have appeared on the scene, fought the good fight, and saved the day. Indeed, they have extended the boundaries of the known and cultivated lands and have left a larger heritage to the generations following them.

In the recent world crisis, man was once again faced with the threat of annihilation by the archaic forces of the daemonic unconscious, and once again we looked for a leader or hero to overcome the dragons for us and to show us the way to victory. By this I mean not just victory over our military foes, but rather psychological victory over the hostile and devastating forces that are still threatening all that has made for civilization and cultural development in mankind. It is these evil powers in the psychic realm that are symbolized as dragons. It follows that this type of victory is complete only when it is achieved by the combatants of both sides. If it is attained by one side alone, while the other remains a victim of the dragons, world-wide peace will not follow the cessation of hostilities. Not until the dragons are overcome all over the world can a universal peace be established. Unfortunately, past history gives us very little encouragement to hope for such a desirable outcome of world conflict. As of old, when the general populace remained indifferent to the dragons or passively suffered their tyranny, so today the great majority of men are concerned more with how to get worldly advantages for themselves than with the moral problems on which man's well-being, possibly even his survival, depends.

In the legends, the men who were aroused to the necessity of combating the dragons were few, but their influence on the progress of civilization has been inestimable. Therefore it may be worth while to enquire what kind of men these were who are reputed to have performed the feats recorded, for it is probable that the same qualifications will be necessary for one who would repeat their exploits. Provided we know how to interpret the legendary material, we shall find that the wisdom it contains is directly applicable to our modern problem.

The heroes of legend, as has been pointed out above, fall into two distinct classes. First there are the divine or semidivine heroes: many of this type could be named from among the great figures of different religions. Examples are the various avatars of Krishna, the god-born heroes of Greek story, the Volsungs of Nordic saga, and Christ himself, who might be considered the supreme example, although, as he was "very man" as well as "very God," he is nearer to the character of the everyday human hero than to that of the gods or demigods of legend.

The god or godlike man looks down from his exalted abode and pities man's plight; or he is invoked by men in their dire distress and comes to earth out of compassion, prepared to use his superior strength and wisdom to rescue man from evils too strong for him to combat unaided. In the Hindu legends, Vishnu, even when he comes to earth in a human avatar, remains always the god and is not subject to any peril from the ills he comes to cure. The humanity of Jesus in the Christian mystery, however, is more real. The account of his temptation in the wilderness is the story of an actual human conflict, in a realm where many a man of today has had to meet his own personal devil. As the writer to the Hebrews says: "For we have not an high priest which cannot be touched with the feeling of our infirmities; but was in all points tempted like as we are, yet without sin." [4] The hero of legend, though reputedly an actual, historical man, is usually presented as a glorified figure, having certain general characteristics that are no longer human attributes but belong to the archetypal image of the hero that arises from the unconscious in the hour of need. This heroic image is perceived in projected form in the exploits of a gallant man. It is the source of the stories and furnishes the impetus for the creation of such a legendary figure.

In marked contrast to this compassionate superman is the other type of hero. He is entirely human, often pitifully weak and fallible. He undertakes his heroic task not at all for altruistic reasons; in fact, he usually does not realize at all that he is setting out on a hero's task. His motives for action are very different from those of the god-saviour, for he is caught in the problem and threatened by the danger; he must fight or die as a matter of his own necessity. This contrast may be made clearer by an analysis of a well-known example of each type.

As often happens in the case of legendary heroes, the records about St. George, who will serve as the example of the glorified hero, are rather vague and confused. It is hard to determine what is history and what is legend; furthermore, the stories from different parts of the world do not tally. Each shrine or sacred place dedicated to the memory of the hero has its own version. So far as church history is concerned, St. George [5] seems to have been a hero of eastern-Mediterranean lands. There is a noted shrine dedicated to him in Abys-

4. Heb. 4:15.
5. E. G. W. Masterman, "Saints and Martyrs, Syrian," in Hastings, *Encyclopaedia of Religion and Ethics*, XI, 81 ff.

sinia, and another in the village of Al-Khudr, which lies between Hebron and Jerusalem in Palestine. The village takes
its name from that of the saint Al-Khudr (identical with Al-
Khidr), who is also venerated there; the Mohammedans identify him with Elijah and the Christians with St. George. St.
George's Day in England is April 23, while Al-Khudr's feast
day is April 26; this is another evidence of the identification.
The latter day is called "the Feast of Spring, which makes
everything green"; Al-Khudr means "the Green One" or
"the Ever Living One." This saint, under the name either
of George or of Al-Khudr, was believed to have peculiar
powers—in particular, power to heal lunatics. The procedure
prescribed to bring about a cure was as follows. At the time
of the saint's feast, the sick person was brought to the shrine
and a lamb was offered in sacrifice. The sick man was then
shut into a dark cavern at the back of the shrine, where he
spent the night alone.

This was obviously a measure intended to put the patient
in touch with his unconscious, under favourable auspices as
it were. A similar technique is followed in certain yoga practices, in which sacred pictures are meditated upon until they
appear to come to life and unfold spontaneously before the
mind's eye.[6] In the Middle Ages the alchemists [7] evoked similar
visions by watching the chemical changes in their retorts, while
various esoteric societies had other methods designed to
produce cures by influencing the patient's unconscious. The
"trumps major" of the tarot cards were used for this purpose.
A series of archetypal themes was represented on the cards
and these were meditated upon by the disturbed individual,
under the guidance of a teacher, with the expectation that the
so-to-speak right or healthy images pictured would gradually
replace the faulty or disorganized contents of the patient's
psyche.

Similarly in ancient Greece sick or mentally disturbed
persons repaired to the temple of Aesculapius and there slept
in the Court of Dreams. The dreams that came to them at

6. See below, chap. 11.
7. See below, chap. 12.

night were interpreted by the priest or seer and were believed
to give healing guidance. Among some of the North American
Indians similar practices were common up to the coming of
the white man, and in some instances they persist to the present
day, still forming part of the puberty initiations. The Navahos,
the Sioux, and the Crows use them in their healing ceremonies.[8]

In all these instances the purpose of the meditation is obviously to put the sick person into a positive relation to his
unconscious. Naturally the primitive or the man of antiquity,
and even the mediaeval practitioner, did not formulate the
rationale of the procedure in psychological terms. Such techniques must have been evolved empirically. At first perhaps
by a happy chance, someone whose intuition in such matters
was sound had an experience of being healed through meditating on a phantasy or dream. If so, he was like the hero who
dares to explore unknown regions, braving dangers but bringing
back a treasure. Then others in need of similar help would
pluck up courage to follow his example, till gradually a method
grew up and came to be safeguarded with rules of behaviour
and prescribed rites that had to be followed if the results were
to be favourable and dangers avoided.

In analytical psychology today we follow a somewhat
similar procedure. An attempt is made to restore the individual
who is suffering from a psychological conflict, or from a
mental disturbance, to a positive relation to his unconscious.
But as we have no preconception of what the nature of that
relation ought to be, we must proceed in an entirely undog-
matic way, taking the material that arises from the unconscious
in dreams and phantasies, and trying to understand the guidance it gives as best we can.

After this digression, let us return to St. George. The details outlined above belong to the earlier tradition. In mediaeval times tales about St. George were told much like the
popular romances about King Arthur and the Knights of the
Round Table. According to these stories, George was born

8. Cf. F. B. Linderman, *American Mythology*, in Gray, *Mythology of
All Races*; J. G. Neihardt, *Black Elk Speaks*; L. A. Armer, *The Mountain
Chant*, a documentary film of a Navaho Indian ceremony performed for
the healing of a man suffering from a mental illness.

in Coventry, but many of his exploits were carried out in the East, while his first encounter with a dragon took place in Egypt. The passages quoted below are from a seventeenth-century version of the tale.[9]

There lived in the city of Coventry a noble lord, who was Lord High Steward of England. His lady was troubled and said to her lord, "Night by night no sooner would sweet sleep take possession of my Senses, but methought I was conceived with a dreadful Dragon, which would be the cause of his Parents death."

These words struck such terour to his heart [that he answered:] "My most dear and beloved Lady . . . never shall rest take possession in my heart, nor sleep close up the closets of mine eyes, till I understand the signification of these thy troubled dreams."

Since Kalyb the enchantress might be able to interpret these visions, the husband set out to seek her; he went "without any company, except another Knight that bore under his Arm a white Lamb which they intended to offer unto the Enchantress."

In this mediaeval version of the legend of St. George, a lamb is killed as an offering to the enchantress whose aid is sought toward alleviating bad dreams, just as in earlier times a lamb was sacrificed when a lunatic sought healing at the shrine of Al-Khudr. This lamb is related to the paschal lamb sacrificed by the Children of Israel as a substitute for their own children when the angel of the Lord slew all the first-born of the land of Egypt. We recall also the substitution of a ram in the sacrifice of Isaac by his father, Abraham. The paschal lamb was adopted as the symbol of Christ sacrificed to redeem mankind, and in the Apocalypse those who were rescued from the accuser when the dragon had attempted to devour the newborn hero at his birth, were saved "by the blood of the Lamb." [10]

The story of St. George goes on to recount that presently the two knights came to a cave in the midst of a dark and

9. R. Johnson, *The Famous Historie of the Seaven Champions of Christendome*, pp. 3-4.

10. Exod. 12:3-14, 21-24; Gen. 22:1-14; I Cor. 5:7-8 ("Christ our passover is sacrificed for us: Therefore let us keep the feast"); Rev. 12:11.

dreadful wood, and having sacrificed the lamb, they drew near to the cave, "whose Gate of Entry was of Iron, whereon hung a Brazen Horn for them to wind that would speak with the Sorceress." A hollow voice then issued from the cave, saying:

> Sir Knight from whence thou cam'st return,
> Thou hast a Son most strangely born:
> A dragon that shall split in twain
> Thy Ladies Womb with extreme pain:
> A champion bold from thence shall spring,
> And practise many a wondrous thing.
> Return therefore, make no delay,
> For it is true what I here say.

This was repeated three times. The Lord High Steward listened in silence and in doubt, "but being persuaded by the other Knight not to move the impatience of Kalyb he rested satisfied with the Answer" and returned home. Here he found that his lady had died while giving birth to a son. The child had been stolen from her side and no one knew where he was. But strange tales were told of him: "Upon his breast nature had pictured the lively form of a Dragon, upon his right hand a blood red Cross, and his left Leg a Gold Garter." And his mother had called him George.

This story is similar to the Welsh legend of the birth of Pryderi, son of Pwyll, king of Annwfn, the underworld, and Rhiannon, whose voice was as the song of nightingales. On the night when Pryderi was born, six women were brought to watch by the mother and her infant son.

And the women slept, as did also Rhiannon, the mother of the boy. And the number of the women that were brought into the chamber was six. And they watched for a good portion of the night, and before midnight every one of them fell asleep, and towards break of day they awoke; and when they awoke, they looked where they had put the boy, and behold he was not there. "Oh," said one of the women, "the boy is lost!" . . .

Now at that time Teirnyon Twryv Vliant was Lord of Gwent Is Coed, and he was the best man in the world. And unto his house there belonged a mare, than which neither mare nor horse in the kingdom was more beautiful. And on the night of every first of

May she foaled, and no one ever knew what became of the colt. And one night Teirnyon talked with his wife:

"Wife," said he, "it is very simple of us that our mare should foal every year, and that we should have none of her colts."

So he caused the mare to be brought into a house, and he armed himself and began to watch that night. And in the beginning of the night, the mare foaled a large and beautiful colt. And it was standing in the place. And Teirnyon rose up and looked at the size of the colt, and as he did so he heard a great tumult, and after the tumult behold a great claw came through the window into the house, and it seized the colt by the mane. Then Teirnyon drew his sword, and struck off the arm at the elbow, so that a portion of the arm together with the colt was in the house with him. And then did he hear a tumult and wailing both at once. And he opened the door, and rushed out in the direction of the noise, and he could not see the cause of the tumult because of the darkness of the night, but he rushed after it and followed it. Then he remembered that he had left the door open, and he returned. And at the door behold there was an infant boy in swaddling-clothes wrapped around in a mantle of satin. And he took up the boy, and behold he was very strong for the age that he was of.[11]

Teirnyon and his wife kept the child till it was four years old; then, because of its resemblance to Pwyll, they realized that it must be his lost son, and so they returned the boy to his parents.

In similar fashion George was spirited away from his mother's side by "the fell Enchantress, who tendring him as the apple of her eye, appointed twelve sturdy Satyrs to attend his person." When he was fourteen years old George demanded to know who his parents were. Kalyb told him and also showed him how she was holding captive six of the bravest knights of the world. These were St. Denis of France, St. James of Spain, St. Anthony of Italy, St. Andrew of Scotland, St. Patrick of Ireland, and St. David of Wales. "And thou," she said, "art born to be the seventh, thy name S. George of England."

Then she gave him a horse, named Bayard, and a sword and suit of armour, saying:

11. Guest, "Pwyll Prince of Dyved," in *The Mabinogion*, pp. 26 f.

Thy Steed is of such force and invincible power that whilst thou art mounted on his back there can be no Knight in all the World so handy as to conquer thee: Thy Armour is of the purest Lydian Steel, that neither Weather can pierce, nor Battle-Ax Bruise: thy Sword, which is called ascalon, is made of the cyclops; that it will separate and cut the hardest Flint and hew in sunder the strongest Stone: for in the Pummel lies such precious Vertue that neither Treason, Witchcraft, nor any other violence can be offered thee, so long as thou wearest it.

Then, however, the sorceress tried to entice him into a magic rock in which she had imprisoned many "sucking babes." But he got the better of her and shut her into the rock instead. Then he freed the six imprisoned champions, and they all set off together on their adventures. Each of these heroes became a dragon killer in the course of time, but George remained their leader.

He journeyed to Egypt, where a powerful dragon had cast a strange horror over all the people. "True virgins" had been offered to appease him, and "now there is not left one true Virgin but the King's Daughter throughout Egypt." George immediately determined to fight this dragon and save the maiden. He rode into the valley where the dragon abode.

The dragon no sooner had sight of him, but he gave such a terrible Peal, as though it had thundered in the Elements: the bigness of the Dragon was fearful to behold, for betwixt his shoulders and his tail were fifty foot distance, his Scales glittering as bright as Silver, but far more hard than brass, his belly of the colour of Gold, but bigger than a Tun. Thus weltered he from his hideous Den, and so fiercely assailed the sturdy Champion with his burning Wings, that at the first Encounter he had almost felled him to the ground; but the Knight nimbly recovering himself gave the Dragon such a thrust with his Spear, that it shivered into a thousand pieces; whereat the furious Dragon so fiercely smote him with his venemous Tail, that down fell man and horse, in which fall two of S. George's ribs were sore bruised; but yet stepping backward, it was his chance to leap under an Orange Tree, which tree had such precious Virtue, that no venemous Worm durst come within the compass of the Branches, nor within seven foot thereof, where this valiant Knight rested himself until he had recovered his former strength; who no sooner feeling his spirits revived, but with an eager Courage smote the burning Dragon under his yellow burnished Belly, with his trusty Sword Ascalon, whereat came abundance of ugly Venome, his Armour burst in twain, and the good Knight fell into so grievous a dead swound that for a time he lay breathless; but yet having that good memory remaining that he tumbled under the Branches of the Orange Tree, in which place the Dragon could proffer him no farther violence. The fruit of the Tree being of such an excellent Vertue, that whosoever tasted thereof should presently be cured of all manner of Ordeales and Infirmities whatsoever. So it was the noble Champions good and happy fortune, a little to recover through the virtue of the Tree, and to espy an orange, which a little before had dropped down, and made his Divine Supplication to Heaven, that God would lend him (for his dear Sons sake) such strength and agility of Body, as to slay the furious and terrible Monster; which being done, with a bold and courageous heart, he smote the Dragon under the Wing, where it was tender without scale, whereby his good Sword Ascalon, with an easy passage, went to the very Hilt through both the Dragons Heart, Liver, Bone and Blood, whereout issued such an abundance of purple gore, that it turned the Grass which grew in the valley into crimson colour, and the Ground which was before parched through the burning stench of the Dragon, was now drenched with overmuch moisture proceeding from his Venemous Bowels, where at last through want of blood, and long continuance in fight, the Dragon yielded his Vital Spirits to the force of the conquoring Champion. . . . During this long and dangerous Combat, his trusty Steed lay altogether in a swoon without any moving, which caused the English Champion with all speed to crush the juyce of an Orange into his mouth; the vertue whereof presently expelled the venemous poysen, and recovered his former strength again.

George then returned to tell the princess of her rescue and later married her and took her back with him to England.

Such is the story of St. George, a man of miraculous birth, destined from the beginning to become a dragon slayer, marked with the sign of the dragon and the cross, brought up by a sorceress and armed with invincible weapons. The human hero has no such stigmata and no such supernatural aid, nor does he have assurance of victory before the trial begins. But George was hailed as "S. George of England" by the sorceress before ever he undertook his exploits. This incident conforms to the pattern for divine heroes; Buddha, for example, was saluted at his birth by celestial beings who acclaimed him saviour of the world; Jesus of Nazareth was hailed as "Son of God" at his baptism, which marked the beginning of his life as hero, and which was followed immediately by his encounter with Satan in the temptation in the wilderness. Satan is of course a personification of the same psychological forces that are represented as dragons in the St. George legend. In the Apocalypse, Satan is expressly called a dragon:

And there appeared a great wonder in heaven; a woman clothed with the sun, and the moon under her feet, and upon her head a crown of twelve stars: And she being with child cried, travailing in birth, and pained to be delivered. And there appeared another wonder in heaven; and behold a great red dragon, having seven heads and ten horns, and seven crowns upon his heads. And his tail drew the third part of the stars of heaven, and did cast them to the earth: and the dragon stood before the woman which was ready to be delivered, for to devour her child as soon as it was born. And she brought forth a man child, who was to rule all nations with a rod of iron: and her child was caught up unto God, and to his throne. And the woman fled into the wilderness, where she hath a place prepared of God, that they should feed her there a thousand two hundred and threescore days. And there was war in heaven: Michael and his angels fought against the dragon; and the dragon fought and his angels, and prevailed not; neither was their place found any more in heaven. And the great dragon was cast out, that old serpent, called the Devil, and Satan, which deceiveth the whole world. . . . And they overcame him by the blood of the lamb.[12]

This vision of St. John gives the salient points of the typical hero legend.[13] We have the child threatened at his birth by powers already fully developed while he is still a helpless in-

---

12. Rev. 12:1-11.
13. For a fuller interpretation of this material, see C. G. Jung, "Answer to Job," in *Psychology and Religion: West and East* (C.W. 11), pp. 438 ff.

fant; the flight of the mother to the wilderness; and the overcoming by means of the sacrifice of a lamb.

George was marked out in a similar way as being an extraordinary child. He was snatched away by evil powers immediately after his birth and was brought up by a sorceress, as other heroes were reared by Titans or kabiri or other nature spirits. Particularly interesting are the marks upon his person. The dragon on his breast marks him as having kinship with the dragon that he is to conquer. It is as though the dragon could be overcome only by the dragon's child. In some of the legends the hero has to taste of dragon's blood before he is strong enough to give the *coup de grâce* to his daemonic antagonist. Many indications suggest that there is an essential kinship between the dragon and the dragon slayer; for the dragon power is positive as well as negative. The renegade in man is closely related in its nature to the slothful aspect of the dragon, while the forward-going, heroic element in him is more nearly related to the energy of the dragon. Thus the human being who has conquered the dragon and assimilated its power through tasting its blood or eating its heart becomes a superman. He transcends the consciousness and therefore the powers of his contemporaries, because he has to this extent overcome the unconscious, which previously functioned, as it were, entirely outside the human psyche. Through his exploit, however, a further area of psychic life is brought within human range, thus enlarging the sphere of man's conscious control.

This is only one of many instances in which the hero is said to be akin to the dragon he overcomes. For instance, he is frequently said to have snake's eyes, and the magician or medicine man, whose task it is to control and exorcize the denizens of the daemonic world, also acquires snake's eyes as a result of the experiences by which he is made into a magician. For in many primitive tribes the discipline and ordeals prescribed for his training are so severe that they drive the candidate to the borderline of insanity. The man who is to exercise power over the daemons must himself be touched by the daemonic, and ever after there is something strange and glistening in his glance that is described as snakelike. This is a quality frequently seen in the eyes of persons who have been overwhelmed by the unconscious. They see, but their eyes give no human response.

A modern woman, whose intuitive perception of the unconscious brought her very close to that strange and incomprehensible realm, once dreamed that a man of her acquaintance was claiming to be a magician, and that to prove his power he was about to produce a vast and devastating flood in the Himalayas. She and all the inhabitants of the valley were terribly alarmed and started to flee. When she reached the other side of the valley, she looked back and saw the man sitting like a huge Buddha on a mountain on the farther side of the valley. At this she recollected herself and thought: "If he is really a magician he will be able to bring about this terrible disaster and will do so regardless of the human suffering it will involve. In that case he will have snake's eyes; but if his eyes are human, then this is only an idle boast and nothing will happen."

So she got a telescope and looked at his eyes, and to her great relief she found that they were "not quite" snake's eyes. When the flood began she knew therefore that it would only irrigate the valley and not inundate it. Then she found herself wading in a river that rose up to her knees but did not drown her. This dream had a prognostic significance in regard to the outcome of the case, for it indicated that the danger of invasion from the unconscious would pass without a flood. Clearly also the man of the dream stood for the hero who bears the equivocal mark of the serpent: he might cause destruction, or he might prove to be the very defender who would subdue the serpent-dragon and release the fertilizing streams that it forever guards; this would mean that the power of the unconscious would be brought into such a relation to consciousness that it could be used creatively.

There are many other instances demonstrating the existence of a relationship between the hero and the serpent. For example, in ancient Greece, when the spirit of a dead hero was to be consulted, certain mantic rites were performed at his grave. It was believed that his soul would come forth in the

form of a snake, to which the suppliants would offer a bowl
of milk, and when the hero in this guise had drunk he would
answer the questions put to him.[14]

An anonymous sect of Gnostics, whose ideas are preserved
in the writings of Irenaeus,[15] taught that the serpent in the
garden of Eden was actually the Son of God, who came to
earth to lead men out of their condition of unconsciousness
and to make them more aware, so that they might be free.
This teaching seems to be substantiated in our canonical scriptures by the passage in which Christ compared himself to the

Fig. 9. Snake as the Soul of the Dead Hero

serpent that Moses lifted up in the wilderness,[16] obviously referring to his own crucifixion, which he foresaw would have
a healing effect on mankind, just as the brazen serpent Moses
made healed the people who had been bitten by poisonous
snakes.

The theme of a serpent hanging on a cross is also to be
found in mediaeval alchemy. Nicolas Flamel (1330-1418)
speaks of such a figure in his description of an ancient book
that he is reputed to have found as a young man. This book
contained both writing and pictures, one of which represented,
as he says, "a Crosse where a Serpent was crucified." This is

14. J. Harrison, *Prologomena to the Study of Greek Religion*, pp. 325,
352, and see figure 9.
15. G. R. S. Mead, *Fragments of a Faith Forgotten*, pp. 189 f.
16. John 3:14.

reproduced in figure 10.[17] A similar situation is depicted in the drawing by a modern woman, in figure 11, where a serpent is seen sacrificed on a vine-covered cross. This would mean that her instinctuality in its cold-blooded form is sacrificed—not repressed—but sacrificed, so that it might live again in a new form, redeemed through its ritual death. And here it should be recalled that, before Jesus said "I am the vine" and later declared that the wine of the sacrament was his own blood, Dionysos had been known as God of the Vine, whose spirit gave its intoxicating power to the juice of the grapes. So when the cross on which the snake is hung is covered with vine leaves it would indicate that the sacrifice of the auto-erotic aspect of the instincts is thereby healed, or transformed into the emotion of love.

There is also a Matsys painting of St. John carrying in one hand a chalice in which there is a small dragon, and with the other hand making the sign of the cross over it.[18] Here obviously the dragon represents the spirit of Christ, for the wine, transformed by the mystery of the Eucharist into the blood of Christ, is the symbol of the life or spirit of the Redeemer. A similar motif is seen in plate XI, where St. John holds a chalice, over which hangs a snake, clearly representing the "spirit" in the consecrated wine.

To return to St. George, the first danger he encountered was the attempt of the sorceress to entomb him in the rock cave, and his first heroic act was to overcome this powerful foster mother who tried thus to enchant him. This is always the first task of the potential hero, who must free himself from the mother before he can set out to enlarge the field of human endeavour, by meeting and overcoming his particular dragon.

The dragon, we are told, was covered with metal scales; this recalls the metallic dragons of alchemical writings, in which the contents of the unconscious are symbolized as mercury,

17. A. E. Waite, *Lives of the Alchemystical Philosophers* (1858), quoted in J. Read, *Prelude to Chemistry*, p. 60.

18. See plate X, and also Jung, *Symbols of Transformation* (C.W. 5), "The Dual Mother," where a fuller discussion of this whole subject may be found.

Fig. 10. The Serpent on the Cross (after Nicolas Flamel)

Fig. 11. The Serpent on the Cross (modern drawing)

lead, copper, etc. The monster's burning wings and venomous tail were so powerful that the hero was unhorsed, his magic spear was broken and his armour burst asunder. It seems that the dragon had knowledge of the properties of these magic gifts, for in his assault upon the hero he always attacked in such a way as to void their protection. The hero could not be hurt when mounted on his horse, so he was first unhorsed; his armour could not be pierced by any weapon, so it was shattered by venom.

St. George would have been overcome by these tactics had it not happened that an orange tree with life-giving powers was growing near by. This too is typical. It is just in that place where the venom of death threatens most direly that the life-giving plant appears. The orange, the golden fruit resembling the sun, is symbolic of consciousness. In one of the Gnostic sects the communion was celebrated with another sunlike fruit, the melon. This tree also recalls the tree of life growing beside the river in the New Jerusalem; it bears a different fruit every month and its leaves are for the healing of the nations. The tree of life in the garden of Eden also conferred immortality and therefore invulnerability. When St. George ate of the oranges he was healed of the wounds inflicted by the dragon—meaning that an access of consciousness repaired the damage suffered by the personality under the onslaught of the daemonic forces of the unconscious. A charming touch is given to the story by the fact that George gave an orange to his horse, so that it too was healed of its wounds. Not only is the conscious side of the hero victorious, but his animal instinct also, his libido, is restored to its full vigour after the exhausting struggle.

In spite of the shifting luck of the battle, it was obvious from the first that the dragon was doomed, for this combat was a drama, a ritual action, in which the characters play an ordained or archetypal role, while the humanness of the champion was in abeyance. As to what St. George was in himself, the nature of his experience as a man, all clue has disappeared. He may have belonged originally to the second hero class, but as we know him in these legends he is resplendent in his saintliness and heroic quality. His valour has become proverbial, and his deeds inspire courage in all his followers. He has become the patron saint of England, as the sorceress foretold. His cross, the square red emblem on a white ground, is combined with the white cross of St. Andrew of Scotland and the red cross of St. Patrick of Ireland to form the triple cross of the Union Jack.

St. George is depicted on the sovereign and the crown, coins of the British realm, each of which bears a symbolic name. As the contest is shown in these designs, it is obvious that the dragon does not have a chance. An amusing anecdote illustrates the attitude of the unlettered folk of a generation ago in England towards these symbolic forms. An old Devonshire man, keeper of a toll-bridge, was offered a crown in payment of the toll. He turned the coin over and looked at the picture on the reverse side, saying: "St. Garge and the dragon! I read about that in a buke. A wouldn't 'v bin frightened of un; 'er was no but a fish."

"Oh," the traveller replied, "but it was a very terrible fish. Why, fire came out of its nostrils."

"I do not care," said the old man, "I wouldn't 'v been frightened of un—why, 'er couldn't get out of the water with a tail like that!"

What is this tail that holds the dragon down in the water? The dragon, as indicated above, is nature itself, the power of primordial life stuff, the blind urge of living matter that has not yet been "psychized," to use Jung's term. When this symbol appears in the dreams or phantasies of a modern person, or when some problem or situation in the outer world looms before him huge and menacing like a veritable dragon, it means that the life energies within his psyche are stirring. But these ancient instinctual forces have very deep roots. They have functioned in us and in our ancestors from the beginning of life on the earth, compelling the generations to fight for food and shelter and a chance for reproduction against all the hazards and hardships of ruthless nature. These dragons, with their long tails reaching back to the beginnings of life on earth, are tenacious of being—but of being in the old pattern, not in the new. Consciousness to them is anathema, for consciousness is set against the unconsciousness of natural life; consciousness seeks after spirit, understanding; the dragons cling to matter.

And so it is said that when the hero attacks the dragon from in front, he must beware of the tail, for the dragon will swing it around and sting him from behind.[19] The hero then falls over backwards—as it were, into an opposite attitude. How often do we see this happening! If a man makes a direct attack on his particular dragon—inertia, for example—there is grave danger that he will become dominating, aggressive, egotistic, driven by a very daemon of work, so that his spirit is just as surely killed by compulsive activity as it might otherwise have been by laziness. That is, he has been poisoned by the venom of his foe. For the dragon always represents a pair of opposites. The hero can be overcome by the dragon's fiery breath, or, in guarding himself from this danger, he may be overwhelmed by a dose of the dragon poison from behind. In either case the dragon draws its victim slowly but surely down to oblivion, back into unconsciousness. At this crucial point the orange, bestowing the life-giving force of the sun—consciousness—is invaluable.

St. George and the other dragon slayers braved these perils and by their acts of aggressive heroism not only overcame their own particular dragons, so saving themselves from annihilation, but in addition wrested a treasure from the dragon's hoard. Thus lands that had been under its domination were opened up for the pioneers of a coming age: a new phase of culture was initiated. These conquests could with relative ease be made a permanent heritage for mankind by other, lesser men who could follow where the heroes had opened the way: by walking in their steps and following their example, these smaller persons could become heroes by proxy, as it were.

The new lands represent an aspect of life that previously had functioned only autonomously and that had been experi-

19. Cf. Baynes, *Mythology of the Soul*, pp. 315 ff., where a modern illustration of this situation is given, together with an exhaustive discussion of the problem.

enced only passively. The values it contained came to man purely as a gift of the gods; he could not augment them by his own effort, and if they were withheld he could but endure the deprivation as best he might. He was a helpless puppet of natural forces that might be kind or cruel, or, more accurately, utterly indifferent to his personal interests and welfare. The same complete helplessness prevailed where the dangers of the unknown were concerned. But when the land was freed from the control of the dragon by the exploits of a hero, it was made available for all men to explore and to develop by conscious effort and ingenuity.

The symbol picture is clear enough. In psychological terms it means that where we are unconscious we are merely puppets of the nonpersonal forces of nature, which act in the inner world of the psyche just as they do in the outer world of objective reality. For example, it is notorious that primitive tribes are fickle and unreliable in their allegiances. They may swear eternal friendship one day and on the next, because of some quite unaccountable change of mood, may fall upon their erstwhile blood brothers and treacherously destroy them. Even among Western peoples examples of a similar instability are not far to seek. In the realm of feeling particularly, Western man is apt to be the puppet of his unconscious moods. The primitive has to await the coming of his thoughts as well as of his feelings; the civilized person can usually attend to a given subject of thought on demand. Few persons, however, are even aware that it is possible to summon feeling at will, and furthermore to learn to feel correctly about a situation, instead of merely reflecting in one's feeling judgments an undifferentiated agglomeration of personal reactions.

For instance, a woman is in the midst of preserve making; perhaps her jelly has reached the critical moment, so that it cannot be left without risk of spoiling, when her telephone rings. No matter what the communication may be that so peremptorily demands her attention, her spontaneous reaction is apt to be one of irritation, and her tendency is to say no to the telephoned request, even though she may hide her feelings under a mask of good manners. This type of reaction is so common that it is a matter of everyday diplomacy to wait for a "good moment" before broaching a question of importance, especially to one who is known to be irascible, for fear that the request may be judged subjectively on the basis of the listener's immediate feelings rather than objectively on its merits.

In these cases the realm of feeling is obviously not really free. The dragon of unconsciousness still rules there, in greater or lesser measure. But so general is the condition that few people realize how unfree they are in this respect—a state of affairs comparable to that in the legends when the dragons sleep and the human beings make shift to live in their own restricted domain. But when a life situation arises in which such an unconscious way of reacting will no longer suffice, because it threatens some real value, there comes a challenge to wage war on the dragon of unconsciousness and establish conscious control over reactions that till then have been autonomous and therefore auto-erotic.

Such a situation not infrequently arises when a man who has allowed his feeling function to remain unconscious falls in love and marries. Then, instead of being able to get along without developed feeling, as perhaps he has been able to do in his business, possibly by dint of having a secretary to humour his whims and adjust things to his moods, he finds himself confronted with a woman who requires a real reaction, an attitude springing from his true relation to the subject under discussion and dependable even in face of difficulties. If he gives a response determined only by his subjective state, misunderstandings and difficulties will surely arise, and no real relationship can be worked out between the two persons. When it becomes necessary for him to clarify his reaction, commit himself to a taken attitude, and he does not find himself in the right mood to do so, even though a decision is imperative, his feeling, represented by the anima, withdraws from the situation, and he just feels blank. When his wife challenges him, seeking a genuine reaction, he feels pushed or pursued. The reply he now gives to her questioning is quite likely to be a reaction to this sense of being pushed—a reaction that becomes more and more compulsive and is less and less under his conscious control, the more she presses for a decision. In terms of the myth, the maiden, the anima, is given over to the power of the dragon, and the situation goes from bad to worse.

When the anima is lost in this way, the man may find himself incapable of any articulate response and may simply fall into a mood of black despair whenever he is confronted with a question that demands a feeling reaction. If he gives way to these moods or allows them to become still more autonomous, producing actual illness—headaches, indigestion, or the like— it means that he is following the renegade tendency in himself, hoping, albeit unconsciously, to return to that blissful state of infancy in which a beneficent fate, an all-loving mother, arranged matters for his comfort and well-being without his having to move a finger to help himself.

Perhaps his wife consents to play the mother role, and possibly this works for a while. But life is no kindly mother, and sooner or later fate forces the issue. For the wife cannot permanently play the part of providence. She too is a human being. Perhaps her own health breaks down under the strain of carrying a double load of adult responsibility. Something within her may eventually rebel at being God to a childish husband. Or possibly some crisis arises that threatens her adaptation as well as his, and it becomes obvious that the dragon is about to devour all they hold dear in life.

Under such conditions the situation can be saved only if the man is able to undertake a heroic quest and redeem his lost soul, the anima. It was in such a desperate situation that St. George set forth to conquer the dragon that held Egypt in thrall and to rescue the princess from her dire fate. It is perhaps worth noting that to the people of the Middle Ages, Egypt was on the one hand the land of magic power and on the other a byword for lust and self-indulgence. Thus the legend is an allegory of the anima captured by the dragon of greed or auto-erotism. In our example the husband is childishly auto-erotic because his anima has not been differentiated from instinctive self-indulgence; and so it is still in the custody of the dragon of selfishness. St. George attacked the dragon and overcame it. Analogously it is recognized in our civilization that a man and woman ought to be able to deal with emotional problems without being swamped by selfish or auto-erotic compulsions. The injunction, "Do unto others as ye would that they should do unto you," represents this rather elementary first step in feeling culture. It is expected of us, and we expect it of ourselves, that the fair land of human relationship should be available to us. But we forget that the dragons of self-indulgence always retake land that is not cultivated, and when an individual hopes that someone will tend his emotional needs as a mother tends a child, he leaves the field of relationship open to the dragon of self-love.

The individual concerned probably has not the slightest inkling that this is what he is doing. He has merely left a whole realm of life to itself, on the assumption that the conditions of childhood will persist throughout life, and before he knows it he is assailed by one of the dragons of the unconscious, who, wily beasts that they are, often appear in disguise and fall upon a man without warning. They give no alarm but creep upon him insidiously. They never announce themselves by saying, "I'm the dragon that St. George slew," or "I'm the demon overcome by St. Michael." And so, as they are not recognized, their intended victims do not call upon the saints for aid. To put it in psychological terms, it is the unawareness of danger that constitutes the greatest threat to one who is assailed by an uprush of primitive libido from the unconscious. If he could see the threat or temptation clearly enough to call it by its true name, half the battle would be won; for such an honest naming of the peril acts like a clarion call summoning all the forces of consciousness to the contest. This is the modern equivalent of calling on the saints for aid; by such an act of conscious discrimination one summons the hero, the valiant Champion of the Light, to give help against the renegade, who always seeks to conceal himself in the shadowy land of unconsciousness.

Not infrequently, when an individual is in danger of falling prey to unconscious psychic elements, the delicate balance between sanity and insanity depends on whether he can gain and hold on to insight into his condition. His physician has the difficult task of deciding whether or not to press him to recognize that his strange ideas and feelings are of subjective origin. If the patient can grasp this, he turns his face towards sanity. But these contents of the unconscious are so remote from his own conception of himself that he usually experiences them as though they were objective, coming into his consciousness from outside—that is, as though they originated in the machinations of other persons or in an uncanny world of spirits.

For this reason there is always a grave risk that if the physician calls these projected and unassimilable elements by their rightful names he may cause a panic, and the attempt to reinforce the patient's conscious standpoint and sanity may precipitate the final plunge into the maelstrom of the unconscious that it was designed to prevent. If, however, the manoeuvre is successful, and the patient comes to recognize his strange ideas as phantasy or illusion, as projections that distort his understanding of the world about him, he will not become insane, even though the illusion, the projected material, remains to be dealt with. He will recognize that it is a nonpersonal power of the unconscious that is assailing him—a dragon to be fought on the subjective plane and not an objective reality to be combated by overt action.

This situation is obvious in the case of insane persons. When for instance a paranoid patient makes a murderous attack on his wife or on someone else in his circle, the onlooker is aware that the man's suspicion and hatred are the result of a delusion and that his action is evidence of the unbalanced condition of his mind. But it is not so easy to recognize in one's own case, when one is beset by unreasonable resentments towards a loved companion, or by revengeful feelings over imaginary slights, that one is oneself suffering from similar illusions. The blindness to one's own condition may be even greater than this statement of the situation indicates, for the words "unreasonable" and "imaginary" both imply insight. Many persons who feel themselves to be injured or misunderstood are actually obsessed as much by the "reasons" for their hostile feelings as by hostility and resentment. Such reasons are nothing more than rationalizations, which are in themselves evidence of a predominance of unconscious functioning.

In a woman, the rationalizations usually occur in the form of the so-called "ten thousand reasons" produced by the animus from the storehouse of the age-old experience of all possible causes of anger, hatred, and enmity. In a man, the rationalizations will occur in the form of the "ten thousand resentments." The reasons for his anger reflect not logical thoughts so much as reactions due to frustration of unconscious feeling expectations that he does not voice to himself and can hardly bring sufficiently into consciousness to express when questioned. This is because the anima has remained buried in the womb of the mother and gives him understanding of the feeling world only in terms of a personal comfort provided "of course"—unasked and without obligation.

Because the expectations of such an unconscious person do not correspond with the reality of human experience, they are naturally doomed to disappointment. Inevitably life itself sooner or later frustrates them. Usually this comes about through impact with some other human being, who fails to fulfill the unexpressed desires. Then all the individual's negative feelings, which are the other side of the unconscious demand that life give him what he wants, settle upon this unfortunate other being as a sort of scapegoat or bête noire whose every act and look are interpreted as hostile or dangerous. The term bête noire is surely a recognition in popular speech of the fact that the evil characteristics really emanate from the accuser: they are in fact projections. It is his own "black beast" that a man sees mirrored in one who irritates him so especially.

In Evans-Wentz's *Tibetan Book of the Dead*, a translation of an eighth-century text of Mahayana Buddhism, there is a passage that throws a very interesting light on this problem. It sets forth instructions for a dying man concerning the experiences he will meet with after his soul leaves the body. It tells him how to behave in the bardo, the realm intermediate between this life and the next. His reactions to the situations he meets there will determine whether his soul is to be reborn on earth or in one of the heaven or hell worlds. In this way, he becomes as it were his own judge after death—from the psychological point of view, a most highly developed conception.

At one stage of his journey he will meet the "wrathful deities," who will appear as terrifying demons of lust, anger, and hatred. The instruction given him is as follows: "O nobly born, whatever fearful or terrifying visions thou mayest see, recognize them to be thine own thought-forms." [20] If he is able to overcome his fear and achieve this degree of insight, he will be released from their power. Their menacing forms will melt away, and he will be free to pass on to the next ordeal. This means that as soon as man becomes conscious of the fact that the devils who appear to be external are really just reflections of the unrecognized and threatening nonpersonal forces operating within his own psyche, he is freed from their power. A similar instruction is given in regard to the beneficent deities who will likewise be encountered in the course of the journey through the bardo. This clearly shows that man may no more remain under the spell of the good than of the evil aspect of the daemonic powers. He must recognize both as his "own thought-forms," if he is to be freed from their domination.

Unfortunately, however, we are given to understand that many departed souls cannot meet this ordeal successfully. Perhaps it requires a hero with the valour of a St. George to do so unaided. However, as has been said, heroes are of two types. In addition to the saintly or divine figures that come to rescue mankind, there is the ordinary, mortal man who is compelled, often against his will, to undertake a campaign against one of the dragon foes of progress. Such a one was Jonah.

The story is told in the Bible as if it were purely history, and, just as in the case of the accounts of St. George, it is impossible at this distance in time to determine what part of it is fact and what part legend. From the point of view of the psychologist, the distinction is not as essential as it is for the historian, for the story surely portrays the inner experience of its author and in all probability also the typical experience of the generation to which he belonged. Reading between the

20. W. Y. Evans-Wentz, *The Tibetan Book of the Dead*, p. 147.

lines, we see that Jonah was no outstanding figure in his environment. He is described as just a commonplace small citizen, a timid man, not very highly thought of by his neighbours. Apparently he had no regular occupation, and so fell to brooding and to thinking about how the times were out of joint. And the voice of the Lord came to him, as it often does, the world over, to those who meditate instead of acting. It told him to go to Nineveh, the capital city, and preach against its people because of their wicked ways. But Jonah said to himself that he was only a little man, by no means able to assume such a difficult and important mission, and that surely his inner voice had made a mistake. Only a superiority complex could account for the idea that he should undertake anything so conspicuous. How could he, a small-town man, and unlettered, preach to all those important people and hope to get a hearing? And many other objections and excuses doubtless crowded into his mind.

However, as the voice was urgent, he concluded that he really was intended to accept some sort of mission, though naturally nothing so big or so important as going to Nineveh. So he went to the port and took the first ship that was sailing—it happened to be going to Tarshish—thinking that he could start a revival there instead. For Tarshish was a much more modest place; besides, it was overseas, and as he was unknown there none of his friends would be likely to hear about it even if he failed, as he felt he well might, and so he would not be ridiculed and made to look like a fool. Then the storm came up and he was ignominiously thrown into the sea to appease the wrath of the elements. That is, the unconscious would not tolerate his cowardly retreat; his rejection of the inner command caused a commotion in the depths of his own unconscious that everyone near him could see. His cowardice was exposed and he was cast out from among his fellows. But now comes the strange part, for final escape was denied him. God had already prepared a great fish—as though in the unconscious it was foreknown what course he would take, and preparations had been made to meet the situation—and so he did not die but was swallowed by the "dragon" of the sea.

A fourteenth-century alliterative poem describes Jonah's plight in touchingly picturesque language:

As a mote in at a Minster door, so mighty was its jaws,
Jonah enters by the gills, through slime and gore;
he reeled in through a gullet, that seemed to him a road,
tumbling about, aye, head over heels,
till he staggers to a place as broad as a hall;
then he fixes his feet there and gropes all about
and stands up in its belly that stank as the devil;
in sorry plight there, 'mid grease that savoured as hell
his bower was arrayed who would fain risk no ill.
Then he lurks there and seeks in each nook of the navel
the best sheltered spot, yet nowhere he finds
rest or recovery, but filthy mire
wherever he goes; but God is ever dear;
and he tarried at length and called to the Prince.

.   .   .   .

Then he reached a nook and held himself there,
where no foul filth cumbered him about.
He sat there as safe, save for darkness alone,
As in the boat's stern, where he had slept ere.
Thus in the beast's bowel, he abides there alive,
Three days and three nights, thinking aye on the Lord,
His might and his mercy and his measure eke;
Now he knows Him in woe, who would not in weal.[21]

Jonah, falling into the vast sea of the unconscious, was swallowed up. And in that period of complete solitude and introversion, when there seemed no escape from his horrible doom, he thought over his foolish rebellion and repented. Naturally, there was no one to talk to except for his inner voice, and his conversation with this other within him changed his whole attitude to life. Meanwhile the whale swam slowly to land and unceremoniously vomited him ashore. Here we see that Jonah's refusal to follow the voice from within left him completely at the mercy of the unconscious. After that he could only suffer his fate. Such is man's vaunted freedom and hybris. Unless he accepts his own inner guidance, he becomes

21. Cf. *Patience*, pt. III, in R. Morris, ed., *Early English Alliterative Poems*, p. 100.

a mere puppet of fate. If he sets himself up against the inner voice, asserting that he is free to choose what he wants, he inevitably becomes the victim of the dragon. Only when he voluntarily chooses that which he inexorably must do, has he any free will at all. For the command from within is his own inner law, and he disobeys it at his peril. So Jonah got dried out on the shore and started off for Nineveh. That is not the end of the story, but we have as much of it as concerns us here.

This tale of Jonah is a very instructive myth. Translating it into psychological terms, we see that life challenged Jonah with a task, represented by the call to go to Nineveh. This he undoubtedly should have attempted, but he was afraid of the responsibility involved, and being headstrong and self-willed, he said that he would choose his own task. His refusal to accept life on the terms offered him caused a disturbance in his unconscious, a storm. This means that when he started out to take up the self-chosen work instead of the job he should have shouldered, he fell into such conflict, and acted in so unbalanced and unadapted a fashion, that everyone noticed it. In fact, his attitude jeopardized the whole enterprise. So his companions cast him into the sea, having first consulted the unconscious by throwing lots. This would be equivalent to the modern step of calling in a psychiatrist to interpret the dreams of one who is acting strangely or to carry out psychological tests before taking action in the case. The act of casting him into the sea would be the equivalent of sending him to a mental hospital; he would disappear from society, to experience in solitude the immersion in the unconscious, from which he might never return.

In interpreting the material in this way, I am taking Jonah's companions quite literally as the actual persons close to the patient; but there is another way in which they can be understood, namely, as the parts of the psyche not directly affected by the renegade factors that have tried to take over complete control. Under this assumption the interpretation would be that at the point in the story when the companions threw Jonah out, a decisive split occurred in his psyche. This is the moment at which the neurotic conflict goes over into the schizophrenic state, and the cast-off part of the psyche falls into the ocean of the unconscious. This is the critical change that Jung speaks of as the primary symptom of the psychosis:

The real trouble begins with the disintegration of the personality and the divestment of the ego-complex of its habitual supremacy. . . . It is as if the very foundations of the psyche were giving way, as if an explosion or an earthquake were tearing asunder the structure of a normally built house.[22]

In our legend Jonah represents the ego complex, and the crowd of companions represents the multiplicity of habitual reactions that go on autonomously without the direction of consciousness. When Jonah was thrown into the sea—that is, when the ego lost control—these "companions" took over. Jonah disappeared from sight in the ocean or, psychologically speaking, in the incipient schizophrenia, or splitting of the psyche, the conscious personality vanished.

But, we are told, God had prepared a great fish that swallowed him up. That is, he went into a profound introversion; this was not willed, in a conscious attempt to face and struggle with the problem; it was forced upon him by his breakdown, and for this reason it is better called a regression.

Jonah's regression threatened to take him right back into the chaos of undifferentiated beginnings (the ocean); but before this point was reached it was checked by the intervention of the fish-dragon so providentially at hand. Jonah's regression took him into the great monster's belly—a symbol of the womb—where he found the shelter of the unborn state. The fish-dragon plays a dual role in the drama, for while it swallows up Jonah, it also saves him from drowning. This is characteristic of the mother archetype.[23]

When he found himself trapped in the belly of the whale, however, Jonah began to call upon God. This is evidence that he had not completely regressed into chaos, for in his distress his relation to the unconscious reasserted itself. When an individual suffers a psychological split, he cannot assert himself

22. Jung, "On the Psychogenesis of Schizophrenia," in *The Psychogenesis of Mental Disease* (C.W. 3), p. 240.
23. Jung, *Symbols of Transformation.* Cf. chap. vii, "The Dual Mother."

against the swirling currents in which he is tossed about help-lessly; still less can he do so if his ego consciousness is, as it were, dissolved. If, however, he can feel himself as an entity over against the chaos of the waters, there is at least a chance that he may still be rescued. This Jonah was able to do. In his isolation and imprisonment he called upon God, and in the darkness he saw the light. In this story of the hero and the dragon the light symbolizes a moral or spiritual insight. For the Jews, of whose mythological store it forms a part, had a developed moral consciousness at a time when their neighbours could perceive their psychological experiences only in terms of projections, as doings of the gods. Thus it is more usually related that the hero, having been swallowed by the dragon, makes a fire in its belly, or finds that the dragon's heart is on fire; or it is so hot inside the monster that the hero's hair is ablaze when he emerges. That is, out of the heat, the emotion of the experience within—out of madness—light or insight is created.

The theme of the light that is found in the darkness forms a familiar mystery teaching. In the Scriptures we read of "the light which shone in the darkness." "They that walk in darkness shall see a great light." These are allegories of the spirit that is inherent in matter. As is recorded in Genesis, when God had created man's physical body he breathed into him the breath of life, namely, his own spirit.

It is customary among us to think of matter and spirit as antithetical. Spirit or consciousness is considered to be entirely separate from matter: the two are thought of as complements, as opposites, eternally at war. But the mystery teachings of many religions and philosophies state that it is in matter that spirit is to be found. According to alchemistic teaching, it is the *lumen naturae* hidden within the stone, or the image of the sun buried in the centre of the earth. Therefore the philoso-pher's gold, which is the sun's reflection, namely, the light of consciousness, is to be found inside the earth's substance. The earth is taken to correspond to the body; therefore the teach-ing is that the spirit, the light, actually inheres in the body.

This is an extremely important and interesting point of

view and a very modern one, though it runs counter to the generally accepted idea, namely, that the body is void of spirit, which shines upon it from without or is "inspired," breathed, into it from on high. In a similar way it is usually assumed that a patient who is mentally ill has unhealthy ideas in him and can be cured only by getting away from himself, by being distracted; he is urged not to be so "morbidly introverted" or is persuaded that he will be cured by the instillation of some spirit or idea that is to come from some external source. However, modern psychotherapeutic experience, especially as based on depth psychology, corroborates the mystery teaching outlined above. It is well recognized today that the insight or guidance needed to bring the schizophrenic patient back to the world of reality must come from within his own psyche; it cannot be imparted from without. No matter how clearly the physician understands what is happening, he cannot give the patient his insight. The latter has to find his own ground of understanding; the most the physician can do is to guide and encourage him on his inner journey, helping him to comprehend the experiences through which he is passing, until of itself the light dawns upon him, often in a way quite unforeseen by his doctor.

Thus the myth relates that Jonah's recovery and return to the world of men was not his own doing, nor was it brought about by human aid, for he was taken to shore by the forces of nature, the great dragon that had swallowed him and that carried him for the appointed three days and three nights of the undersea journey and deposited him by a strange new birth upon the land.

In the Persian miniature reproduced in plate XII, Jonah is seen emerging from the mouth of the whale. He is naked, with his knees drawn up in the foetal position, so that it is obviously a birth that is intended. But as he is fully bearded it cannot be the birth of an infant, but must be rather the rebirth of an adult man. He is greeted by an angel, who offers him a new robe. The gift of a new robe is one of the regular features of rebirth and initiation rituals, and it symbolizes the completely new attitude and adaptation needed by the newly born one.

An experience such as this is encountered by all who undertake the "night sea journey" through the unconscious. The prolonged introversion, represented by the three days and three nights lost in the abyss, not only in the Jonah story, but also in the descent of Christ to the underworld after the crucifixion, are lived symbolically. There the shadow qualities are encountered and the dragon that must be overcome, and this is followed by a rebirth. A new adaptation, a new garment, almost a new skin, become necessary to meet the world, which has taken on an entirely new aspect as a result of the change the individual has undergone.

This sequence of events occurs regularly during psychological analysis, as part of the transformation process. But when an individual becomes alienated from himself, as Jonah obviously did, and a pathological introversion sets in, there is little that friends or even the physician can do to help. He can perhaps suggest the attitude that will bring the patient back into relation with his inner voice; for the rest he can merely watch the stages of the regression, hoping that the sufferer will hear the inner voice in time to allow of his return to the world of men. If, however, the individual is not completely alienated—that is, if he is only threatened by an invasion of dynamic material from the unconscious—he may be able to retain his contact with reality, even though his attention is largely withdrawn from it. In these cases the psychologically trained physician can obviously do much more to help.

The question whether an invasion of strange material from the unconscious is to be considered as the sign of a lowering of the threshold of consciousness within normal limits—an *abaissement du niveau mental*—or of schizophrenia, is often difficult to decide. The difference between these conditions is largely a matter of degree. Some individuals remain so fluid and unformed that they can stand an amount of inner chaos that would drive a more conscious person crazy. Thus for any given person sanity depends on not falling below his own level of integration—a point overlooked when insanity is described as "going over the border," as though there were a definite, fixed boundary between mental health and mental sickness.

In true schizophrenia, however, the material presented is more disorganized and far more archaic than it is in neurosis or in a temporary invasion from the unconscious. But the differentiation must be based not primarily on the nature of the material, but on the extent of the patient's insight into his condition, and on the question of his ability to take the problem underlying his illness as a moral one, instead of being fascinated and swamped by his strange experiences. The attitude required can be described only as one of inner morality or integrity—loyalty to the law of his own being. This obviously has little relation to the collective morality, which depends on conformity to an outer standard. Indeed, acceptance of the problem as a moral dilemma usually involves a separation from the accepted moral code, for elements discarded under the group sanctions have become activated in the individual and must be recognized; further, an attempt must be made to assimilate them into the totality of the psyche.

Whenever there is an upsurge of highly activated unadapted material into consciousness, the task of assimilation becomes urgent. This holds true whether the new material is valuable, creative stuff or merely archaic phantasy that bespeaks more a morbid exuberance than a prolific creativity. The assimilation of the new material demands a fresh standpoint, which implies a recognition of the relativity of all former judgments. What was formerly considered unqualifiedly good must now be judged in the light of the new and enlarged understanding; the same must be done with that which has been considered bad. If the work of assimilation cannot be accomplished, the effect of the uprush of new and strange material may be to unseat the judgment, or the centre of equilibrium may be displaced, so that the whole psyche suffers such a disorganization that the very structure of the personality may be broken up and its elements dispersed in the shifting currents of the collective unconscious.

The first powers to be lost when there is a lowering of the level of consciousness are those last attained in the process of development, namely, the higher critical and moral functions of the personality. A similar deterioration of consciousness can be observed whenever the threshold is lowered by exhaustion or the use of depressant drugs. The critical judgment is impaired and good taste and the finer feeling discriminations are blunted long before control of the motor functions is lost.

These considerations raise a question regarding the relation of insanity to the ethical or moral problems of the individual. Persons who are deliberately immoral, either by conscious choice or because of an innate lack of discrimination, do not as a rule become insane. If, however, a conflict arises within an individual because certain of his actions or attitudes do not accord with the rest of his psychology, his realization of his lack of integrity may be sufficiently disturbing to cause a neurosis; on the other hand, if the conflict remains relatively unconscious, so that its effects all occur below the surface, the more serious illness, schizophrenia, may result.

When we approach the problem from the other end, asking whether it may not be said that the crux of insanity in general is an unsolved moral conflict, the considerations become highly involved and difficult, because so many factors enter into the picture. But there is a good deal of evidence to suggest that in cases of insanity of psychogenic origin, a moral problem usually lies at the bottom of the difficulty. Frequently, however, the situation involves a peculiar aspect of morality. For it is connected with the problem of psychological development, even with that of evolution. At one stage of development, the psychic organism will tolerate acts or attitudes that at a higher level would cause serious disturbance. The regression that occurs in psychosis, and in lesser degree in neurosis also, is nature's attempt to find a level at which the new material can be tolerated. If recovery takes place, a new attitude is built up from the lowest point reached in the regression; in this way the patient is enabled to assimilate the contents of the unconscious that have so disturbed him, or at the least to make a new adjustment to life on a firmer foundation.

In some cases of schizophrenia the regression stops at the infantile level. Childish responses and patterns of life are reactivated and lived through; in favourable cases, this stage of the illness is followed by a recapitulation, in condensed form, of the psychological growth from infancy to adult life. In others, the regression goes to deeper levels, and much more archaic impulses are brought to the surface; unless the regressive process is reversed within certain limits, a deterioration of the psychic structure apparently takes place and full recovery cannot be expected. In the deteriorated dementia praecox patients who form a large part of the permanent population of our hospitals for the insane, the regression failed to come to a halt and the movement was never reversed.

The modern so-called shock treatment for schizophrenia is a technique by means of which far-reaching regressions of this kind can be artificially brought about under the control of the physician. The aim of the procedure is to find a level that can be used as a firm base for the reconstruction of the personality. Such techniques are still in the experimental stage, and it is not yet clear what role they will ultimately play in the treatment of schizophrenic patients.[24] However, they offer a hope of establishing an acceptable social adjustment for many individuals who would otherwise be condemned permanently to institutional life. The aim of these treatments is the restoration of function. They are not designed to give the patient insight into his problem or understanding of his psychotic experience. Consequently when he returns to ordinary life he has no greater psychological defence than he had before his illness. If, however, the patient with incipient schizophrenia is treated by psychological analysis, the situation is entirely different. For this method is designed to enable him to understand the alien material that has broken through into consciousness and to help him to reconcile it with his former attitudes and values. Under this technique the patient may gain from his psychological illness a higher level of consciousness and greater inner integrity.

The story of Jonah is capable of a different interpretation, one which the Catholic Church usually gives, basing its understanding on the reply Jesus gave to the Pharisees when they asked him for a sign. He said, "There shall no sign be given

24. Jung, "On the Psychogenesis of Schizophrenia" (C.W. 3).

. . . but the sign of Jonah, the prophet; for as Jonah was three days and three nights in the belly of the whale, so shall the Son of man be three days and three nights in the belly of the earth." [25] On this interpretation we see that Jonah's sojourn in the belly of the whale can be taken as representing not only Christ's descent to the underworld in the days between the crucifixion and the resurrection, but also the night sea journey that is an almost constant feature of the hero ordeal, as Frobenius clearly demonstrated.

And so we see that a descent into the depths can result either from a voluntary encounter with the powers of the unconscious, undertaken as part of the mystery initiation of the hero, when we speak of an introversion; or it can result from an inability to meet the demands of life, with a consequent flight from life's tasks, when we speak of a regression.

In the case of Jonah, he had refused to tackle his life's task and so had regressed to a very serious degree. But the regressive movement was halted at the moment when he came to terms with his inner voice and so metaphorically saw the light. When this happens in a patient of the present day, it is a particularly favourable sign, for it is an indication that in all probability the sufferer will be able to return to the everyday world, bringing with him a new insight regarding the strange contents by which his disturbance was caused. If he returns without this insight, his recovery will be only relative or partial. Jonah realized where he had gone wrong and was able to change his attitude. When he reached dry land, he found that he would have to take up his moral problem at the point where he had deviated. He had to face his headstrong self-will and learn to accept life on the terms it gave, as is told in the story of the gourd that follows the tale here discussed.

In his ordeal Jonah showed himself but a sorry hero. He would much have preferred to remain unknown, living out his life in obscurity and ease. He was forced to play the hero role and to brave the perils of the deep because he could not face the task that life had prepared for him. He ran away like any other coward. It was the renegade quality in him that got

25. Matt. 12:39, 40.

him into this predicament. Not infrequently, indeed, the renegade furnishes the stuff out of which the hero must be forged.
For the accepted and acceptable elements of the psyche that
make up the moral and conventional "good citizen" are only
a part of the individual. Those elements which were left over
and discarded when this role was formed are the only material
available for the creation of any additional structure or role.

The discarded or outcast parts of the psyche correspond
to the "black sheep" in the community—the man who of
choice or necessity lives without benefit of society. If these
elements are in the minority in a given person, or if the psychic
police force is sufficiently strong to keep them in the background, the conventional adaptation may prove adequate and
successful. But if the balance is tipped in the other direction,
the unadapted and unconventional factors may take the lead;
the individual will then be regarded with suspicion by society
and may actually be excluded. Such a one has to create a new
way, whether he wants to or not. The fact that he cannot fit
in compels him to make a way of his own, to create an individual as over against a collective adaptation.

A man who has succumbed to the renegade tendency
always expects good things to come his way, or thinks that
they ought to, without effort on his own part. He does not
think of life as holding out to him a challenge to develop
his own potentialities in face of indifferent nature, a chance
to discover what stuff he is made of. Rather, he regards it as
solely a medium for satisfying his needs. He approaches the
problem of living with the greedily opened mouth of the
fledgling, and reacts to life almost as if it were a person, an
indulgent or, conversely, a stingy parent. He considers himself the favoured son of fortune, so that he can afford to pick
and choose; and if the opportunities that come his way do not
measure up to his requirements in every particular, he feels
free to reject them. In applying for a job, for example, such a
man will ask first what advantages he will get from it and what
privileges are allowed, and will consider later or not at all what
he can give that would make him a desirable employee. Mr.
Micawber was an outstanding example of this type of mental-

ity. He had the optimistic outlook of one who knows without any shadow of a doubt that the gifts of fortune are his due. Consequently he never faced himself as the failure he actually was—an attitude of mind that was buttressed by the maternal adoration of his wife.

In other cases, far from thinking himself a favourite of fortune, an individual of this type may see himself as life's stepchild. Then he will spend his time in envy and resentment of those whom he considers more fortunate than himself. But the result is the same. In either case, this type of man is a shirker: he expects success to come his way unearned and thinks that life ought to bestow on him what he is too lazy, too self-indulgent or shiftless, to create for himself.

And so the renegade drifts through life, choosing always the easiest way, seeking only the satisfaction of the moment. He takes all that he can get and never creates anything by his own effort. But presently the good is all consumed and only the bad remains; by and by things become intolerable, till even he can stand it no longer. By this time, however, his selfishness has probably alienated his friends and neighbours. For in refusing to conform to the elementary law of society—namely, that in order to eat one must work—he forsook the collective way and the community life; thus in his time of need no one remains to whom he can turn for help or advice. He finds himself alone and is compelled, whether he wants to or not, to pull himself together and fight his dragon by himself. It is no longer of any use to dream of better times or to phantasy a way out. He is inexorably confronted with a choice—either to perish or to summon whatever inner resources he possesses to attempt that heroic act by which wishful thinking is transformed into the will to create.

What exactly is this dragon that the renegade must face and overcome? We have spoken of the dragon on the one hand as personifying the blind urge that keeps life going, often under seemingly intolerable conditions, and on the other as symbolizing the mother depths, the unconscious in which all life is rooted and which produces life and yet more life regardless of how slender the chances of survival may be. The primal instincts or life urges function in human beings just as they do in all living creatures. The lowest forms of life seem to consist solely of these instincts; but in man another principle, ego consciousness, has asserted itself over against the blind interplay of creative and destructive life instincts. We human beings are not composed solely of the life urges. My ego, my consciousness, is something separated from the unconscious life impulse and is often set over against it, having certain aims that may prove to be actually in opposition to the urge of instinct. Yet, because the effort to keep oneself conscious is both painful and exacting, every individual longs to relax his efforts and to fall back on the blind strength and age-old wisdom of instinct; thus the dragon threatens to overwhelm his hard-won consciousness and to devour him again. If he cannot summon his energies to resist the dragon, he allows himself to sink back into unconsciousness, into the mother.

The strength of this backward longing is the measure of man's childishness and of his desire to be spared effort and responsibility, his almost ineradicable desire to have someone decide for him, do for him—always, however, arranging matters in the way he would like. Even when the individual has outgrown the desire to return to the actual mother or to some mother substitute, even when he has set aside the desire to be understood and approved, he still feels the pull back into unconsciousness, especially when some step forward is demanded of him. For unconsciousness means freedom from responsibility and is in fact frequently offered as an excuse for default. A man who has injured his neighbour by some careless act, may, instead of apologizing, simply protest, "But I did not know," or "I did not see"—when obviously he should have known or seen. In denying knowledge of something he has done, he feels himself completely exonerated of all guilt or responsibility in relation to it. This is the condition of avidya, not-knowing, which Buddha described as the supreme obstacle in the way of enlightenment. For primal sloth, the inertia of matter, of the body, can be overcome only when it is impregnated with the spark of the divine spirit, of consciousness.

One of the most important accomplishments of psychological analysis relates to just this problem, as concerns not only those in imminent danger of psychic illness but the so-called normal person as well. For as an individual takes up the situations and experiences of his life, step by step, from the very beginning, and brings before the bar of his adult consciousness the acts of his ignorant and unconscious former self, he finds himself obliged to take responsibility for certain acts, performed in ignorance, for which at the time he could not take responsibility. Yet all through the years these particular experiences have remained latent in the personal unconscious, where they may have caused all sorts of disturbances. The very fact that they have remained not neutral but energized, which is attested by the emotion and sense of guilt with which they are brought back into consciousness, means that there was already present in the individual at that stage—albeit unknown even to himself—a potential self that could not be content to let these things, these particular things, rest as unconscious, therefore innocent acts. Other actions, in themselves perhaps just as wrong as these, but truly innocent—that is, in no way detrimental to or in opposition to the individual's potential character—remain neutral.

As the individual follows through this process of taking responsibility for his former unconsciousness, the actions that were at that earlier time outside of his control, completely autonomous, lost to the personality, are joined to consciousness. Something of himself that has been in the possession of the dragon is redeemed, and that amount of the dragon's energy is captured for the individual's own use. Thus the process of analysis involves not only a review of the patient's life but also an actual reliving of past experiences together with their emotional content. The going back into childhood with all its affects means also a going back to the mother. Old childish reactions are reactivated and must be resolved in a new and more adequate way.

Through this reliving of the past, parts of the psyche that have been repressed and cut off from the total personality are restored, and their energy is released for creative living in the present. Of even greater importance, however, is the fact that such unacceptable contents are as a rule repressed because they are contaminated with nonpersonal material belonging to the collective unconscious, and when reactivated through the attention bestowed upon them in analysis, they become available for understanding and furnish the energy and the new standpoint from which a new psychic structure can be fashioned. To go back to the mother, not just regressively, but through a deliberate act of introversion, may bring new life, rebirth. But always when such a quest is undertaken, there will be an encounter with the dragon that guards the treasure, and if the individual is not to fall victim to its stealthy power, it will be found necessary to overcome the childishness that longs to renounce all individual effort and find peace and security in the mother's protection.

Yet it would be a mistake to suppose that the conscious personality can assume entire responsibility for the nonpersonal impulses that assail it from within, or that the dragon's powers are the personal possession of any individual, or even that they can ever be entirely assimilated. A part of that which we have designated as the dragon belongs in the individual's psyche; but for the rest the dragon represents a nonpersonal factor, the activation of which entails problems that must be met by creating a relation between the conscious psyche and the powers of the collective unconscious. But however much these forces are explored and domesticated, there will always remain collective forces that seem to be outside the psyche. "Canst thou draw out leviathan with an hook?" [26] No human being can ever assimilate the whole of the dragon power, for it is the inexhaustible life energy of the collective unconscious.

But, it may be asked, if the dragon is nonpersonal libido, why does it seem at times as though it pursued its prospective victim personally, with malice and aggressive energy? Why in dreams does it single out the dreamer in order to devour him? This question opens up an important problem. In ordinary times, when the daily round of common tasks makes up the content of individual life, the forces of the collective unconscious remain latent and quiescent; the inner ocean sleeps

26. Job 41:1.

peacefully. At such times the dragon is neutral towards the conscious personality. But a moment may arrive when the individual should wrest a further quantum of energy from the dragon powers; or it may happen, as at the present time, that his whole generation is living on a level of consciousness below that which nature and the inherited civilization demand. Then childish inertia and fear, the inevitable concomitants of living below one's level, together with the renegade tendency that exists in all men, add themselves on to the eternal reluctance of the unconscious to yielding up its treasure. The sum of these factors makes up the personally menacing aspect of the dragon.

Two cases may serve to illustrate this point. The first patient, a woman, dreamed:

I was walking on a sunny beach. The sand was smooth and golden. At some little distance children were playing in the ripples at the edge of the sea. The whole scene was peaceful, with a joyous holiday feeling. I came to a depression in the sand, left by the tide. There I saw a lump of black stuff, tar or jet. I picked it up; it seemed very precious to me. Immediately the scene changed. The sky became overcast. An angry gust of wind blew in from the sea. It caught at my clothes, hampering me as I started to hurry home before the coming storm could catch me. But I found I was in quicksand, in which my feet were engulfed. I struggled against the fury of the wind and the sucking sands that threatened to swallow me up.

Here we see that as soon as the dreamer finds the dynamic, baffling stuff, the *nigredo* of the alchemists, the pleasant scene of play and innocence changes. Nature herself becomes angry and tries, as it seems, to prevent the finder from securing her prize, even threatening to devour her.

In the second case, a woman had the following dream early in her analysis.

I was standing on the shore, where the sand was golden and the sun shone brilliantly. Then I was alone in a canoe, paddling along parallel to the shore. My paddle was highly finished and I was amazed at the speed and ease of my progress. The water was quiet and clear and shallow. I could see beautiful shells on the bottom.

Presently the bottom fell away over a shelf. Here the water was dark and cold, and I noticed the paddle was now rough and crudely fashioned. Suddenly I was in the water, swimming. All at once I looked ahead and saw white objects; as I approached them, one began to move slowly, lazily, and I saw it was a shark. It came towards me, jaws spread, dripping blood and froth. I realized my danger and knew that my only chance lay in facing it. The creature came nearer till I could feel its breath; it was only afterwards I realized that sharks don't breathe! [Thus it was a veritable dragon.] I began to wonder if anyone else was in these dangerous waters. I looked and saw my sister, who could not swim well, and called to her to get behind me. She did so, but I had to hold her up, putting my left hand behind my back in order to do so. The weight on my back added to my distress and danger. Other sharks gradually closed in upon me and I was nearly exhausted, but managed to swim back to the shallow water and somehow scramble up the shelf into safety.

The dreamer awoke terrified and shivering with cold.

This dream and its associations offer material clearly showing that the qualities of the woman's shadow,[27] represented by her sister, were involved in this dangerous situation. Succeeding months were devoted to realizing and assimilating these shadow qualities, and again the woman dreamed. This time in her dream she deliberately went swimming. In the previous dream she had been in a canoe, and had apparently fallen out, for she said, "I found myself in the water." But now it was a consciously undertaken enterprise.

I swam across a pond and had taken only a few strokes when I found myself slithering through weeds. "Oh, how unpleasant those long fingers, coiling and uncoiling," I remarked, and fearing lest my feet get entangled, I kicked my way out, then with firm strokes struck off across the lake.

27. *Shadow* is the term used by Jung to designate the repressed part of the personality. The shadow is the personification or representative of the personal unconscious and often figures in dreams as a rather shadowy other of the same sex as the dreamer. This shadow may accompany the dreamer in much of his dream activity. As it represents the unacceptable part of the personality, it frequently has a negative or even sinister quality. It embodies all those qualities that the individual most dislikes or fears in himself. Cf. also Jung, *The Integration of the Personality*, pp. 20, 22, 88, 91, 173; and see below, chap. 10.

A young girl followed me, nipping at my heels. I was very much annoyed with her. When I reached the wharf several people came to meet me, and I complained in no uncertain terms, saying, "She might have made me drown."

"Oh no," someone answered, "she only wanted to have someone to play with."

This dream is in marked contrast to the former one. The shark has been replaced by the water weed. The dreamer personifies it in a sense by speaking of its fingers, but even in the dream she is not really afraid of getting caught and can easily free herself, for the weed does not pursue her; it remains where it is, and she does not need to go to that part of the pond. It is a place of danger, but entirely without personally directed menace. The emotion of the dreamer, which in the first dream was a very legitimate terror of the man-eating sharks, is here transferred to the perfectly harmless and playful girl who pursues her and tickles her heel, which she associated to the story of Achilles' heel. The heel of Achilles is the vulnerable spot, the place covered by his mother's hand when she dipped him in the Styx. Thus it means that at that spot where one is still related to the mother in a dependent way one is vulnerable when engaged in the hero ordeal. The dreamer felt threatened by the teasing and laughter of the young girl who was a new aspect of her shadow, a part of herself, that was apparently aware of the dreamer's weakness and willing to expose it, even at the risk of throwing her into a panic. With this part of her problem she will have to come to terms. But the enemy is no longer a threatening dragon-shark; it is clearly shown by this dream that her enemy is her own childishness, and this can endanger her by its treacherous activity.

What, then, are these shadow or renegade qualities in ourselves that turn us over as a prey to the dragons? The list is a long one and could be indefinitely extended, but here are a few of the commonest of these factors: inertia and laziness; greed, egotism, and lust; and last but not least, the desire to have one's own way and dominate others, either directly by aggression, or indirectly through demanding attention by weakness—that is, the will to power in both its positive and negative aspects, its sadistic and masochistic forms. These instinctive urges are particularly dangerous when they remain unrecognized. Unconsciousness is for the modern Western man the greatest hindrance on the way, just as avidya, unknowing, is for the Buddhist.

The aspects and qualities of the shadow always appear first in projected form; this is the manner in which they manifest themselves in consciousness. It seems that it is not I who am greedy or selfish, but that someone else has taken what surely should be mine. As the schoolboy in the story complained: "Isn't Charlie greedy—he has taken the biggest piece of cake, that I wanted!" An epitaph on an old gravestone reads:

> The faults ye see in others take care to shun,
> If you'll only look at home there's enough to be done.

This doggerel verse embodies the same warning as Christ's saying: "Cast out first the beam out of thine own eye, and then shalt thou see clearly to pull out the mote that is in thy brother's eye." [28]

Obviously therefore the first step towards a greater consciousness is to make these unknown qualities clear—to bring them out of the shadowed land where they have been hiding and look them squarely in the eye. Few are able to do this unaided; self-examination rarely penetrates below the threshold of consciousness, while the shadow qualities remain unconscious. Consequently introspection not infrequently serves to enhance the one-sided attitude of the ego, whose dominance is thus increased, to the disadvantage of the whole personality. Not until the repressed elements have caused some disturbance of adaptation does the ego even recognize that there is something wrong. The disturbance of adaptation that forces itself on consciousness may be an outer one, affecting the work adjustment or the emotional life, or an inner, subjective one. Whenever elements too incompatible to pass unnoticed are harboured in the unconscious, conflicts or anxieties or psychosomatic symptoms of some kind are likely to arise.

28. Luke 6:42.

If the individual then begins to investigate his unconscious through a psychological analysis, these hidden characteristics and reactions will become clear to him. Thereupon the entire situation changes. As a result of his new insight, what was formerly an illness or an anxiety becomes a moral problem. If he is able and willing to look at the shadow qualities as his own and to recognize that they emanate from himself, instead of seeing them only in others, a change will take place in his reactions. His anger and resistance will no longer be directed against the neighbour who has seemed to embody the faults in question, but will be applied instead to eradicating these defects from his own conduct. If, however, he is not willing to undertake this task, though, because of the insight he has gained through the analysis, he is no longer able naïvely to attribute the difficulty to his neighbour, the rejected attributes will be projected upon the analyst, and the resistance will be directed against the doctor—for has he not been instrumental in bringing these unpleasant facts to view?

Thus the analyst will replace the dragon and will appear to the patient to be as dangerous and hostile as the latter. Furthermore, the energy wrested from the dragon by means of even this very limited degree of understanding will be used to obstruct the analysis and to prove the analyst to be in the wrong, instead of being applied to correction of the fault. But if this very natural desire to blame the analyst can be sacrificed, the first round in the fight against the dragon, the first battle with the renegade tendency, will have been won. Then at last the energies of the patient can be directed to exploring the faults themselves.

On first examination these may seem to lie merely in the natural weakness and self-indulgence of the ordinary human being; they may seem to be little defects that one is quite justified in condoning in oneself. But as soon as they are faced squarely, the little faults will be found to be no longer little. They cling like limpets, and every attempt to overcome them seems to make them swell and become more and more menacing. Obviously something of far greater seriousness has been hiding behind the appearance of little natural weaknesses.

This problem is so commonplace and so banal that only a very banal illustration can well demonstrate it. I put it in the first person because this is the sort of experience with which nearly everyone is familiar. Realizing one day, for instance, that things are not going well with me, I say to myself that I am wasting too much time—that is the reason why my work is always in a muddle. So I determine to overcome my lazy habits and promise myself to get up betimes in the morning, to attend to all the neglected little things that accumulate so alarmingly and hamper me all day. But then I oversleep, or the alarm clock "finds itself," as the French would say, run down. Of course I never forget to wind it! A whole series of misadventures intervenes, so that I am prevented from inaugurating the new regime on Monday. Probably my employer takes this opportunity to remark that I am late again. There is nothing like a determination to tackle a fault to make others conscious of that particular flaw; one's own concentration on it brings it into focus, as it were. So I stifle my irritated speech of self-justification, and determine to do better tomorrow. But on Tuesday the same performance is repeated, and so again on Wednesday. By Thursday my affairs are in such disorder that I can barely keep my head above water, promising myself that Sunday will be the day for clearing up the unfinished business. On Sunday, however, a little voice whispers:

Isn't it a shame to do chores on Sunday,
When there's Monday, Tuesday, Wednesday, Thursday. . . .
Oh isn't it a shame to do chores on Sunday!

The probabilities are that by this time unconsciousness reigns securely once more, and I fall sound asleep—that is, if I have not been dismissed from my job. But then comes a nightmare, or a nervous headache. The dragon gives a menacing grunt as it were, spits out a little derisive smoke, and I either beat a hasty retreat or else open one eye to enquire what is happening.

Our pet little sins are not so very little after all. They represent the natural reactions of the unconscious organism; they are the evidences of the renegade tendency in man that will not tolerate the control of any purpose higher than the desire to exist merely for the sake of continued existence. The church named these same little weaknesses "deadly sins." They are the factors in man that correspond to the dragons of greed and lust and avarice, of anger or power, with their sinister aftermath of treachery and deceit; and everyone has that inertia or sloth which seeks to bind the spirit forever with the uncomprehension of insensate matter.

The alchemists met with this problem in projected form when they saw the contents of their retorts turn black before their eyes as the result of heating or from the action of chemicals, so that it looked as if the whole laborious work would end in disaster; instead of the precious gold, or the elixir, they had produced only blackness. However, they found that in some instances this was but a stage in the whole process of transformation, a stage that they named the "nigredo."

Many of them realized that the chemical process in some way corresponded to their own spiritual or, as we would say, psychological condition, and cried to God to be relieved from the terrible blackness of their souls. Jung quotes from *Splendor solis* [29] by Trismosin as follows: "The old philosophers declared they saw a Fog rise, and pass over the whole face of the earth, they also saw the impetuosity of the Sea, and . . . saw the king of the Earth sink, and heard him cry out with eager voice, 'Whoever saves me shall live and reign with me for ever in my brightness on my royal throne.'" This situation is represented in plate XIII, where the White Queen is seen receiving the "black" one as he emerges from the sea. The White Queen represents the albedo, the alchemical stage that follows the nigredo, and also represents the coming of the feminine element, the eros, bearer of feeling, into the situation. For the blackness of the shadow must be recognized not only legalistically, as it were, that is, with thinking, but must also be dealt with by feeling. For unless there is a reaction from the heart there can be no transformation. Jung comments on this legend, saying: "The king sinking in the sea is the arcane substance

. . . [that] corresponds to the Christian dominant, which was originally alive and present in consciousness but then sank into the unconscious and must now be restored in renewed form." [30]

In those centuries when the three great lusts were dealt with as deadly sins, an attempt was made to overcome them by asceticism and discipline. Much of the training of the young in Christian countries has been directed, up to quite recent years, to the gaining of control over these basic faults. But control or repression leaves the human being relatively empty. His life becomes a petty routine. The three great dragons are replaced by a host of little dragons—little selfishnesses, trivial greeds, furtive lasciviousness—while some of the little dragons are even decked out as virtues. Childishness is renamed affection for family; greed hides behind hospitality; egotism is whitewashed as proper self-interest or even self-respect; lust is legalized under the sanction of marriage rights and the double standard; and moral indifference struts openly in the market place, bearing the label of tolerance.

Such things go on for a time, a hundred years or so perhaps, unrecognized; little by little the easy way becomes habitual, everyone evades hardship and responsibility, the renegade is accepted as a very civilized chap. But then the dragons become restless and begin to breathe more menacingly. They ravage the outlying districts and even invade the streets of the cities, at first cautiously by night; but gradually they become bolder, and the citizens get accustomed to seeing them. Then one day people awake to find that their city is infested and rapidly becoming rotten from within.

It becomes appallingly apparent that a new hero is needed, if the dragons are to be conquered once more. At such times the aroused energy may find its expression in a crusade; or a new religion may clothe the eternal truths in fresh symbols that have power to touch men's hearts. Or a new philosophy may arise, capable of expressing the old truths in a new way. This is what happened when Freud began his explorations of the unconscious. Through his work with his patients he un-

30. Ibid., § 466.

masked one of the dragons, lust, and made its defeat and re-demption his life work. His explorations were followed by those of Adler, who attacked the dragon of ego power. Jung, who came next, directed his attention to selfishness, that is, to the concern with oneself, and also showed how the energy inherent in these instinctive drives must be wrested from them, for it is needed to build a house for the individuality. Out of the understanding of the dragon powers gained by these men of science, three redeeming values have been brought within the reach of all: a new attitude to sexuality and greed, that is, to the biological urges brought to consciousness in the autos; a new attitude to the will to power of the ego; and a new con-cept of the Self.

IO

The Psyche as a Whole
DRAWING THE CIRCLE

IN THE PRECEDING CHAPTER, the problem of the relation of man to the undeveloped and untamed forces of the unconscious was outlined under the symbol of the dragon and the hero. It was shown how from time to time these forces become active and therefore dangerous to individual man as well as to the collective culture and civilization. For when some part of the primitive energy that has been held inert in the depths of the unconscious passes from the latent to an active state, it threatens to overrun the little realm lighted by consciousness, and there is grave danger that the spark may be extinguished. When such a catastrophe happens to one individual, he falls into disintegration and his psyche is overwhelmed by archaic and incomprehensible contents. If, however, the calamity is not a matter of one man's experience, of one man's sanity, but is far-reaching, affecting groups of people, perhaps whole nations, then culture in its entirety is threatened and society may disintegrate into a state of collective madness, which is barbarism.

This is the condition we have witnessed in the world during the last few decades. Energies that are ordinarily latent in the unconscious, and that have not been adapted to civilized values, burst forth into the outer world and were lived once more in all their primitive or archaic violence. This is indeed a state of madness. In the totalitarian societies in which this phenomenon came so prominently to the fore, the leaders themselves spoke of the spirit that possessed them as a dynamism—an energy, without form, without limits, and without goal, an energy that is total, that is, absolute, not relative, and therefore even in principle, as it proved itself in practice, entirely impervious to scruple, amenable to none of the recognized codes of values, either of religion or of civilization.

The unprecedented violence of this dynamic outburst belongs to the twentieth century. Such a thing has not happened in the world since the days of the breakup of the Roman Empire at the beginning of the Christian era. In the intervening centuries, the unconscious psychic forces were, it seems, relatively quiescent. Such disturbances as arose—and there have been numbers of them—usually remained more or less local. Even when outbreaks on a larger scale did occur, some remnants of the Christian code of conduct were maintained, at least as an accepted ideal—certainly as regards societies within Christendom. For the forces of the unconscious have been held in leash in some measure by the Christian symbol. As Jung says:

Thanks to the labours of the human spirit over the centuries, these images have become embedded in a comprehensive system of thought that ascribes an order to the world, and are at the same time represented by a mighty, far-spread, and venerable institution called the Church.[1]

But recently in our day, wherever the dynamic outburst of unconscious energy was given full sway, all safeguards of human value and of human freedom were thrown into the discard; civilization itself was threatened, not only in the totalitarian countries but throughout the world. This breakdown is closely related to the neglect and depreciation of the symbols of religion, which no longer seem to have the vitality necessary to contain the dynamic power of the unconscious forces. To most people in Christian countries today Christianity has become little more than an ethic. The symbols and symbolic

1. "Archetypes of the Collective Unconscious," in *The Archetypes and the Collective Unconscious* (C.W. 9, i), p. 8.

dramas that in earlier centuries contained and adequately represented the mystery of the life processes as they unfold themselves eternally in the unconscious, are either discarded by us as unscientific, untrue to life, or are retained as so many meaningless pictures and stories, sanctified indeed by age and tradition but—except to the few who are more than just nominally Christian—now so unimportant that for the most part it does not even occur to us to enquire what they mean. A similar movement away from ancestral religion has also occurred in the non-Christian countries.

When the symbols of a religion are depotentiated in this way and no longer avail to mediate between the human being and the nonhuman forces of creation and destruction that underlie conscious life, man is left undefended in face of an outbreak of this archaic energy. If these energies are not to destroy the whole world they must be gathered up into a new container. Sanity itself is threatened by a too immediate contact with the powerful and fascinating images in which the forces of the unconscious are expressed. This is a numinous experience,[2] awe-inspiring, terrifying, a *tremendum;* it is fraught with an intimation of the holy and the dread before which the human being shrinks in awe, if indeed his very reason does not totter and fall.

It is therefore most urgently necessary for the individual in face of such an experience to find a container adequate to replace the vessel formerly supplied by the church. But what can constitute such a container? Religious symbols are not man-made; they cannot be invented or contrived. They arise spontaneously out of life. As Jung says: "Religious symbols are life-phenomena, plain facts and not opinions."[3] In religious terminology it is said that they are "given of God" or "received by revelation" or "by inspiration." The same fact is expressed in modern psychological terms by saying that they arise spontaneously from the unconscious and appear in consciousness under the guise of dream symbols or phantasy images or other unwilled, autonomous contents—such as thoughts that

2. R. Otto, *The Idea of the Holy*, chaps. ii-iv.
3. *Psychology and Alchemy* (C.W. 12), p. 121.

come unbidden, pictures that obtrude themselves before the inner eye, tunes arising of themselves to haunt one, anger surprising to oneself, and so on through the whole gamut of unsought, unpredictable psychic happenings.

That these subjective images, which are sometimes trivial-seeming, though at others impressive and even terrifying, could have any importance or could in any way contribute to the solution of the problems of personal and collective sanity instanced above, is a startling thought to most people. During all the years when the Catholic church held sway over the conscience of mankind, it claimed to be the sole mediator between man and the unseen world. Personal or individual revelation was frowned upon, if not entirely excluded. Now, however, not a few people feel an urgent need to effect a direct personal relation with the inner realm. Our own generation has developed, in psychological analysis, a technique by means of which individual persons can become acquainted with the happenings in the unconscious. By this means the ancient symbols are rediscovered, and because the individual undergoing analysis does not merely learn about them but experiences them, they come forth with a new and more direct meaning and endued with the energy needed to enable them to live again.

Foremost among these symbols are those which carry the value of wholeness. Man could be whole! This idea, revolutionary today, though well known to the ancients in terms of Plato's "spherical man" and to the Middle Ages under the concept of the *rotundum*, arises anew in the dreams and phantasy images of many persons when, on account of mental conflicts, they undertake a serious study of their own unconscious contents.

Anyone who works faithfully to reconcile himself with his other, his unconscious and hidden side, will find such a symbol emerging from the unconscious, and if he follows the guidance afforded through understanding of the dream images, he will be led step by step, in the gradual unfolding of the symbolism, towards the realization of wholeness within his own life. By this I do not mean that the unconscious is to be taken as the sole determinant of conscious action; rather, this inner and usually disregarded aspect of psychic reality should be taken into account as one factor in all important decisions. For the unconscious complements and frequently compensates the one-sidedness and partialness of the conscious attitude. When its functioning is regularly observed, it will be found that the dream symbols do not remain static or stereotyped; moreover, they do not merely compensate the conscious attitude but manifest a life of their own. They change and evolve, and gradually develop a pattern or theme—very similar to the themes of myth or religious ritual—that is not meaningless or fortuitous but has a goal or outcome of great significance.

The fact that the path unfolds in this way, step by step, leading the individual on, often by quite unexpected turns, towards the goal of wholeness, must mean that there are in the psyche patterns or rules of development analogous to the patterns operative in the physiological realm—such as that, for instance, which leads to the growth and development of the embryo. Surely we should not be surprised to find in the psychic life such a priori patterns, for we take the physiological patterns entirely for granted. We expect that lungs will develop in the unborn infant, ready to react to air at the moment of birth, although up till that time it has been a creature of the water; we are moreover astonished when nature's patterns do not work "normally" and the living being fails to develop or react as experience has taught us to expect. Yet Jung's brilliant demonstration of these patterns of psychic life—the archetypes,[4] as he has called them—has met with considerable opposition and resistance. However, the presence of these unconscious themes can be demonstrated by anyone who follows the leading of the unconscious symbols. If he is able to interpret them rightly, he will find himself participating in a process of psychic development called by Jung the process of individuation. The goal of the process is wholeness, and the achievement of this

---

4. *Two Essays on Analytical Psychology*. For definition, see First Essay, chap. v. The whole of the book from that chapter on is an exposition of the theory of the archetypes. Cf. also "Archetypes of the Collective Unconscious," in Jung, *The Archetypes and the Collective Unconscious* (C.W. 9, i).

aim is of the greatest importance not only for the individual but also for society.

Thus if ordinary men and women of good will could realize —make real, or accomplish—such wholeness in themselves, they would not only be freeing themselves from the conflicts and divisions of their own lives but would also be doing something constructive towards the solution of the very problems that are devastating mankind.

Individuation is, then, a modern term for that process by which the individual progresses towards completeness within himself and becomes most truly man. It was dimly recognized and foreshadowed in many systems of religious discipline and initiation whose aim was the development or completion or, as it has more commonly been called, the redemption of man. But we are indebted to Jung for having discovered by scientific methods that these systems had their origin in unconscious processes occurring also, as he has demonstrated, in modern persons, in whom a natural evolution of the unconscious symbols often leads to a similar entirely natural goal. Most of his recent writings have been concerned with this aspect of psychological experience.[5]

In his discussion of the histories he presents, notably in "A Study in the Process of Individuation" and in "Psychology and Religion," Jung deals with the evolution of symbols of wholeness that have a general or collective validity and occur widely throughout history—as for example the mandala, or magic circle,[6] which is to be found in the earliest known drawings of primitive man, as well as in the iconography of many if not most of the highly developed religions of the world. Identical symbols occur frequently in the unconscious products of modern men and women, and it is these phenomena that form the main theme of Jung's chapters, though for understandable reasons he has had to omit the personal aspects of

5. *The Integration of the Personality; The Archetypes and the Collective Unconscious; Psychology and Alchemy; Psychology and Religion: West and East; The Spirit Mercury.* The same theme was treated in a series of lectures given at the Eidgenössische Technische Hochschule, Zurich, from 1939 to 1941 (unpublished).

6. See below, chap. 11.

his patients' material. This method is necessary and even desirable in a theoretical presentation; at the same time it leaves out something of the human and personal aspect of the given situation—a lack that makes the whole process seem rather cold and leaves the reader, if he has not himself undergone a similar experience, somewhat baffled as to how or why the process is set going in the persons described.

It is certainly true that the dream and picture series presented by Jung are not the stuff of ordinary experience, and that such occurrences are not likely to arise in persons entirely occupied with the outer aspects of life. These dreams or phantasies reflect rather the hidden, subjective, or background aspect of a particular and therefore not usual phase of an individual's life. In the case of the woman [7] whose pictures are reproduced, Jung tells us that she had come to the end of a stage of her life and was in considerable conflict and depression because she felt herself to be "stuck," as if the normal flow of her life had come to a standstill. Of the man whose extraordinary dreams form the basis of discussion in "Psychology and Religion" as well as in the chapter on "Individual Dream Symbolism in Relation to Alchemy," [8] Jung tells us only that he was a patient; thus we must conclude that he was facing some difficulty of a psychological nature that similarly served to set the process going.

This phrase, "to set the process going," is significant, for the transformation process cannot be initiated at will. If the development is to go forward to completion, it is necessary for the individual to take part actively in the work with a conscious and willed effort; in its essence, however, the process is not under the control of the will. It originates autonomously from a movement in the unconscious, and may be likened to physiological processes that go on without conscious control or assistance.

Symbols relevant to the process of becoming whole sometimes arise from the unconscious in quite irresponsible persons

---

7. "A Study in the Process of Individuation," in *The Archetypes and the Collective Unconscious* (C.W. 9, i), pp. 290 ff.
8. *Psychology and Alchemy* (C.W. 12), part II, pp. 39 ff.

who have no intention of taking them seriously or of following the course of action they indicate. This may happen in normal persons if they are not awake to the importance or significance of the happenings in the unconscious; it can also be observed in the insane, who, unlike so-called normal persons, usually attach great importance to their dreams, visions, and hallucinations. Unfortunately these individuals take such experiences to be objectively valid and so do not seek out their subjective or symbolic significance. In either case, whether the dream symbols are disregarded as of no importance, or are taken to have only objective reality, their true significance is missed, and the process takes a cyclic form; that is, the symbols evolve up to a certain point and then regress again to the aspect from which they started. Conscious participation is needed to convert this ebb and flow of the unconscious into a continuous line of development.

To put it in another way, the supreme value represented by the term individuation lies hidden in the unconscious. It is like a golden fish in the ocean. If a man wants to catch it, it is obviously of no use for him to stay inactive on the shore; he must take a boat and go out and fish. This requires a conscious and willed act, possibly hard work and persistence; but unless the fish rises of its own accord, all his fishing will be in vain. The old alchemists used to say of their work that it required effort, and that this effort could be successful *Deo concedente*, only if God concurred in it.

In the following chapters I propose to take up various points bearing on the quest for individuation and to deal with them as simply as possible, omitting the technical considerations that necessarily apply in any particular case. I shall concentrate on those well-known happenings in daily life which, common as they are, can nevertheless open the door to this inner experience.

The term individuation means a becoming whole and therefore implies the necessity of reconciling the conscious and the unconscious parts of the psyche. In practice the process involves two steps. The first is that of searching out and recognizing all the scattered parts of the psyche and bringing them together; the second is that of amalgamating and co-ordinating them, together with the energies that inhere in them, so that they will make a meaningful whole—a cosmos, not a chaos. These two processes naturally go on simultaneously in actual life. It is only for the sake of clarity that they are separated in this discussion.

The elements that have to be brought within the psyche include not only the conscious and accepted factors organized under the ego, but also certain other factors that have remained hidden in the unconscious, unrecognized by the ego. These unconscious elements can be divided into two groups. The first comprises the unrecognized components of the personal psyche—the personal unconscious, which is personified in the figure of the shadow,[9] and of which most persons prefer to remain unaware.[10] The second includes those elements of the collective unconscious which lie nearest to the conscious psyche and are personified in the figure of the anima (the feminine soul in a man) or of the animus (the masculine soul in a woman).[11] This figure provides a contact with the nonpersonal forces described in the preceding chapters; for the anima and animus are defined as the function of relationship between the I and the not-I—the liaison between the personal psyche and the collective unconscious.[12]

As long as this psychic element—the anima or the animus—remains unassimilated, it will be relatively unconscious and

9. See above, note, p. 295.

10. "Medical psychology has recognized today that it is a therapeutic necessity . . . for consciousness to confront its shadow. In the end this must lead to some kind of union, even though the union consists at first in an open conflict, and often remains so for a long time. . . . What the product of the union will be it is impossible to imagine. The empirical material shows that it usually takes the form of a subjective experience, which . . . is always of a religious order" (Jung, *Mysterium Coniunctionis* [C.W. 14], § 514).

11. Jung, *The Archetypes and the Collective Unconscious* (C.W. 9, i), pp. 25 ff., 284; *Aion* (C.W. 9, ii), pp. 11 ff. Cf. also Jung, *Two Essays on Analytical Psychology*, Second Essay, pt. ii, chap. ii, "Anima and Animus," and M. E. Harding, *The Way of All Women*, chaps. i and ii.

12. It is not possible to go further into this aspect of the subject here, as it is too extensive to treat in passing. Cf. Jung's own writings, especially *Two Essays on Analytical Psychology*, and "Archetypes of the Collective Unconscious," in *The Archetypes and the Collective Unconscious* (C.W. 9, i).

autonomous. It may appear in consciousness only in the guise of unaccountable subjective happenings, such as emotional disturbances or feeling-toned moods in the case of the anima, that is, in a man, or as unfounded assumptions and judgments in the case of the animus, that is, in a woman. Or it may appear in personified form in visions or daydreams. In other cases it will be encountered in the outer world, the anima projected upon a woman, the animus upon a man. But when this element has been brought up to consciousness and its activity taken over as a function of the psyche, other archetypal figures appear to replace it. For behind the area of the unconscious represented by the figure of the anima or animus lie deeper layers, further reaches of that mysterious psychic domain stretching we know not how far into primordial depths of unknowing, from which emanate those intimations which, given favouring conditions, can cause panic, terror, or strange elations even in those protected from superstitious fears and emotions, as they think, by the bulwark of a rational and scientific attitude.

These deeper layers of the unconscious are represented by other archetypal figures, which appear from time to time in dreams and play their ambiguous role in myth and religion. They usually are of bivalent quality, having both an attractive and repellent effect—in such concepts for example as hero-renegade, wise man-black magician, mother-witch. Inasmuch as they represent the unconscious, they are always equivocal in purport—good-bad, favourable-ominous, etc. If individuation is to be complete, these figures must also be assimilated by the individual and so converted into functions of the psyche. But complete individuation in any absolute sense is little more than an abstract concept. For the problems connected with the remote and inaccessible regions of the collective unconscious become more and more indefinable and abstruse the farther we go, till our baffled understanding halts before impenetrable darkness. About this part of the problem, therefore, we can say only that it consists in achieving a satisfactory relation to the nonpersonal energy of the unconscious, the source of life itself, which is manifested in or expressed by the archetypes, and that some transformation of this energy is accomplished by the work done on the psyche during the quest for individuation.

When the shadow and the soul figure (anima or animus) are progressively assimilated by an individual in the course of his psychological development, an increase in the range and intensity of his consciousness is achieved, for a certain portion of the unconscious has been redeemed and added to that part of the psyche presided over by the ego. The individual becomes aware of contents and subjective reactions formerly hidden from consciousness or perceived only in projected form. From this point on, therefore, it is necessary to distinguish what may be called the conscious personality from the ego complex. The individual in whom this process of development is taking place will of course still think of himself as "I" and may not even realize that this new I is different from his old ego. It is just such subtle changes of venue that make the discussion of psychic experience and development so difficult and confusing. In the Orient these changes in the character of the I have long been recognized as occurring in regular gradation with the advance of psychological development, as a result of the religious disciplines of initiation or enlightenment. In a number of systems—the Tantric form of Buddhism, for example—seven stages of consciousness are described, though for practical purposes the count can be reduced to five, since the two highest stages are rarely met with on earth, even among adepts. Each of these stages is held to have as its centre a different I, much as our Western psychology recognizes that the first-formed I of the child, the autos, is gradually replaced by a socially oriented I, the ego.

When the shadow has been made conscious and has been accepted as part of the personality, its contents and part of its energies are added to those of the ego, so that a further development of the I results. Similarly, when the anima or animus has been united to the conscious psyche by a process described in many religious systems as an inner marriage,[13] a further enlarge-

13. On the *hieros gamos*, see below, pp. 432-33, 450 ff.; and cf. Harding, *Woman's Mysteries, Ancient and Modern;* on *coniunctio*, cf. Jung, *Psychology and Alchemy,* "Psychology of the Transference," in *The Practice of Psychotherapy* (C.W. 16), and *Mysterium Coniunctionis.*

ment of consciousness results, and the conscious personality begins to display those qualities of dignity and stability which are the marks of the unique or individuated personality.

However, through the bringing to consciousness of the shadow and of the soul figure, only a part of the energy they contain is made available for conscious daily life; another, and that the greater part, retreats into less accessible regions of the unconscious. This elusive part is the numinous element—that component which has power to move us with fear or dread, which can "make us to quake." It is the uncanny or awe-full element to which H. Rider Haggard referred when he drew that extraordinarily true picture of the anima, the figure he called "She-who-must-be-obeyed." The emotions aroused by this numinous aspect of the unconscious act through the sympathetic or autonomous nervous system, which is not under the control of the voluntary centres or of the conscious will. They therefore produce a direct effect in the body, such as strange reactions and sensations in the intestines, or palpitations of the heart; or they may cause the hair to rise or a cold sweat to break out, though the day is warm and from a superficial view all seems well.

Reactions of this kind take place regardless of the individual's conscious attitude, and it often requires a high degree of discipline and inner development to hold one's ground in face of them. That intangible something called morale depends not a little on this ability. For experiences of this kind attack a man at the point where he is least protected. They can unseat his reason or make him act quite strangely; they can throw him into a panic or in extreme cases even into insanity. This is the work of the mana aspect of the archetypal figure. When one such figure is brought up and assimilated to consciousness, its mana retreats farther into the unconscious depths and is taken over by or rather devolves upon the archetypal figure that stands next behind it—as for instance the anima or animus, standing behind the shadow, becomes increasingly important as the shadow is taken up into the conscious personality.

Apparently each layer of the unconscious is represented by an archetypal figure personifying that particular stratum and possessed of the power or mana inherent in that psychic realm; thus the image of the Old Wise Man or the Great Mother may be constellated—activated by an access of energy, and come to dominate the individual's psychology. This domination will continue until he can redeem the value represented by the figure and create out of its energy a new attitude or psychic function for integration into his personality. If on the other hand he does not develop such inherent potentialities, he remains the puppet of the archetypal figures. For example, if his thinking function is insufficiently differentiated, or if he has not troubled himself to think adequately about the problems of the world, the figure of the Old Wise Man will continue to carry for him all the potencies of wisdom or of understanding, even though he has reached a time of life when he should be making a contribution of his own to the sum of human understanding.

This figure of course symbolizes the father, but it is of more weight than the personal father: it has an impersonal and incontestable authority, an aspect of the kind described above as numinous. If this figure is projected into the outer world, as often happens, the individual will find himself overawed by learning in others, or he will be resistant to those who have or are supposed to have authority in intellectual realms; that is, the figure of the Wise One will be overly powerful and will in consequence tend to paralyse his efforts to gain understanding. Such a man will remain diffident and childish, or will compensate for his inadequacy and inferiority with an egotism and self-assurance in no wise based on competence.

Further, a potentially great man, a person destined to become a leader in the world of ideas, may in his formative years project the archetypal image of the Wise Man upon an actual leader or teacher or upon some figure that lives only in his creative imagination; it was thus that Zarathustra served Nietzsche, who, however, did not live to redeem the wisdom he envisioned in the ancient religious teacher who speaks with such authority by his pen.

The power that such a figure wields over a young man is really a measure of the psychic values accessible to him—some part of which he will gradually assimilate and express in his subsequent lifework and personality. Thus the constellation of the archetype may mean that the individual is below the average level of the civilization in which he lives, or that he is potentially above this level but has not yet attained his full stature.

When the archetypal figure is not projected to a human being in the outer world but acts from within a man's own psyche, it influences him in strange and unaccountable ways. In such a case we say that the individual is identified with the archetype, or has suffered an inundation from the unconscious, or is possessed. Primitive man in such a case thinks of actual possession by a spirit, a demon or ghost. That this kind of thinking really represents the situation in a certain way is suggested by the fact that in modern language the terms that come most readily to the tongue imply that the sufferer is the victim of an alien agency. Even though we have discarded all belief in spirits as superstitious, we still say of a man under the influence of an archetype that "he is possessed by an idea," "something has got into him," "he will come to himself when the mood leaves him": we are really saying that a spirit not his own has temporarily taken possession of his faculties and is speaking and acting for him. There is this difference, however, that while the primitive thinks of the "spirit" as a separate being, a ghost or demon, or one of the pixies, fairies, will-o'-the-wisps, etc., of folklore, modern man refers not to some airy or ghostlike being but to autonomous psychic factors. These in their functioning may, however, still be spoken of as a spirit, for example, a warlike spirit. We shun the plural of the word, which sounds too highly personalized in our ears.

In *Two Essays on Analytical Psychology* [14] Jung describes how such an archetypal figure may become so activated through the accumulation of psychic energy that it breaks through into consciousness, causing disturbance of the personality and adaptation of varying degrees of severity. He speaks particularly of the effect of identification with the mana of the Old Wise Man, which produces what he has called the mana personality, and refers to H. G. Wells' *Christina Alberta's Father* for illustration.

14. Cf. Second Essay, pt. II, chap. IV, "The Mana Personality."

He might as easily have taken a historical figure for his example, as for instance Joan of Arc. Here the archetype of the hero led a human being through incredible difficulties, transforming a little peasant girl into the saviour of her people and upholding her with a sense of her mission even through torture and death. Or if these essays had been written fifteen years later (they were published in English in 1928), Jung might have chosen Hitler for his illustration. In this case too an unknown, poorly educated person came to be possessed by an archetypal figure, manifesting itself in quite typical fashion. Hitler's ecstasies of oratorical afflation, the consultations with his voices, the hypnotic effect of his personality on the mob, are all characteristic of a domination by a mana factor of the unconscious.

When such an invasion from the collective unconscious affects only one individual, it produces a result correspondingly limited to this single human life and its environment. But when the unconscious in many persons, even of whole nations, is simultaneously activated, it happens not infrequently that one particular individual among them voices or embodies the archetype for the entire group; then an upheaval of the existing order results, and a formless and chaotic energy of enormous power, a dynamism, may be loosed upon the world. Thus, when one personality alone is so affected, there will be at the worst one insane man; where, however, the occurrence is widespread, epidemic, it may well produce the phenomenon of a nation gone mad.

When, through some life experience, the energy or mana of some archetypal figure is released in an individual, the problem of how to deal with it in a constructive way becomes urgent. If it is not dealt with constructively it will assuredly produce destructive, perhaps even disastrous effects. For it is an uncanny and inhuman power, like a daemon, or a djinn escaping from the bottle in which for some thousands of years he has been more or less securely corked up.[15] When this djinn awakens in an individual, or is let loose in the world through

15. Jung, *The Spirit Mercury*, trans. pub. by the Analytical Psychology Club of New York Inc. with permission of Bollingen Foundation; to be included in vol. 13 of the Collected Works.

the inadequacy or breakdown of the old religious holds, he cannot be put back into the old bottle. It will be recalled that Christ applied this metaphor to the problem of the seething unrest of his own day—which in this respect was not so very different from the twentieth century. A new spirit had been released in men and had been focused and brought to a head through his own unconventional and revolutionary teachings. Then he said that this new spirit, this wine, could not be put back into the old bottle of Judaism; it needed a new bottle. The new bottle was the Christian church together with its dogma, which were gradually elaborated and established, in the centuries following his death, by the Church Fathers, beginning with Paul. It is this bottle of the Christian form that, after two thousand years, is apparently proving to be in turn no longer adequate to its task of containing the spirit of the unconscious for all the people.

The increasing rationalism and materialism of Western civilization have undermined the authority of Christian morality and ethics; indeed, they could hardly be expected to stand without the foundation of Christian symbolism on which they were built and the "divine" nature of which furnished their authority. The fundamental Christian beliefs have thus been widely discredited and in many places—even in certain Christian churches—largely or entirely discarded, on account of their strange and irrational character. For the modern scientific spirit rejects doctrines manifestly opposed to reason—as that a virgin should bear a child, or that three persons should be one person, or that a man should rise from the dead and be carried up into a material heaven literally as to a continent invisibly poised in outer space.

Modern scientists, with the exception of a few psychologists, have not yet found the clue that could resolve the enigma —namely, the realization that the mystical formulations of a religion may, and indeed do, refer to the psychological realm and not to the external world. They are symbols of the actual contents of the unconscious. The failure of the modern intellect to grasp this fact has contributed to the breakdown of a two-thousand-year-old order, permitting the energy of the unconscious, that potent wine which is at once a life-giving drink and a death-dealing poison, to be poured out over the nations, to their destruction and to the irreparable waste of the values it holds. If the world is not to suffer a double disaster, this potent spirit, this energy, must be gathered up again into a vessel that can contain it.

This is the task of the second part of the process of individuation. When this energy is gathered into a suitable vessel or symbol—by "suitable" I mean one that can safely contain it and adequately express it—that symbol becomes the centre of the individual psyche, at once the source of its power and the safeguard of its integrity. It is the centre and also the container of the conscious individual. The supreme psychological value is characterized by this paradox. For it is a value always beyond us, in a different dimension, as it were; thus it is incomprehensible and can be represented only by a symbol. The idea that the Self is at once the centre of the personality and its container is equivalent to the statement that God, the supreme value, is the centre of a circle and also its circumference—by which the theologian intimates that it is not possible to say whether God is within man or whether God is all, man being but a speck in the infinity of God. Or rather, he declares that the statement is true in either aspect, according to the standpoint from which the incomprehensible fact is viewed.

The problem of enclosing the dynamic and nonpersonal energy in a container can be made clearer by comparing the psychological conditions in this modern age, in which we have seen the dynamism of the unconscious breaking loose from its holds, with those periods in our history when these energies were really contained in a symbol. Among these, the period with which we are most familiar is of course the Christian epoch—by which I mean those centuries when the symbolism and ritual of the church really lived, not just for a few persons here and there as they do today, but for the great majority of people in Christian countries. The unconscious in individual men was adequately represented by the symbolic and ritual happenings re-enacted over and over again as the seasons of the church calendar recurred throughout the year. For the men and women of those centuries their own inner, psychic drama was played out by the persons of the sacred story. They really felt themselves to be renewed at Easter through participation in the ritual reliving of the death and resurrection of Christ. They were actually released from the sense of sin by the rite of confession and absolution; for them, Christ was in very fact sacrificed anew at the celebration of the mass, and by witnessing the mystery of transubstantiation they too were transformed, redeemed, and made one with him. These ceremonies were not a mere expression of beliefs, lightly held, but actual psychological experiences that satisfied the individual's unconconscious needs.

The unmediated experience of the spirit, however, in all its numinous power, came to only a few isolated individuals. That it was an awe-inspiring experience, a *tremendum*, is amply shown in the accounts of the early Christians, as for example in the descriptions of the descent of the Holy Spirit at Pentecost and of the vision of Paul on the way to Damascus. Many similar experiences are recorded, so that we can read how it was with the saints and mystics whose visions and dreams produced ecstasy or terror. It was only later that these experiences were organized under fixed symbolic and ritual forms to make a church in which the many could find a solution of life's problems and rest for their souls. The fact that this could happen is evidence that the original experiences, while occurring to a few only, had yet a general validity; the few had the necessary vision to perceive the psychic reality that was present, unseen and unrecognized, in the unconscious of the large majority of their contemporaries. This is the function that the artist and the seer have performed in all ages.

But when the content of the numinous experience is organized in this way, and, as it were, stereotyped by being formed into a doctrine and ritual, the untamable spirit is caught and limited and bound. For many centuries this limitation was tolerated by the spirit, which could function adequately for men through the meaningful services of the Christian church. Moreover, through the familiar and well-loved forms the common man was able to participate in the mysteries, though he could not comprehend them; thus the very limitation sufficed to safeguard the individual from the direct impact of the unknown and terrifying forces of the unconscious. But eventually these broke loose from the forms that had become meaningless. However, when the form is discarded the spirit is not thereby dissipated or destroyed. As an American poet writes:

> [Men] built their temple-walls to shut thee in,
> And framed their iron creeds to shut thee out.
> But not for thee the closing of the door,
> O Spirit unconfined!
> Thy ways are free
> As is the wandering wind.[16]

Since the present age possesses no collective symbol adequate to contain the dynamic spirit, each of us who voluntarily or involuntarily explores the unconscious realm is abandoned to the danger of a direct experience of that mighty and awe-inspiring force. Fortunately, when outer organization fails us, we are not left entirely alone in face of this *tremendum*, for the work that has been accomplished in past ages by the best and bravest of mankind has left a residuum in the human psyche. If an individual's conscious attitude is right,[17] the archetypes lying deep within him will arise in helpful guise when he is beset by the terrors of the unknown and will mediate between him and the inchoate and threatening dynamism that might so easily destroy his slender consciousness.

When at such a time a man turns in all seriousness to the unconscious for guidance, it may well be that a symbol will appear for him, like those which appeared in times past for his ancestors—a symbol that will gather up into itself the energy threatening to destroy him, as it has been threatening also to destroy civilization itself. Many symbols will be found on the

16. H. Van Dyke, "God of the Open Air," *Poems*, p. 72.

17. The attitude of the conscious I towards the unconscious is "right," in the sense used here, when the energy of the unconscious is channelled into life in a meaningful way. Then the life stream can flow on unobstructed, the unconscious remains quiescent, and the dreams and phantasies show that the inner life too is moving forward steadily to its goal.

road to the goal; the central one is called by Jung the symbol of individuation or the Self.[18]

The practical search for individuation involves two steps that must be undertaken by conscious effort if the work is to progress. The first is to collect within *my* psyche all that belongs to *me;* the second is to find a right relation to the nonpersonal energy that manifests itself in me—in my instincts, and in all those experiences, arising either in my environment or within myself, which have mana, that is, power to move me or arouse in me unruly or compulsive emotions.

In actual life these two processes must be carried on simultaneously, but the emphasis is sometimes on one and sometimes on the other. Beyond these two steps lies another, which cannot be initiated by conscious effort, though it occurs as a result of the conscious work. This is transformation of the nonpersonal energy, and its embodiment in a symbol, a "body," having the mana or power formerly hidden in the unconscious. This symbol becomes the new centre of the psyche, the Self.

This value corresponds to the final product sought by the alchemistic philosophers [19] under many names and many forms, such as *aurum nostrum* ("our gold"), the *rotundum* ("round thing"), the philosopher's stone, the elixir of life, etc. More than a hundred names for this final product of their work have been collected from the literature, showing that the value for which they stood was intuited or experienced but not fully understood, so that it continued to defy definition. It was always something beyond the content expressed by any one term: for it contained the unknown mana of the unconscious, which is illimitable and therefore in the last analysis inexpressible.

Three symbols have been selected to portray the successive steps of the individuation process—the circle of the psyche, the mandala, and the hermetic vessel. They have not been chosen arbitrarily, for in all probability any individual in whom the process of individuation is taking place will meet all three in some form or other in his own dreams and phan-

18. See Jung, *Aion* (C.W. 9, ii), esp. chaps. IV and V.
19. See below, chap. 12.

tasies. However, they will not necessarily occur in the order given here, and they are not likely to appear exactly as described; for the forms under which the basic ideas represented by the fundamental symbols can appear are truly legion. For instance, the circle of the psyche can be represented by any circular object, or by a group of people sitting or dancing in a circle, or in any other of a thousand ways. The mandala, which is only another aspect of the circle of the psyche, can be represented similarly by a circular object, or, when its own particular function of reconciling the opposites is implied, by a circle in relation to a square, a cross, or a triangle, this being represented either in a diagram or by means of an arrangement of objects—for example, a square box standing on a round table, or a round building in a square field.

The hermetic vessel too may be indicated under many guises, as by a cooking pot, an egg, or a womb symbol (the number of these is uncounted), a cauldron, a chalice, a retort or other chemical vessel, and so on through the whole range of containers in which a fundamental transformation takes place. The transformation itself may be represented in as many ways—as by the idea of cooking, of fermentation, or of the incubation of an egg. It may be put in terms of a chemical or a physical transformation, such as the precipitation of an insoluble salt, the formation of crystals, etc., or of the transformations symbolized by religious rituals, which in turn are usually based on natural phenomena, such as the renewal of the snake by the sloughing of its skin, or the metamorphosis of the caterpillar into a butterfly.

Although these symbols vary greatly as regards both the form and the order in which they occur in different individuals undergoing analysis, they do roughly correspond to stages in the developmental process. In actual experience, the first stage is not necessarily completed before the next begins to appear; more usually, the individual seems to accomplish one stage in a certain measure and go on to the next, only to return to the earlier one to experience it more thoroughly before proceeding further. The alchemists, who certainly experienced something like this in themselves, though they perceived it only in projection in the occurrences in their retorts, constantly stressed the necessity of repeating the processes of their work. They said for instance that the steps of solution and fixation (perhaps crystallization, possibly sublimation) must be repeated seven times. According to John Read, *"when repeated many times* it [the process] was supposed to furnish the 'quintessence' of the material concerned." [20]

The circle as used to represent the psyche may denote merely a single individual—"myself," complete, whole, separate from all other persons. The majority of people would assume that such a diagram would truly represent their own psychic status; this is an illusion, however, for, it is actually by no means easy to determine, in the psychic realm, what belongs to oneself and what does not. Furthermore, many an individual suffers not a little from a sense that he is incomplete, as if something that should be present within him were lacking. Others at times seem to lose themselves in a quagmire of depression, or in an unreal elation from which they recover only to find themselves depleted and unwhole. Others feel themselves to be divided: such an individual seems to himself to be two persons, or even many persons, and not one. Still others are so carried away by the demands of the outer world, or by interesting and exciting collective activity, that they lose their identity completely; they no longer know what they themselves think, and when they are alone they feel empty and utterly bored. In none of these situations could a circle be said to represent truly the actual condition of the psyche.

Certain schools of psychology speak of the I and the not-I as if these were a priori categories that no normal adult would confuse, any more than he would be confused about his own separate bodily entity. Infants, it is true, have to learn even this degree of discrimination, and adults may on occasion lose it. Thus the analogy of circle and individual does not always hold even on the physical plane, where it seems so obvious. It is hardly any wonder that in the psychological realm the difficulty and confusion are even greater.

20. J. Read, *Prelude to Chemistry,* p. 138. The italics are mine.

The relation of the personal part of the psyche to the non-personal part, also called the not-I, will be deferred for the moment, in order that we may explore first the ostensibly much simpler question: What are the boundaries of my own psyche —where do I leave off and where does the other fellow begin?

It is usually assumed that everyone knows exactly what belongs to himself, what originates from himself, what he is responsible for. Yet it is by no means always easy to determine the line of division between oneself and others. Even in the realm of direct, sensory experience—"what I have seen with my own eyes" or "heard with my own ears"—there is often ground for doubt. To demonstrate this point, it is necessary only to question two or three "reliable" witnesses about the details of an automobile accident. The infant does not even know the bodily I from the not-I, as anyone who has observed a baby's discovery of his own toe will have seen. His consciousness, his discrimination, does not as yet reach to the limits of his own body.

As we grow to adult awareness we do learn to recognize the connection of ourselves with our own bodies, but it takes only a slight lowering of consciousness to dissolve even this perception. Many of the amusing stories told about drunkards hinge on this circumstance. Similarly, preoccupation with some inner concern can produce a condition of absent-mindedness in which the most absurd lapses may occur. Such things are at times exceedingly funny, like the perennial story of the old gentleman who hunts for his spectacles unaware that they are still on his own nose. Or they may be embarrassing, like the situation occurring not uncommonly in dreams, and occasionally in actual life, in which a person goes out oblivious of the fact that he has not put on some essential article of clothing. In other situations absent-mindedness may not be so amusing. Many an accident has occurred because someone in a daydream did not look where he was going, but was allowing his autonomous functions to carry on while he moved about in a hazy, dreamlike state. An adult who has not learned to be more aware of himself is considered by primitives to be only a part man, possessed of the animal soul with which he was born, but lacking a human soul, which they believe must be acquired through undergoing the tribal initiation ceremonies.

A man who has only an "animal soul" would, in psychological terms, be said to have only somatic or body consciousness; when he gains a "human soul" he acquires object consciousness. This is the condition demanded and developed by Western education. In our extraverted culture it has been raised to a high degree of efficiency. But beyond the fact of object awareness lies the question: Who is it that is aware? This posits the problem of self-consciousness. Self-consciousness, in the sense here intended, means an awareness of myself and of the part I play in the happenings I observe, and also awareness of the subjective life going on within me, which is related to the external life around me, though independent of it.

Society in general is made up of persons in all stages of psychological development, in whom consciousness varies enormously, not only in extent and degree but also in kind. Many, and these by no means only the uneducated, are entirely in the dark so far as consciousness of self is concerned. They may even reject the idea that there is such a thing as a self-existent psychic life, being at the same time convinced that they know exactly what is I and what is not-I. Others, in whom some development has occurred, may find their complete certainty on this point challenged, even though self-consciousness in them is still rather dim and rudimentary. This state is like that of the young man who went to a dance after fortifying himself with several cocktails; he stood at the door of the ballroom and watched the whole floor and all the dancers seemingly swaying in time to the music, and murmured to himself: "Am I, or is it?"

As regards the physical I and not-I, that is, on the level of body consciousness, most people can discriminate. Even here, self-awareness may not be very profound. Many a woman has at some time or other found tears trickling down her face though she was not aware that she was crying, and some persons never seem to be able to determine whether their feelings of exhaustion indicate that they are sick or only tired and hungry. Physiology students are put through a little experiment designed to impress upon them the relativity of personal observation and the necessity of taking into account what is aptly called the "personal factor." In this test the left hand is placed in cold water for two or three minutes, while the right is kept in hot water; then both hands are put together into a bowl of tepid water. The fallibility of subjective judgment is startlingly demonstrated by the contradictory sensations that result. For when the two hands touch the tepid water, it is as though an argument arose between them. The left hand asserts that the water is quite hot; the right hand emphatically contradicts this judgment, for to it the water is cold, and so convinced is each of being entirely right that even a thermometer may hardly avail to settle the dispute. It takes a considerable degree of disidentification from one's own sensations for the I to be able to accept this impersonal evidence, and to realize that the testimony of the hands may be deceptive.

Examples of this sort of thing could of course be multiplied indefinitely; yet to many persons it comes as a surprise to discover that on a higher level their ability to discriminate between the I and the not-I is even less developed than it is on the somatic plane. Few individuals realize to what an extent they project their subjective reactions, and how much of what they see in the world about them originates in the hinterland of their own psyches. We dimly see this in others and we all know theoretically that "we view the world through our own glasses." When one has met with disappointment or is depressed, everything looks gloomy; when one is happy the sun seems to shine, even on a cloudy day. That these impressions are the result of inner states may be perfectly obvious when we observe them in others; but relatively few persons recognize such mechanisms in themselves clearly enough to be able to disentangle themselves from their moods of happiness or despondency, and to turn their attention inward to seek out the real cause of the seeming brightness or gloom of the outer world.

When the unrealized subjective state is completely projected into an object, the individual will be entirely unaware of the source of his reaction and will be convinced that what he likes or dislikes is a quality of the object and does not relate to anything in himself. A homely illustration is the attitude of the child who protests at dinner, "Mother, why do we have to have that horrid dessert?" The child does not realize that the trouble is not with the food, which is pleasing to the rest of the family; the difficulty is that he happens not to like it. But to him it is the food that is horrid. It is only a step beyond that for him to feel that his mother is horrid or unkind in providing such horrid food. This is in miniature the beginning of a persecution complex.

If in the experiment of the hot and cold water the parties to the argument were two different persons instead of the two hands of one individual, it is easy to see how difficult it might be to settle the dispute. Each person will be entirely convinced of the correctness of his own conclusion. His anger and general unreasonableness will be proportionate to his inability to realize that his observations may be relative or perhaps entirely personal; if he is blind to this possibility, the other person will necessarily seem to him to be wrong and unaccountably stubborn, or, worse still, bent only on contradicting him and picking a quarrel. It is amazing how easily even the most reasonable of human beings can impute to another a motive of which he would not willingly be guilty himself. It rarely occurs to the ordinary man that he is subject to just such limitations in consciousness at some point or other, and that his view of the world and of his environment is restricted both in extent and depth and is usually quite self-centred. It takes a special kind of education to enable us to see, in a psychological sense, any point of view other than our own.

To almost everyone other human beings exist, have life, only when they are in the immediate neighborhood. Then the light of one's consciousness illumines them for a moment; as soon as they are out of sight, however, they might as well be nonexistent for all the awareness one retains of them. Of course one can by an act of thought remember their existence, bring them to mind, as we say. One can speculate as to where they are and what they are doing, but as soon as one desists from this conscious effort of attention they drop back into the twilight, perhaps even disappear altogether. The situation is aptly summed up in the White Queen's remark to Alice: "You don't really exist, you are only a creature in my dream!" It is as though other people, as soon as one stops looking at them or thinking of them, were consigned to a state of suspended animation until one remembers them again; then they come to life like the people in the story of Sleeping Beauty. This is exemplified in the dream of a modern woman, in which a voice said: "They all go to sleep in a glass case." One knows they are there, but they don't do anything, or think anything, or affect anything.

The light of ego consciousness is very feeble and intermittent, and until a greater light is kindled in us, only a very small part of the world is illumined for us at any one time. This symbolism is so true to the facts of experience that anyone who has lost consciousness temporarily will almost invariably describe his experience in terms of a dimming of the daylight. He may say, "Everything became dark," or "The room was blotted out"; that is, he suffered a physical or psychological blackout. From the point of view of one who has achieved a higher awareness, the relative darkness of the ego consciousness seems to keep the individual in a state very much like this.

But when a new light, greater than that of ego consciousness, is kindled within, it is as though the psyche were illumined by an inner sun, and the range of psychological vision is greatly increased.[21] When this light shines it is no longer necessary to make a conscious effort to put oneself in another's place or to recall him to mind; he will remain alive not only for himself but also for him in whom the light has been kin-

21. This is surely the light to which the alchemists referred when they spoke of their stone as "the light that conquers every light." Jung, in "Dream Symbols of the Process of Individuation" (*Psychology and Alchemy* [C.W. 12], p. 76), quotes the following passage from a treatise ascribed to Hermes: *Intelligite, filii sapientum, quod hic lapis preciosissimus clamet . . . et lumen meum omne lumen superat ac mea bona omnibus bonis sunt sublimiora. . . . Ego gigno lumen, tenebrae autem naturae meae sunt* ("Understand, ye sons of the wise, what this exceeding precious stone sayeth . . . 'And my light conquers every light and my virtues are more excellent than all virtues. . . . I beget the light, but the darkness also is of my nature . . .'").

dled. For the sun shines on all men alike. And my friend stands plain to me in the light of this inner sun.

Just as the child's ego does not start out with a complete view of the universe, nor even of his own world, so his psychological awareness too is very limited. Although the light of ego consciousness increases as development progresses, its range at best is limited to the realm of the I; much even of the outer world that might be known remains unexplored, and all the vast reaches of the inner, psychic world remain unlighted. It is as though little islands of awareness emerged one by one from the dark waters of the unconscious. In the development of consciousness these are gradually pieced together, until something that seems to be a complete picture of the environment is formed. But this picture is by no means whole and is often far from accurate, although it is the mark of a rather high degree of consciousness to be aware that there are gaps in one's vision. The less educated and the more limited a person is, the more sure is he that he knows all about everything. This accounts for the prejudice so characteristic of the unconscious person's opinions and for his dogmatic or fanatical way of upholding them. A cultured and experienced man, in contrast, is far more willing to admit a doubt, recognizing that his views are necessarily relative and that there are two sides to every question.

The unconscious parts of the psyche are actually, as the term implies, unknown—a fact not infrequently overlooked, for it is hard for anyone to believe that factors of which he knows nothing are functioning autonomously within his own psyche. Even when their presence has been demonstrated conclusively, it is often hard for the individual to admit their existence even to himself, for this means also the admission that instead of his being the master who initiates and controls his own thoughts, actions, and emotions, the part he is enacting may have been assigned to him by "another"—an unknown other—by reason of whose unrecognized influence he is revealed to be the unsuspecting object of the action rather than the self-determining subject. He may in fact be but a servant in his own house, not the master; at times he may suspect that he is a dupe, for he finds that what he has done is actually not what he intended to do, is possibly even the direct opposite of his purposed act.

The unconscious factors of the psyche not only pull the strings in this secret way within man; they also affect him from without, for they are mirrored from the objects in his environment. Whenever something in life interests a man, or exercises an attraction, either positive or negative, in a measure disproportionate to its actual value, it is carrying the image of some psychic element that has lain dormant in the unconscious and is now so activated that it begins to manifest itself in the mirror of the world, where it is at last within reach of the conscious psyche. If it could then be disentangled from the object in which it is reflected, it could be taken back into the psyche and assimilated to consciousness.

These psychic elements lying behind the ego in the individual's unconscious are projected, that is, they are reflected or mirrored externally, in persons and things and situations which therefore acquire for him a significance and power of attraction borrowed from the unknown aspects of his own psyche. It is this psychological mechanism that is represented in the Hindu concept of maya, as used to refer to the phenomenal world; for one of its meanings is "illusion," and to the Hindu philosopher our concern with outward existence is a manifestation of the fact that some of our psychic values exist, as yet, only in the projections we make to the world around us.

This phenomenon of projection is a very important one, for it is one of the principal means by which unconscious contents obtrude themselves on consciousness. To a very unconscious person the world about him may even be peopled by objects that seem to be alive and have the ability to act or speak by virtue of the power of the unconscious psychic stuff projected into them, or, as it seems, residing in them. The term projection is not a very well-chosen one. For the situation is not that the factors illusorily perceived in the other person or in the object were once included in the conscious psyche or possessed by the ego and were deliberately "thrown upon" the person or object now carrying the projection. Rather, it is just those "should-be-conscious" contents which have remained unconscious, and therefore outside of consciousness, that are met or discovered in the projections. Of persons who carry such projections for us we are very apt to say: "I would never dream of feeling like that or of acting as he did; it is the last thing I would ever do." Yet the very fact that the individual feels the given behaviour to be so incompatible with his conscious standpoint, while he is at the same time so emotional about it, should give him pause. For these are the hallmarks of projection: they are the characteristic reactions to those psychic contents we are unaware of in ourselves.

In children and primitives so much potential psychic energy remains unconscious and unassimilated that the whole world around them comes alive with it. Inanimate objects seem to them to move and speak and live a life of their own, while animals seem to be endowed with consciousness and other human characteristics. The psychological attitude denoted by the anthropologists as "animistic" rests on this phenomenon of projection; through it the primitive contacts those elements of his own psyche that are still unknown to him and have remained as it were outside himself. When a tree speaks to him, telling him things that a more conscious man would recognize as his own thoughts, it means that he is not capable of articulate thinking; inasmuch as he may be nonetheless an intelligent man, thinking of a sort goes on in him, but as this is an unconscious process, the results are voiced to him by the tree.

When the primitive tribesman consults his snake, it is his own instinct that he confers with; or, as among the ancient Greeks, it is the spirit of the ancestors or of some hero of the past that assumes the form of the snake to give an oracular answer to a perplexing question or to speak the word of wisdom in a crisis. In a more developed society, the ancestral wisdom or the tribal experience is formulated into a code of behaviour, into laws, customs, and historical precept. But even in such a community, when an unusual situation arises, the old ways may recur spontaneously, awakening from the unconscious in the hour of need, and some village seer or prophet will once more consult his snake or his voices and on this basis claim a more than human authority. We are very prone to apply the term superstitious to these ways of acting as they appear so overtly in the primitive, and to assume that we of the present day have long ago outgrown them.

But is not a modern man acting very much like the unlettered primitive when he cannot make up his mind about some matter of importance until he has talked it over with the woman he loves? For the thoughts on which his decision must be based "come" to him as a result of his talking with her, although she is incapable of helping him with any knowledge of her own. Where then do the helpful and pertinent ideas come from? Obviously they must come from the man's own unconscious, where they lie all ready to hand; yet they remain entirely inaccessible to his conscious mind until they are found in the particular woman who embodies the projection of his anima and is therefore endowed with all the wisdom of the unconscious. To him, however, it seems as if the actual woman were the source of the new ideas. The fact that they are only reflected back to him from her could easily be demonstrated by questioning her about the subject. Yet the man may remain blind to her real limitations.

It is strange that we are so little conscious that our view of the world is so inaccurate. Practically every individual has some psychological blind spot of which he is blissfully unaware until it is encroached upon, when an unreasonable emotion is likely to flare up. This is perhaps not very easy to appreciate in regard to the psychological sphere; but a roughly analogous phenomenon is found on the physical plane. There is in actual fact a blind spot in the retina, which can be demonstrated by a very simple experiment; but we are rarely conscious of it and do not take it into account in everyday life. Instead, we automatically fill the gap in what lies before us with an imaginary object conforming with the rest of the picture, or we cover the whole area before us by moving our eyes. In other words, we do not see a blank space; it fills itself, as it were. For example, in facing an audience a speaker observes a sea of faces. Theoretically he may know that somewhere in the field there is a blank area, but he does not see a hole, although he automatically compensates for it by turning his eyes first to one side, then to the other. Even if he keeps his eyes still and looks straight ahead, he does not see an empty spot in the general picture. The people in that part of the room seem to merge together—it might be said fancifully that he invents an extra, quite indefinite person to fill the gap.

If we now carry this description over to the psychological realm, we might postulate a corresponding mechanism as serving to fill in the field of the psychological blind spot, the area of unconsciousness. By a stretch of the imagination one could conceive of a play written around the idea of this physical peculiarity, with a villain who would be able constantly to conceal himself by taking advantage of someone's blind spot, as a sort of invisible man—invisible to his victim, but plainly in view to the rest of the group. Such a story would seem too fantastic, however, because most people are unaware of the retinal blind spot and its customary compensation.

Yet an analogous drama is constantly being played in real life on the psychological plane, the villain of the piece being an unconscious element of the individual's psyche obtruding itself in the form of a projection. For all unconscious psychic factors are autonomous and have a marked tendency to become personified, acting like part souls, little persons. This is found to be true in regard to the shadow, the anima or animus, and the mana personality.

Any of these figures may play the part of the villain who keeps himself hidden from his victim while quite probably remaining visible to everyone else. Naturally such a situation can make for great misunderstanding; but this is nothing compared with the confusion that inevitably arises when the areas corresponding to the psychological blind spots of two different persons happen to coincide. In such a case each will confuse the villain—the one who does the "dirty work"—with the other person; all the libido of both will be drawn into fixing the blame, and none will be left over for "fixing" the situation. If only the antagonists could realize that there is indeed a villain in the piece, but that neither of them is "it," something might be done to clear up the misunderstanding. They are so busy belabouring each other, however, or so overwhelmed by hurt feelings over mutual suspicions and accusations, that they fail entirely to be aware of the actual villain and so do not even attempt to catch him or to "frustrate his knavish tricks."

I have used the term "it" here in the way in which it is used in childish play. Children do not stop to analyse or to ask why but live out their phantasies quite naïvely. Consequently their language, especially as used in games, often reveals a hidden psychological reality. For instance, this "it" of the child's game is quite a valuable formulation. In tag or blindman's buff the players are "it" in turn; the "it-ness" is worn like a garment that can be passed from one to another. It is put upon one of the players—"You're it!"—and as such he will be avoided or feared. The others will hide from him or run shrieking when he appears, as if he were a powerful and evil monster. But when he is divested of the role, by passing it on to another, he loses this extrahuman quality and is accepted once more as one of the group. And as the children all understand clearly the difference between the individual in his own person and the role he is playing, no vestige of the "it" feeling remains in a given child after he has doffed the part.

If only we could follow this example in our grown-up game of blindman's buff, in which the "it" is the unconscious factor intruding itself into our conscious human relationships, we should be enormously released. To accommodate this factor, Jung suggests, we should do well to create a personification for the unseen mischief or evil, something like the children's "it." This personification would have to take the form of a creature recognized by all involved as having only psychological reality, such as a "jinx" or a "gremlin."

In certain folk rituals the participants vent their wrath on one who carries the projection of unseen evil forces. Actually this is an attempt to exorcize the demons of evil by separating them from the life situation and dealing with them within the frame of the ritual, thus deflecting their destructive potentialities from human lives and relationships. But the participants in such a ritual may not be aware of the actual significance of their actions; consequently at times, because its purpose is not understood, the rite that should be an exorcism serves instead to keep alive the angers and resentments clinging to the memory of the evil, which "seek" to be avenged on the person of the scapegoat.

Rituals of this nature are to be found in the burning in effigy of some long-dead enemy of society, as on Guy Fawkes Day in England—an occasion sometimes used, if the mob spirit happens to be aroused, to vent current social or political animosities by giving to the "Guy" the name and appearance of some living enemy. In this case the mob is usually satisfied with the symbolic vengeance. But the mechanism underlying the compulsive and violent passion that takes possession of ordinarily sober, law-abiding citizens under the influence of the group emotion is very similar to that which underlies the far more sinister ritual of lynching. The victim of the lynching may have only the slenderest connection with the crime that is being avenged so violently and so lawlessly; yet he immediately becomes almost a demon or a devil to those caught up by the mob spirit. The evocation of this spirit in modern times rests upon exactly the same psychological impulse that impelled the ancient Greeks to sacrifice a corn man at the harvest. Still, when Guy Fawkes is burned as if he were the devil, there is more insight in regard to his existent nonexistence than there was in ancient Greece in regard to the corn man, or in mediaeval times in regard to a witch burning or to the practice of ascribing all the evil in the world to Satan, whom the majority not only of the common people but also of the educated conceived of as an actual being.

If we today, while recognizing the psychological nature of such evil forces, could learn how to create a form equivalent to that of the devil, or Guy Fawkes, or the "gremlin" of the airmen—all the time knowing what we were doing—our private devils would no longer be able to dog us unseen, ready at any and every opportunity to manifest themselves in misunderstandings and the other unaccountable disturbances that so often mar our human relationships. For they would be caught, contained, imprisoned for examination at leisure.

It is not enough just to be released from the daemonic

forces that can so disastrously obscure our understanding of any given situation. This step, it is true, will help to give us an unobstructed view of the personal field. But just as the excitement and interest of the children's game depends on the function of the "it," without which there could be no game, so for adults the significance of life, and its deeply fascinating and exciting elements, come from the untamed, the unknown, the unexplored regions of the psyche, the nonpersonal realm, rather than from the obvious, the understood, the cultivated precincts. In the game, the drama and *élan* depend on the "it"; for here the players are dealing with the unknown, the nonpersonal. It is uncanny, perhaps, as in blindman's buff or hide-and-seek, but on that very account alluring, fascinating, exciting, even a little frightening—for it carries, albeit only in play, a touch of that unknown quality which belongs to the realm of the gods and demons. It is the numen, the *tremendum*, at once terrifying and fascinating, awe-inspiring and infinitely desirable.

Before the individual can become rounded out, he must first of all recognize those psychic elements which live outside his own psyche, as it were, in the projections that have such power to fascinate him and attract either his love or his hate. When this nonpersonal factor has been aroused and recognized as such in some life situation, he faces the problem of how to separate the elements that belong within his own psyche from the projections in which they have been concealed. When this has been done the nonpersonal energy, the "devil," remains to be mastered. If this energy, being no longer contained by the projection, is not dealt with adequately, it will be free to work its mischief unchecked, as in the parable of the man from whom the devil had been cast out. It is related that the unclean spirit went forth and wandered in waterless places, and on returning found his old dwelling place empty, swept and garnished; then he took seven other devils worse than himself to live with him there.[22] In other words, when a man does not take moral responsibility for the inmates of his psychic house, the nonpersonal elements will take over like a troop of devils.

22. Matt. 12:43 ff.

The psyche of the individual is not a simple, homogeneous entity; rather, it is an extended realm, a domain that has a certain organization, and the elements belonging to it have a certain affinity. The organization may be very loose, however, or even entirely latent. Furthermore, the realm of the individual psyche extends in all directions around that spark of light which each of us calls "I"—into the outer world through contacts with family and friends, with business and social circles, and, beyond these, with national and world affairs, and into an inner world where the unseen subjective life is affected by influences of a psychological nature that are as real as concrete phenomena. A demonstration of the power of psychological factors has come to us forcibly in recent years in the "war of nerves" and in the organized propaganda aimed to influence morale—itself a psychological quality—not only through the information, true or false, that it offers for the conscious consideration of the listener, but still more through the effects it has on the unconscious.[23] An individual may be entirely without knowledge of what psychological influences are affecting him, except as they show themselves in the dreams, phantasies, moods, obsessions, or even physical symptoms they produce.

Thus the individual psyche is an indefinite formation of unknown or largely unknown constitution and extent. If it is to be consolidated—individuated, to use the technical term —it is necessary first of all to determine its boundaries. Then all that belongs to the psyche must be brought within these boundaries. Finally, a centre must be established that can control the functioning of the whole structure.

To any individual who has not undertaken a special study of the matter, the range of his own psyche with respect to the outer world is known only very roughly. As this range increases progressively during at least the first half of life, merely finding the outer limits of the psyche is a difficult task in itself, requiring not only many years for its accomplishment but also a true and deep devotion, for it involves the necessity of investing the whole of one's potential energies in it as a

23. Cf. V. O. Packard, *The Hidden Persuaders.*

life enterprise. Furthermore, even if an individual could gauge with accuracy the range of his psychological interest, there would still remain the problem of determining what part of those things which concern him belongs to his own psyche and what part belongs to others involved in the same situation.

In the course of my daily work as an analytical psychologist, I constantly see evidences of the difficulty of this differentiation. However, when an individual comes to me torn by some conflict that he has been unable to resolve unaided, that is threatening his adaptation or his health, the procedure of merely laying before him the conflicting elements of his story as he himself tells it, and of pointing out to him that he is divided in himself and needs to be whole—that he actually could be whole, even though the conflicting elements in his environment remained—brings an immediate response and a certain release from distress, so that he can begin to face the problem of how to gather up the scattered parts of his psyche and integrate them. If this is true in the case of individuals who have about reached the end of their endurance, how much more valuable would it be for others, not so hard pressed, to seek a measure of integration while they have the opportunity, and before the stresses of life have pushed them to extremity.

This task in relation to the outer life, difficult as it may be, is still easy as compared with the task of finding the limits of the psyche in its inner or subjective range, for there it stretches back indefinitely into the dark regions of the unconscious. Yet, difficult and almost impossible as it seems, the task of becoming whole is one that cannot be ignored. The majority of persons recognize instinctively that wholeness is essential for psychological health, while to be dispersed and disintegrated spells sickness and suffering. Thus certain persons find themselves obliged to undertake the task of individuation as a conscious willed enterprise, even though the quest promises no definite ending. Once it is undertaken, however, aid comes from an unexpected source, namely, from the unconscious itself. For symbols of wholeness begin to appear in dreams and phantasies and in other products of the unconscious, pointing the way that must be taken, even if this way leads towards an unknown goal.

Thus the quest for wholeness shows itself to be in line with an archetypal trend inherent in the psychic structure of the human being. This trend is akin to an instinct and, like the instincts, is capable of showing the way to be taken by the developing organism. The instinct leads towards a goal, although the individual in whom it operates may be completely unaware what that goal is. The instinct of a newborn infant causes it to make sucking movements when it is put to the breast, an activity it has never before undertaken. During all its intra-uterine life its nourishment came to it via the blood stream, but now, taught by an inner wisdom, it makes its first attempt to feed itself, not in the old, established way but by a new and untried technique. This first effort, blind though it seems, begins a process that leads step by step towards the goal of independent existence. In the same way, the archetypal trend directed to the goal of wholeness or individuation seems to be blind; for the individual in whom the process is taking place may not and usually does not know the goal, nor the road that must be taken in order to reach it.

In the example given above, the unconscious child can neither assist nor retard the instinctive process tending to the goal of independent individual life. The adult similarly cannot assist nor retard the natural development of the psyche, unless he can find some means of acquainting himself with the inner trend, with which he can then cooperate. If in addition he is able to form even a dim picture of the goal to be achieved, he may be able to cooperate more effectively. Unless he is willing, however, to subordinate his preconceived ideas to the instinctive wisdom inherent in his own psychic laws, he may find that his attempts to aid only confuse and distort the issue. To avoid this unhelpful kind of interference, he must be prepared to respect the intimations arising spontaneously within him.

In the quest for individuation, much of the conscious work must of necessity be done on that part of the psyche which impinges on the outer world, for this is the part accessible to consciousness. As the outer boundaries are gradually delimited, a parallel process proceeds within the psyche; the problem of delimitation of the inner bounds begins to clarify itself, and as a result, consolidation or crystallization of a central area begins. Consequently the individual engaged in this work comes to feel within himself the formation of a psychic body having a certain weight and solidity; this foreshadows the emergence of the true centre. This centre is obviously not the ego, which is related only to the conscious part of the psyche. Further, inasmuch as the psyche is partly unconscious, the true centre must remain to that extent unknown, even though its presence and influence are recognized by the conscious ego through the effects it produces. Thus the conscious I turns with ever increasing assurance to this true centre as it learns more and more to rely on the validity and greater cogency of its judgments.

To find this centre, or rather to evoke it—I hesitate to use the word create, for that may give a quite false impression—is, therefore, the goal of the quest. It is the centre of a new kind of consciousness quite different from ego consciousness, whose light is like that of a candle, while the light of the new consciousness is far-reaching and impersonal like the sun's. This goal, however, cannot be sought directly with willed intent, for it is necessarily entangled with factors and processes that are and remain in the unconscious, beyond the control of the ego. The work in its early stages, however, is concerned with that part of the problem which does lie within the competence of consciousness and must therefore be undertaken as a conscious task.

The first problem, then, is to determine the extent and limits of the psyche, or, to put it still more simply, the boundaries of oneself. An individual finds his outward limit when he ascertains how far his interest naturally flows out when unhampered by artificial restrictions and limitations, such as those imposed on the one hand by the family, by moral codes, or by conventions, and on the other by assumptions arising from within him, from his unconscious as voiced by the anima or by other archetypal figures. In the course of analysis the sub-

ject is constantly being asked to find out *what he himself
really wants*, for only so may he learn to know himself. The
clue to his real nature and dimensions is given not by that kind
of wanting which is no more than wishful thinking, but by
an active wanting that can stand the impact of reality and has
power to release him so that he can put forth his greatest effort
and to sustain him through all difficulties and frustrations
until he attains his wish.

During this stage of the analytical work he may have to
experiment with all sorts of things, many of which do not
remain as part of his personality. But so long as he retains a
secret desire to do something that has always been forbidden
to him, or to be something he has never dared to attempt to
be, or so long as he harbours a resentment over the fact that
these things were denied him, he cannot know himself. The
necessity of experimenting with these things may be very
trying both to himself and to his associates, but it is part of
the price of becoming an individual. Moreover, while such
experimenting may be costly, it may also bring a great reward.
Through daring to seize his personal freedom, the individual
may find himself gaining not only release from invisible bonds
and restrictions but also a sense of joy and new power that is
of the utmost value. He feels as though he had been born anew.

As the work progresses, it gradually uncovers the essential limits of his energies and desires—limits which are felt to
be natural and right, within which he can function without
any sense of crippling restraint or frustration. In this way any
excesses that may have threatened during the experimental
phase are brought within bounds, and the new liberty is found
to augment the creative powers of the psyche rather than to
dissipate them.

During this phase of the analytical work it will almost
certainly be found—if indeed this was not the reason for undertaking the analysis in the first place—that the wishes released
within the individual are opposed by conflicting attitudes and
desires that have an equally great if not greater value for him.
In everyday life, when such a conflict arises, the conventional
way of disposing of it is to choose one or the other course of

action and to repress the opposed wish. In relatively unimportant matters this may work, at least for a time, but it does not dispose of the problem, for the repressed desire continues to live in the unconscious and will seek all sorts of clandestine ways of fulfillment, without the knowledge or consent of the conscious I. And the energy with which the impulse is endowed, as represented by the amount of desire associated with it, will be lost to the conscious part of the psyche, being submerged together with the repressed content. Consequently the individual feels himself to be divided: he cannot live the chosen role with undivided loyalty, he cannot put himself wholly into it, and his interest naturally flags.

When in the course of analysis the individual begins to investigate his natural boundaries, this repressed inclination will surely reappear in consciousness, and a renewed conflict will arise between it and the chosen way. In certain instances, the desire that has been repressed may be so at variance with the general character of the individual that he may be able by an act of self-control to keep it in check without again denying or repressing it. When the occasion is not too important, his natural desires in regard to food, possessions, sex gratification, or ego recognition can be curbed in deference to his sense of the consideration due to other people or of the justice and equity of the situation, though he will also have to assimilate this unacceptable bit of psychic stuff that he declines to live overtly. But where the natural desire is of greater significance and moves him more deeply—namely, where an instinct is involved and the daemonic or nonpersonal energy inherent in such a fundamental urge is aroused—the conflict between the primary need and his civilized feelings and code of behaviour may become acute, and some means for reconciliation of the two desires will be sorely needed if the individual is not to be fundamentally split. A conflict of this kind is likely to give rise to all sorts of more or less violent emotions—anger, jealousy, hate, and so forth—for, as Jung points out, "passionate emotionality . . . precedes the recognition of unconscious contents," [24] that is, emotional outbursts usually occur in cases

24. Jung, *Mysterium Coniunctionis,* § 404.

of insufficient adaptation due to unconsciousness. This is the problem with which the mandala symbolism is concerned.[25]

The individual begins to discover the limits of his own nature by continuing to apply the method of exploring his own impulses and desires. He allows his wishes to flow out as far as his capacities permit, and finds out what these capacities really are. He puts his dreams to test; he outgrows the infantile state of being a "man of promise" and becomes a "man of actuality."

In the course of this development, which usually takes years of effort, a man will almost invariably find himself sooner or later—usually sooner rather than later—in some situation in which his desires and capacities come into conflict with those of another person, or with some external reality that prevents his natural self-fulfillment. He cannot go ahead or claim place unchallenged by reality. Such experiences will come to him in the objective world and also in his subjective life. In the objective world he may find that the position he wants has been given to another, that the enterprise in which he has invested money and effort is failing through some factor he could not foresee, that his research has been forestalled, that the woman he loves is marrying someone else; or perhaps illness and death put a limit to his desires. The list of mischances could be multiplied indefinitely through an array of all the possible frustrations of this mortal life. In the subjective sphere too he soon discovers that he is not the sole protagonist: his will, his desire, his sense of the importance of his ego may conflict with the demands of another. It is as though the psychic world were filled with entities that take up space just as the physical world is filled with tangible bodies. These entities are sparsely scattered in some areas and thickly clustered in others. Where they are scarce, the bounds of the individual must be determined according to the farthest point to which his interest flows out; where they are closely packed, his limits must be accepted as falling at the line of his contact with his neighbour.

25. See below, chap. 11.

The picture reproduced in plate XIV was drawn by a woman during the course of analysis. At the time she made the drawing she was occupied with the problem created by the fact that the numerous interests of her life demanded her attention so insistently that she began to feel herself getting lost among her many concerns. Was she to be divided up into little pieces, giving part of herself to this interest and part to that? She felt that if she allowed this to happen, she would be split and dismembered, and would lose touch with herself. Then she had a vision of how things could be. She saw a circle with many other circles impinging upon it, and began to speculate about the geometric technique for finding the centre of a circle by using the tangent at a number of different points. She was so intrigued by the psychological implications of this idea that she worked out her problem in this drawing. The circles filling the entire space stand for circles of interest. The large circle enclosing several smaller ones represents the natural field of interest of this individual, the external range of her psyche. The circles within the enclosing circle represent the different spheres of her life. The larger ones, which are coloured in the original, stand for the functions of sensation, thinking, feeling, and intuition, which give access to the four categories of knowledge of the world; the others represent other realms of interest—family, friends, work, etc.

In one feature this drawing is not like the conventional mandalas of organized religions—for instance, those used as *yantras* in Buddhism [26]—for the main circle overlaps other circles that do not, however, belong entirely within it. This circumstance reflects the problem with which the maker of the drawing was concerned. The partially included circles represent the many interests that she felt to be encroaching upon her individuality. The overlapping segments are lighted up with colour; that is, these areas take on colour and emotional interest because the psyche is impinging upon them. The colour spreading beyond the main circle marks psychic stuff that is still embedded in persons, situations, and objects outside the

26. See below, p. 380.

psyche, thus indicating projections that need to be assimilated.

If these other circles happen to represent other persons, an entanglement may well arise in the area of encroachment. Such an entanglement may consist in an emotional involvement of a positive nature, such as a love affair; or it may take the shape of a dispute, a rivalry, or some other negative or power involvement. Such situations constitute what may be called points at issue: at these points an increase of consciousness could take place. In the absence of such points at issue, it will obviously be more difficult to determine one's boundaries.

On the other hand, so long as some of the colour of one's own psyche is or seems to be in another individual, one is not free but is unconditionally bound to that person and to the situation. For they hold a part of oneself, they control this part and manipulate it, or seem to do so, quite independently; when they pull the strings one must dance, whether one wishes to do so or not. It recalls the situation of the giant in the fairy tale of Goldilocks. The giant, a wicked ogre, caught little children and kept them in his castle in order to eat them at leisure. But Goldilocks and her brother escaped. They journeyed to the country of the spider people (the mothers) and obtained from the greatest spider the giant's heart, which had been left in the spider country for safekeeping. The children put it in a bag, and whenever the giant threatened one of them they squeezed a little spider juice on the heart, at which the giant fell down in a fit, suffering great agony. By thus dominating the giant they rescued all the children in the castle and destroyed the power of the giant. Here we have a picture of the effects of projection. The giant has left his heart in the keeping of the mother, but it is stolen away by the golden-haired darling—that is, he falls in love with a girl who captures his anima projection. She then has complete power over his feelings and can bring him under her domination by appealing to his filial tie to the mother (spider juice symbolism), which is now transferred to her.

To return to the drawing under consideration: If the projections represented by the colour could be withdrawn from the adjacent circles, the entanglements due to psychological involvement would be resolved. This would result, theoretically at least, in the gradual withdrawal of all colour into the main circle. We must not argue from this, however, that for one who is completely individuated, the world becomes a colourless place. In one sense this is probably true, for the bodhisattva, as the Buddhists call such an individual, is by definition one who is completely released from the illusion of the world. Yet he retains a profound concern for the welfare of mankind, expressed as infinite compassion. This is for us of course only a theoretical goal in any final sense; but it is important to realize that individuation, even in the very limited form in which one can hope to achieve it, does not make one indifferent to the world, although the nature of the involvement changes. As the projections are gradually recognized and assimilated, the character of an individual's relation to the world undergoes a profound alteration. The identification with an object, the *participation mystique*, which depends on projection, is dissolved, and the individual's attitudes and reactions to persons and situations become freer and far more objective. He is no longer at the mercy of another's actions or moods; instead, the source of his feeling lies within himself. He has become autonomous and so, in a very true sense, his own master.

By means of her diagram the woman described above gained insight into her problem. She had supposed that her sense of being split up into little pieces was due to the number of the interests that so insistently demanded her attention. After she had drawn the picture, however, it was obvious that their power over her came not from them but from the projections she had made to them. Consequently, if she could withdraw the projections she would not only be released from her bondage but would also find herself greatly enriched.

The idea of the colouring in the picture bears out the statement that the psyche extends as far as one's interest can go; but the quality of the interest involved must also be considered. When G. K. Chesterton asked, "Are we really broader than our fathers, or are we only spread out thinner?" he was referring to the whole generation, but the question is relevant here too. Interest that is merely idle curiosity will not further psychological development. That demands an interest so vital that we must be ready to put time and work into its development, and a determination not to be discouraged even if at first we meet with little encouragement or success. Perhaps the sense in which "interested" is used in business here in America embodies the essential nuance. When a businessman is asked, "Are you interested in this proposition?" he understands the question to mean: "Are you willing to put time, attention, even money into it, to hold on to it and compel it to yield interest on your investment—thus to incorporate it into your sphere of interest, in some measure into your actual life?"

It is in this sense, with an equivalent emphasis on seriousness of purpose and responsibility, that one must ask himself what the limits of his interest are. Whatever concerns an individual in this vital way, so that he is held to it through thick and thin, that, we may be sure, contains something that is his business, his interest—something that he needs if his psyche is to be whole.

Things that are interests of ours in this sense will intrigue us, as a rule, and lead us on with an absorption that is one of the great delights of living; they attract us and make it easy to work at them and to take the rough with the smooth. If for instance an individual is interested in gardening, he pursues it with joy despite the backaches it produces. Perhaps some intellectual subject thrills him, and he thinks nothing of the hours spent poring over a book. Or it may be old ruins that he dreams about by night and reads about by day, until at last the time comes when he can set out to explore them in person; on that trip neither heat nor rain nor fatigue can spoil his pleasure. Such interests we are all likely to follow spontaneously, if we can succeed in freeing ourselves from the conventional holdbacks warning us that a well-conducted person never does more than one thing devotedly and indulges in any hobby or avocation only mildly. As the lure here is a positive one, we all follow it gladly when we dare. But there are other things that concern us—matters in which we do not listen so gladly to the voice that calls us, insistent questions that obtrude themselves in a far from agreeable guise.

Perhaps one goes to bed some night and tries to compose oneself to sleep. Darkness and oblivion should descend; instead it seems as if a light were turned up in another part of the room, and interests and concerns put aside during the day begin to stir and enter claim for attention. Some issue ostensibly settled demands reconsideration and will not be silenced by the arguments that seemed so convincing by daylight. A conflict settled too casually, a problem dismissed with a conventional argument—"Of course it must be done thus and so"—, a friend whose need was set aside with a perfunctory expression of sympathy, some bit of chicanery allowed to slip by in the hurried daytime, all come stalking out of the shadows. Thoughts crowd upon one, coming apparently from outside; they go on of themselves, they act as if they had a life of their own, they seem to be entirely autonomous. They will not let one sleep.

In such confrontations we experience in actuality the situation in the nursery story that tells how, as soon as the children are safely asleep, the toys come out of the toy box and begin to carry on a life of their own. Their loves and hates, their quarrels and friendships, are lived out in the nighttime while the children are inactive and helpless. The toys now have all the life and energy, and they do not by any means always play the parts assigned to them by the children. They are no longer the subservient puppets of their little masters; in this night world they have opinions of their own, which may be exceedingly critical of the humans who think themselves so completely dominant. As the children wake up, the toys all slip quietly back into the box and patiently play the children's game until night comes again; then once more they throw off their bondage.

But how is it that the toys have this life? Where does it come from? When the children grow up and go away from home, most of the toys die. One or two perhaps retain a faint vitality, but for the most part they become mere wood and tin and paint. For the energy that animated them has gone away with the young people and is now vested in a different set of "toys." The tin soldier is discarded for a motorbike or a baseball bat that in turn takes on a life of its own, while the doll with her pink cheeks and golden hair lives in a precarious incarnation in the vanity box and mirror of her little mistress. But normally a large part of this libido is utilized in the larger sphere of work and dream that must be explored and filled with interest; while the remainder, the part that is not used,

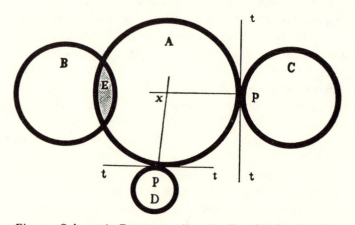

Fig. 12. Schematic Representation of a Psychic Involvement

A subject's psyche
B, C, D objects of interest impinging on the psyche
E area of involvement
p point of contact (point at issue)

tt tangent to A and C or A and D (impartial line of judgment)
px perpendicular to tangent (line of force representing irrational emotion)
x centre of the psyche

perhaps cannot be used in daily life, slips away behind the veil of unconsciousness. For the vitality of the toys was drawn from the energy of their owners: it was the psychic stuff the boys and girls had not as yet assimilated into themselves.

And when in the nighttime the adult finds certain things stirring, beginning to talk, refusing to be silenced, he may be sure that the voice comes from a bit of his own soul stuff housed in the person or situation that pursues him and disturbs his rest. If, instead of trying to solve his problem merely in an external sense, he takes the occurrence as an opportunity to find out what bit of his soul stuff is so concealed, he will

be working creatively towards determining his own boundaries. At the same time, because the objective situation will
be cleared of that ambiguous factor which really belongs
within his psyche, the resolution of the outer conflict will be
greatly facilitated. When this clarification has been achieved,
the conflict can fulfill its real function, namely, that of fixing
definite psychological points from which the search for the
centre of the psyche may be started.

This was the second piece of insight that the woman who
made the drawing gained from her work. Her meditation on
the circle had led her to the problem of finding the centre.
Her picture was drawn freehand, without a compass, so that
in the actual drawing the centre was not marked. But if
tangents were drawn at the points where the smaller circles
touched the larger one, and perpendiculars to the tangents
were constructed at these points, the centre of the circle could
be found. Thus the question arose whether in the psychological realm analogous points of contact might not be made to
play a corresponding role in determining the still unknown
centre of the psyche.

The situation could be shown in simplified form as in figure 12. Here *A* represents the psyche of the subject; *B*, *C*, and
D stand for persons or situations that hold interest for the
subject. The overlapping at *E* represents an involvement that
has aroused emotional reactions disproportionate to the situation. If the projection implied in *E* can be withdrawn by means
of a clarification that establishes an impartial line of demarca-
tion, the two spheres of interest will be separated, and the new
situation can be shown by the relation of *C* to *A*. The impartial
line here is represented by the tangent *tt*. The passionate emotion released from the situation is the force opposed to the
impartial judgment. These two lines of force are represented
by the tangent *tt* and the perpendicular *px*. When similar
perpendiculars are drawn at several points, their intersection
(*x*) establishes the centre of the circle. In our analogy, we
may take this point as representing the centre of the psyche.

An illustration will make the psychological procedure
clearer. In the dispute about the temperature of the tepid

water,[27] a thermometer would serve to establish an impartial judgment; this would correspond to the tangent of the diagram. If similarly two individuals are involved in a controversy as to whether a room is too hot or too cold, they may well be unable to reach agreement solely on the basis of their sensations. A thermometer will furnish an impartial decision, a factual "truth" that each can accept, at least with that part of him which is under the control of reason. This impartial truth, like the geometric tangent, does not encroach upon the subjective territory of either person.

This very simple example has been chosen because the issue is so clear. The principle involved could be applied equally well to other controversies of a much more complicated and serious nature. However, a situation trivial in itself is not necessarily insignificant in its consequences. It seems hardly credible that a difference of opinion about a matter so easily checked as temperature could cause a quarrel between adults, yet such things can happen. Where, for instance, a number of persons work in one office, a disagreement as to what room temperature should be maintained may become both persistent and acrimonious, and can gradually attract to itself so many latent jealousies and egotisms that it can become the focal point of a feud of quite menacing proportions. In order to be able to accept an impartial judgment reached by comparisons based on thermometer readings, the individuals concerned would have to be able to make a distinction between that which is reasonable within them and that which is unreasonable, as irritation, anger, jealousy, will to dominate, namely, the irrational emotion aroused by the point at issue, no matter how trivial-seeming it may be.

This is a very difficult thing to do, for the emotions represent the unconscious factor, the villain of the blind spot. Many people brought up to follow the Christian way—this means of course the conventional Christian way—try to be reasonable and swallow their wrath. This is frequently more than a mere metaphor, for the psychological effort to repress the emotional factor is often accompanied by swallowing

27. See above, pp. 326-27.

movements of the throat. In fact, if this practice is indulged in too persistently, the resultant neurosis is likely to be associated with symptoms of indigestion. The unconscious factor, being possessed of a dynamic power, cannot be disposed of so easily; the repression will inevitably cause some ill effect. Yet rarely do people take an adequately responsible attitude towards their irrational reactions. The individual concerned usually identifies himself with his more reasonable part and says: "I was not quite myself—something must have got into me to make me act in that way." For one almost always speaks of this unreasonable factor, the sudden and uncontrollable emotional reaction, as something apart from one's true self.

In a sense this is correct, for the irrational emotion is a nonpersonal manifestation. It is not adequately amalgamated with the I and is certainly not under its control. It appears in consciousness without respect to the wish of the I, and when it disappears again it is as though it had never been; it then remains utterly inaccessible until evoked once more by some similar situation. If one is striving to become whole, every effort should be made, when this factor is aroused and thus becomes accessible, to prevent its escaping again into the unconscious. It should be caught and anchored to consciousness by every means that can be devised. Usually one who has suffered such an emotional upheaval prefers to forget it as soon as possible, but if he is seeking wholeness he should take exactly the opposite course. It is a very good plan to write for oneself as detailed and accurate an account of the events as possible—both those which led up to the outburst, and, so far as they can be recalled, the events of the storm itself. Having done this, it is often exceedingly valuable, where feasible, to review the happenings with the other person involved. Confession of guilt to this person or to some confessor, priest or analyst or understanding friend, can also serve to attach the nonpersonal factor more firmly to consciousness; while the insight that results from getting an impartial judgment, or better still a professional analysis of the occurrence, can be most helpful.

Among primitives and children, and adults as well, there

is a strong tendency to recount or re-enact, over and over, happenings that have a numinous or mana quality. In this way they are assimilated to consciousness; their overweight of emotion is gradually lightened, their daemonic quality is exorcized, and the whole experience is made more acceptable. This instinctive way of dealing with the awe-full or dread aspect of unusual happenings has been made a procedure of the psychotherapy originated by Freud; it is called abreaction, and has been extensively used in military medicine in treating "battle neuroses." The technique produces very favourable results in cases in which the aim is to prevent or cure neurotic symptoms resulting from terrifying and abnormal experiences. Naturally, however, where the object is to return the man to his regiment or to everyday civilian life, there is no thought of using his experience to enlarge consciousness, let alone to aid in the quest for individuation or psychological wholeness.

But where no such crisis as war is the cause of the emergence of the nonpersonal factor, and where the aim is not only to release the individual from the devastating effects of his experience but beyond that to produce an enlargement of consciousness and of the personality, it is necessary not only to exorcize the daemonic force by some psychotherapeutic technique, such as abreaction or confession, but also to attempt to establish a relation to it. For this reason it must not be allowed to drop back into the unconscious. It must be caught and given reality, a form of some sort; at the least it must be given a name. If it cannot be accurately described or identified, it can still be given an indefinite name, such as "third factor," or, as in the children's game, simply "it"; or if its activity is very destructive it might even be called the "devil." It can then be recognized and identified in situations in which it may function somewhat differently. Gradually, if an accurate record is kept, a picture of its nature and activities can be built up by putting together many experiences.

When in any given situation the irrational factor has been recognized, it can in this sense be removed from the external controversy, so that reason can once more prevail. Naturally this procedure does not dispose of the nonpersonal emotion, or, as we might say, of the devil aroused through the dissension or whatever else may have produced the point at issue. In terms of the geometric diagram in figure 12, this irrational energy is represented by the line directly opposed or at right angles to the line of impartial truth. This line passes through the centre of the circle. In our psychological analogy, therefore, what we have done in separating the unreasonable or emotional factor from the rational and impartial reality of the disputed situation is to establish a line of force leading to the centre of the psyche.

In actually coming to grips with such a situation, the individual may be able to agree to settle the external dispute according to reason or justice; and if he really recognizes that this is the way the external situation should be dealt with, the agreement may be not merely a gesture or face-saving device but a genuine acceptance of a truth of greater validity than his own wishes. Having done all this in good faith, he may still, when he goes to bed at night and is alone with himself, find unbidden thoughts and phantasies arising to harass him—ideas that do not agree with the accepted decision. When he faces these unsatisfied thoughts—one might say these insatiable emotions—and tries to trace them to their lair, he usually finds that they have to do with some complex, some unconscious assumption that caused him to get emotionally disturbed about the external situation. This complex may involve a determination to be master, or a compulsion to have matters arranged in a certain way because that is "the way they should be done" or "the way the parents ordained them." It may be that the situation has revealed a weakness or inferiority, which can arouse a fear bordering on panic. Or the anger may have to do with a yellow streak in his make-up, or with an anxiety lest his integrity be destroyed. He may be struggling with a half-conscious sexual involvement. Or the problem may be even more illusive, more difficult still to define, turning possibly on a sense of the sacredness of some threatened value, something that touches on the religious realm. In other words, the complex may lie in the area of the power problem, or the parent problem, or sexuality, or in any other of the basic realms of life

where primitive instinct rules until challenged by a more profound allegiance.

Thus the force of the emotion running counter to the impartial truth pierces deeply within the circle of the psyche,
and the procedure is bound to be not just an academic one.
For it really does pierce to the very heart. If it does not go

Fig. 13. Spontaneous Drawing Made by an Individual
Attempting to Find the Cause of Her Depression

The disks within the circle of the psyche represent the
knotty points in the subject's life situation. The lines
projected from these points cannot reach to the centre
because it is guarded and concealed by a coiled serpent.

as deep as that, it means that the particular point at issue is
too slight or not sufficiently important to involve the centre.
It can lead to deeper layers within the psyche, but before
the centre can be reached a more fundamental issue must
arise.

A drawing corresponding to such a situation is reproduced in figure 13. This picture was also made by a woman
undergoing analysis. The disks on the circumference of the
circle stand for points at issue in the subject's psychic impasse. These arise from the impact of problems of her work
and of her relationships with fellow workers as well as with
friends; they are in fact knotty points in her situation. As in

plate XIV, the tangential lines do not appear in this drawing; but as the perpendiculars to such tangents are drawn, we must conclude that this woman too had been struggling to separate the objective facts from her emotional reactions to the difficult problems her life presented. These lines go towards the centre but do not reach it; they are stopped short by a serpent, whose coils enclose and hide the centre. This serpent is the embodiment of the cold-blooded instinct. It is the snake Kundalini, the serpent power,[28] described in the Tantric system of Buddhism as lying asleep in *muladara*, the "root base"—psychologically speaking, in the depths of the psyche at the root or origin of consciousness. She sleeps there until she is aroused either by some happening in life or by application of a technique designed to arouse her. In the Tantric system the yogic exercises, meditation, and discipline are directed towards arousing Kundalini and leading her up through *sushumna*, the channel piercing the spinal cord—meaning that the instinctual force is to be led up by the route of consciousness. In her journey she progressively opens and illumines the chakras, or centres of consciousness, which correspond to the different stages of development of the I.

Yogic practices would of course not be suitable for the West, even if we knew how to employ them; but in the disciplined work undertaken in analysis the instinct power is similarly separated from the external situation and followed through evolutionary changes that profoundly affect the very character of consciousness. In the Orient it is recognized that yogic practices should be undertaken only under the guidance of a guru, a teacher, because without this they would be either sterile or dangerous; similarly, it is not likely that the psychological procedure outlined here will lead to the desired results without the guidance of a trained analyst. But in analysis the slumbering power of instinct is not aroused by following a prescribed course of physical or psychological exercises or devoting oneself to meditations. Instead, it comes into view of itself whenever the situations in life that I have called points at issue are tackled in the way described above. For the snake

28. Cf. A. Avalon, *The Serpent Power* and *Shiva and Shakti*.

Kundalini is a personification of the instinct that may not be stirred without risk of blind emotional turmoil.

In the quest for the treasure symbolized here as the centre of the psyche, the Self, it will be necessary to take up many such points at issue, one after another, as they arise in life. They must each be dealt with conscientiously, however distasteful it may be to stir up trouble by scrutinizing them. Then some day a situation may arise that has power to move the seeker so deeply that the very core of his being is touched. After this he may go on for a while meeting only with the everyday happenings; sooner or later, however, a vital situation arises again, perhaps in an entirely different realm of his life. Once more he seeks out the impartial line of truth or justice, holding his emotional reaction in check; and so the tangent is truly drawn, and the perpendicular, the line of the instinctual force that is opposed to—runs at right angles to—the impartial, reasonable solution, pierces to the very depths of his psyche, moving him strangely and disturbing his inner peace. It may be that when this has happened many times, the lines penetrating the circle begin to converge, and it becomes apparent that the central point is being neared.

How many such experiences are needed before the lines meet in the true centre no one knows, for the process is far more complicated than this simplified exposition would suggest. Furthermore, the progress of the development varies greatly in different individuals. But at least we can say this: When the lines do actually meet, there will be formed a star that begins to glow, foreshadowing the coming of that radiant "crystal body" whose name is Self.

The Reconciliation of the Opposites
THE MANDALA

M AN COULD BE WHOLE. The pattern of wholeness is inherent within his psyche, albeit unrealized. This pattern is not just a static image or ideal; it is dynamic—a trend, functioning like an instinct, leading towards the achievement of wholeness as towards a goal. This goal of the psychic urge can be disregarded by man's conscious ego, even frustrated in some measure by his self-willed and purblind consciousness; if the individual realizes, however, what the inner impulses connote, he can use his will power and disposable energy in their service. Division within himself means sickness and misery; wholeness means health—healing for all those inner feuds and self-frustrations which make so many lives meaningless and tragically unsatisfactory.

It has already been noted that the psyche comprises not only the conscious personality but also elements from the personal unconscious—represented by the shadow—and beyond these still others, coming from the deeper layers of psychic experience, the collective unconscious, represented by the archetypes. Viewed in this comprehensive way, the psyche is aptly represented by a circle. This picture commends itself to the intellect: it serves as a diagram of an ideal condition. When used in this way the circle is a sign, not a symbol. The meaning of the term symbol as used in analytical psychology, as well as its differentiation from the term sign, is very important for this and the following chapter. Jung discusses the point at length in *Psychological Types:*

> The concept of a symbol should, in my view, be strictly differentiated from that of a mere *sign.* . . . For instance, the old custom of handing over a sod of turf at the sale of a piece of land, might be described as "symbolic" in the vulgar use of the word; but actually it is purely semiotic in character. The piece of turf is a *sign,* or token, representing the whole estate. . . . Every view which interprets the symbolic expression as an analogous or abbreviated expression of a known thing is *semiotic.* A conception which interprets the symbolic expression as the best possible formulation of a relatively unknown thing which cannot conceivably, therefore, be more clearly or characteristically represented is *symbolic.* . . .
>
> In so far as a symbol is a living thing, it is the expression of a thing not to be characterized in any other or better way. The symbol is alive only in so far as it is pregnant with meaning. But, if its meaning is born out of it, i.e., if that expression should be found which formulates the sought, expected, or divined thing still better than the hitherto accepted symbol, then the symbol is *dead,* i.e., it possesses only a historical significance. We may still go on speaking of it as a symbol, under the tacit assumption that we are speaking of it as it was before its better expression had been born from it. . . .
>
> An expression that stands for a known thing always remains merely a sign and is never a symbol. It is, therefore, quite impossible to make a living symbol, i.e., one that is pregnant with meaning, from known associations.[1]

When the image of a circle arises spontaneously in dream or phantasy and is progressively delimited and built up during the unfolding of the unconscious material, over weeks or months perhaps, it is no longer to be considered as merely a sign, a representation of a wished-for ideal. Rather, it is a true symbol picture, representing a potential reality or a reality having its existence in the unseen psychic realm. It is a living experience.

The preliminary work required to establish the limits of the

---

1. *Psychological Types,* chap. XI, "Definitions," under "Symbol," pp. 473 ff.

circle of the psyche—its circumference—has been discussed above, and the further step that must be accomplished, that of finding the centre, has also been indicated. The drawing of the circumference has to do with the psychological separation of the individual from his environment. The search for the centre is a more internal, a more subjective problem. When the circle has been drawn around him, so to speak, the individual may find, indeed inevitably will find that this inner domain, where he might expect only his own will to rule, only his own voice to be heard, is inhabited by others as well. Other voices, other wishes and impulses than those which he can ascribe to his ego, clamour to make themselves heard. The question arises: Who is master in this domain?

The governor of a circle is of course its centre, around which everything revolves. In the psyche likewise, the centre is ruler of the entire man. In the conscious realm the ego is master, but in this larger sphere the ego is only one voice among many. The ruler here must transcend the ego. It must be a suprapersonal value that can command the allegiance and obedience of the ego, just as the ego, through the development of consciousness, comes to transcend the autos. This ruler Jung has called Self.

The discussion of the psyche under the symbol of a circle has involved an implicit assumption that living entities consist of body and spirit. Just as in the physical realm we deal with matter, body, and energy, so also in the psychological realm we deal with something that is as it were the equivalent of matter—this might be called the "body" or structure of the psyche—and the energy inhering in it. The concept of the psyche as being a body of some kind corresponds to a universal feeling, present in every human being, that in the psychological dimension he occupies a certain space and has a definite position. In addition, he feels himself to be possessed of a certain energy inherent in his psychic contents. This psychic energy, or libido, seems to follow laws corresponding to those which govern physical energy.[2]

2. C. G. Jung, "On Psychic Energy," in *The Structure and Dynamics of the Psyche* (C.W. 8).

Naturally the analogy between psychological and physical energy has only a relative validity, for we cannot demonstrate a visible or tangible body of the psyche distinct from the energy inhering in it. But in the realm of physics also, where our hands and eyes tell us there is a solid body, our intellects are faced with the paradox that this so solid-seeming body may be nothing more than a form of energy; thus it is more than likely that the psyche too is only a form of energy. Still, for practical purposes we continue to make the distinction between matter and energy, and in the psychological realm likewise it may be helpful to think of a body of the psyche, animated by psychic energy.

Just as the manifest energy of physical bodies is only a small part of their total store, so too only a small part of the energy residing in the psyche is at the disposition of the conscious ego and under the control of the personal I. The larger part of physical energy is locked up inside the atoms, and the larger part of the psychic energy is similarly locked up in the instincts, the patterns or forms of biological behaviour, and in the archetypes, the patterns or forms of psychic behaviour. In animals the instincts dominate behaviour and function quite autonomously; in human beings, too, they assert themselves autonomously until the individual has evolved a conscious standpoint strong enough to stand over against them, to control them and mediate them to the world in human and conscious behaviour. For it is only when the human being really *knows* what he is doing that he can be called self-conscious and responsible. The person who is guided by his ego alone is not self-conscious in this sense, for he is limited in his self-knowledge to the conscious realm only, and beyond this terrain yields himself blindly to the obscure urges and devious impulses of the unconscious.

In outlining the steps that can be taken in daily life to transcend the limitations of ego consciousness, I have spoken of the emergence of points at issue, by which unrecognized parts of the psyche can become accessible to consciousness. The natural tendency is to avoid these points at issue and to gloss them over, because they always raise unpleasant controversy and often threaten the relationship concerned as well as the individual's self-esteem. Or, if he is of a different temperament, he may make a practice of attacking such situations on sight, hoping to win his point by a kind of psychological blitzkrieg. He avoids them or attacks them because he senses that they carry an unknown and dangerous emotional charge.

Nothing is fundamentally gained by either course, however, for the unconscious element remains unrecognized and its projection into the outer world, either to the situation or to the opponent, is only reinforced. For every time that unconscious material is allowed to pass unrecognized when it could have been made conscious, the projection gains as it were a verisimilitude and validity confirmed by experience, so that it is more difficult to recognize its true nature subsequently, just as the actual facts of the situation, if they are allowed to rest unclarified, will be harder to unravel at a later date. Thus, in spite of the fact that if such points at issue, such contretemps, are looked into too closely or are handled too roughly, emotions, angers, fears, anxieties can easily be released, with most painful and destructive results, the man seeking a truer relation to life and to himself must face this danger.

When an individual, caught in some such situation, summons enough courage to tackle his problem and clarify it, using all the patience and good will of which he is capable, he finds that energy is released, generally in the form of emotion. This energy must then be separated into two parts, or, to use the physical analogy, resolved into two lines of force at right angles to each other. One of these lines of force is represented by the tangent between the two circles that have come in contact. It does not cut across the domain of either nor transgress their rightful boundaries. It represents the objective truth of the situation, the impartial "right," the line of equity or justice. The other component is the perpendicular to the tangent, which penetrates within the circle and, if continued, will pass through its centre. It represents the emotion that does not really belong to the external situation—the energy belonging to that part of the psychic contents which was unconscious and so has been projected into the outer situation.

This energy, being released from the projection, pierces into the interior of the circle of the psyche.

That part of the energy which belongs to the life situation, being released from entanglement with the unconscious projection, will begin at once to function in life. The individual will experience a sense of liberation and release of tension; the impasse that has been blocking him, in his activities or in his relationship with his friend, will melt away, and he will find a new joy and ease in that entire aspect of his life. His sense of gain will be greater or smaller according to the importance of the situation, but will depend even more on the value of the unknown psychic content formerly entangled in the projection.

Now these two forces represent a fundamental opposition. In the examples discussed in the preceding chapter, the first was equated to the reasonable factor, which enables a man to recognize and accept an impartial standard. The second was equated to the unreasonable and dynamic factor, which compels a man to deny any possibility that his own experience or point of view might be fallacious and makes him declare: "It *is* that way, and that is the way it is!" He cannot concede even that modicum of relativity which would allow him to say, "That is the way I see it," recognizing that someone else may see it differently.

These two forces operate in every one of us, and if we are to travel the road leading towards consciousness and individuation, we must each sooner or later face the problem created by their fundamental opposition. For one represents the rational attitude to life, the form-creating relation, which on the human level is the product of ego consciousnes, of scientific thought and of logic, while on the cosmic or universal level it is expressed as the law of God or the logos. The other represents dynamic energy, formless and goalless, quite devoid of logic, being, as we say, irrational—following only the *ratio* of nature, as water does, or wind or fire. On the human level it is emotion, especially emotionality, panic, rage, passion. In its unconditioned, daemonic, or divine aspect it is that principle, called *eros* [3] by the Greeks, which "binds together and delivers"—the principle of dynamic relatedness. Or it could be called the blind urge of instinct, Kundalini, the serpent power that, according to the teachings of Tantric Buddhism, lies coiled up at the root of all psychic life, dormant in unawakened instinct.

When an individual becomes aware of forces so fundamentally opposed operating in his own life, motivating him in his attitudes and actions, the ensuing conflict may be so severe as to paralyse his every effort. When he says yes to the rational tendency and represses the other, it may look like the right decision; everything appears quite in order, and it seems as if he had reached a satisfactory solution of the problem. But the zest goes out of living, and he begins to feel depressed or suffocated. If he takes the opposite course and says yes to the dynamic urge, courting the emotions and yielding himself to what D. H. Lawrence calls the "flow," his life may come alive; but then he finds himself swept along by the current of his emotions, and may be seized by a panic fear of being carried away into all kinds of excesses, or into strange regions of inner experience where he can no longer make an adequate contact with his fellow men, where perhaps he will not be able to make himself understood at all.

The extent of the distress and pain caused by a conflict of this character can hardly be realized by anyone who has not experienced such a state. The validity of everything the individual does seems to be destroyed. He may attempt to resolve the dilemma by following the reasonable and logical way, building his house foursquare, taking into account all sides of any situation, so far as he can see them, and ruling out every other consideration. This course of action may seem to work for a while, a few days perhaps or even a few weeks; then it goes stale or is threatened by some extraneous influence—his wife's irrationality, for instance, or he may be seized by a quite unreasonable emotional outburst that yet obviously holds

---

3. Cf. M. E. Harding, *Woman's Mysteries, Ancient and Modern*, which is largely concerned with the laws of eros and woman's relationship to them; also Jung, "Woman in Europe," in *Civilization in Transition* (C.W. 10).

value, possibly something of the value of the completeness of himself. He may feel more at one with himself while acting in this irrational fashion than he did when measuring his actions with care, and he says to himself: "When I go with this impulse, I feel whole." But shortly a doubt arises as to where this irrational impulse may lead. "Is it not just arrant selfishness," he asks himself, "to follow my own desires in this way?" He begins to wonder what all the self-controlled, disciplined leaders he has always admired would say to such "self-indulgence." And so he swings back to the constraints of accepted law and order, burdened still further by a sense of guilt at his defection.

The conflict has been described here as if it were conscious, but it is not necessarily so. More usually, the battle goes on in a subterranean place and almost completely unrecognized, the sufferer being aware only of the stultifying effects it has on his life and not at all of the conflict itself as a psychological or moral problem. Under such circumstances it will probably break through into the conscious life under the guise of physical symptoms—actual paralysis sometimes, or less serious illness, such as severe headaches having a paralysing effect. Sometimes the difficulty may show itself in psychological guise, even though its origin is still completely unknown to the individual, who suffers from unexplained depressions or from inertia and fatigue, which prevent him from accomplishing anything: every attempt at activity requires a herculean effort that has a nightmarish quality, as in that not uncommon dream in which one is unable to move because one's feet are too heavy to be raised or so light that they can get no grip on the ground. Indeed, a conflict of this sort can produce an almost complete paralysis of the life.

Where the situation is more conscious than in either of the foregoing instances, the sufferer is aware that his difficulty is due to an inner conflict, although he is unable to make clear to himself the precise nature of the values that are opposed in him, or so to disentangle them that he can make a valid choice. Naturally there are many different ways in which the values of life can divide into irreconcilable opposites. The opposition between the rational attitude and the dynamic one is a very common expression of the impasse. In political terms it takes the form of the right versus the left, or the conservative versus the revolutionary. In religion it becomes the schism of the Catholic as against the Protestant point of view, or the question of formalism as against mysticism—as Paul puts it, of works or grace—while in everyday life it sets the plodding scientific attitude in contrast to creative flight. There are of course innumerable other lines of cleavage—extraversion versus introversion, the individual versus the collective aim, material versus spiritual values—any one of which may posit the insoluble dilemma and bring life to a standstill.

When this happens, the problem of what to do about these contradictory, seemingly irreconcilable factors has to be faced, for it is undeniable that both are indwellers of the kingdom of the psyche. They are actually more than indwellers: they are organic components of it, making up perhaps the majority element and wielding greater power than the reasonable and conscious minority. If the psyche is not to be a house divided against itself, which obviously could not stand, some means of reconciling the opposites must be sought.

The conflict between the conscious and the unconscious elements has been taken as illustration because it is obvious and well recognized by anyone with even a modicum of psychological insight; it is not, however, the sole or even the most difficult aspect of the problem. For the daemonic energy manifested in the emotion aroused by the point at issue, and represented or personified by one of the archetypes, is not single but dual. In the archetypes the urges of the unconscious have not as yet been differentiated, for differentiation is a function of consciousness. Therefore they appear in ambiguous or dual form, in fact as pairs of opposites—as good-bad, favourable-harmful, spiritual-demonic, and so on through the whole range of possible dichotomies. The fundamental opposition may similarly be represented by other irreconcilable pairs such as male-female, yang-yin, sun-moon, animate-inanimate. This inner duality of the nonpersonal energy awakened by the life situation is not a matter merely of philosophical or academic interest. To the individual torn by conflict it is of the deepest concern, even a life-and-death issue; for until he can find some way of reconciling the opposition within himself, his life will remain suspended and his soul will be a battleground.

In attempting to resolve a fundamental psychological conflict, a thorough survey of the problem at the conscious level must first be undertaken. If this approach does not yield a satisfactory solution, it will be necessary to scrutinize the unconscious data for further evidence as to the cause of the difficulty and also for guidance as to its solution. When this course is followed, it is usually found that factors reaching beyond the personal life of the individual are involved. For example, the opposition inherent in the conflict may be bound up with or represented by the two parents, who—apart from their individual characters and temperaments, which may or may not be in accord—have of necessity a certain incompatibility, from the child's point of view, owing to the fact that they are of opposite sex. Yet if the child is to become an individual in his own right, he must find some way of amalgamating the essential qualities of both parents existing within him; for each is part of the very stuff of his being. This is a problem with which every child has to deal, and the task may prove a difficult one even when the parents have somewhat similar tastes and temperaments. When, however, as not infrequently happens, the parents married not because of their likeness but because of their dissimilarity, being attracted to each other by their very difference, the child's problem will be severe, especially if neither parent has worked to assimilate psychologically the values represented by the partner.

In such a situation the child will probably identify himself with one parent; he will love, admire, emulate everything that this parent does and is, and will turn away from the other. Jung states the case most trenchantly when, writing of the child negatively related to the mother, he says: "The leitmotif of this type is: Anything whatever, so long as it is not like Mother!" [4] Or, if the child's positive feeling goes to the

4. "Psychological Aspects of the Mother Archetype," in *The Archetypes and the Collective Unconscious* (C.W. 9, i), p. 90.

mother, the corresponding negative feelings of resentment and resistance, even of hate, may devolve upon the father. A markedly negative attitude to the parents is particularly apt to develop when there is lack of harmony between them, and inevitably produces serious psychological results. In such families the husband and wife may each ascribe to the other all the difficulties of the marriage and even of life itself, and the projection to the partner may not stop with this. The husband represents to the wife her animus, her unknown, other side, and the wife similarly carries the projection of the husband's anima. Thus, if either person lacks insight regarding his own character and the less obvious contents of his psyche, he may all too readily project these to the partner: consequently he will consider the other to blame for temperamental problems and conflicts stemming in reality from his own unwholeness.

When it is the wife who makes this massive projection, she will feel that all the misfortune of her lot derives from her husband and his family, while all its desirable factors are to be credited to her own people. Her greatest reproach to her child will be: "You are just like your father." Now it goes without saying that in some respects the child probably is like his father, from whom half of his heritage comes—a fact for which the child can hardly be held responsible. But faced with this repudiation of the father's traits within himself, he may follow the mother's lead and despise all that the father stands for, rejecting the father character not only in his own parent but in all other men as well, and, with far more devastating effects, in himself. On the other hand, the child may love his father best; then, resenting the injustice of the mother's accusations, he will take the opposite attitude and side with his father against her. In this event he will be compelled to champion the characteristics of the father, whether they are desirable ones or not, in season and out, to the detriment of his own critical powers.

No matter which of these attitudes the child takes, as he comes to maturity the conflict between the inharmonious parental elements within him will absorb an increasing proportion of his energy and will hold it anchored in the unconscious.

For he dare not allow himself to become aware that his chosen attitude is challenged or even contradicted by a different set of values lying dormant within his own nature—namely, the values associated with the parent whom he has elected to despise and, psychologically speaking, to repudiate. Instead he will hold to his conscious standpoint with a tenacity not untinged with prejudice and fanaticism, because it stems from the unconscious root of the positive bond with the favoured parent; thus it necessarily exerts an autonomous and compulsive influence on his consciousness. Or it may be that even though he remains unaware of the contradictory elements within him, he allows them free play, so that they function unchecked in his daily life. He will then fall into hopeless inconsistencies, so that what he does or says today may have no connection with his actions or convictions of yesterday or of tomorrow. Obviously a life so wanting in consistency may easily come to a complete deadlock.

Before the modern discoveries in regard to the unconscious had become matters of common knowledge, it might have been expected that any individual would automatically outgrow his parents and their influence, and, having left the conflicts of childhood behind, would be free to go on to live his adult life unhampered. However, the researches not only of Freud and his followers, but of many other psychologists as well, have made it clear that in the psyche of the child the actual parents, and still more what Freud calls the parent imagoes, or, as Jung prefers to call them, the parent archetypes, carry dynamic values of their own and are possessed of specific energy that cannot be entirely disregarded or repressed.[5] Psychological energy, like its physical counterpart, is indestructible, and any quantum that is repressed into the unconscious will not cease to exist; instead, it will activate a relevant archetype, causing disturbances in the unconscious and eventually breaking through into consciousness.

Archetypes have an essential ambiguity or duality. If one of the opposed values of a given archetype is chosen by con-

5. See Jung, "Analytical Psychology and *Weltanschauung*," in *The Structure and Dynamics of the Psyche* (C.W. 8), p. 373, § 723.

sciousness, the other, being repressed, will carry with it into the unconscious the specific energy inhering in it. One cannot choose in a seemingly rational way to go to the right, strictly eschewing the left; for each of the opposing tendencies is dynamic and will not brook complete denial or repression. This is quite clear where an individual's conflict stems from a difference between the father and the mother, for the opposed values are both a part of himself, having their origin in the parents who loomed over his infancy, beings of seemingly superhuman size and power, and who continue to exert, from the depths of his unconscious, an overwhelming influence upon his life even as an adult. To the infant, father and mother are more than mortals; they are all-powerful, incomprehensible, awe-inspiring; their yea and nay are law even though they are at the same time familiar beings, possibly indulgent, always taken for granted. In them the child gleans his first impression of the meaning and the power of the gods.

Yet every man—in the very genes that determine what manner of man he is—bears his father within him, and so also his mother. He cannot escape this dual fate or any of its implications by rooting out the father and allying himself only with the mother; nor can he deny the mother and follow the father alone. To do so would spell dismemberment—mutilation and death. Dreams of mutilation—self-inflicted or imposed by someone else—may have this meaning, namely, that the dreamer is trying to identify himself wholly with one parent or with one side of his nature alone, and so is compelled to cut off those members which represent the other parent or the other side of his being.

According to a passage in the First Gospel that seems strangely out of keeping with the context, Christ advised and even commanded self-mutilation as a means of dealing with unacceptable or sinful aspects of the character. The saying is recounted twice, in slightly different settings. In the second version we read:

> Wherefore if thy hand or thy foot offend thee, cut them off, and cast them from thee: it is better for thee to enter into life halt

or maimed, rather than having two hands or two feet to be cast into everlasting fire.[6]

This advice would seem to be valid if one's aim is to reach a certain standard or to fit oneself to a given pattern of perfection. But when wholeness is the aim, all the members must find some place within the individual's life and their differences and incompatibilities must be overcome through transformation rather than through suppression. Judging from the context of the passage quoted above, it seems that Jesus himself was not quite satisfied with the teaching of self-mutilation, for both here and in the earlier version [7] the injunction is coupled with another of quite different significance. Thus he goes on immediately to say:

Take heed that ye despise not one of these little ones. . . . For the Son of man is come to save that which was lost.

This is followed [8] by the parable of the lost sheep, in which, far from being discarded, cut off, the one that was lost is regarded as of more value than the ninety-and-nine that were never endangered. This seemingly illogical judgment rests on the fact that the lost one not only represents the value of one sheep out of a hundred but also signifies that which is needed for wholeness: without this one the flock is incomplete. In the quest for wholeness of the psyche, in an exactly similar way, the repressed and despised element—the wandering missing sheep—carries an incomparable value, for its presence is essential if the psyche is to be healed and made whole.

This teaching is still further emphasized in the Gospel, for the parable of the lost sheep is followed by the story of the two brothers who were at variance. In chapter 18 the conflict is left unhealed, but in the story as it is told in the earlier passage we read:

Therefore if thou bring thy gift to the altar, and there rememberest that thy brother hath ought against thee; Leave there thy

6. Matt. 18:8.
7. Matt. 5:29, 30.
8. Matt. 18.

gift before the altar, and go thy way; first be reconciled to thy brother, and then come and offer thy gift.[9]

In an uncanonical version [10] of the same story, the brother is represented as the man's other self, and the saying reads: "First be reconciled to thyself and then go and offer thy gift."

Self-mutilation is therefore obviously not recommended as a satisfactory solution of the problem of the opposites within oneself. If only a single part of the psyche is lost, it will have to be sought again with pain and difficulty, involving perhaps even a journey to hell (cf. the expression, "cast into everlasting fire")—that is, to the unconscious, regardless of the hazards and suffering that such an adventure entails. For only when the lost members are all retrieved and given their rightful place will the psyche be made whole.

On the biological plane the irreconcilable elements of father and mother, of male and female, are reconciled on a new level in the child, who carries in his own person physical characteristics and psychological components derived from both parents. It is not surprising, therefore, that in the images of the unconscious a child frequently appears as the symbol of reconciliation on the psychological plane within the individual. In religious symbolism, the Christ Child, who is Son of God, his Divine Father, and son of Mary, his human mother, reconciles God and man in his own person. The alchemistic philosophers relate how the vision of the mysterious embryo they called homunculus took shape in their retorts; and over and over again in the dreams and phantasies of modern persons, the Self is represented as a little child.[11]

In the creation of the child, nature actually reconciles the opposites. But in the psychological realm, nature's way has been challenged and often interfered with by man's development of ego consciousness, which has given him the power to choose for himself and so to defy nature. It is on account of

9. Matt. 5:23, 24.
10. This version of the parable and its interpretation were brought to my attention by Dr. Jung.
11. See above, p. 171; also plate V.

this very power that man's life is distracted by conflicting values. For the animals no such problem exists. They accept what nature provides, be it good or bad, and abide by her law; but man undertakes to work out his own adjustment to life and its conditions. If these do not suit him, he endeavours to choose the favourable factors and to eliminate the unfavourable ones. And when the discarded elements are not dealt with and assimilated but are merely repressed, the conscious adaptation will be threatened by their inherent energy. Yet, just because the discarded values have been pushed into the unconscious, the individual may be completely unaware of the nature of his difficulty. In such a case some technique is needed for finding out exactly what the values are whose opposition is causing disturbance in him.

The painstaking analysis that is needed should be undertaken only with the help and under the direction of a competent analyst, since conflicts of such severity as those here under consideration touch the most sensitive and delicate aspects of the human psyche. The analysis will begin with a review of the patient's life story, especially that private and subjective aspect of it which seems to be of importance to no one but himself. This will be followed by or interwoven with an analysis of his dreams and phantasies, which are likely to play a considerable part in the work, as they are the chief source of information in regard to the contents of the unconscious. But not infrequently the patient is unable to make clear in words the nature of the forces that he feels are in conflict within him; his dream images may not represent them adequately, or perhaps he cannot remember his dreams. In this case he may spontaneously try to depict them in a diagram or picture—much as was done in the drawings of the circle discussed in the preceding chapter—in order to convey to his analyst some understanding of the distress he is suffering.

On many an occasion when I have asked a patient who was obviously in great trouble, "What is it that distresses you so?" I have received the answer, "It's here"—with a gesture to the heart or abdomen—"it's like a great lump here"; or, "It is a burning fire here"; or, "It is a mass of blackness"; or, "A turmoil is going on here." Evidently these persons do not know what it is that distresses them; furthermore, though they know that their distress is psychological, they experience it in their bodies. This means that because the difficulty is unconscious, it is projected into the body. In such cases I ask the patient to make a drawing of what it is that is within him, or by active phantasying to try to learn something about it in story form. Sometimes the patient is able in this way to portray the unseen factors that are disturbing him. If he succeeds in making a picture of them, that is, in objectifying them, they will become accessible to consciousness and he will begin to be able to handle them.

This way of attempting to reach unconscious contents is in line with a natural psychic law. As Jung points out:

An unconscious event which eludes the conscious mind will portray itself somehow and somewhere, it may be in dreams, visions, or fantasies. . . . Such a content is an autonomous complex divorced from consciousness, leading a life of its own in the psychic non-ego and instantly projecting itself whenever it is constellated in any way—that is, whenever attracted by something analogous to it in the outside world.

In such visionary images . . . there is expressed the whole phenomenon of the unconscious projection of autonomous contents. These myth-pictures are like dreams, telling us that a projection has taken place and also what has been projected.[12]

In order to allow the projected yet unknown psychic contents to unfold themselves truly, undistorted by conscious interference, it is necessary to lay aside all preconceived ideas of what the drawing should be like. The hand and pencil must be used as if they were a sort of recording apparatus making a picture of the psychic reality. This does not mean that the actual drawing is done unconsciously, like automatic writing; on the contrary, much conscious attention and effort must be put into it. But the content of the picture is not consciously chosen, nor is it constrained into a preconceived form; it is conceded a certain autonomy. It is as though the picture already existed and the artist were merely redrawing it from

12. *Psychology and Alchemy* (C.W. 12), pp. 288 ff.

memory. Or it is made as a child makes a little world from the toys on his sand tray—a device extensively used in the play technique of child psychotherapy. From the nature of the world that the child creates, one learns the secrets of his inner world and so uncovers the difficulty that is disturbing him.

When the right attitude is achieved, the individual making such a drawing feels that he is not the creator choosing the objects he draws; rather, it seems to him as if the objects themselves were the originators of the picture, directing him to portray them. This sense of being merely the medium, the chosen instrument, as it were, of an autonomous image or idea, is very frequently found also in the creative artist or writer. The situation is portrayed exactly in a statuette of Mark the Evangelist, who is shown sitting, scroll on knee and pen poised in hand, with his head half turned to the lion [13] apparently whispering in his ear what he is to write.

When an image arises that so to speak wants to be drawn, the subject allows his phantasy to play with it, and the changes occurring in the image are elaborated in the drawing; or he may make a series of pictures showing the progressive changes —the story, as it were, of the image. Throughout, the eye rather than the mind must be the judge of what belongs in the picture. Sometimes it is not a phantasy image arising spontaneously that intrigues the individual; he may wish instead to draw a picture or diagram of some situation or representation that has occurred in a dream and that holds interest for him beyond the meaning he has been able to extract by the methods of free association and elaboration usually employed in the interpretation of dreams.

13. The lion is more than the emblem of Mark. He is rather the personification of the spirit—or, as the mediaevalists would say, the "angel"— that inspired Mark in his work as evangelist. The four evangelists were represented by the bull, the lion, the eagle, and the angel. These forms are also to be found representing four "angels," or four aspects of the divinity, in Ezekiel's vision; they correspond to the four sons of Horus, who play such a conspicuous part in Egyptian burial rites, as funerary figures placed at the corners of the catafalque—a custom that calls to mind the childhood bedtime prayer: "Matthew, Mark, Luke, and John, Bless the bed I lie upon." In ecclesiastical art, and especially in mystical drawings and sculptures dealing with the esoteric aspect of the Christian religious experience and dogma, the evangelists are nearly always represented by these four figures, instead of being portrayed in their natural forms as human beings.

In such so-called unconscious drawing, it is very important to avoid analysing or interpreting the material while the work is being done, for such conscious evaluation almost inevitably leads to distortion of the images or to disturbance of their spontaneous unfolding. Analysis and criticism must be applied to elicit the meaning of the drawing, but this must come at a later stage. It is by no means easy to concentrate one's utmost attention and effort on the task and yet refrain from conscious interference. However, difficult as it may be, it is an essential condition of the work. For this is no idle pastime, but a serious attempt, first, to discover what the unseen inner reality is and, second, so to work over it that the effort expended on the drawing, and the concentration of attention on the inner problem portrayed, may produce an effect on the psychic situation that could not be obtained by direct means.

For this reason it is of no use merely to draw circles or squares, as anyone with a compass and ruler can do. Nor is there any magic healing in making pictures of meaningless forms or of external objects. In the inner world things are as obstinately real as they are in the physical world. When someone says, "That is only psychological," he does not credit this reality of the psychological world, but assumes that psychological phenomena are only airy nothings, stuff of the imagination that has no substance or body but can be changed at will or by wishful thinking, and that can therefore be disregarded by practical men.

But this is not true. Psychic material is real and has weight and can be changed only by real work done upon it. The kind of drawing discussed here is an instrument, a technique by means of which conscious effort can be applied to psychic reality. For when one succeeds in drawing a true picture of the inner situation, and continues working with the materials, submitting oneself, as it were, to what they want—obeying that which wants to be drawn—then, strangely enough, the psychic situation actually undergoes a change corresponding to the changing images in the picture. It has been noted that unconscious factors activated by some conflict in the life situation are readily projected into an outer form. The image with which the individual is busying himself may seem to have no direct connection with his conflict, but if it attracts his attention sufficiently to interest him, even fascinate him, his libido—the energy of the unconscious contents—will flow into it. The very fact that the image fascinates him signifies that unconscious factors have been projected into it. In pursuing the object of his interest the individual is really seeking himself, his unknown, unconscious contents.

Modern art is based upon a very similar psychological mechanism, although most artists apparently do not fully or even correctly understand the psychological import of their own products. The artist of a nonrealistic school does not aim to reproduce the manifest appearance of things, but seeks instead their nonobjective meanings. He allows an object or situation to work upon him, to develop in him its own innate quality, and then tries to express what he has experienced. He calls this the essence of the object, its inner reality or *surréalité*, and he does not realize that the reality he perceives in this way does not belong to the object per se; if it did, all artists working on the same material would reach similar conclusions about it, which is obviously not the case.

Rather, the reality he perceives is an emanation or reflection from the object. It is the "superreality" not of the object but of himself, the subject; it is his psychological reality or truth. Thus what he actually perceives is his own psyche, his own unconscious content projected into the object and revealed to him as if it were the inherent quality of the object itself, its ultimate reality. If the artist could view his picture in this way, he might learn far more about himself than he ever does about the nature of the object. Moreover, if he is a genuine artist, his pictures will portray not only his own inner condition but also the unconscious psyche of his time.

In a similar way a patient's drawing may yield much helpful information about his actual psychological situation.[14] In addition, if he has worked with a devotion to the truth of his subjective experiences comparable to the true artist's fidelity

14. For an illuminating and full discussion of this technique as a whole, cf. H. G. Baynes, *Mythology of the Soul*.

to his sense of the essential inner truth of the object, it will produce an effect on his inner condition and may even have power to point the way to a solution of his conflict.

The patient's work with his drawing resembles the opus of the alchemists, who experimented so persistently with material substances and chemical reactions. The transformations that took place in their retorts occurred simultaneously, as some of their records tell us, within themselves. The psychologist understands this effect as being due to the projection of the alchemist's unconscious psychic life into the unknown and to him mysterious materials with which he was working. Jung writes:

> The real nature of matter was unknown to the alchemist: he knew it only in hints. Inasmuch as he tried to explore it he projected the unconscious into the darkness of matter in order to illuminate it. In order to explain the mystery of matter he projected yet another mystery—namely his own unknown psychic background—into what was to be explained: *Obscurum per obscurius, ignotum per ignotius!* [15]

Consequently in working on the substance in his flask he was at the same time working on that part of his own psyche which was projected into it:

> Strictly speaking, projection is never made; it happens; it is simply there. In the darkness of anything external to me, I find, without recognizing it as such, an interior or psychic life that is my own.[16]

Thus what happened in the experiment happened also in the experimenter; as the alchemists themselves used to say, *Tam ethice quam physice*—as it is in the physical realm, so it is in the psychic realm. Jung continues:

> It would therefore be a mistake in my opinion to explain the formula "tam ethice quam physice" by the theory of correspondences, and to say that this is its "cause." On the contrary, this theory is more likely to be a rationalization of the experience of projection. The alchemist does not practise his art because he be-

15. *Psychology and Alchemy* (C.W. 12), pp. 233-34.
16. Ibid., p. 234.

lieves on theoretical grounds in correspondence; the point is that he has a theory of correspondence because he experiences the presence of the idea, or of spirit, in physical matter. I am therefore inclined to assume that the real root of alchemy is to be sought less in philosophical doctrines than in the projections experienced by individual investigators. I mean by this that while working on his chemical experiments the operator had certain psychic experiences which appeared to him as the particular behaviour of the chemical process. Since it was a question of projection, he was naturally unconscious of the fact that the experience had nothing to do with matter itself (that is, with matter as we know it today). He experienced his projection as a property of matter; but what he was in reality experiencing was his own unconscious. . . . Such projections repeat themselves wherever man tries to explore an empty darkness and involuntarily fills it with living form.[17]

He [Zosimos, an alchemistic philosopher of the third century] must have experienced, in matter itself, at the very least an identity between the behaviour of matter and the events in his own psyche. But, as this identity is unconscious, Zosimos is no more able than the rest of them to make any pronouncement about it. For him it is simply there, and it not only serves as a bridge, it actually *is* the bridge that unites psychic and material events in one, so that "what is within is also without." [18]

In a number of religious systems, drawing is used as one method of promoting spiritual growth in the novices. In some instances the sacred pictures are merely contemplated; in others they are faithfully copied, as an aid to meditation and as a means of concentrating the attention on the subject to be contemplated. In the Tibetan lamaseries to this day the young novices copy the designs of the temple banners. The Buddhists use sacred pictures and diagrams as *yantras*,[19] much as the Catholic contemplates the Stations of the Cross, or other sacred pictures, as a means of furthering the development of his soul.

Sometimes the drawings consist of intricate geometric de-

17. Ibid., p. 234.
18. Ibid., p. 288.
19. A "geometric diagram of mystical significance" by use of which the yogin aims "to establish telepathic and even more intimate communication with the deities that he invokes to assist him in his *yogic* endeavors." Cf. W. Y. Evans-Wentz, *Tibetan Yoga and Secret Doctrines*, p. 29.

signs having an esoteric meaning; they are drawn repeatedly—
an activity not unlike the elaborate dances and physical exercises used in certain forms of yoga and in the initiation training of many other religions. It is possible that the scrollwork
so often used in the illumination of religious manuscripts in
Christian monasteries had some such use; while the artisans
who worked on the carvings of similar decorative and symbolic designs in the churches and cathedrals of Europe may
well have been doing it for the good of their souls as well as
the glory of God.

In such cases the design used is a more or less fixed form
conventionalized and sanctified by the associations of many
years, possibly many centuries, of religious culture; the avowed
purpose is to bring about a particular effect in the heart or,
as we should say, in the psyche of the novice. On the other
hand, where the quest is not for "perfection" but for the
wholeness of the individual, it is obviously not possible to
know in advance or to prescribe what thing should be drawn
or what ideal should be sought by means of the drawing, since
individual experience is unique. It follows also that one who
sets out to depict his inmost personal problem must be entirely free to choose his own symbols. Paradoxically enough,
however, he is not free to choose them; instead, the symbols
choose themselves, as it were, and he is obliged to let his hand
and his pencil function in the service of such symbols as choose
him for their portrayer.

When this condition is faithfully adhered to, the result of
the work is unique and individual, an expression of the most
intimate aspect of the given person's life. Yet a survey of a
collection of such personal drawings, all of them dealing with
the problem of the conflict between the opposites, reveals
striking similarities among them. Many of them denote the
psyche by means of a circle,[20] while the conflicting values are
represented symbolically either as invading the circle from
without, or, if an acceptable solution has been found, as en-

20. See Wilhelm and Jung, *The Secret of the Golden Flower,* for illustrations of typical mandalas. See also Jung, "Concerning Mandala Symbolism," in *The Archetypes and the Collective Unconscious* (C.W. 9, i).

closed within the circle. Sacred sculptures and paintings of many religious systems contain similar designs, which often represent in symbolic language their deepest truths or most hidden teachings. But while the drawings made by persons undergoing psychological analysis have to do with their individual problems and difficulties, a design that has become an accepted religious symbol no longer has this personal quality; it has been depersonalized through use by many generations and through the modification entailed in such use. Elements that were merely personal or incidental have been gradually eliminated, and the final product, thus purified of the ephemeral concomitants of some single human experience, is left as an abstract, symbolic formulation of a problem or truth that has a much wider, even a universal, application.

So long as such a drawing really represents the archetypal drama that is being lived in the unconscious, it has power to attract and fascinate the attention of the religious devotee. Through his contemplation of it his individual problems and difficulties may find an appropriate solution. In Mahayana Buddhism such a figure is called a mandala, and Jung has adopted this term to describe all such drawings. He writes:

> The term "mandala" was chosen because this word denotes the ritual or magic circle used in Lamaism and also in Tantric yoga as a *yantra* or aid to contemplation. The Eastern mandalas used in ceremonial are figures fixed by tradition; they may be drawn or painted or, in certain special ceremonies, even represented plastically.
>
> It seems to me beyond question that these Eastern symbols originated in dreams and visions, and were not invented by some Mahayana church father. On the contrary, they are among the oldest religious symbols of humanity and may even have existed in paleolithic times (cf. the Rhodesian rock-paintings).[21]

Figures that are true mandalas occur in Christian iconography, especially in the esoteric or secret aspects of it, and similar representations are to be found among the symbols of many other religions. They are frequent in Celtic religious art, and occur among the art forms of many of the Indian tribes

21. *Psychology and Alchemy* (C.W. 12), pp. 91 f.

of Mexico and Central America, for example the ancient Mayas, while the so-called sun wheel found in palaeolithic cave drawings is very probably, as Jung points out, an early form of mandala, for the sun as an external object could never have been portrayed as a circle with a cross in it. This device is surely an art form—that is to say, it originated in the imagination of the artist, or derives from an archetypal image that he perceived and reproduced pictorially. Whether it had to do with a conflict of opposites in him we can never know; but we do know that this form, the circle divided by a cross, has persisted through the centuries and still attracts the eye and the imagination of modern persons, for some of whom at least it represents an opposition corresponding to their own psychic duality.

The word mandala means circle and is used especially to denote a magic circle. In religious usage, however, it has a technical meaning: "a *mandala* is a symbolical geometrical diagram wherein deities are invoked." [22] When such a figure is drawn in a ceremonial, the aim is twofold: first, to delimit a space wherein the worshipper will be safe from foreign influences; second, to heal his sickness, whether of soul or body, through identification with the supreme deity symbolically enshrined in the centre. Healing of the soul is here the equivalent of enlightenment. The psychological significance is that the mandala is used to isolate the personal psyche from the not-I, to keep out or exorcize foreign influences, and to unify the disparate psychic elements under the rulership of a new centre, that is, to replace the partial rulership of the ego with the accepted dominion of the Self.

The circle as a magic means of protection is a familiar concept. When a magician is about to call up spirit forces he usually draws a circle around himself. He then invokes the aid of that spirit or daemon from whom at his initiation he received his occult powers, and commands or beseeches him to protect the circle. This he does by drawing a portrait or symbol of the spirit or daemon, or by writing the secret name of this being on the ground inside the circle, or perhaps by laying

22. Evans-Wentz, *Tibetan Yoga and Secret Doctrines*, p. 72.

the contents of his amulet or medicine bag in the place where he wishes the daemon to stand guard. Alien spirits are unable to cross the line he has drawn; thus he remains safe from their influence.

A somewhat similar technique is used when at moments of danger, especially psychological danger (the modern formulation corresponding to the older notion of threat from evil spirits), there is an implied insistence that the circle must not be broken. For instance, it is expected that no one will leave the room during an important conference, while even in a social situation there is an uncomfortable feeling if anyone leaves the table early, especially if the meal has a ritual meaning, as in the celebration of a birthday or a feast with a religious background, like Christmas or Thanksgiving. Where a spiritistic medium has invoked her control and made contact with spirit forces, to use the language of the séance, it is considered even dangerous for the circle to be broken; if it does happen, the medium may have difficulty in coming out of her trance and resuming the conscious state.

Peter Freuchen [23] relates that once when he was living in the most inaccessible part of Greenland, he was present at a magic ceremony in which the medicine man undertook a journey to the spirit world in order to purify the water supply of the village, which had become polluted. This enterprise was believed to be fraught with many dangers. The entire population of the village gathered in the medicine man's hut while he lay on his cot and began to chant. Gradually he passed into a state of trance; his voice grew fainter and fainter, seeming to draw off into the distance as he went farther out on his spirit journey. The emotional tension grew until the people in the hut were nearly frantic. Presently it became too much for one man, who started up and dived right through the snow wall of the hut and made his escape. Immediately the voice of the medicine man showed that he was in distress. He lost his way in the spirit world and had the greatest difficulty in getting back to the hut and re-entering his body; indeed, he

23. *Arctic Adventure*, pp. 132 ff.

nearly died, and the man who had broken the circle was considered to have committed a serious crime.

The taboo against breaking the circle accords with psychological laws. If the ring is broken and anything leaks out, it may be impossible to finish the business in hand; conversely also, a newcomer entering a group already deep in some undertaking may bring in a foreign influence disturbing or even destructive to the enterprise. When the matter to be dealt with involves something not quite clear, which therefore predicates unknown elements, partly understood potencies or unconscious dynamic factors, it is particularly necessary to keep the circle closed. In addition, it must be further protected by steps ensuring that the participants safeguard their thoughts and attention, and restrain their emotional reactions, so that other unconscious elements may be debarred from entering and adding their quota of undisciplined emotion to the situation.

Thus far the circle symbolism has been applied to the problems of group activity and human relationship. Beyond this it has a more direct bearing on those of the individuation process. The preceding chapter has stressed the more personal aspects of the question, such as the necessity of collecting all the bits of psychic stuff that have lived only in projections, of disentangling them from the situations in life that made them apparent, and of bringing them back within the circle of the psyche. If an individual has projected a large element of himself into another human being or into an idea and is quite unaware of the psychological fact behind his enthusiasm, it may happen that his whole demeanour changes whenever this interest is alluded to, though he himself is quite unaware of his reaction. In ordinary speech we say that he is fanatical about it. He may be quite unable to discuss it on its merits; instead, mere mention of the subject moves him as automatically as any puppet pulled by an invisible string, though about other matters he may be a reasonable and thinking person.

Thus a projection that is unrealized as such will function as an autonomous complex, with the characteristic manifestations of a part personality. This mechanism may be so deceptive that the individual's own observation of the circumstances will be seriously distorted. He may even be ready to swear that the person who carries his projection did or said something that he actually did not do or say; in a less exaggerated situation, the psychic projection gives a false colour to what was actually said or done, so that the action is seen in a wrong light.

Such distortions of reality can occur as the result of either a positive or a negative projection. There are many expressions epitomizing both types. For instance, it is proverbial that "love is blind," that is, the lover sees the loved object always in a good light. The aphorism, "Give a dog a bad name and hang him," implies that when once a projection has loaded an imputation of villainy on some person, everything he does will be distorted in the eyes of the individual who has made the projection.

Naturally the task of recognizing and assimilating the projected psychic material is neither short nor easily accomplished, because so far as is known there is no limit to the problem of projection. Each step of assimilation only clears the way for a recognition of further projections. Yet there are certain obvious projections that must be made conscious if the individual is not to fall below the general cultural level compatible with his position in life. For each level of culture correlates roughly with a certain level of consciousness, and the obvious duty of each individual is to strive to attain the psychic level corresponding with his cultural status. When a man has done this he is no longer infantile; he is fully adult and may be said to be up to date, to be truly living in his own era. One who rises above the general level of his time becomes what Jung has called "truly modern"; he stands like a spiritual pioneer facing the problems that will confront civilization tomorrow.

As recognition of the projections advances and the lost elements are collected within the circle of the psyche, a considerable conflict is likely to arise between them. This is understandable, for some of these factors come from the father or mother, others from more remote ancestors; beyond these still other elements whose origin cannot be traced, and whose manifestations are often strange and baffling in the extreme, press into consciousness and make their influence felt. These strange, sometimes even nonhuman elements in the psychic inheritance are aptly represented in fairy tales as the good and bad gifts of the fairy godmother. It is small wonder that a lack of inner harmony results. The marvel is that there is not a perpetual state of war within the psyche, for each of these elements is endowed with energy and so cannot die. Fortunately for our sanity, many of these irreconcilable elements lie deep within the unconscious, locked in primordial sleep; those which may have stirred are shut away in separate compartments. But as life progresses and an increase of consciousness is achieved, the inner conflicts awaken, and the problem of reconciling the oppositions they reveal has to be undertaken as a serious and urgent task.

It is at this time that the mandala symbolism begins to appear in dreams and other unconscious products, pointing the way in which the conflicts can be resolved. It must always be remembered that a real mandala is a living symbol and cannot be made as a deliberate device. Manufactured diagrams obviously have no power to change or influence the condition of the psyche. But a symbol arising out of unconscious depths is not made; it is a true mirror image of how things are in the unseen part of the psyche. This is a real picture, and if it can be grasped by consciousness it can be made real in consciousness too. About this problem Jung writes:

All that can be ascertained at present about the symbolism of the mandala is that it portrays an autonomous psychic fact, characterized by a phenomenology which is always repeating itself and is everywhere the same. It seems to be a sort of nucleus about whose innermost structure and ultimate meaning we know nothing. We can also regard it as the real—i.e., effective—reflection of a conscious attitude which can state neither its aim nor its purpose and, because of this abdication, projects its activity entirely upon the virtual centre of the mandala. The compelling force necessary for this projection always lies in some situation where the individual no longer knows how to help himself in any other way.[24]

24. *Psychology and Alchemy* (C.W. 12), p. 175.

The mandala usually contains a square, a cross, or occasionally a triangle or star form within or surrounding a circle. The relation between the square and the circle has symbolized for many people through many centuries the problem of the relation of two incompatible values. The square represents the earth, which is, as we say, foursquare reality; it is the indisputable fact, the logical or rational principle, and symbolizes human consciousness and understanding. The circle is complete in itself, without beginning and without end; it represents the heavens, the cosmos, and symbolizes the sphere of the absolute, the divine. Through the ages the endeavour to solve the mathematical problem of squaring the circle [25] embodied man's attempt to reconcile these two realms.

The absorption of thinkers and philosophers of past epochs in this and similar problems indicates that more was involved for them than the external and apparent enigma. They could not be content as we are to state the area of a circle as πr^2. We are satisfied with this formulation, so that further concern with the problem seems to us useless, merely puerile. But for the *mathematici* of ancient Greece and the philosophers of the Middle Ages, many of them men of outstanding intellectual gifts, this was not enough. They were fascinated by such insoluble problems and felt compelled to exercise themselves in attempts to solve them, and above all to discover their hidden philosophical import. They were held to this work in much the same way as the alchemists were held to the problem of their opus, which was concerned with the secrets of matter.

From this circumstance we must conclude that the external problem, whether mathematical or chemical, bore a hidden psychological value. The unknown within the learned searcher after a truth that was hidden in darkness found a resting place in the objective problems of mathematics or of matter. This view is further supported by the fact that in many religious

25. This is the attempt to find a square whose area will be exactly commensurate with that of a circle, so as to make it possible to say that the area of the circle is known. But as this area can be expressed only with the use of an unknown and unknowable quantity represented by π, the problem remains unsolved. Cf. Michael Maier, *De circulo physico quadrato,* an alchemistic treatise.

systems a figure formed by combining a circle with a square or with some other form of ascertainable area, such as the triangle, is one of the symbols of the secret or esoteric teaching or dogma of the group, and is regarded as the revelation of a truth inexpressible in intellectual terms, for it represents the relation between the human and the divine. These figures are true mandalas.

For the initiated such a form has an esoteric meaning and represents the highest truth, the reality that can be grasped only through undergoing the training or discipline leading to initiation or enlightenment. The ordinary worshipper, who as a rule makes no effort to understand what he is taught, simply takes the sacred pictures for granted, or uses them in a quite superstitious way as a means of influencing the spirit world—to exorcize the demons or to compel the gods to grant him favours—just as a magician uses the magic circle to keep out evil spirits.

In the East, the mandala is used by the generality as a magic means for the reconciliation of the opposites and to heal the sick, though the initiated understand its use differently, as will appear later. The Pueblo and Navaho Indians make a sand painting of a mandala on the ground, and the Sioux map out such a form in the figures of a sacred dance as part of the ordinary religious ceremonials and also in the rituals performed to heal the sick. These American Indians hold the belief, very common among primitive peoples, that illness is caused by evil spirits invading the body or the mind of the sick man and warring against his true spirit. He is therefore placed on the ground and a mandala of healing is drawn or danced around him. The power residing in the centre of the mandala, as the result of the reconciliation of the opposing forces, enters into him and he is returned to his "true" state, that of normal well-being.

In discussing the value of the mandala symbolism, Jung writes:

The mandalas used in ceremonial are of great significance because their centres usually contain one of the highest religious figures: either Shiva himself—often in the embrace of Shakti—or Buddha, Amitabha, Avalokiteshvara, or one of the great Mahayana teachers, or simply the *dorje*, symbol of all the divine forces together, whether creative or destructive in nature.[26]

In the mandalas of the sand paintings, the central power is often represented by a picture of Father Sky and Mother Earth. Or it may be symbolized simply by pollen, the golden dust whose miraculous power to fertilize the corn has fascinated the religious thought of the Navahos, and corn meal, the female seed—the one representing the father, the other the gift of Mother Earth's own body. In Buddhist mandalas, as Jung points out, the central symbol is often a representation of the god Shiva and the goddess Shakti [27] in eternal embrace; in the mandalas of Northern Buddhism in Tibet, it is usually the dorje, which is both a double sceptre and the thunderbolt, representing unlimited power and its control. We may also find in Tibet a representation of one or another of the gods of the pre-Buddhist Bon religion, frequently in wrathful aspect, occupying the centre of the mandala.

In Christian mandalas, Christ Triumphant appears in the centre, surrounded by the emblems or symbols of the four evangelists—the bull, the eagle, the lion, and the angel—representing the four manifestations or emanations of the divine power in its relation to man. Sometimes the central figure is Mary enthroned, seated with God the Father and God the Son, or holding on her lap her Son, crowned—signifying that God, who became man through a human mother, has reassumed his divine power and now rules triumphant in the central place. In the mandalas of later centuries the centre is sometimes occupied by an abstract design, such as an eye enclosed in a triangle, meaning perhaps the all-seeing divine consciousness enclosed in or manifested through the Trinity. These are all conventionalized or fixed ritual forms. Doubtless each originated in the vision of some person whose numinous experience presented itself in this guise, and gradually through the cen-

26. *Psychology and Alchemy* (C.W. 12), pp. 93-94.
27. Shiva, the masculine (or positive) aspect of the universe-embracing forces of the Cosmic Mind, is a personification of the male half of the duality of deity; Shakti, the female (or negative) half, is commonly personified as a mother goddess. Cf. Evans-Wentz, *Tibetan Yoga and Secret Doctrines*, p. 28.

turies, as one and then another found that his own experience could be expressed in a similar way, the original image underwent modification, until at last a definite form was crystallized out of the experience of the many and became established in the ritual as a sacred picture showing "the way things are."

When Dr. Jung was in India he talked with a Lamaistic abbot about the use of the mandala in Tibetan Buddhism, and was told that the ritual mandalas to be found in every temple are not venerated in the services but are used as an aid to meditation, in this way they serve as models for active imagination, for "building up" the individual mandala. If a man has a religious conflict or a serious personal problem, he builds for himself a mandala and by this means works out a solution of his conflict.

This is an exceedingly interesting parallel to the observations reported by Jung and confirmed by others working along the lines he has laid down, namely, that when in the course of a psychological analysis a seemingly insoluble problem is encountered, work performed on the images arising from the unconscious by drawing or painting them may lead to a resolution of the conflict. Drawing is of course not prescribed as a remedy, and even when the patient has a spontaneous impulse to draw, he is left entirely free in the choice of his figures, since, as said above, the whole meaning and purpose of the activity would be vitiated by any attempt on the part of analyst or patient to influence the free expression of the unconscious contents. Obviously no particular virtue, no magic power, is to be won by merely drawing circles and squares. Furthermore, it is inappropriate for the patient to draw a mandala unless it presents itself spontaneously in a dream or phantasy image. For the mandala represents an effort of the unconscious to compensate a state of disorder or confusion in the conscious realm. It arises therefore in that moment when the lack of order in the life situation has been brought most clearly into consciousness by concentration of attention upon it. Such a heightened awareness of conflict often occurs in an individual undergoing analysis, as a result of discussion of his problem with the analyst.

The true purpose and use of mandalas can perhaps best be understood from a study of their ritual use in Tibet, where they play a most important part. In addition to the permanent drawings kept in the temples for use in the services and for the contemplation of novices, special mandalas are made for many occasions. These may be drawn on the ground with coloured sands, just as the Navahos make their sand paintings, and for much the same purpose. Or they may be made of dishes of offerings for the gods whose aid is being invoked, the offerings being placed in geometric arrangements that have ritual significance. Or the mandala may be traced out in the patterns of a dance. In each case the particular mandala used belongs to the ritual appropriate to the special occasion.

The mandala plays an especially important part in a little-known Tibetan ritual by means of which the yogin seeks to transcend ego consciousness and attain to consciousness of the Self. The text states it as follows:

> Thus may my divine mission be crowned with success,
> And may I attain to the body of Glory.

This rite is described in a Lamaistic text of the Ningmapa school of Padma Sambhava, which is of pre-Buddhistic, i.e., Bon origin. Evans-Wentz gives us the text as translated by the late Lama Kazi Dawa-Samdup.[28] It dates from the eighth century A.D. and is entitled, "The Path of the Mystic Sacrifice: The Yoga of Subduing the Lower Self." The ritual to which the text applies is called *chöd*. It is concerned with the sacrifice of the ego personality and the attainment of union with a divine consciousness.

The doctrine of the All-Consciousness transcending the consciousness of man is fundamental and central in Buddhism. The object of these yogic practices and of the prolonged training of the Mahayana, Zen, and other schools is to achieve enlightenment, which means to experience the light of the All-Consciousness and thus to be released from the wheel of birth and death through the realization that the phenomenal world

28. Evans-Wentz, *Tibetan Yoga and Secret Doctrines*. The description and quotations below are taken from this study.

is but maya, whose reality depends for each individual on his psychic attitude alone.

I have already referred to these teachings as paralleling in a certain way the experience of modern psychologists, who also find that when the consciousness of an individual is increased through recognition and assimilation of his projections, his unconditional commitment to the world is relaxed, and he begins to see that the emotions and involvements that formerly held him were really due to a projection of intrapsychic factors. This surely corresponds to the Buddhistic teaching that the demons and gods, that is, the psychic powers of fear, hate, and anger, or of desire and fascination, are manifestations of "thine own thought-forms," as it is expressed in the ritual for guidance through the after-death state.[29] If the modern individual can recognize his "demons" and "gods" as his own thought forms, they will lose their power over him.

The ritual of *chöd*, which is practised by the advanced yogin as part of his secret initiation, is also enacted as a so-called mystery play

performed for the purpose of expelling the old year with its demons of ill-luck, through winning the aid of the deities by means of human sacrifice (nowadays made in effigy) and thus safeguarding the crops and cattle and assuring divine protection for the state and triumph over all enemies, both human and spiritual. Primitively, a sacramental eating of the flesh and drinking of the blood of the sacrificed one was probably associated with the rite.[30]

When, however, the rite is undertaken by a Tibetan yogin seeking enlightenment at an advanced stage in his training, it no longer has the character of a mystery play performed before a whole village to the accompaniment of feasting and merriment. It is a severe ordeal that might well terrify the hardiest devotee.[31] The yogin retires to an isolated place, often high up in the mountains, and carries out the ceremony entirely alone. It consists of a weird dance, performed at night, frequently on

29. Evans-Wentz, *Tibetan Book of the Dead*, p. 147.
30. Evans-Wentz, *Tibetan Yoga and Secret Doctrines*, p. 285.
31. See A. David-Neel, *With Mystics and Magicians in Tibet*, pp. 148 ff., for an eyewitness description of the rite.

a burial ground or in a place where the decaying bodies of the dead are exposed to the vultures. The solitary worshipper seeks to identify his own body with the rotting corpses around him and to concentrate his thoughts on the transitoriness of life. The uncanny setting and the gruesome details of the rite serve to arouse his imagination, so that the emotions of fear and horror lying dormant in the unconscious may be stirred, or as the Tibetans would say, that the wrathful deities may be moved to come to him. In this solitude he struggles with the psychic forces thus unleashed upon him; if he is successful, he conquers the demonic powers and dances upon them. This means that he overcomes his own instinctive impulses and desires. For *chöd* means

"cutting [off]" with reference to egoism, as represented by the human fleshly form together with all its passions and *karmically*-inherited predispositions constituting the personality. . . . In virtue of the mystic sacrifice of his own body, the successful *yogin* breaks asunder the fetters of personality, of passion, of separateness, of all *maya*, or illusion; and transcending Ignorance, of which these are the sources, attains to *yogic* insight into the true nature of human existence. Once having realized the illusory character of all phenomenal appearances, which the unenlightened hold to be real and external and separate . . . the *yogin* sees the many as the One, and the One as All, and knows that the sole reality is Mind.[32]

The ritual "cutting off" of egotism corresponds to the psychological process by which the dominance of ego consciousness and of the instincts is challenged, even broken, through a coming to terms with the unconscious—a process leading to the discovery of a new centre of the psyche and corresponding to the realization of the yogin that Mind, or All-Consciousness, is the supreme power. This realization is similar to the culmination of the process of individuation. The remarkable correspondence between the teachings of Eastern esotericism, and the findings of analytical psychology in its

32. Evans-Wentz, *Tibetan Yoga and Secret Doctrines*, pp. 277, 281. "Mind," as used in Buddhistic texts, never refers to intellect, but corresponds rather to the idea of superconsciousness, or to the Greek concept of nous.

exploration of the unconscious in modern persons, is startling. Jung in his commentary on a Chinese esoteric text writes:

My experience in my practice has been such as to reveal to me a quite new and unexpected approach to eastern wisdom. But it must be well understood that I did not have as a starting point a more or less adequate knowledge of Chinese philosophy. On the contrary, when I began my life-work in the practice of psychiatry and psychotherapy, I was completely ignorant of Chinese philosophy, and it is only later that my professional experiences have shown me that in my technique I had been unconsciously led along that secret way which for centuries has been the preoccupation of the best minds of the East. . . . [This Chinese text] shows striking parallels to the course of psychic development in my patients, none of whom is Chinese.

In order to make this strange fact more intelligible to the reader, it must be mentioned that just as the human body shows a common anatomy over and above all racial differences, so too does the psyche possess a common substratum. I have called the latter the collective unconscious. As a common human heritage, it transcends all differences of culture and consciousness and does not consist merely of contents capable of becoming conscious, but of latent dispositions toward identical reactions. Thus the fact of the collective unconscious is simply the psychic expression of identity of brain-structure irrespective of all racial differences. By its means can be explained the analogy, going even as far as identity, between various myth-themes and symbols, and the possibility of human understanding in general.[33]

According to the Lamaistic teaching, the replacement of the ego by a superior consciousness is something to be directly sought after by definite means prescribed in the ritual. In this respect the yogic way is utterly different from the procedure in analytical psychology. As Jung himself says:

There could be no greater mistake than for a Westerner to take up the direct practice of Chinese yoga, for then it would still be a matter of his will and consciousness, and would only strengthen the latter against the unconscious, bringing about the very effect which should have been avoided. The neurosis would then be increased. It cannot be sufficiently strongly emphasized

33. Wilhelm and Jung, *The Secret of the Golden Flower*, p. 83.

that we are not Orientals, and therefore have an entirely different point of departure in these things.[34]

Nevertheless, the experiences that occur spontaneously during the process of individuation resemble in certain ways those described as resulting from yogic disciplines; moreover, the symbols arising in the former frequently have a remarkable similarity to those employed in the latter. Obviously both of these undertakings are concerned, though in very different ways, with those contents of the unconscious which are experienced as split-off psychic factors. The yogin deliberately courts such a splitting off by conjuring up terrifying thoughts and visions, and by practising his disciplines in an isolated spot where the ordeal is enhanced by the physical hardship he must endure. The modern Occidental comes upon these autonomous psychic factors while seeking to clarify problems arising over what I have called the point at issue, or when he is confronted with some experience that has a deeply moving, even numinous quality; for such *tremenda* all contain projections functioning as autonomous psychic complexes that in naïve men give rise to belief in demons and ghosts, gods and spirits.

The recognition that the split-off psychic forces are not actual demons or gods is possible only

in so far as consciousness has begun to detach itself from its contents. However, the latter is only the case when life has been lived so exhaustively, and with such devotion, that no more unfulfilled life-duties exist, and when, therefore, there are no more desires which cannot be sacrificed without hesitation. In a word, this detachment of consciousness can only begin when nothing remains to prevent an inner superiority to the world. It is futile to lie to oneself about this. Whenever one is caught, one is still possessed; and when one is possessed it means the presence of something stronger than oneself.[35]

The progressive assimilation of the split-off psychic forces results in an increase of consciousness leading to the ultimate goal, the supreme value, represented by the symbol of the Self. The road by which one must travel to reach this goal

34. Ibid., p. 87.
35. Ibid., p. 112.

passes through certain definite regions, as it were, where typical experiences are met with, as Frobenius has shown in regard to the hero myth, the dragon slaying, and the night journey.[36]

According to the Tibetan text I am about to describe, the ego, represented by the human body, is sacrificed and devoured by the gods and demons at the invitation of the yogin. This parallels the implications of the visions of Zosimos, in which the priest, who is called the "sacrificer," tore off pieces of his own flesh and ate them. Zosimos writes:

> I was filled with fear. . . . And I saw a little man, a barber white with age, who said to me, "What are you looking at?" I replied that I was amazed to see the agitation of the water and the men burned, yet living. He replied in these terms: "This spectacle that you see, is the going-in and the going-out and the mutation." I asked him again: "What mutation?" He replied: "It is the place of the operation called maceration; for those men who wish to obtain the virtue [French *vertu*, meaning inner essence or power] enter here and become spirits, after having fled the body." Then I said to him: "And you, are you a spirit?" And he replied: "Yes, a spirit and a guardian of spirits." [37]

In the earlier stages of the Tibetan initiation, a mandala is drawn on the ground, and the deities presiding over the psychic realms whose secrets are to be revealed, and whose powers are to be conferred on the neophyte, are invited to be present and to occupy the spaces in the mandala reserved for them. During the ceremony, if the postulant receives the inner illumination, his attainment is confirmed by his seeing in the sky, above the earthly drawing, another mandala—the "true" one. This true mandala is exactly like the one drawn on the ground except that the deities are visibly present in their prescribed places, conferring upon the neophyte understanding of the realms of psychic reality over which they rule. At the end of the initiation, the neophyte receives a new name, regarded as sacred.

After he has received enlightenment by passing through

36. Cf. also Jung, *Symbols of Transformation* (C.W. 5), p. 210.
37. M. Berthelot, *Collection des anciens alchimistes grecs,* Traductions, II, 118 f.

several such initiations, of differing degree, and has thereby become possessed of much spiritual power, he is considered ready—in his own judgment or that of his teacher—to undertake the difficult and hazardous experience of *chöd*. In this rite he strives to gain control of the demons—i.e., the psychic non-ego—and to overthrow their dominion over his body.

The ritual of *chöd* begins with a "Dance Which Destroyeth Erroneous Beliefs," in which the yogin identifies himself with the Goddess of the All-fulfilling Wisdom, who sits in the centre of the mandala. Being thus protected, he begins to visualize the demons and to summon them to come to him. They are (1) the "King Spirits of Hatred and Wrath," (2) the "Head of Pride," embodied in Yama, "Lord of Death" and controller of rebirth, who manifests himself in the eight worldly ambitions, namely, profit, fame, praise, and pleasure, and their opposites, avoidance of loss, defamation, disparagement, and pain, (3) the "Ogress of Lust," embodying greed and sexual desire, (4) the "Mischievous Spirits of Jealousy," (5) the "Vampire of Stupidity." When these demons have become visibly present to his inner eye, he begins to dance upon them, saying:

> I, thy *yogin*, who practise the Dauntless Courage,
> Devoting my thought and energy wholly to the realizing
>   that *Nirvāna* and *Sangsāra* are inseparable,
> Am dancing this measure on [the forms of] spiritual beings
>   who personify the self;
> May I (be able to) destroy the *sangsāric* view of duality.[38]

He then calls on the Heroes and Heroines to come and dance on the demons whom he has subdued. They dance in the four quarters—the four chief "continents" (that is, worlds) oriented about Mount Meru as the centre—bestowing their efficacy:

> When dancing in the Centre of the Perfectly Endowed Spot,
> The arena for the dance of the Heroes and Heroines is blessed
>   [with their divine influence];

.   .   .   .

38. Evans-Wentz, *Tibetan Yoga and Secret Doctrines*, bk. v, "The Path of the Mystic Sacrifice," pp. 302 ff.

The joyous songs of *Hum*, of the Wisdom of the Real Essence, sound melodiously.[39]

Next he calls upon the five goddesses embodying the divine antidote to the five passions composing egotism, and adjures them to transfix these egotistic passions or demons with their celestial spears. There follows an instruction to the yogin:

Having recognized the Elementals, Hatred or Wrath, Pride, Lust, Jealousy and Stupidity, of which egoism is composed, now thou must recognize the sacrificial gift of thy body.[40]

According to another version of the text, the "mandala of sacrifice" is then drawn, and offerings are placed in the sections of the drawing. The yogin concentrates upon it in meditation, and the realization comes to him that the mandala is his own body and that he is himself the sacrifice offered within it.[41] The ritual instructs him:

Then in offering up the circle of offerings,
Imagine the central part [or spinal column] of thy body to be
    Mount Meru [in the Hindu idea, Mount Meru is the central
    pillar of the universe],
The four chief limbs to be the Four Continents,
The minor limbs to be the Sub-Continents,

39. Ibid., p. 306.
40. Ibid., p. 307.
41. Cf. Jung, *Mysterium Coniunctionis*, § 511-13: "But when [a man] loses his own values he becomes a hungry robber, the wolf, lion, and other ravening beasts which for the alchemists symbolized the appetites that break loose when the black waters of chaos—the unconsciousness of projection—have swallowed up the king.

. . . "If the projected conflict is to be healed, it must return into the psyche of the individual, where it had its unconscious beginnings. He must celebrate a Last Supper with himself, and eat his own flesh and drink his own blood; which means that he must recognize and accept the other in himself. . . .

. . . "The miraculous feeding with one's own substance—so strangely reflecting its prototype, Christ—means nothing less than the integration of those parts of the personality which are still outside ego-consciousness. Lion and peacock, emblems of concupiscence and pride, signify the over-weening pretensions of the human shadow, which we so gladly project on our fellow man in order to visit our own sins upon him with apparent justification. In the age-old image of the uroboros lies the thought of devouring oneself and turning oneself into a circulatory process, for it was clear to the more astute alchemists that the prima materia of the art was man himself."

The head to be the Worlds of the *Devas* [the gods],
The two eyes to be the Sun and Moon,
And that the five internal organs constitute all objects of wealth
and enjoyment amongst gods and men.[42]

After the mandala has been offered up in worship, the
yogin is directed as follows:

Having done so, mentally absorb the [visualized] objects into thyself,
And keep thy mind in the equilibrium [or quiescence] of the non-
two state.[43]

Having done this he prays:

This illusory body, which I have held to be so precious,
I dedicate [in sacrifice] as a heaped-up offering,
Without the least regard for it, to all the deities that constitute the
visualized assembly;
May the very root of self be cut asunder.[44]

He then imagines

this body, which is the result of thine own karmic propensities, to
be a fat, luscious-looking corpse, huge [enough to embrace the
Universe].[45]

Here he calls upon the gods and demons:

Come ye all here where devotional penance is being observed.
This day, I the fearless *yogin*,
Am offering in sacrifice this illusory body of mine,
This body which createth the distinction between the *Sangsāra*
and *Nirvāna*.
Having made the skull as vast as the Third-Void Universe
And filled it with inexhaustible quantities of Elixir of Wisdom.
To all of you, enjoying the miraculous power of appearing in
whatever shape desired,
This gift is offered most ungrudgingly and without the least feel-
ing of regret. . . .[46]

42. Evans-Wentz, *Tibetan Yoga and Secret Doctrines*, bk. v, "The Path
of the Mystic Sacrifice," pp. 324-25.
43. Ibid., "The Fundamental Essence of the Subtle Truth," pp. 324 ff.
44. Ibid., bk. v, "The Path of the Mystic Sacrifice," p. 309.
45. Ibid., p. 311.
46. Ibid., p. 313.

The concluding instructions are:

Then offer the feast and dedicate the act [of having offered it] . . . [and finally] dedicate "the Merit of the Act of Sacrifice." [47]

Thus, through the sacrifice of his fleshly body—"thou strippest the hide from off thy body, which is the dregs of egoism" (cf. Zosimos, *Il a enlevé toute la peau de ma tête*)—the yogin is released from the conflict of the opposites within him and remains in the "non-two" state, which is samadhi, enlightenment, in which it is realized that all dualism is transcended.

This climax of the ritual corresponds remarkably with the psychological data we are considering. The yogin's recognition that the mandala he has drawn stands for himself, corresponds to the realization that the symbol of the circle arising from the unconscious represents the psyche and its boundaries. The instruction by which the yogin sacrifices his body and its desires, in order thereby to come into the non-two state of consciousness, parallels the observation made over and over again in analysing persons in conflict—namely, that if the opposites are to be reconciled, the ego must be renounced in favour of a new, nonpersonal centre of the whole psyche.

When the yogin is directed to place his offerings in a circle, he is first instructed to meditate on the mandala thus formed, contemplating it as a whole, as representing himself. Next he must consider his own body as representative of the whole of creation. His spinal column, which corresponds to the chakras in the closely related Tantric yoga—symbolizing the unconscious psyche—is to be envisioned as Mount Meru, the pillar supporting the universe. His head is to be realized as the world of the gods; that is to say, the mind, as consciousness, is the dwelling place of the gods, who are thus seen to be not external beings but psychic forces. In the same way the *Book of the Dead* adjures the deceased to recognize that the gods and demons are all his "own thought-forms." The various organs of the body are to be considered as representing all the physical desires and their satisfactions. Thus the stomach stands for

47. Ibid., pp. 313 ff.

the instinct of hunger, the genital organs for sexual desires, and so on. All these things the yogin is to absorb into himself, thereby becoming reconciled to everything in the universe, good or bad. In this way he becomes able to hold himself in the nondual state.

In this most instructive religious ritual, the reconciliation of the opposites is achieved by the yogin through sacrifice of his personal needs and desires and relinquishment of his relative standpoint as based on the separateness of the ego. In place of this he accepts life in its entirety, where some are filled and some go empty, some are loved and others experience loneliness. He sacrifices his individual being and renounces his personal fate, receiving instead a share in the total fate of mankind.

On the death of a man who has received this highest initiation, a special ritual is used at the burial, in which the mandala again figures as the central symbol. A funeral mandala is drawn on the ground and the corpse is placed in its centre, so that once again, and for the last time, his duality as a human being may be resolved and he may be made one. It is recorded that at the funeral of Milarepa, one of Tibet's great saints, five *dakinis* or goddesses appeared and sang a hymn beginning with an invocation to the seed of eternal fire, *Rom*.

> *Rom!* the divine fire of the Vital Force
> Having been ever contemplated [by Him],
> What power hath the fire [of this world] over Him?
> For Him, who hath long been engaged in devotion,
> Meditating on His organic body as a shape divine,
> What need is there to leave behind a fleshly corpse?
> For the *yogi* who hath the perfect Divine *Mandala*
> Well defined in His own body,
> What need is there of the *Mandala* outlined on the ground?

The chant then outlines the blessings the yogin leaves behind, and ends thus:

> Unto the life which ye have chosen
> Many interruptions come; so perform ye rites in secret.
> From the admonitions by your wondrous *Guru* given
> There shall come a blessing; so cast all doubts aside.

.   .   .   .

For all the beings here to-day assembled
No birth in the Unhappy Worlds shall come, O ye of human kind.
For the *Mandala* of the Thatness,
Appearances external and the mind are one; shatter then your
theory of duality.[48]

"The Thatness" means the fundamental reality behind all phenomena; realization of it constitutes liberation from ignorance and attainment of the true state, in which all dualistic concepts are transcended, and all phenomenal things merge in transcendental at-one-ness. The last couplet of the hymn could therefore be paraphrased: "In the mandala of fundamental reality, external appearances (that is, the concrete reality of the world) and the mind (psychic reality) are one; shatter then your theory of duality." From the point of view of the enlightened man, duality is seen to be only an illusion.

In the case of the Tibetan yogin, as we have seen, a long period of preparation is required before the initiation at which he will receive illumination can be undertaken. At this time he will have a vision of the reconciliation of the opposites, not just as a concept but as a profound realization. If the preparatory work has been effective, and the initiation is successful, the mandala drawn for the ceremony becomes alive for him; he sees it filled in actuality with the potencies he calls deities, wearing the forms familiar to him from religious pictures and teachings. This vision is of course a religious experience of great intensity and awe, a numinous perception. From that moment on, for the rest of his life, the reality of the unseen is an ever present fact to him.

Important as this realization is, it still does not solve the problem of the opposites, for the two realities, the seen and the unseen, still exist side by side, and often are opposed. The gods are still external; the potencies they represent have not yet been assimilated. It is only later, in the ceremony of the visualization of the sacrifice, in which his own body is both the sacrifice and the place of sacrifice—the mandala—that his duality is finally healed. This initiation is accomplished alone, without the assistance of a guru, and is attained only by the most advanced yogins.

48. Evans-Wentz, *Tibet's Great Yogi: Milarepa*, pp. 277 ff.

In the course of psychological analysis a very similar sequence of symbols and subjective experiences may gradually unfold in the stages of the individuation process. As the limits of the psyche are gradually defined, and the projected elements are first recognized and then accepted as part of the whole psyche, the full impact of the conflict of the opposites makes itself felt. As a rule it is only after the opposition has been realized in its fullest measure that what may be called "mandala psychology" develops. It arises as the outcome of severe conflict resulting from the realization that certain things one has refused to look at, or has recognized only in others, are actually a part of one's own psyche.

In the two cases described by Jung [49] this symbolism played an important role, and it is plain to see from the material itself how difficult the inner transition must have been. The struggle is particularly evidenced in the dream series, in which the emergence of a real mandala,[50] having power to reconcile the conflict, came about so haltingly. For obvious reasons it has been necessary to omit all mention of how it felt to the persons concerned to be caught in such far-reaching conflicts, so that from the available account it would seem to have been easy. I doubt very much, however, that this was the case. During my more than twenty-five years of analytical work [51] I have been privileged to observe similar transformations many times, and my experience is that these fundamental changes are usually associated with much pain and distress. It is as though they demanded a ritual sacrifice and death similar to the self-offering described in the Tibetan text. The sacrificial aspect of the experience is in fact often emphasized in dreams. The dreamer may find himself stretched on the cross of the mandala as though crucified; or in the dream he may have to dissect his own body, or paint the mandala with his own blood.

A few illustrations may make clear how such terrifying dreams can have a positive, spiritual significance.

The first turns on the dream of a woman who for many

49. *Psychology and Alchemy* (C.W. 12).
50. Ibid., p. 191 ff.
51. This was written in 1947. The number of years of my analytic work is now (1961) just over forty.

years had suffered from a serious conflict between the irrational, creative, in a certain sense mystical side of her nature,
and her rational, not to say skeptical intellect, which was
usually represented in her dreams by a certain cynical brother-
in-law, whose "hard-boiled" attitude had often made the
dreamer withdraw into herself, feeling very small and foolish,
when she had overcome her usual reticence and voiced some of
her philosophical ideas. During her analysis she would no
sooner begin to move along what was obviously her own inner
road than the brother-in-law would appear in one of her
dreams and with a sarcastic remark destroy all she had been
building with such care. In the dream she would be impotently
angry at his interference, and when talking about the dream
she would protest that her own more spiritual view was the
true one. But as his scathing comment held a good deal of
common sense, she could not deny it completely and would be
thrown into indecision, in which condition she naturally could
make no progress. Her conflict seemed impossible of solution;
both her analysis and her life were hampered by it, for the two
sides of her nature were forever obstructing each other.

One night she dreamed that she was heir to a fortune left
by an aunt. In the dream she was in the aunt's house, having
gone there to see about the inheritance. But there was also a
sinister manservant about, who wanted to do away with her
in order to possess himself of the fortune. Here she learned
secretly that there was a second fortune, larger than the first,
which only this man knew about, and it was this treasure that
he was so anxious to secure for himself. The clue to its where-
abouts was in some way connected with a square of black cloth
that the man had taken and secreted before her arrival. This
cloth was drugged, and the man was planning to use it to kill
her. He approached her, hiding it in his hand, and with it
touched not her but her friend. The friend fell unconscious.
The dreamer was horrified and terribly afraid, but she seized
the square, holding it as far from her face as possible, and fled,
pursued by the man. She evaded him and dashed through the
house, looking for a safe hiding place for the valuable and
dangerous square. She could not throw it away, for it held the

clue to the fortune; yet it was lethal. As she ran through the dining room she saw a golden dish on the sideboard. Under that she hid the black square. Then she awoke.

The next night, in a half-waking state, she had a vision of a golden sphere standing on a rectangular golden box and surmounted by a cone, the whole making a structure that she described as "like a church."

The dream and the vision together exemplify the making of a mandala, and warrant a rather full analysis. The inheritance left to the dreamer by the aunt represents some value that is to come to her from the ancestors, a treasure held in the family that she has not yet come into possession of in her own right—the family code still controls it. In addition to this there is a second fortune—some value beyond that which is generally recognized. This means that there is a secret lying buried in the collective unconscious; it is this fact that she has become aware of in her analytical work. The sinister manservant is the only one who knows about this treasure. He represents the dark aspect of her animus. He is connected with the former owners, corresponding, perhaps, to the manifestation of the secret value in the Christian teaching; for though the patient was of Protestant ancestry, she was not a practising Christian.

This interpretation of the manservant accords with the fact that the animus is the mediator between the conscious and the unconscious, and also connects the individual with the past by which the archetypes within him have been moulded. The manservant wants to keep all knowledge of the treasure from her, just as the animus, so long as it is an autonomous function, "wants," so to speak, to keep the knowledge of the unconscious values from being exploited by consciousness.[52] Until the animus is overcome as an autonomous function, that is, until the dreamer learns to think for herself instead of allowing herself to be swayed by pre-conceived judgments and opinions, and until she has broken the projection of her animus to her brother-in-law, it will keep from her the values of the

---

52. Cf. the story of the Garden of Eden, or of the theft of fire from the gods, etc. In these accounts the treasure is guarded by dangers and withheld from man by threat of dire punishment.

unconscious that, as an adult, she should now "inherit." Until then they will remain only intuitions or mystical dreams and ideals.

The clue to the treasure lies in the black square, suggesting that the secret is a dark one. To the alchemist the "black substance," the nigredo, was the first stage in the process of transforming the prima materia from which the philosopher's gold must be made. It was therefore essential to the work. Here the black substance is a square; it represents the earth, the dark, chthonic prefiguration of the Self. In the dream this is poisonous to the dreamer. The danger arises because the image of the Self is unconscious and so is distorted by her animus thinking—just as in life her brother-in-law's critical thinking has a destructive effect on her. Because she has not adequately developed her own power to think creatively, his thinking, so specious to her, can drug her intellect, represented here by the friend, namely, her shadow, the carrier of the inferior function. It is this inferior side of herself that is overcome by the poison. She runs away, as she has done many times in reality when confronted by the problem. This can be taken as referring both to the occasions when she has abandoned her guns in face of a challenge from the actual brother-in-law, and to the occasions when she has turned away from her inner quest, becoming sceptical of the reality of an inner way and of the value of developing wholeness within herself. In the dream, however, it was apparently just the right thing to run away.

Here is a point at which the analyst needs to take note of a lesson. It is all too easy to reproach a patient when he is unable to face his problem and runs away. But experience teaches that the leading of the dream symbols is a more reliable guide than the wish of the analyst as to what the patient can and should do. Thus when the dreamer runs away she successfully evades the sinister manservant, and in the dining room, in the place where food is taken, she finds a secure hiding place. The theme of the dining room perhaps refers to the analytical situation, in which psychological food or ideas are laid before the patient for assimilation. In this place she finds the round golden dish. Gold connotes value, and roundness suggests wholeness.

A dish is, further, a container. The covering of the black with the gold again corresponds with alchemical procedures, in which gold is "projected" upon the inferior substance that is to be transmuted.

The appearance of the golden vessel is connected with the fact that the dreamer has possessed herself of the square. But evidently she is not to keep that poisonous foreshadowing of the Self; it must be placed under the golden symbol of completion, the circle. Thus there emerges a mandala, symbol of reconciliation of the opposites. Then in the vision of the following night the transformation has taken place. The dish has become a sphere, the square has become a box; both have become three-dimensional, that is, they are now solid realities and not merely ideas; furthermore, the black square has itself become golden. The gold has been successfully "projected" upon the black, to use the alchemistic phrase, which means that the inferior function has been transformed. Its nature is no longer black and poisonous; it now partakes of the nature and value of gold.

The square, the circle, and the triangle—or, correspondingly, the cube, the sphere, and the pyramid or cone—are three of the five elements constituting the stupa, which is venerated throughout the East. It is to be found on temple altars and also supplies the form of sacred edifices circumambulated by worshippers in a rite symbolizing the following of the Way, for the structure of the stupa represents the Way to Nirvana. The square, solid base represents the element earth; the globular part represents a drop of water—the element water; the spire rises like flame and represents fire; the crescent, as the inverted bowl of the sky, represents air; and the acuminated circle and flamelike apex represent space or ether. Thus the stupa is the symbol of the universe. In the churchlike structure of the patient's vision, two of the stupa elements are missing—the crescent and the flame. As the flame represents ether, complete consciousness, it could hardly be expected to appear here. The absence of the crescent has the same implication as the anomalous shape of the box, which is elongated, rectangular, instead of square. The mandala of the man whose dreams and visions are discussed by Jung[53] went through a similar incomplete phase. Jung calls this the "distorted mandala."

Therefore another element or function will have to be added before the present subject's mandala is complete. To put it in psychological terms: Although she has become conscious that her thinking is inferior, and in her dream has wrested it from the control of the animus, another, now "missing" function (one still in the unconscious) will have to be brought up to consciousness and assimilated if her psyche is to be whole. This is the function symbolized by the crescent. In the stupa it corresponds to the element air and the region of the sky. It represents the feminine principle, of which the moon goddess is symbolically the bearer.[54] In the second chakra of the Tantric system the crescent symbolizes water, the unconscious or instinctive state, also ruled over by the moon goddess. In the case under discussion, the omission of the figure means that the dreamer is lacking in feminine instinctiveness. A woman can never grasp reality with her thinking only. Her perception must be based on something much deeper within her, an instinctive feminine wisdom that is the human counterpart of the fundamental principle of eros, just as a man's insight must be based on that part of his masculine nature which corresponds to logos, the rational principle. If the eros principle is insufficiently developed in the case of a woman, or if the logos principle is defective in a man, the psyche will lack stability and weight.

In her vision of the golden structure the dreamer felt it to be like a church. It is the stupa, the shrine that will house the new value—or, as the dream put it, the heritage "accruing" to her, which will have for her the significance of a redeeming value, equivalent to the redemption her forebears found in the Christian church. For her this value is symbolized not by the cross alone nor by the Trinity, but by the stupa, which represents the universe in its entirety, and is thus a symbol of completeness.

Dreams of this character are not very common, being

53. *Psychology and Alchemy* (C.W. 12), p. 184.
54. See Harding, *Woman's Mysteries, Ancient and Modern.*

always the outcome of a long period of development and preparation. They are the so-called big dreams; that is, they are "big" in their significance, though they may not be very impressive or extensive in their manifest content. Such a dream is the following.

The dreamer had been experiencing a conflict of opposites within herself similar to and perhaps as serious as that of the woman just described. Then one night she dreamed that she was given an instrument like a stereoscope [55] and two cards, one with a cross on it, the other with a circle. In her dream she was told to look through the instrument and try to bring the two images together. She attempted repeatedly to do this but could not. The effort was most painful, and the task seemed entirely beyond her power. Almost in despair she was about to give up, when she was told to try once more. Again she looked through the stereoscope, and to her great joy she saw the circle with the cross in its centre.

Here again is the formation of a mandala. The exertion imposed on the dreamer reflects a prolonged effort made in real life, so that this dream, like the one previously described, represents a sort of culmination point foreshadowing the resolution of the conflict and the achievement of a certain unification within the psyche. This dream, however, differs from the other woman's in that the formation of the mandala occurs only in a visual image perceived by the dreamer through the stereoscope. The instrument refers to the analytical procedure, which has given the subject a new way of viewing life. In the dream she is instructed to use this new instrument to view her problem, when she will find the conflicting elements combining in a meaningful symbol. The stereoscope gives to a two-dimensional picture the semblance of solidity—of reality. Hence the dream also means: The problem of the opposites cannot be solved in an abstraction, theoretically; the reality of the opposing values must be restored by the analytical process, and then the view of them will have changed.

55. An optical instrument by means of which two pictures, taken from slightly different points of view, are combined in vision to produce a single three-dimensional image.

Thus the dreamer had gained insight as to how the problem could be solved; for its actual solution, however, a further step was necessary, for the opposing factors would have to be reconciled in actuality and not only in her view of them. This step, however, could not be accomplished save at the cost of something far greater than the effort and eyestrain of the dream. In the case of the first dreamer, the mandala was created only under threat of death. In the Tibetan initiations, the yogin has to realize that inner reconciliation is to be achieved only through the sacrifice of his own body and of his instinctive desires. So likewise wholeness of the psyche is to be attained only through the sacrifice of ego dominance and replacement of it by a new centre of control, the Self.

Oriental mandalas that have been venerated by successive generations and have become fixed or conventionalized forms are usually foursquare in design and are decorated with four principal colours (though other colours may play a subsidiary part), representing the four aspects of the deity, while the Christian symbolism of the Trinity accepts only the Three in heaven and disregards the fourth, relegated to hell, corresponding to the underworld, the unconscious. This difference in symbolism corresponds with the fact that Oriental thought concedes to the unconscious a much greater place in the psyche than we do; consequently "evil," the destructive aspect of the life force, is not excluded or repressed but is recognized as the negative or dark aspect of the deities. So Kali is but the devouring aspect of the Mother Goddess, while Shiva is both Creator and Destroyer.

The goal of perfection for the Oriental is not identification with the All-Good, as it so often is with us; rather, he seeks that enlightenment through which good and evil are recognized to be relative, a pair of opposites, from whose domination the individual can be released by acquiring a new standpoint and a new centre of consciousness.

The mandalas made by individual persons as part of their analytical work have to do, as a rule, with one particular aspect or phase of the reconciliation of the opposites. The undertaking is accomplished in successive steps; it may require a whole lifetime for its completion, until finally the opposition of life and death must be faced. Consequently these personal mandalas are usually partial, while the ritual mandalas of the Orient are much more complete. But even there, it is to be noted, the experience of any one person is expressed by a series of initiation mandalas, just as in the Kundalini yoga the progressive stages of consciousness are symbolized by a series of chakras or mandalas that represent centres of consciousness corresponding to successive regions of the spinal cord and the body areas related to them.

In these chakras a progressive reconciliation of the opposites takes place. The energy released by the resolution of the conflict in each chakra rises to the next higher level, potentiating the central symbol of that chakra, until in the highest, *sahasrara*, nothing is left but the ineffable centre, all else having been absorbed.

Thus, while personal mandalas represent highly individual experiences, the religious ones displayed in temples and churches have a typical, a more general, even a universal validity, as though the experiences of the whole of mankind had been amalgamated in one expressive symbol. A Chinese mandala of this type is reproduced as the frontispiece of the Wilhelm and Jung edition of *The Secret of the Golden Flower*, supplying a sort of pictorial commentary on the text, which is concerned with a form of meditation designed to produce a psychological change leading towards enlightenment in much the same way as the Tibetan rituals described above.

This mandala is drawn as resting half in the earth and half in the heavens. (See plate XV.) At the level of the earth it is surrounded by mountains, whose peaks symbolize the gradual ascent through the stages of consciousness. Their summits are illumined by the rays of the sun, representing the enlightenment that crowns the successful climber. In the heavens are seated those who have attained Buddhahood, whose blessing is sought by the one who aspires to follow in their steps.

The mandala itself is enclosed by a wall, so that nothing it contains may escape and no foreign influences may enter.

This wall is of fire; it is the circle of light that, according to the text, is made to rotate by the power of the creative meditation of the yogin. The fire signifies desire, even desirousness, which is hot, and in ordinary course streams out to objects in the outer world. Here, however, the flames are intercepted by the rotation, that is, the outward-flowing desires are checked by the inward movement of the meditation and turned back within the psyche. The rays of light, the psychic energy, streaming out from the centre of the mandala, the source of life, are in some instances represented as reaching to the boundary walls, where they are deflected and turned back towards the centre, thus augmenting the inner heat. A mandala of this type represents a deeply introverted state corresponding to the condition of meditation described in the text.

If the light rays originating in the centre, together with the fires of desirousness, were to stream out into the world unchecked, they would seek fulfillment in material and worldly satisfactions. Perhaps this energy would be dissipated in what is rightly called "dissipation." It might on the other hand be used for constructive activity in the outer life, producing a work adaptation, a family, perhaps, or some other creative result. But when, as in this mandala, a protective wall prevents such an outflowing, this energy is turned back towards the centre and thus performs its creative function within, in the depths of the psyche.

So too when this vital energy meets with no gratification in the outer world, but instead finds itself frustrated by illness or death, by failure or misfortune, it recoils and flows back into the psyche, and the individual is, as we say, thrown back upon himself. The great danger at such a time is that the vital energy may fall into inaccessible depths of the unconscious and be lost; this occurs inevitably if the individual is unable or unwilling to face the pain of frustration, but instead seeks forgetfulness in distractions. If such loss is avoided, the libido turned back from the outward goal will flow into the psyche and activate it. If in its reflux it reaches to the centre, an inner work will be initiated, from which will arise the Holy Embryo of the Chinese text. This inner creation is called by many other names, such as the Golden Flower or the Diamond Body. In alchemistic language it is the philosopher's stone or the *aurum nostrum* or the *rotundum*. For the value that is designated is beyond rational comprehension or description and can be indicated only by a symbol. Interestingly enough, while occasionally one of the conventional Christian symbols occupies the centre in mandalas drawn by modern persons, it is more usual to find a figure that has no formal religious significance, such as a flower, a crystal, or a star. These symbols arise directly from the unconscious and so are still plastic and capable of holding the living meaning that flows into them from the awakened life springs within.

To return to the Chinese mandala: Within the wall is a garden with flowers and fruit trees, representing the fruitfulness of the personality that achieves inner unity. Within this in turn is a foursquare city with open gates; this is called the Yellow Castle or the Palace of Jade. In Christian symbolism it is the New Jerusalem, which is also described as a foursquare city with gates at each side.

It is significant that in Revelation the symbol of individuation is a city or palace, a man-made structure, while the Garden of Eden, its prototype in nature, is pictured in Genesis as a natural growth. This change in the conception of paradise indicates that in the original state of unconsciousness, before the ego principle arose, there was personal unity, selfhood of a sort, naturally existent as in animals, whose dignity and completeness put many a man to shame. But when personal consciousness raised its claim to self-determination, at-one-ness with God, wholeness, was shattered and—for all that the break was due to an instinctive prompting—could be regained only by human effort consciously undertaken and persevered in. This is the fact symbolized by a city or a palace. For a city or a house does not come into being of itself. Planning, foresight, and long, patient effort are needed for the construction of either.

It is important for our purpose to note some of the implications of this widespread intuition that represents the place of individuation as a city. For a city must not only be built, but, being built, must be kept in repair. If it should fall into decay or be destroyed, it will not grow up again of itself. Only man can rebuild it. This is of course true of all man's works. They have no life of their own; nature's works alone have the power to reproduce themselves. Therefore if civilization, that most precious flower of man's long struggle towards the light, is overthrown or destroyed, only the effort of men and women who have retained the vision of its value can rebuild it, and the rebuilding may take as long as or longer than the original construction, for what remains of it as ruins will hinder rather than serve in the work.

Within the walls of the city of the Chinese mandala is the central place, circular in form, that contains the holy mystery. It is represented here by the double dorje, mystical symbol of supranormal efficacy, the sceptre of the gods, which has power in heaven and on earth. This is surrounded by twelve smaller dorjes arranged in a flower-like pattern, while similar symbols guard the four gates. Thus the centre of the mandala is the seat of the most concentrated and terrific energy— namely, that energy of the psychic nonego which the human being experiences through the instincts and especially through their frustration. It may be aroused when issue is taken with an unconscious assumption or may flare up when the individual's will power is inadequate to control a situation threatening some essential, possibly vital value. Lastly, it may come to expression in an individual, though he knows not why, in the form of a numinous experience, a *tremendum*.

In the Garden of Eden, this nonpersonal or daemonic power was represented by the Lord God, Yahweh, who wielded an unquestioned authority. That is, in this story the energy of the collective unconscious is not recognized as functioning from within the human being, but is exteriorized and personified in the figure of a manlike being who walked in the garden at evening. But shortly there appeared the serpent, personifying the instinct of man himself; he induced our first parents to rebel and learn for themselves the meaning of good and evil. One of the Gnostic sects, whose doctrines are discussed by Irenaeus, taught that the serpent of Eden was actually the Son of God—Son, that is, of the highest God, the Father of Light—sent to arouse men from their unconsciousness:

Adam fell again under the power of Ialdabaoth (Yahweh) and the Elohim; then Sophia or Wisdom sent the "serpent" ("mind") into the Paradise of Ialdabaoth, and Adam and Eve listened to its wise counsels, and so once more "man" was freed from the dominion of the Creative Power, and transgressed the ordinance of ignorance of any power higher than himself imposed by Ialdabaoth. Whereupon Ialdabaoth drove them out of his Paradise together with the serpent.[56]

In Tantric yoga, the daemonic power of the nonego is the goddess Kundalini. She too is represented by a serpent. The yogic exercises are designed to arouse her from her age-long slumber in the instincts and to cause her to rise through the chakras. Within these a progressive transformation of the instinctive energy takes place, and thereby the opposites are reconciled. This progress, however, is achieved only through a prolonged discipline of the instinctual desires. In the Tantric system it is sought through a prescribed course of training. In the biblical story it is accomplished through the ritual death of the Messiah, who likened his crucifixion to the raising of the brazen serpent on the pole. And as we have seen,[57] there are Gnostic art forms in which a serpent is impaled on the cross, and the same symbol is employed by the alchemists, and occasionally appears in modern dreams.[58]

In figure 13, the second drawing discussed in chapter 10, the lines of nonpersonal energy piercing the psyche do not reach the centre, but stop at a layer where the Kundalini serpent lies asleep. If one of these shafts should penetrate with sufficient force it would arouse the serpent—the ancient, sleeping might of nature—which would then begin to take a part in the process, but in the case of the woman who made this picture such a thing had never happened. She was still living in an unawakened state, like a child.

56. G. R. S. Mead, *Fragments of a Faith Forgotten*, pp. 189 f.
57. See above, p. 264.
58. See above, pp. 266-67, and below, p. 446.

But in the mandalas reproduced in plates XVI and XVII the penetration has taken place. The serpent has begun to uncoil and has bitten to the centre. This represents a kind of fertilization. Immediately the whole structure of the psyche is thrown into great activity, similar to that which occurs in the ovum when it is fertilized, and a whole series of changes, resembling a psychic pregnancy, is initiated. For the energy that has been aroused, and, caught within the psyche, is the means by which a transformation of the whole personality is brought about. The psychic event here pictured is the beginning of a renaissance or rebirth, often symbolized as the birth of the "holy child." The modern mandala reproduced in plate XVIII shows the outcome of such a happening. The dragon, symbol of the transformed instinctive energy, here guards the supreme value represented by the gemlike centre.

Thus the work of the mandala, as instrument for the reconciliation of the opposites, is completed. A new psychic individual has been born, who will grow and develop, as living things do; for the outcome of the conflict is not a rationally conceived solution, not a mechanism, however ingenious, but a living individuality—a Self.

12

The Transformation of the Libido

THE HERMETIC VESSEL

THE INITIAL STAGES of psychological transformation have been outlined in the two preceding chapters in terms of two symbols—the circle of the psyche, and the mandala. These symbols represent distinct aspects of the experience and emphasize successive steps that must be taken by the individual who embarks on the process of individuation.

Under the symbolism of the circle, two problems have been discussed. The first, that of finding the true limits of the psyche, leads directly to the second—namely, the problem of collecting within the I those lost or vagrant or unrealized bits of psychic material which can hardly be called psychic contents as long as they exist only in projected form. The process of retrieving these separated pieces of psychic stuff from the projections concealing them usually effects a differentiation of two elements in the libido involved. One is the component really belonging to the situation that has given rise to the point at issue: this is the personal or conscious aspect of the libido, pertaining to the ego. The other is the component that does not belong to the external situation nor to the conscious ego personality: it is nonpersonal, arising from those parts of the psyche which have their roots in unconscious, instinctive urges.[1] The fact that the individual concerned usually feels in-

---

1. These are the elements that Jung later described as *psychoid*, namely, those phenomena that occur at the limits of consciousness and represent the areas where psychic processes come into contact with their physical substrate. See "On the Nature of the Psyche," in *The Structure and Dynamics of the Psyche* (C.W. 8), pp. 173-84.

volved in a peculiarly personal way when this aspect of the libido is impinged upon, does not refute this statement. We always do have peculiarly personal feelings about just those subjective reactions which are aroused in us by collective or instinctive urges, on either the somatic or the emotional plane, though as a matter of fact they occur in everyone.

The symbolism of the circle has suggested a technique by which these two parts of the libido can be differentiated. That part which belongs to the situation is freed from the nonpersonal elements involved and can be applied directly to life, being dealt with as a problem of the external adaptation. The other part is taken back within the psyche, to be dealt with as a concern of the inner life. The opposition between these two elements of the libido, together with the dualism inherent in its nonpersonal part, creates a conflict of major proportions. It is with the solution of this conflict that the symbolism of the mandala is concerned.

Two further problems must inevitably be considered. During the work of bringing the scattered parts back into the circle of the psyche, it becomes evident to the individual concerned—often painfully evident—that all sorts of odd fragments of psychic material will have to be recognized and accepted as his own. Such fragments are by no means always compatible, as they may derive from remote and often archaic sources, so that after they have been gathered together it is necessary to find a means of reconciling them and fusing them into a whole, lest they fall apart again.

The points at issue that bring the projections into focus induce violent emotion or other expressions of libido. This is so unacceptable to our civilized attitude, and so unadapted to conventional standards, that a large part of our social and moral education of the young is concerned with disciplining or even repressing this very factor. When an individual in some contretemps discovers this primitive force alive within him, like a ruthless and cold-blooded daemon, he must find some method by which it can be transformed into a different kind of spirit, if he is to avoid a regression to a level of civilization far below his conscious standard.

As the projected elements are gradually recognized and accepted, the pieces of the psyche that belong together are progressively gathered up and arranged to form a whole, much as the pieces of a jigsaw puzzle or of a broken mosaic are fitted together. In the ruined temples of Chichen Itzá in Mexico, many gigantic puzzles of a similar sort have been worked out in the restoration of the ancient stone carvings. Here, however, two distinct methods have been used. In the buildings where the work was being done for the government, the pieces of sculpture were arranged to form a pattern. If some parts of the design were missing, other carved stones were fitted in to make a plausible whole, even though the added pieces sometimes had to be put in upside down. Carnegie Institute scientists excavating other mounds worked differently. They numbered each piece as it was uncovered and recorded its position on a chart. These pieces were then fitted together in their order, regardless of whether at first sight they promised to make a plausible whole or not. At first the restoration looked like a perfectly hopeless jumble; but as the pieces were painstakingly put together, with fidelity to the reality they presented and without interference from preconceived ideas, unexpected patterns evolved out of the disorder.

Strangely enough, when the scattered fragments of the psyche are gathered up, an exactly similar discovery is made. If, with similar respect for realities, preconceived ideas can be kept out of the picture, as the pieces are fitted together, bit by bit, the true form of the individual will begin to take shape, and it will become apparent, often to his own great amazement, that his personality is actually built on a pattern. Its precise form may be dissolved or overlaid, but it exists fundamentally, and therefore cannot be replaced simply from imagination or wishful thinking.

At this stage of the work, symbols of individuation begin to appear in the dreams and other unconscious products, and it seems as if the purpose of the quest were really about to be achieved. All too often, however, something unfortunate happens; some external difficulty, some inner impediment jolts the psyche and the whole matter falls apart, just as a puzzle or a mosaic does when the table is suddenly jarred, and there is nothing left to do but to begin the tedious process all over again.

After several such accidents, the individual concerned may begin to despair. If he is made of sterner stuff, he looks around to see whether there is not some method of welding his pieces so that they will hold together and not fall apart at every strain. At this point he is lucky if he has built a secure containing wall around his psyche. Then at least the pieces will not be lost altogether but will remain in consciousness. If he has no strong wall, his fragments may be scattered anywhere—as we literally say it, he may "go all to pieces"—and the task of finding the missing parts again may be even harder.

Thus there is need of a vessel to contain the materials that must be fused together and transformed. These terms—vessel, material, fusing, transforming—are all alchemistic in origin. The present chapter indeed makes free use of alchemistic writings and symbols to elucidate the development of the supreme symbol of the Self. Jung's researches [2] into this slightly known and even less understood field have made a rich source of knowledge available to us, and through his profound understanding and skilled interpretations of its obscure symbolism, this treasure has become comprehensible. Alchemistic symbols and references are very common in the dreams of modern persons; it would therefore seem indispensable for the analytical psychologist to have some understanding of the experiences of our immediate forebears, which were really concerned with the psyche, although they were conducted under the guise of chemical research. It was actually the unconscious of the ex-

2. At the time this chapter was written the only paper Jung had published in English on this subject was "The Idea of Redemption in Alchemy," in *The Integration of the Personality* (1939). Since that time most of his major works on the subject have been published in the Collected Works: *Psychology and Alchemy*, vol. 12 (1953); "Psychology of the Transference" in *The Practice of Psychotherapy*, vol. 16 (1954); *Aion*, vol. 9, i (1959); *Mysterium Coniunctionis*, vol. 14 (1963).

During the war years, 1939-45, no contact with Dr. Jung's work was possible, though a personal contact was maintained. However, he had discussed some of this material with me prior to 1939, and a friend had translated for me some of the German articles dealing with the subject.

perimenter that was being explored, while consciously he was seeking the hidden secret of matter.

One of the chief difficulties besetting the alchemists in their search for the "indestructible and immortal stone," *lapis incorruptibilis et immortalis*—without doubt a symbol of the Self—was the tendency of materials to fall apart or to be disintegrated by heat or pulverization, etc. They realized that they needed a means to join the constituents of their stone in such a way that they could never again be separated. As their custom was—they were often called natural philosophers—they looked around in nature to see whether they could not uncover there a secret way of uniting things and adapt it to their purposes. They found various examples of such a process, three of which impressed them especially, indeed fascinated them; that is, these processes became to them symbols dimly showing forth the unseen workings in the unconscious. They meditated on these natural transformations, trying especially to imitate them in their art, seeking thus to produce the miraculous effects they desired. These phenomena were the hatching of a chick, the baking of bread or cake, and the marriage of male and female. A saying ascribed to Hermes, quoted in *The Philosophical Egg*, reads: "If two do not become one, and three one, and the whole composition one, the desired end will not be attained." ³

An egg is obviously a closed chamber into which nothing extraneous can enter. At the outset it contains nothing but the white and the yolk; yet after a short brooding period a living chick emerges. The alchemists explained this transformation as due to a blending of the yellow and the white substances, which they thought were liquefied and transmuted, and they realized that this change was brought about by the body heat of the mother hen, since the egg will not produce a chick unless it is incubated. They therefore defined the first grade of heat necessary for the opus as the heat of the brooding hen.⁴

3. M. Berthelot, *Collection des anciens alchemistes Grecs*, Vol. 2, Traductions, p. 21 (my translation).

4. *Tapas*, connoting in Hindu yoga the generating of warmth by creative meditation, as a means of bringing about psychological transformation, means literally "to brood as a hen."

The second change that impressed them was the one that occurs in the kitchen. They saw that heat produces a somewhat similar change in the ingredients of a cake, which are only mixed together by the cook, but are fused and transformed by baking. The philosophers were impressed with the fact that here also the change takes place through the action of heat—equal, as they said, to the heat of the sun when it is in Leo, that is, in August. Thus they concerned themselves greatly with the action of heat, or, as they usually called it, fire, and expended much research and ingenuity on designs for furnaces and retorts and on methods of regulating heat. In accordance with the thought of that day, heat or fire was considered to be a substance—phlogiston, one of the four elements of which the universe was thought to be composed. To them it was something concrete that is added to the other ingredients.

The third change, the marriage of male and female, or, more generally, the union of opposites, *conjunctio oppositorum*, was so important to them, and indeed is so important in relation to our problem, that it must be considered at greater length later.

In the first example of transformation, the hatching of the chick, the miraculous change takes place only in nature. Even here, however, as Solomon Trismosin [5] points out, the work of the brooding hen is needed for the successful consummation of the work. In the second, the baking of a cake, the fusion of the substances does not occur in nature but is brought about by human art. And so some alchemistic philosophers taught that the fusion of elements needed for making the *aurum nostrum* ("our gold") or the philosopher's stone—in psychological language, the Self—could not occur in nature. Nature by herself, they said, could not produce the result. What was needed was a co-operation of nature and art: the opus called for human effort and ingenuity, but this was of no use unless it was combined with divine grace. However, some disagreement is to be found among the various philosophers on this point, for some assert that nature unaided actually can make

5. *Splendor solis*, p. 19.

the stone, though it requires aeons of time and the process may be greatly hastened by art:

> What nature cannot perfect in a very long space of time, that we compleat in a short space by our artifice: for art can in many things supply the defect of Nature.[6]

This saying corresponds with the thesis of the present volume, which is concerned with the evolutionary changes that take place very gradually through the centuries of human culture but can be quickened by the use of a technique, religious or psychological, that supplies means for working directly on the nonpersonal, unconscious elements in the psyche.

The following passage from Trismosin's *Splendor solis* states the case very clearly. The writer begins his treatise by saying:

> The Philosopher's Stone is produced by means of the Greening and Growing Nature.
>
> Hali, the Philosopher, says thereof: "This Stone rises in growing, greening things." Wherefore when the Green is reduced to its former nature, whereby things sprout and come forth in due time, it must be decocted and putrefied in the way of our secret art. That by Art may be aided, what Nature decocts and putrefies, until she gives it, in due time, the proper form, and our Art but adapts and prepares the Matter as becomes Nature, for such work, and for such work provides also with premeditated Wisdom, a suitable vessel. For Art does not undertake to produce gold and silver anew, as it cannot endow matter with its first origin, nor is it necessary to search our Art in the places and caverns of the earth where minerals have their first beginnings [i.e., by delving into the unconscious as if the precious thing could be found only there]: Art goes quite another way to work and with different intention from Nature, therefore does Art also use different tools and instruments.
>
> For that reason can Art produce extraordinary things out of the aforesaid natural beginnings such as Nature of herself would never be able to create. For unaided Nature does not produce things whereby imperfect metals can in a moment be made perfect, but by the secrets of our Art this can be done.
>
> Here Nature serves Art with matter, and Art serves Nature

6. From Geber, "Summa perfectionis," ed. Holmyard, p. 43.

with suitable Instruments, and method, convenient for Nature to produce such new forms; and although the before-mentioned Stone can only be brought to its proper form by Art, yet the form is from Nature [i.e., the form of the Self is already present in the psyche, like the pattern underlying the jigsaw puzzle]. . . . But it must be borne in mind that the essential form cannot originate in matter unless it is by the effect of an accidental form, not by virtue of that form, but by virtue of another real substance, which is the Fire, or some other accidental, active heat.[7]

This whole passage might have been written as an account of the process of analysis. The "matter" found in nature is the ordinary human being, with all the happenings that make up his life situation and contain the projections of the unconscious parts of his psyche. Trismosin says that these materials, if left to nature, will never be changed into the precious stone; as we should say it, individuation or consciousness of the Self is not likely to result from the ordinary experience of life. The kind of development required for this transformation occurs only, as Trismosin says, "by art," which must supply a form— "a suitable vessel"—and must also apply the fire. However, he concedes that such a change might take place without a direct application of the alchemist's art, when he says that sometimes an "accidental form" occurs, though here too it is the fire or other accidental heat that brings about the change. This statement bears on a question often asked, namely, whether consciousness of the Self, or individuation, can come about in persons who have not undergone psychological analysis.

The answer is that a development analogous to the process of individuation can take place without application of this very modern technique. There have been in the past many systems with very similar aims, as is plain in the evidence amassed by Jung from many epochs and many sources. But in such systems there is a difference in point of view as to what it is that is sought, and perhaps also in psychological understanding. In addition to these numerous examples of transformation—in which the change was after all brought about by art, for religious initiation would fall under this heading—there are also instances of persons who have achieved development in our

7. *Splendor solis,* p. 17.

specific sense without the aid of analysis or any similar procedure. They are the persons who, in Trismosin's phrase, have found an accidental form by virtue of an accidental heat. T. S. Eliot's play *The Family Reunion* describes just such a situation. A most unusual concatenation of circumstances brings the hero to what is called "the loop in time," and the realization born from this joining of past and present will, as the action suggests, enable him to come to terms with the fate figures of his own unconscious. This concept, "the loop in time," is strangely reminiscent of the *ouroboros* of the alchemists, the serpent that eats its own tail, thus symbolizing a cyclic action— an eating of the past, or an assimilation of the unconscious. This is one way in which the individuation process may be initiated. But, as pointed out in the *Summa perfectionis*, art can greatly speed up the process.

The form or vessel of which Trismosin speaks represents for modern thought the psyche of man. The alchemists, however, were still completely conditioned by the illusion produced by the projection of the unconscious, and so did not realize this vessel to be a symbol analogous to the circle and the mandala. They concerned themselves with spherical and egg-shaped alembics; they accepted the fire or heat likewise as an external agency and debated at length about the four degrees of heat, though some of them apparently suspected that this heat was also a manifestation of psychic energies or instinctive emotions—*tam ethice quam physice*.

Trismosin distinguishes very carefully between the functions of these two agents, the vessel and the heat, in the alchemical process. The vessel, he says, has a determining effect; the change is produced, however, by virtue of the fire. It is the energy of heat, its power or fieriness, that causes the change in the alchemist's material.

The process by which the change is brought about or accelerated is referred to not only by Trismosin but regularly by all alchemistic writers as an art, a technique devised and applied by man. Its practitioners are called by various names, such as artificer, magister or master, more often philosopher— meaning not one who deals in concepts only but rather one who loves wisdom in any form. The alchemists always point out to any who want to make "our gold," or the philosopher's stone, that the work in itself is hard and exacting and beset with many pitfalls for the unwary or the uninstructed. The texts repeatedly cite the qualifications required before an aspirant can safely and profitably engage in alchemy. Indeed, so difficult was it to find the right way, and so obscure were the directions given, that it was called the secret art. No doubt some of the obscurity was deliberately cultivated by the alchemistic writers, in order to protect themselves from persecution and exploitation; but much more of it was due to the nature of the experiences they encountered in their work—happenings they were quite incapable of explaining to outsiders, or even of portraying adequately to themselves, except in parables and symbols.

Instructions with regard to the attitude requisite in the seeker if he is to undertake the work with any hope of success are given by various writers. Their texts might have been written for the benefit of a reader about to undergo a psychological analysis in the present day. For example, Heinrich Khunrath (born in 1560) writes in the *Amphitheatrum sapientiae aeternae:*

> The successful adept must be endowed with a knowledge of the material of the Great Work; also with faith, silence, purity of heart, and prayerfulness. After passing through the gate surmounted with the hieroglyph of philosophic mercury he traverses the seven angles of the citadel, representing the chief operations of the Great Work—calcination, dissolution, purification, introduction into the sealed Vase of Hermes, transference of the Vase to the Athanor [furnace], coagulation, putrefaction, ceration, multiplication and projection. And even upon reaching the *Petra Philosophalis*, he finds that it is held in custody by a formidable dragon.[8]

Thomas Norton in his *Ordinal of Alchemy* (1477) [9] describes the art as being sacred:

8. J. Read, *Prelude to Chemistry*, pp. 82 f. See plate XVIII, where a dragon guards the central treasure.
9. In A. E. Waite, *The Hermetic Museum*, vol. II, art. 1, pp. 12-24. The passages here cited are taken from this volume.

We know . . . that the science of this Art has never been fully revealed to anyone who has not approved himself worthy by a good and noble life, and who has not shown himself to be deserving of this gracious gift by his love of truth, virtue and knowledge. From those who are otherwise minded this knowledge must ever remain concealed. Nor can anyone attain to this Art unless there be some person sent by God to instruct him in it.

The analytical psychologist would say it thus: The problems of the personal life, such as egotism, will to power, self-indulgence, laziness, lack of discipline, etc., must be dealt with before an individual is ready to embark on the more specific problems of the individuation process. Furthermore, it is well recognized that an instructor is needed in the more advanced part of the work. Interestingly enough, Norton's description of a good master is not inapplicable today as a criterion for a good analyst. A satisfactory teacher, he says, is of lofty character, he is not induced to instruct a pupil by reason of selfish motives, nor does he offer his services, for "such a man stands more in need of you than you of him." And he continues:

If your master be at all such a man as mine was, you can have no excuse for doubting him, for mine was noble and true, a lover of justice and an enemy to deceit. Moreover he was a good keeper of his secret, and when others ostentatiously displayed their knowledge, he held his peace as if he knew nothing.

Norton then takes up the difficulties marking the path of seekers of this art. These again are strangely like the problems that beset the individual seeking greater psychological maturity:

For many who have now departed this life have gone widely astray before they finally succeeded in their search after our Stone. Either at the very outset, or at a later stage of the work, all are liable to error, until they are enlightened by the teaching of experience, and hit upon the proper regulation of heat and cold. Nobody is more liable to error in respect to this matter than your bold and overconfident enquirer. Nobody sooner mars our work, than he who is in too great a hurry to complete it. The man who would bring this matter to perfection should set about it cautiously and heedfully. The most grievous circumstance connected with our Art, is that if you make a mistake in any part of it, you have to do it all over again from the very beginning. . . . When you have found a truly learned master, you have not yet by any means left all your troubles far behind you. If your mind is devoted to virtue, the Devil will do his utmost to frustrate your search by one or the other of three stumbling blocks, namely haste, despair or deception. For he is afraid of the good works which you may do if you succeed in mastering this secret. The first danger lies in undue haste, which destroys and mars the work of many. . . . Rest assured that haste will precipitate you from the pinnacle of truth.

The individual who goes to an analyst expecting to solve all of life's problems in one or two interviews is in like case. Norton cautions further:

It is the Devil's subtlest device to ensnare us; for this haste is an *ignis fatuus* by which he causes us to wander from the right path. . . . Be on your guard against hurry. . . . If the enemy does not prevail against you by hurry, he will assault you with despondency, and will be constantly putting into your minds discouraging thoughts, how those who seek this art are many, while they are few that find it, and how those who fail are often wiser men than yourself. He will then ask you what hope there can be of your attaining the grand arcanum; moreover, he will vex you with doubts, whether your master is himself possessed of the secret which he professes to impart to you; or whether he is not concealing from you the best part of that which he knows. . . . The third enemy against whom you must guard is deceit, and this one is perhaps more dangerous than the other two. The servants whom you must employ to feed your furnaces are frequently most untrustworthy.

The writer was speaking of the men and women employed in the laboratories; but his words are by no means irrelevant to our situation if these attendants are taken to represent the individual's inner, psychic servants, his power of concentration, his feelings and moods, etc., for these are often as untrustworthy and dishonest as the alchemist's helpers. Norton goes on:

Some are careless and go to sleep when they should be attending to the fire; others are depraved and do you all the harm they can; others again are either stupid or conceited and over-confident and disobey instructions; some have fingers retentive of other people's property.

This might be applied as a parable to persons of today trying to solve their psychological difficulties by appropriating another's truth, or by embracing strange and esoteric doctrines or half-understood formulas; for only that truth which is genuinely one's own can cure the sickness that afflicts one's own soul. The alchemist's further admonition is also in point:

Or they are drunken, negligent and absent-minded. Be on your guard against all these if you wish to be spared some great loss. If servants are faithful they are generally stupid; those who are quick-witted are generally also false; and it is difficult to say whether the deceitful or the stupid are the greater evil of the two.

Norton discusses three things that are necessary for the great opus. These are the vessel, the contents, and the fire.

The alchemical vessel or *vas Hermetis* is pictured in the old drawings and described in the texts as made in various shapes, but all these vessels, whatever their shape, have one characteristic in common. They are all designed to be securely sealed. The *Turba philosophorum* directs: "Strongly close the mouth of the vessel." Our modern term "hermetically sealed" originates from the instructions given for sealing the vessel according to the alchemical laws ascribed to Hermes. For one of the strictest requirements of the art was that during the process of transformation nothing must escape and nothing must be allowed to enter.

The vessel of the alchemists, like the circle of the psyche and the mandala, must be closed if the transformation process is to proceed satisfactorily. For the alchemists, the process took place in the material substances collected in the retort. For us, this is a symbol representing a similar process taking place within the psyche. Thus it is said that a wall must be securely built about the psyche before the reconciliation of the opposites can take place within it, and before the new centre of the individual can be created. The transformation process that takes place in the hermetic vessel generates great heat, which may burst the vessel if it is not made of strong material; or the gases and spirits given off in the process may escape, so that an essential element of the product may be lost. For this reason the problem of sealing the vessel was considered supremely important. When an individual is undergoing the process of individuation in analysis, he has a similar constant concern.

But what is this hermetic vase, and how did the alchemists regard it? The Greek alchemistic texts describe it as the container of the four elements that must be fused to make the round stone, the *rotundum*. By some it was regarded as a symbol of the whole creation, the cosmos, as made up of the four elements—earth, air, fire, and water. It is also a symbol of the little creation, the microcosm, man himself, whose body is likewise composed of the four elements, and whose psyche is compounded of the four aspects of the world, the four realms of being mediated to him through the four functions. The hermetic vessel of the alchemists is indeed analogous to the circle of the psyche and to the mandala, for each of the three in its own way represents the individual man—a fact that some of the alchemists themselves surely understood dimly.

The hermetic vessel is oneself. In it the many pieces of psychic stuff scattered throughout one's world must be collected and fused into one, so making a new creation. In it must occur the union of the opposites called by the alchemists the *coniunctio* or marriage. It is also the secret chamber of the miraculous transformation that will make the "precious gold" out of common metal, or, as it is also said, change the cheap and ignoble stone of nature into the "noble stone" of the philosophers. Some of the later alchemistic philosophers seem almost to have recognized that their opus was in reality performed on themselves. In the *Aureum vellus*, published in 1598, this is stated in practically so many words:

> Study what thou art,
> Whereof thou art a part,
> What thou knowest of this art,
> This is really what thou art.

> All that is without thee,
> Also is within,
> Thus wrote Trismosin.[10]

In the illustrated alchemistic texts, the hermetic vessel is often pictured as a simple flask sealed at the top. In the *Mutus liber*,[11] the alchemist and his *soror mystica*, the counterparts of "the ruddy man and hys whyte wyfe," are seen sealing a glass vessel by heating the neck over a lamp by means of a blowpipe.[12] It may be noted in passing that many of the texts indicate that the opus requires the combined work of a man and a woman, who often enact the parts of the male and female elements of the stone, or represent *Sol et Luna* or the "red king and white queen," and in psychological terms correspond to man with his feminine soul, the anima, or to woman with her masculine counterpart, the animus—the union in each case constituting the inner marriage, the *hieros gamos* by which the individual must become whole.

In a treatise entitled *Concerning the Philosophers' Stone*, Alphonso, King of Portugal, wrote in 1653:

The forme of the glasse must be of the forme of the Sphere, with a long neck [often called the philosopher's egg]. . . . Even as there be in a naturall Egge three things, the Shell, the White, the Yolke; even so there be in the Philosophers Stone three things, the Vessell, the Glasse, for the Egge shell, the white liquor for the white of the Egge, and the yellow body for the Yolke of the Egge; and there becomes a Bird of the yellow and white of the Egge, by a little heate of the Mother, the Egge-shell still remaining whole untill the Chicken doe come forth; even so by every manner of wise in the Philosophers Stone, is made of the yellow body and white Liquor by mediation of a temperate heat of the mother the

---

10. *Trismosin's Alchemical Wanderings and Adventures in Search of the Philosopher's Stone*, in *Splendor solis*, p. 88.

Jung quotes Dorn: "What more do ye seek, ye anguished mortals? Why, poor wretches, do you trouble yourselves with infinite cares? What madness is it, pray, that blinds you? seeing that all that ye seek outside yourselves and not within yourselves is within you and not without you" (Jung, *Mysterium Coniunctionis* [Swiss edn.], II, 21, § 25, f.n. 69).

11. A supplement to Manget's *Bibliotheca chemica curiosa*, 1702. Cf. Read, *Prelude to Chemistry*, pp. 155 f.

12. See plate XX and pp. 450-51.

earthly substance *Hermes* bird, the vessel still remaining whole, and never opened untill his full perfection.[13]

Philalethes writes: "Let the glass be clear and thick . . . in order to prevent the vapours which arise from our embryo bursting the vessel." [14]

The vessel was known by various names: it was called an alembic, the vase of Hermes, the "house of glass," the "prison of the king." In the pictures in *Splendor solis* (pl. XIX), it is a simple flask; sealed at the top, with the neck circled by a crown, and appears enshrined in a gilded niche. Sometimes the vase is of more complicated form—as for instance the *pelicanus*, a vessel with a long neck curving around so that the mouth opens into the belly of the flask, making a condensing or distilling retort. This vessel was likened to the pelican because of the popular belief that the female bird wounds her own breast in order to nourish her young on her blood—a myth that had great significance for the alchemists. Its meaning obviously relates to the same self-contained activity that is represented by the *ouroboros*, the serpent eating its own tail, and to the circulation of the light that appears in the mandala symbolism. There is also depicted a double retort, called gemini or twins (fig. 14), which is so constructed that the distillate of one of its vessels discharges into the belly of the other, and vice versa, so that the contents are intermingled again and again. This action corresponds to the *coniunctio*,[15] which is not infrequently represented as a marriage of twins, or of sister and brother—as for example of Isis and Osiris, Beya and Gabricus (or Gilbran), Diana and Apollo.[16]

13. Read, *Prelude to Chemistry*, pp. 149 f.
14. Ibid., p. 150.
15. Cf. Jung, "Psychology of the Transference," in *The Practice of Psychotherapy* (C.W. 16), where the subject of the *coniunctio* is treated at length in connection with the picture series in the *Rosarium philosophorum*. Unfortunately this book was not available when the original version of the present chapter was being prepared.
16. This is of course an incestuous relationship, one that on the objective plane is quite illegitimate, although it was considered normal for the gods, and in ancient times also for royal personages (as, for instance, among the Pharaohs). Jung explains its meaning when it occurs in alchemical phanta-

Fig. 14. The Gemini or Double Pelican of the Alchemists

Rotatory movement, or circulation, is emphasized not only by the alchemists; it also has a prominent place in the exercises of Tibetan, Chinese, and Hindu yogins, for whom the circulation of the light is an indispensable factor in the process of transformation.[17] As the mandala symbolism teaches, when the fires of desirousness are checked or frustrated, the individual is thrown back upon himself, and his thoughts begin to go round and round. So long as this circulatory activity is concerned only with seeking for a means of escape, like the movement of a squirrel in a cage, no transformation can take place. But when the thoughts are held by a conscious effort to exploring the meaning of the experience, the circular movement becomes a spiral leading down into the underlying and unconscious roots of the occurrence. The meditation with its inner concentration, like the light rotation of the mandala symbolism, prevents the energy from flowing outward and leads ever deeper into the unconscious, where it activates the latent creative source at the centre.

Being thus charged with energy, the central symbol gives forth rays of light that flow out and meet again the wall of fire

---

sies. He writes: "Incest expresses the union of elements that are akin or of the same nature; that is to say the adversary of Sol is his own feminine chthonic aspect which he has forgotten" (Jung, *Mysterium Coniunctionis,* § 506.

17. See Wilhelm and Jung, *The Secret of the Golden Flower.*

created by the frustration, or, in the case of the yogins, by the
life of concentrated introversion and seclusion that constitutes
a self-imposed frustration of all natural desires. The energy
is thus deflected back again to the centre in a continuous process closely resembling the action of the reflux condensers of
the alchemists. As a result of this circulation, the centre is re-
charged with energy again and again, so that the emanating
rays become progressively more powerful. These are in turn
deflected and thus an intensifying process is set up; in *The
Secret of the Golden Flower* this is called the "circulation of
the light."

The alchemists' vessel has to be sealed most carefully, just
as the mandala must be guarded by a continuous wall. The
psychological meaning is that a watertight, even gastight vessel
must be created before the psychic transformation can take
place. For if anything is lost the process is nullified and the
final product will be incomplete, imperfect. So long, for instance, as the individual continues to project his deficiencies,
or his values, upon circumstance or upon another, he does not
have an impervious vessel.

Further, the container must be made of strong material;
otherwise, as soon as the individual gets into difficulties, and
things begin to get hot and uncomfortable, a leak will develop
in the vessel, or, to use a slang expression having an alchemistic flavour, he will "blow off the lid." (It is amazing how
often alchemistic thought tinges modern speech, especially in
its more colloquial forms.) Then the hot liquid will boil over
in scalding reactions, and the heated vapours, the spirit, will
escape. (Each of these terms has a double meaning; in the alchemistic usage the physical and the psychological meaning
are amalgamated or perhaps not yet differentiated.) The alchemists repeatedly warn against allowing this to happen. For the
purpose is to transform the spirit: if that escapes, the whole
undertaking will be ruined. In the *Turba philosophorum* it is
said:

The spirit being separated from the body and hidden in the
other spirit, both become volatile. Therefore the Wise have said

that the gate of flight must not be opened for that which would flee, by whose flight death is occasioned.[18]

In the alchemical experiments this vapour was frequently derived from mercury, which as the *spiritus mercurius* was considered to be a spiritual being, and was at times equated to the Holy Spirit. Mercury, the metal, on account of its anomalous properties, was a source of never ending wonder to the alchemists. It was the quicksilver, the *argentum vivum*, whose droplets ran together in so spritely a fashion—even to this day we speak of a mercurial disposition. It was "our heavy water" —the term water was used for all liquids—or "dry water" that would not wet the hand. Above all, it was the spirit personified as Mercurius, he who took wing and flew away when he was heated, which no other metal would do, and then miraculously recreated himself on the cooler parts of the condenser; he alighted upon or, as the alchemists said, he "projected" himself upon the glass or upon the base metal, turning it to his own silver colour.

Thus, in the psychological experiment that so closely resembles the alchemical one, it is the "hot air," the vapour, the incorporeal spirit, that must be transformed or, at least, is essential for transformation. Those alchemists who had most psychological insight sensed that this was really the goal of their endeavour. For instance, in the *Turba philosophorum*, one of the speakers, Zimon, says: "For this spirit, that ye seek, that ye may tinge therewith, is concealed in the body, and hidden away from sight, even as the soul in the human body." [19] This obviously has a very important bearing on the problem of the transformation of the instinctual forces. For if the hot reaction is repressed or merely abreacted—as when we say we "blow off steam" or "give vent" to our feelings—something essential for the transformation will be lost. Consequently there comes a time in the individuation process when the individual must "consume his own smoke"—when it is no longer permissible for him to take out his anger or irritation on someone else merely in order to relieve himself. This does not mean re-

18. A. E. Waite (tr.), *Turba philosophorum*, p. 140.
19. Ibid., p. 109.

pressing the affect. Far from it—for if the emotion is repressed the spirit it contains will once more be lost in the unconscious and will inevitably be projected again, and the whole process will have to be repeated.

The course that must be taken is a very different one. When an individual who has reached a certain stage in his psychological opus encounters a point at issue—one of those points at which unconscious reactions interfere with rational behaviour —he must separate the elements in the situation according to the impartial line of truth or justice and return the subjective component within the vessel, which is himself. For that quantum of activated spirit or emotion—be it anger, hostility, will to power, fear, sympathy, disdain, love, hate—which is in excess of the requirements of the external situation, is an essential part of his *materia*, and without it the transformation cannot proceed to its appointed end.

Thus the contents essentially involved in the transformation are seen to be the irrational, instinctual, not yet human factors of the psyche, the nonego. The human and civilized factors, those subject to the will, make up the wall of the vessel. This wall of the personality is built of the qualities of the personal character—honesty, fairness, love of truth, honour, unselfishness. The alchemists insisted that these qualities must be present in considerable measure before the novice could undertake the great work; for only then would the vessel he built be capable of containing the very dynamic materials of the experiment. In that aspect of analytical procedure which is concerned with the process of individuation, these qualities must likewise be present as already acquired; that is, the problems of the personal life and the personal unconscious must stand largely solved before the deeper problems of the collective unconscious, of the nonpersonal aspects of the psyche, can safely be undertaken. For unless the container is made of such honest, good material, it cannot be relied on to stand the strain at the critical point.

During the preliminary stages of analysis many dark and unacceptable things lurking like shadows in the background of the individual's life and character must be brought up into consciousness and dealt with. As Jung points out: "One realizes, first of all, that one cannot project one's shadow onto others, and next that there is no advantage in insisting on their guilt, as it is so much more important to know and possess one's own, because it is part of one's own self and a necessary factor without which nothing in this sublunary world can be realized." [20]

When this part of the work has been accomplished it is as if the individual had built a psychic container, and this must be done to the very best of his ability, or it may go to pieces when the strains and stresses of the transformation process begin. For there will still remain certain things, and these usually the very darkest, that will come to light when he explores the unconscious; these are those things he considers the meanest and most contemptible in himself, that he cannot assimilate or dispose of even with the most devoted conscious effort.

These blackest shadows, that the alchemists called the state of nigredo, will probably prove to be connected with the unadapted emotions representing the nonpersonal part of the psyche, and it is most painful to realize that they actually exist within oneself. Jung speaks of this darkness and blackness as referring to a man's sense of confusion and lostness, when he realizes that he is unable to reconcile his dark shadow side with his conscious personality, and writes that this is the state which nowadays gives rise to an analysis.

But the fact remains that the most unacceptable and blackest inner secrets are nonpersonal, even though they always seem to be the most personal part of all life's experiences. They bespeak the individual's peculiar weaknesses, which he is tempted to believe cannot be matched for depravity in any other person. He feels himself to be set apart by the knowledge of his own guilt.

But anyone who has ever undertaken an honest and genuine introversion, whether with the help of an analyst or without it, will have had exactly this experience. Each one of us is burdened with this innermost dark secret. It belongs to that primal earthy mud out of which the human being has grown, and

20. Jung, *Mysterium Coniunctionis*, § 203.

which still lies as a residue within him, untouched by the civilizing spirit, the Pneuma breathed into Adam at his creation. It is frequently a realization of this kind that brings an individual to analysis. And then other elements of the unconscious, the light sparks the alchemists speak of, begin to glow in the dark and a glimmer of light dawns on the individual's consciousness. For as Jung writes:

> The analysis and interpretation of dreams confront the conscious standpoint with the statements of the unconscious, thus widening its narrow horizon. This loosening up of cramped and rigid attitudes corresponds to the [alchemical procedure of] solution and separation of the elements by the *aqua permanens*, which was already present in the "body" and is lured out by the art. . . . The situation is now gradually illuminated as is a dark night by the rising moon. The illumination comes to a certain extent from the unconscious [moon as luminary of the night], since it is mainly dreams that put us on the track of enlightenment. This dawning light corresponds to the *albedo* [the whitening], the moonlight which in the opinion of some alchemists heralds the rising sun. The growing redness (*rubedo*) which now follows denotes an increase of warmth and light coming from the sun, consciousness. This corresponds to the increasing participation of consciousness, which now begins to react emotionally to the contents produced by the unconscious. . . . [This] gradually . . . leads over to the "melting" or synthesis of the opposites. The alchemists termed this the rubedo, in which the marriage of the red man and the white woman, Sol and Luna, is consummated.[21]

For this dark earthy stuff of which man is made constitutes the shadow, but it is more than the personal shadow of the individual, which is but its surface aspect. Its source lies much deeper. It is indeed an archetype, the archetype of the devil—the entirely negative and evil one. So, for instance, Mephisto was at the same time Faust's shadow and the devil incarnate. The alchemists spoke of this element as the Ethiopian, or the Black Man, who must be rescued from the depths of the sea, that is, from the unconscious. Plate XIII, from an alchemical text of the sixteenth century,[22] shows this Black Man being

21. See ibid., § 306-7.
22. Trismosin, *Splendor solis*.

rescued from the sea by the White Queen, who offers him a new robe, just as the angel in plate XII brought a robe for the new-born Jonah. Already the blackness of this shadow element has begun to change, for one of his arms has become white, indicating that when the dark shadow is rescued from the unconscious a mitigation of its blackness begins to take place. And indeed, the dark secret with which we are all burdened begins to show that it contains a value when it is no longer rejected and repressed.

For it is out of this primal material that the new creation must be formed. The alchemist's precious gold cannot be made by refining earthly gold; similarly, the higher value we call the Self cannot be produced by refining or further civilizing the superior aspects of the ego. The precious gold must be made, the alchemists asserted, through a creative transformation of primal elements found in nature—a process similar to but other than that by which nature aeons ago formed the metallic gold in the caverns of the earth—namely, by a fusing of the elements through heat and pressure. So also the Self must be made conscious by fusing the elements of the psyche by means of psychological heat and pressure. But while the ego was formed naturally by an evolution extending over thousands of years, the Self, like the philosopher's gold, must be made conscious by human art, by which the time requirement is greatly reduced. According to the alchemists, "that which Nature only accomplishes in a thousand years, can by virtue of our art take place in the course of one hour."

When the alchemists had found the prima materia, which they repeatedly tell us is scattered everywhere in life—in the market place, in the fields, in the houses, even on the dung heap—they pulverized it and extracted the black substance. Psychologically, the prima materia is to be found in any situation whatsoever in which an individual finds himself emotionally involved. From such points at issue the black substance, that unregenerate old Adam within, can be separated out and put into the vessel, where it is heated up by the fire—the emotion—generated in the separating process.

This emotion has to do with instincts belonging to the carnal man, the earthy or animal residuum that persists as the natural core of the human being. They perform functions that are all-important biologically and in man's ordinary activities in the external world. Without them life itself, living beings, could not be maintained on the earth.

It is told that at the creation God breathed his spirit into the earthy body of the man he had made, and this spirit was in man, but being tempted by the serpent, representing an alien, chthonic spirit, he committed the original sin, so separating himself from God. An earthy nature clung to him and threatened to submerge and deaden entirely the divine spirit. Thus a further infusion of the spirit was needed before the earthy nature could be transformed. Many years later God sent his spirit once again to earth to be incarnated in man; and when Christ was born, the light entered into the darkness, and the darkness comprehended it not—which must refer to the fact that no one would ever expect to find light concealed in darkness. Yet that is exactly the teaching. The alchemistic philosophers also taught that the most precious stone lies hidden, in immature form it is true, yet present nonetheless, within the common stones of earth, overlooked and rejected like that other stone of which it is said: "The stone which the builders rejected, the same is become the head of the corner . . . and it is marvellous in our eyes."

It is not uncommon for individuals in whom the transformation is taking place to dream of finding a light hidden in darkness. It may be a vision of glowing red fire completely concealed in the centre of a black coal; or the dream may show the sun hidden in the centre of the earth; or a common earthenware or stone jar may contain an unsuspected candle burning within it. The forms are many, but the meaning is obviously the same, namely, that the light is inside the darkness. Jung, in *Mysterium Coniunctionis*, quotes Khunrath: "There are . . . fiery sparks of the World-Soul, that is of the light of nature, dispersed or scattered at God's command in and through the fabric of the great world into all fruits of the elements everywhere." [23] These sparks are often referred to as

23. *Mysterium Coniunctionis* (C.W. 14), § 50. See also Jung, "On the Nature of the Psyche," in *The Structure and Dynamics of the Psyche* (C.W. 8), pp. 190 ff.

the glowing eyes of fishes seen in the depths of the sea. They are occasionally to be met with in the dreams of modern persons. Of them Jung says: "The fishes' eyes are tiny soul-sparks from which the shining figure of the filius [the son of the philosophers] is put together again. They correspond to the particles of light imprisoned in the dark Physis, whose reconstitution was one of the chief aims of Gnosticism and Manichaeism." [24] And further on he continues: "Dorn uses the concept of the scintillae [sparks] in moral form. . . . [He writes] 'What madness deludes you? For in you, and not proceeding from you, he wills all this to be found, which you seek outside you and not within yourselves. Such is the vice of the common man, to despise everything his own, and always to lust after the strange. . . . The life, the light of men, shineth in us, albeit dimly, and as though in darkness.' " [25]

The alchemists evidently had similar experiences, for there are many references to the central fires of the earth, and it is also stated that their gold was formed in the centre of the earth by the rotation of the sun, which gradually spun its own image there.

Jung has brought forward a considerable body of evidence showing that the alchemists of the Christian centuries equated their stone with Christ,[26] who was the cornerstone, and in whom the light of the spirit found its dwelling place. But even in the pre-Christian period the stone was the symbol of that which contains the spirit. As Jung points out, Ostanes,[27] who was possibly physician to Alexander the Great, and certainly predated the Christian era, tells the novice in alchemy to go and find a stone by the Nile, that is, in Egypt. For the philosophers of Greece of the syncretistic period, Egypt was the source of secret wisdom and reputedly of alchemy, the very name of which, according to a very old tradition, derives from that of Egypt—al-Khem or Kemia, meaning "Black Earth." But for the Christian church Egypt had another significance dating from the time when the Israelites were in bondage there,

24. *Mysterium Coniunctionis*, § 46.
25. Ibid., § 48.
26. *Psychology and Alchemy* (C.W. 12), pp. 343 ff.; *Aion* (C.W. 9, ii).
27. *Psychology and Alchemy* (C.W. 12), p. 284.

so it represents the place of bondage, that is, of the unfree state, and beyond this, to the Israelites, when they were wandering in the wilderness, Egypt represented the place of plenty. They hankered for the flesh pots of Egypt. So Egypt is a complex symbol—it is the place of wisdom, the place of bondage, and the place of fleshly satisfaction. And the novice is told to seek there for a stone, one that has a spirit imprisoned in it. When he has found it, he is to split it open, reach into its inner parts, and pluck out its heart; for the heart contains the spirit that will furnish the material for his work.

This instruction parallels what has been said about the point at issue. One goes about one's ordinary business in the everyday world until by chance some stone causes one to stumble ("He shall be . . . for a stone of stumbling and for a rock of offence"). Then one discovers that this stone is not dead and inert but acts as if it were alive, coming into consciousness not at call but of its own volition and against one's wishes. When this happens one must split that stone open and withdraw the spirit from it—that is, the unconscious psychic factor that is animating it as a result of projection. This spirit is the material of the opus.

But this saying of Ostanes can also be taken a little differently. He says that we are to take the spirit out of matter. Now the spirit in matter is a cold, inert, heavy spirit; as the mystery saying has it, the spirit wakes in the animal, dreams in the plant, but sleeps in the stone. It is this sleeping spirit that must be awakened and warmed so that it acquires lightness and life. In the solid state, matter is gross and heavy and must be heated, given energy, if it is to become fluid; and still more energy must be applied if it is to become gaseous or spirit-like. So it is also, the alchemists suggest, in the psychological realm.

The stone concealing a spirit is encountered in real life in various forms. When a man comes across something that intrigues him, even though to others it may seem dull and inert, a mere stone, he should suspect that this stone contains for him a spirit. If that spirit calls to him he ought to go and rescue it from its stony prison and make for it a more worthy body, whether in his eyes it seems a precious stone or whether it is that stone of stumbling—a point at issue—which also contains a spirit that will not let him rest in peace until he has redeemed it from its despised condition. In plate XIII we see a black man, the Ethiopian, being rescued from the waters by the White Queen. This is analogous to the rescue of the dark spirit from the gross matter, or, to use psychological terms, it would mean the rescue of the spirit, or energy, from the unconscious.

The spirit that emerges from the stone of stumbling is a spirit of heaviness, anger, egotism, will to power; if it is removed from the point at issue and introverted, it pierces the circle of the psyche and may come upon the Kundalini snake lying coiled about the centre, asleep in the instincts. If now this serpent is aroused and can be caught in the hermetic vessel and heated with a gentle warmth like that of the brooding hen, as in the alchemical incubation—the tapas of the yogic meditation, or creative introversion, as the psychologists would say— it will begin to change, until at last it is transformed into the symbol of central value and wisdom. This is the final mystery of the opus. The alchemistic texts frequently represent it in illustrations showing a winged serpent or fiery dragon within the hermetic vase.[28] In plate XIX, one of the pictures representing the Great Work, the contents of the Hermetic vessel are represented as a three-headed dragon. The margins of the picture show various scenes of collective human activity. In the foreground a king receives honoured guests, on the left youths are engaged in fencing, and on the right some sort of athletic game is in progress, suggesting that when the dragon of lust and warlike anger is contained in the alchemical vessel, these human instincts, that are destructive when in a crude state, then are transformed into social forms leading to co-operative effort and friendship.

The relation between spirit and matter, or spirit and body, was a question of great concern to the alchemists. They saw

28. Easily accessible examples are: *Tripus aureus*, 1677 (cf. Jung, *The Integration of the Personality*, p. 225, pl. VI); Trismosin, *Splendor solis*, 1582, pl. XV (reproduced as pl. XIX of the present volume); Manget, *Bibliotheca chemica curiosa*, 1702; Stolcius, *Viridarium chymicum*, 1624 (cf. Read, *Prelude to Chemistry*, pp. 263, 318); *Rosarium philosophorum*, in Jung, "Psychology of the Transference," *The Practice of Psychotherapy* (C.W. 16). See also plates XVII and XVIII.

this, as they did all psychological problems, as pertaining to the qualities and reactions of matter—a chemical mystery to be solved only in their retorts. But to them the changes observed were more than just the reactions of the substances; according to their own accounts, it seemed to them that the reaction took place within the alchemist and within the retort simultaneously.

Their point of view is very difficult for us to grasp. But perhaps if we recall some of the queer feelings we had about things as children, we shall get a glimpse of how the alchemists were affected by their experiments. For instance, children will often play that they must not step on the cracks of the pavement for fear of some quite undefined ill that would result if they should do so. Some of them have a clear picture of what the ill will be. I remember one child who, when the mood of the game was upon her, believed that fire would dart up through the crack she stepped on; others feel that things will go wrong for the rest of the day—they won't be able to recite their lessons correctly, or "Mother will be cross," or some general ill luck will pursue them. As a rule children do not believe these things to be really so, nor are they always mindful of them; the cracks only at times take on this significant or magic character, which we adults know and even children half know to be due to projection. The alchemists, in respect to their work with matter, were in much the same psychological condition as these children; and we must remember also their precept, *Tam ethice quam physice.*

To return to the problem of the relation of spirit and body: The alchemists knew that the spirit, the gaseous substance, is within matter, but they did not want merely to drive it off by means of heat or by some chemical process, for that would leave matter inert and lifeless:

Cook strongly. . . . For by this regimen the spirit is made corporeal, and the body is changed into a spirit. Observe the vessel, therefore, lest the composition fly and pass off in fumes.[29]

Rather, they aspired to release the spirit from its bondage in matter and then, having purified both it and the "body," to

29. Waite, *Turba philosophorum,* pp. 63 f.

unite them again in a sacred marriage or *coniunctio*—in "the work whereby also spirits take possession of bodies and they become spiritual." [30] There were no means available in the Middle Ages for collecting gases in jars. Robert Boyle, the first chemist to work on the properties of gases, lived at precisely the transition point when chemistry as a modern science was parting from alchemy as a mediaeval art, leaving the philosophical or speculative element to the natural philosophers, such as Jakob Böhme. The alchemists knew that if the gases or spirits were driven off into the air, they simply flew away, escaped. Therefore they sought to make a new kind of container or body in which the spirit might be fixed, so that it could not fly off. The symbol of a serpent nailed to a cross was sometimes used to represent the fixation of the volatile element. [31]

The alchemical problem of gas or spirit in matter corresponds to the problem of spirit and body in the human being: "this spirit which ye seek . . . is concealed in the body and hidden away from sight, even as the soul in the human body." [32] To mediaeval man, the spirit was the divine and immortal part of man, the body the material, temporal part. These two parts appeared forever opposed. To extract the spirit from man, leaving the corporeal part without spirit, would be like driving the volatile elements out of matter in the retort. Even if the spirit could then be purified, released for a life of its own, this would not give a satisfactory solution of the problem. It was of course the accepted theological conception that during life the soul is only latent, a potentiality buried in matter, but at death, when the body returns to the earth from which it was made, the spirit is freed and rises to an ethereal other world. According to this belief, therefore, the soul is the dematerialized essence of man, which does not really function until the earthly life is finished.

When the alchemists heated an oxide or an earth, as they called it, the gas that was given off escaped into the air; in the

30. Ibid., p. 58.
31. See above, p. 416.
32. Waite, *Turba philosophorum*, p. 109.

same way, they felt, this theological doctrine allowed the soul to escape, and it could not be known what became of it. Being realists, they were not satisfied with this formulation, but were eager to solve the much more perplexing problem of making a complete being in this world—as they said, "out of the base material to make the noble"—a being that should consist of spirit and body united in harmony, not continually opposed as they are in the ordinary person.

It is hardly necessary to point out that this objective is very closely related to the aim of completeness or individuation so uniformly revealed in the symbols of the unconscious as the goal of man's quest for psychological health. Naturally this undertaking presented a problem much more exacting than that of purifying a soul for manifestation in heaven only, because the test of validity had to be faced on this earth. Those who sought to make of man a being that was to live a spirit existence in an ethereal world after death, relied for evidence of their success only on an inner sense of transformation or redemption, or on the assertion of the church; they did not have to face a test of reality but only a trial of faith. For the alchemists, however, the place of testing was here and now. They believed that through their art the spirit could acquire a body of its own, a "subtle" body. Thus the transformation of man would become a living reality in this world.

Philalethes in *A Short Guide to the Celestial Ruby* says:

> Listen, then, while I make known to you the Grand Arcanum of this wonder-working Stone, which at the same time is not a stone, which exists in every man, and may be found in its own place at all times. . . . It is called a stone, not because it is like a stone, but only because by virtue of its fixed nature, it resists the action of fire as successfully as any stone. . . . If we say that its nature is spiritual, it would be no more than the truth; if we described it as corporeal, the expression would be equally correct; for it is subtle, penetrative, glorified, spiritual gold. It is the noblest of all created things . . . it is a spirit or quintessence.[33]

Thus the *lapis philosophorum* is the mysterious *rebis*, the "double thing" formed of the union or *coniunctio* of the op-

33. Cf. Waite, *The Hermetic Museum*, II, 247, 249.

posites. It is called the "androgyne" or the "hermaphrodite" and is frequently represented as the "immortal child." The unchangeable quality of that which is formed by this union of opposites, of spirit and matter, is also emphasized in Buddhist texts, in which the Diamond Body is often the symbol of the final achievement. The alchemists likewise sought to produce from these two opposing elements or principles a child or little man, the homunculus—a living being that at the same time was the *lapis philosophorum*. Sometimes it is spoken of as the *rotundum*, the "round thing" (corresponding to the central circle of the Lamaistic mandala), which is a stone, a gem, and yet not a stone, for it is composed of body and soul united to form a spirit.

The alchemist's creation is a living being, product of an act of fertilization—as Alphonso, King of Portugal, clearly indicated when he declared: "The Sperm of Sol [connoting not only the sun but also philosophical gold] is to be cast into the matrix of Mercury." [34] The *Tabula smaragdina*,[35] the "Emerald Table" ascribed to Hermes himself, speaks of it thus: "Its father is the sun, its mother the moon; the wind carries it in its belly, its nurse is the earth." Melchior is said by Stolcius to have described the stone as "a tender babe, which must be nurtured with pure milk." [36] The babe is thus also a stone, a "precious pearl," the *margarita pretiosa*. Its strength and enduring quality were stressed by many symbols; for like the "pearl of great price" that in the parable symbolized the kingdom of God, the precious stone of the alchemists symbolized the central value—the goal beyond all price that has been sought with such persistence and devotion throughout the centuries.

Thus in the making of the stone it was essential to find a means of uniting the opposed "natures" or spirits. These might be conceived of as pairs of opposites—body and spirit, matter

34. Read, *Prelude to Chemistry*, p. 139.
35. A very ancient text of unknown date, possibly of the tenth century or earlier, known in Latin—probably translated from Greek—and also in a corrupt Arabic version called *The Second Book of the Foundation*. Cf. Read, *Prelude to Chemistry*, pp. 51 ff.
36. Stolcius, *Viridarium chymicum*. Cf. Read, *Prelude to Chemistry*, p. 115.

and form, gross and subtle, fixed and volatile, male and female. Or the fundamental opposition might be symbolized as the antithesis of sun and moon (*Sol et Luna*), red king and white queen, brother and sister, lion and serpent, toad and eagle, winged and wingless lion or dragon. The union was represented usually as a mystical marriage—*coniunctio*—taking place within the hermetic vase, or occasionally as a devouring of one element by the other. In the story of Beya and her twin brother Gabricus (Gilbran) recounted in the *Visio Arislei*, both these actions are represented, for during the cohabitation of the royal twins, brought about by the intervention of the alchemistic philosopher, the brother entered into the womb of his sister and disappeared.[37] Jung interprets the death of Gabricus as follows:

> [His] death is therefore the completed descent of the Spirit into matter. The alchemists frequently represented the sinfulness of this occurrence but they never grasped it, and this is why they rationalized or minimized the incest, in itself so repellent. . . . On descending into the unconscious the conscious personality finds itself in a dangerous situation, for it seems as though it were extinguishing itself. It is the situation of the primitive hero who is devoured by the dragon. Since it is a question of the diminution or extinction of the conscious personality . . . the intentional or wanton provocation of this state is a sacrilege or a breach of a taboo, which is followed by the severest punishments.[38]

Other instances of the theme of devouring as a form of the *coniunctio* are: [1] two serpents devour each other, giving rise to a glorified dragon typifying the philosopher's stone;[39] [2] a lion swallows the sun;[40] [3] a king swallows his son and subsequently brings him forth again in a strange rebirth.[41] The union may be represented in other ways. For instance, the

37. See Jung, *Mysterium Coniunctionis*, passim, on the incestuous union of Beya and Gabricus; see also ibid., § 64, where Jung quotes from the second version of the "Arisleus Vision": "With so much love did Beya embrace Gabricus that she absorbed him wholly into her own nature and dissolved him into indivisible particles."

38. *The Integration of the Personality*, p. 242; cf. *Psychology and Alchemy*, p. 319.

39. Read, *Prelude to Chemistry*, p. 107.

40. Jung, *Psychology and Alchemy*, fig. 169.

41. Delphinas, *The Book of Lambspring*, in Waite, *The Hermetic Museum*, vol. I, art. x, pp. 301, 303.

Viridarium chymicum shows two lions meeting and shaking hands. Stolcius, commenting on this in 1624, wrote:

> Behold, twain lions come together with their feet joined, and enter upon a firm pact of friendship. . . . Join the two sulphurs. . . . Let one be constant, let the other fly upwards, but being joined let them stay and remain with agreeing tread.[42]

The two lions represent the fixed and the volatile sulphur. or the male and the female element; more often the combination is mercury and sulphur. Avicenna the Arabian, writing about the middle of the seventh century, says: "Join the toad of earth to the flying eagle and you will see . . . the Magisterium." [43] This means that the seeker after the philosopher's stone should join together "sophic sulphur" and "sophic mercury," or, in psychological language, that the supreme value will be found by uniting the earthly and the spiritual element, or more simply, body and spirit.

The most usual way of representing this union was as a marriage.[44] The two elements brought together in the mystical union are frequently represented as "the red man and hys whyte wyfe" (Ripley), "the faire white woman married to the ruddy man" (Norton), or the thrice purified red or gold king and the purified, immaculate white or silver queen. Of this Flamel wrote in 1399:

> In this second operation, thou hast . . . two *natures* conjoyned and married together, the *Masculine* and the *Foeminine* . . . that is to say, they are made one onely body, which is the *Androgyne*, or *Hermaphrodite* of the *Ancients*. . . . The *man* painted here [he refers to one of the figures in his book of "Hieroglyphicall Figures" [45]] doth expressly resemble *my selfe* to the naturall, as the *woman* doth lively figure *Perrenelle*. . . . It needed but to represent a *male* and a *female* . . . but it pleased the *Painter* to put us there.[46]

42. Read, *Prelude to Chemistry*, p. 265.
43. Ibid., p. 258, and pl. 2.
44. *Rosarium philosophorum*; see Jung, "Psychology of the Transference," in *The Practice of Psychotherapy* (C.W. 16), where this whole text is described and interpreted psychologically.
45. See Read, *Prelude to Chemistry*, p. 61.
46. Eirenaeus Orandus, *Nicholas Flammel* (1624). Cf. Read, *Prelude to Chemistry*, p. 101.

Plate XX, reproduced from the *Mutus liber*,[47] shows an alchemist and his *soror mystica* working with the material of the opus. The picture represents the steps leading up to the consummation of the "great work"—the *coniunctio*. In the first two sections the alchemist and his wife, who here plays the part of the *soror mystica*, are seen weighing out two elements represented by a star and a flower: these symbols indicate that the early stages of the transformation have already been accomplished. These are then transferred to the aludel or hermetic vase. In the third section the flask is being sealed "hermetically," and in the fourth it is being placed in the athanor or furnace, which is built like a tower. The heat is applied from below. But in the picture called "The Tower," one of the trumps major of the tarot cards, which apparently alludes to this phase of the magistery, a man and a woman have been placed in the tower, just as Beya and her twin brother were placed in the triple glass house to be heated up while their union took place. In the tarot picture the tower is struck by lightning and destroyed, while the man and woman escape or are violently thrown out. In the picture in the *Mutus liber*, however, the heat is moderated so that in the last section the work is represented as accomplished. The alchemist and his wife, no longer garbed in their own clothes, take the place of Sol and Luna—possibly Apollo and Diana, another brother-sister pair whose union was interpreted by the alchemists as a symbol of the *coniunctio*. Luna carries a bow, and beside the athanor is a target, indicating that they "have hitt the Marke." The numbers at the right signify the power of the philosopher's gold to multiply itself indefinitely.

We are told that the king, that is, gold or spirit, must be thrice purified; this fact is symbolized by the three flowers frequently carried by the queen. She herself must also undergo a purification, usually represented as a washing or bathing, by which she is changed from the black earth, the nigredo, into the white earth or the silver. Thus another text referring to the

---

47. For a detailed description of this and the other plates of the *Mutus liber* reproduced in the *Bibliotheca chemica curiosa*, cf. Read, *Prelude to Chemistry*.

marriage or insemination reads: "Sow your Gold in White Earth." ⁴⁸ Psychologically this surely refers to the fact that the union of body and spirit or of conscious and unconscious can be safely attempted only when both have undergone a purification brought about by the earlier stages of analysis, in which the conscious character and the personal unconscious are reviewed and set in order.

In the alchemistic literature there is evidence that the mysterious *coniunctio* took place in three stages.⁴⁹ The first is that of the union of opposites, the double conjunction, which chiefly concerns us here. The second stage effects a triple union, that of body, soul, and spirit; or, as it is said elsewhere, "the Trinity is reduced to a Unity."

In *The Book of Lambspring*, published in 1625,⁵⁰ this triple union is represented first by two fishes swimming in the sea, pictured with the legend, "The sea is the Body, the two fishes are the Soul and the Spirit" (see frontispiece), and later by a second picture showing a deer and a unicorn in a forest, with the following text:

> In the Body [the forest] there is Soul [the deer] and Spirit [the unicorn]. . . . He that knows how to tame and master them by art, and to couple them together, may justly be called a master, for we rightly judge that he has attained the golden flesh.

The literature offers far less material about this more advanced stage of the work than about the simple *coniunctio*, and still less about the third stage, the union of the four elements, from which the fifth element, the "quintessence," arises. However, Jung's latest works are largely concerned with the problems of this fourfold *coniunctio*, through which not only are the personal parts of the psyche—ego and anima, or ego and animus—consummated, but these, in a further stage of development, are in turn united with their transpersonal cor-

48. Michael Maier, *Atalanta fugiens* (1618). Cf. Read, *Prelude to Chemistry*, pl. 14.
49. See Jung, *Mysterium Coniunctionis*, chap. VI, where he describes the three stages of the *coniunctio* in detail and interprets the texts in psychological language.
50. Waite, *The Hermetic Museum*, I, 271, 280.

relates—wise man and prophetess, or great mother and magician (under whatever names these superordinate elements are conceived). Jung discusses this problem on several levels: (1) in its primitive foreshadowing in the custom of "cross-cousin marriage"; (2) in the Gnostic symbolism of the Naassenes; (3) in alchemistic literature.[51] The subject is by no means simple, but it amply repays careful study. Unfortunately this material was not available when the present work was written, and indeed we are concerned here only with the first stage, the union between the conscious and unconscious parts of the psyche, as represented by the ego, the conscious personality, in man or woman, and its unconscious counterpart in each, the anima or animus.

In dreams or phantasies this union may be represented as variously as it is in the alchemistic texts. Frequently very similar symbols are used, in particular the symbol of a marriage. Sometimes a wedding ceremony forms the subject of the dream drama, sometimes it is a sexual intercourse. The object of the marriage may not be clearly shown, beyond the aim of fulfillment of the love and desire that are often, though by no means always, a prominent part of the dream experience. But in other instances it is clearly indicated that the change to be effected takes place not in the participants but in the mysterious substance that will be developed or created if the sexual experience leads to a successful outcome.

In one such case, a woman dreamed that she went into an underground cavern that was divided into rooms containing stills and other mysterious-looking chemical apparatus. Two scientists were working over the final process of a prolonged series of experiments, which they hoped to bring to a successful conclusion with her help. The end product was to be in the form of golden crystals, which were to be separated from the mother liquid resulting from the many previous solutions and distillations. While the chemists worked over the vessel, the dreamer and her lover lay together in an adjoining room, their

51. Cf. Jung, "Psychology of the Transference" in *The Practice of Psychotherapy* (C.W. 16), "The Mercurial Fountain," pp. 203 ff., and *Aion* (C.W. 9, ii), chap. XIV.

sexual embrace supplying the energy essential for the crystallization of the priceless golden substance. The dream thus
clearly shows that the work is to be done on the "substance,"
the *materia*, not on the person of the one who undertakes it.

This parallels exactly the objective of the alchemists, who
were concerned with redeeming the spirit hidden in matter,
the ignoble substance, and bringing about its transformation
into "our" noble, precious gold. In psychological language,
the work was concerned with the nonego in the psyche and
the change or transformation that must be accomplished in it.
At the present time it is still generally assumed that the whole
of the psyche is known to the ego—indeed, that the ego is the
whole—and therefore we tend to identify the conscious I with
the happenings in the unconscious. In his discussion of this
aspect of the problem, Jung makes a very clear distinction
between the attitude of the alchemists, who regarded the work
as a task that they themselves had to perform—with divine aid,
it is true, but nevertheless a work they had to accomplish upon
the materials in the retort—and the orthodox teaching of the
church, which was that man merely participated in the benefits
of a work of redemption that had been accomplished and was
eternally being accomplished by Christ and by the priest offi-
ciating at the mass as the representative of Christ.

In the course of the alchemical "work" that forms the
theme of the second part of *Faust*, just when the *coniunctio*
of Sol and Luna is about to be enacted in the persons of Paris
and Helen, Faust in his eagerness identifies himself with Paris
and usurps his role in the visioned drama. With this a tragic
outcome becomes inevitable. Faust here represents modern
man, who no longer reveres the gods but instead identifies
himself with the figures of the unconscious. When Flamel
wrote about the opus that he and Perrenelle, his wife, had carried to success, and that culminated in the *coniunctio*, he was
apparently aware of this temptation and narrowly avoided it.
For the artist who painted the final scene of the marriage between Sol and Luna represented the two protagonists by por-
traits of Flamel and Perrenelle. (See plate XX.) But Flamel
remarks that this was merely a fancy of the painter's; any

man and woman would have done, as "it needed but to represent male and female." Jung writes:

> Faust's sin was that he identified himself with the thing to be transformed and that had been transformed. . . . In a sense, the old alchemists were nearer to the central truth of the psyche than Faust when they strove to redeem the fiery spirit from the chemical elements, and treated the mystery as though it lay in the dark and silent womb of nature. It was still outside them. But the upward thrust of evolving consciousness was bound sooner or later to put an end to the projection, and to restore to the psyche what had been psychic from the beginning.[52]

Thus we come to still another aspect of the problem of the relation of body and spirit as it presented itself to the alchemistic philosophers. From the passages quoted below we gather that their controversies turned on the process by which the end result was to be brought about, as well as on this result itself. For example, in the *Turba philosophorum* we read: "I counsel posterity to make bodies not bodies; but those incorporeal things bodies."[53] Then again in a Byzantine fragment entitled *The Philosophical Egg* we read: "Unless bodies lose their corporeal state and unless bodies assume again their corporeal state, that which is desired will not be attained."[54] Apparently this means that sometimes the work has to be done on the external realities of a situation, and sometimes on its spirit or essential import, even in the absence of any concrete reality. This is rather an obscure statement, but an example will make it clearer.

Suppose it suddenly dawns upon a man in middle life that the slight symptoms from which he has recently been suffering may be due to cancer. What should he do? What must be his inner attitude? The first question is more easily answered than the second. Obviously he must see a doctor at once and have the necessary tests made. But what of his psychological attitude in the interim? For there is more than one way of meeting such a situation. One man will decide to forget about his

52. *Psychology and Alchemy* (C.W. 12), pp. 459 f.
53. Waite, *Turba philosophorum*, pp. 83 f.
54. Ibid., p. 84.

natural anxiety and refuse to worry until there is further evidence. During the daytime he may succeed in doing this, but at night he will probably have bad dreams, which should warn him of the folly of disregarding the inner implications. A man of a different type will let his imagination run away with him and be so upset over all the possibilities of the situation that he will have himself dead and buried a thousand times before he sees the doctor.

Such an obstruction to the normal course of life, with all its possible implications, is a "stone of stumbling," a threatened frustration that might be used for the great opus, but neither of the attitudes described above will serve for this. The first man will need to be more concerned with the possibilities. The significance, the spirit, must be extracted from the concrete fact, from the substance, the body, with which temperamentally he is almost exclusively concerned. The possibilities will have to be used as a touchstone for testing himself and his fundamental attitude to life and death. The other man will need to "hold his horses," namely, to follow the alchemists' advice and keep the vapour inside the alembic; he must refuse to be distracted by all the possibilities and instead face the actual facts.

If an individual, when the shadow of illness and possible death threatens to frustrate all his plans, can free himself from his merely personal reactions, the danger he faces may serve to help him to probe into the secrets of life and death. For these mysteries are no longer just intellectual problems to him, but have become immediate emotional concerns. Such a threat strikes at one of the most fundamental instincts, that of self-preservation, and awakens the fear of death, an emotion with an almost uncanny effect, whose strength few people realize until they actually experience it. It is one of those nonpersonal emotions which have power to pierce to the centre of the psyche. But because the actual situation claims so much attention, and the personal aspects loom so large, it is almost impossible, while the situation is still actively present, to attain an attitude sufficiently detached to be used for furtherance of the "great work," namely, for increasing consciousness in that hidden realm which is ordinarily inaccessible.

To garner the value of an experience of frustration and loss, it is necessary to extract the spirit or essence, the emotion aroused by it, and to introvert it or, as the alchemists would say, to seal it into the hermetic vase and subject it to the various processes of heating, pulverization, liquefaction, etc.; for this is the very spirit required for the transformation. In other words, it is the transformation of the instinctive reaction, in this case fear, that produces the gold. A passage in the *Turba philosophorum* reads:

> For the spirit which ye seek is concealed in the body and hidden away from sight even as the soul in the human body. But, ye seekers after the Art, unless ye disintegrate this body, imbue and pound it both cautiously and diligently, until ye extract it from its grossness and turn it into a tenuous and impalpable spirit, ye have your labour in vain. Wherefore the Philosophers have said: "Except ye turn bodies into not bodies; and incorporeal things into bodies, ye have not yet discovered the rule of operation." [55]

Another alchemistic text runs: "Deprive the shadow of its substance, and perform the work on the shadow." [56] This precept is illustrated by a picture showing a nude woman who bears painted on her breast a heart surrounded by flames, at which Cupid is aiming an arrow. Her shadow lies on the ground, and the alchemist with his instruments is working on the shadow. To the alchemist, the woman with the flaming heart would be Luna; psychologically interpreted, she would stand for the anima. The fact that her image casts so dark a shadow might imply an unhappy love affair. An erotic experience that finds fulfillment leads out into life, into the light of day, and does not cast much of a shadow. But when a man has fallen deeply in love, so that the image of the woman has seemed to him to be aflame—as in this picture in which Cupid,

55. Waite, *Turba philosophorum*, pp. 109 f.
56. Michael Maier, *Scrutinium chymicum*. I am indebted to Dr. Jung for access to this text, and quote it by his courtesy.

the god of love, himself takes a part, which signifies that it was a genuine, divine passion—and the emotions have found no outer fulfillment, but only frustration, the experience casts a shadow on his life that may stretch over all his years. The picture in *Scrutinium chymicum* presents such a situation, and the text states that it is through work on such a shadow that the inner change may be brought about.

There are two classical examples of exactly this situation, namely, Dante's passion for Beatrice, and the story of Francesco Colonna's lost love as he has told it under the allegory of Poliphile's devotion to the lady Polia. In each of these men, the passionate love of his youth was frustrated—in Dante's case [57] by Beatrice's marriage and death, in Colonna's [58] by the death of Ippolita, the young girl whose memory is said to have evoked the dream image of the lady Polia.

In the *Vita nuova* Dante tells us how it was with him when he realized that his love was hopeless. Interestingly enough, he uses the same image of the flaming heart that has been discussed above. He describes his dream in the following words:

> When on a sudden Love before me shone,
> Remembrance of whose nature gives me fright.
> Joyful to me seemed Love, and he was keeping
> My heart within his hands, while on his arm
> He held my lady, covered o'er, and sleeping.
> Then waking her, he with this flaming heart
> Did humbly feed her, fearful of some harm.
> Thereon I saw him thence in tears depart. [59]

At the time, this experience seemed to Dante to hold nothing but suffering and frustration; yet it proved the stimulus to the inner experience described in the *Divine Comedy*, and to the quest that culminated in the vision of the celestial rose, which corresponds to the supreme mandala of Buddhist initiations and to the vision of Selfhood that we have been discussing. In Poliphile's dream Colonna represents the culmination

57. Both *The Divine Comedy* and the *Vita nuova*.
58. Francesco Colonna, *Le Songe de Poliphile;* cf. Fierz-David, *The Dream of Poliphilo*.
59. Norton, *The "New Life" of Dante*, p. 6.

of the inner experience by the marriage with the lady Polia, which corresponds to the alchemical *coniunctio*.[60] This union, however, had to be preceded by Polia's confession of her sin against Poliphile. This episode corresponds to the washing or whitening of the queen, who must be purified before she can be united to the thrice purified king. The king's preparation is symbolized by the long penitence and suffering that Poliphile had to undergo. In actual life it was the suffering that Francesco Colonna himself experienced.

Frustration of love and loss by death of the loved one threw a deep shadow upon the lives of both these poets; yet neither could allow his sorrow to remain merely a burden of human grief, to be carried as best he could, nor could he throw it off by turning to other interests. Dante, as we know, tried this expedient quite unsuccessfully. So deep for each man was the impression made upon him by his love that he was compelled to "eat" it; thus the frustration served as the starting point of an inner experience that was carried to completion only because of the intensity and persistence of the emotional forces set in motion by his love. Each therefore truly consummated an opus that led to a transformation or redemption equivalent to the goal of the alchemistic philosophers, and not so unlike the transformation of the psychic nonego that may result from an exploration of the unconscious by modern methods.

This throws an important ray of light on the meaning of frustration and defeat. Usually, so long as the libido flows out freely and meets with reasonable gratification in the world, the individual is content; but when he meets with frustration, his libido is turned back on itself, and the outcome depends very much on the attitude he takes at this point. If the libido regresses to an auto-erotic level, it will concern itself with childish self-pity. It may drop farther down, so that neurotic, even psychotic symptoms may develop, bringing despair and paralysing inertia in their train. If, however, instead of merely suffering from the effects of the frustration—accepting the

60. Jung, "Psychology of the Transference," in *The Practice of Psychotherapy* (C.W. 16).

shadow—one makes a courageous attempt to work on the inner aspect of the difficulty, the reversed flow of the libido will serve to activate that creative process within the psyche which results in transformation.

This is the reason why the mandala must have a wall around it or be ringed with fire, and why the hermetic vessel must be sealed; should it have an outlet, this must lead back only into itself. The serpent bites its own tail, brother and sister unite in an incestuous union (so that the family-bound libido leads back into the family): these are symbols of the libido that turns back upon itself, not merely in regression, but with the serious aim of creating something new within.

This kind of turning back by no means signifies the same thing as the unbroken auto-erotic circle of unawakened and unconscious infancy, in which the libido is fixed upon itself and its own pleasure satisfactions and shirks the adventures of life. In the picture in which the work is being done on the shadow of the erotic experience, it is clear that the libido of the man who drew it (if we assume the artist to be representing his own life experience) had ventured forth into life and had been caught in a real situation. We cannot, of course, know what was the nature of the frustration suffered so long ago, but certainly the philosopher who made this picture was no renegade from life. When external fulfillment was denied him, he turned back to try to understand his experience and to garner the hidden fruit that grows on the philosophical tree —that tree which is so often depicted as having been cut down in its prime. It is on such a tree that the golden fruit grows.

In ordered and peaceful periods, the problem of dealing with the nonpersonal forces of instinct and the unadapted, daemonic libido originating in the unconscious, is met more or less adequately by the cultural disciplines of society, and more especially by the symbolic rituals and disciplines of religion. In ordinary times these means serve their purpose adequately for the majority of persons. Only those whose lives happen to be touched by some personal frustration, or who meet with some other experience in which they suffer the full impact of the nonpersonal energy, find it necessary to seek for themselves an individual way of adapting to the life forces that are not personal but rather daemonic or divine.

Frustrations of this kind—threat of illness and premature death, loss of loved ones, unrequited love, etc.—occur at all times, in every community, affecting one person here and another there; but they are separate experiences, touching individuals alone, never large numbers of people together, and the problem of dealing with the nonpersonal forces released by the experience must be solved by each person as best he can.

But there are other times, like our own, when the forces of the unconscious have been loosed into the world, and people by the thousands have had to face torture and death, while cataclysmic disaster has threatened countless thousands more. In even more terrifying reality, the unseen powers of evil usually latent in the unconscious have surged up within the psyche in other thousands, inspiring them to plan and execute these dastardly crimes against society. In this twentieth century, the religions of a large proportion of mankind have lost their ancient potency to control and contain the unconscious forces, and so can no longer mediate effectively between humanity and the nonpersonal powers. In such times the problem of finding some adequate relation to these terrific energies becomes universal.

Where the storm actually struck, man's whole attention might well have been occupied in meeting the cataclysm itself, though even here there must have been many who, in the interims of the immediate demands of external reality, were, I am sure, concerned even more with the psychological than with the physical dangers. But where the hurricane has not yet struck, or where its immediate violence has passed, its shadow is still dark upon the world, and as the alchemists point out, it is essential to work on that shadow. Fear, lust, greed, and vengefulness, together with the passionate anxiety to protect ourselves not only from being caught into the maelstrom but also from even realizing what it is that is happening, are all effects of the impact of the unconscious forces, and unless these are gathered up into the vase, that is, the human psyche, and transformed, the very name of civilization may be blotted out from the world.

It cannot be too often emphasized that what is to be transformed in the hermetic vessel is not the personal ego but the nonpersonal part of the psyche. The best that education can offer is a technique for the repression of those instinctive reactions which are beyond the individual's control and therefore in large measure outside the area of his responsibility, while it concentrates on trying to shape the personal character to conform to a cultural ideal. The objective of our religious teaching, too, is to make people better, even to make them perfect. Individuals are drilled to conform to a definite pattern, so that they may comply with conventional expectations. They pray for grace to become "good" or to achieve those virtues which their conscious egos and their religious guides judge to be desirable.

In marked contrast to this ideal is the secret teaching about the transformation. Under this the novice who is about to undertake the great work must give evidence that he is a moral person, of upright and pure life and of diligent and reliable character. In some systems it is also required that he be of mature age, thus having had a full life experience in the world. These things, however, are but prerequisites for the work and not its results. Whether we consult one of the ancient mystery religions, in which the transformation was said to be brought about by the initiation experience, or one of the Oriental religions, in which it is sought through yogic discipline, or the mystical or esoteric teachings of the Christian religion, or whether we search the alchemistic writings, in which the transformation is described as occurring in a chemical retort, we shall find that the moral education of the individual demanded for admission to the deeper teaching is directed not towards making him conform to an accepted pattern of behaviour, but only to putting him into a right relation to the unknown and unseen powers of the spiritual or psychic world.

In psychological analysis, in which the solution of the life conflict is sought in the individual's own psyche, we are obliged to set the same requirement, not because of any arbitrary standard on the part of the analyst, but on account of the manner of the natural unfolding of the deeper layers of the unconscious, which cannot be explored in a constructive way until the earlier stages of the work have largely solved the problems of the personal life and the personal unconscious. This phase corresponds to the process called by the alchemists the "simple magistery" or "little work," which ends with the production of the "white stone" or the "white queen," meaning that the "black substance" or "black earth" has been purified or washed and made white—which would correspond to the taking up into consciousness of the personal unconscious and the shadow. For it is only when an individual has come to terms with egotism and the power motive, with greed and lust, with laziness and the regressive tendencies within him, that he is ready to undertake the more costly and serious enterprise of the "grand magistery," the magnum opus of the alchemists; this stage manifests itself in modern man in dreams and other unconscious products under a symbol of wholeness. Whatever the form it appears in, this symbol represents as the goal of the work not the formation of a more exemplary or more perfect personality, but the development of a complete individual.[61]

If a man could achieve completeness, presumably he would be what he was meant to be. In that sense he would be "ideal" or perfect, not because he would be conforming to a preconceived idea or pattern but because he would thereby be fulfilling completely all his potentialities of growth. Such a person would be truly a whole individual. Indeed, every step taken towards completeness convinces not only the individual concerned but his neighbours too that he is as he should be. For he has the bearing and dignity of an integrated person. This bearing can be seen constantly in animals, who are so completely themselves that they convince by their presence. Occasionally the same quality shines forth in human beings who have come by it naturally, so to speak. The really great among mankind have it, and sometimes quite simple persons—a fisher-

---

61. See above, pp. 310 ff.

man, or a peasant woman—who have no claims either to special goodness or to special worth, yet are so completely what they are that the simple dignity of their state of being carries the weight of psychological maturity and an impress of worth beyond any effect of good works.

If the individual is to be whole, the nonpersonal part of the psyche must be amalgamated under the symbol of the Self. This necessitates a transformation of the daemonic energy associated with the archetypes and the instinctive urges of the unconscious. For if this energy is not transformed, activation of it will either swamp the individual completely, so that his civilized traits will disappear under the flooding from the unconscious, or he will identify with the archetype and allow an unhuman and collective role to dominate his personality. The Self can be formed only through a transformation of the nonpersonal spirit or energy distilled from the prima materia, the black substance, the recognition of which within himself is so painful and disturbing to the man of good will. The alchemists rightly called this part of the work the *magnum opus*, for it is truly a great work.

The character of the individual is naturally changed by this experience, just as it is by that of the simple magistery, the work on the conscious character and the personal unconscious. The change wrought in the individual by the larger undertaking is more difficult to describe in words than that effected by the lesser work, because it is a transformation of the very nature of the instinctive impulses that motivate him, while the lesser work is concerned only with the reactions he consciously accepts and the attitudes he deliberately adopts.

If the libido is in the stage of development represented by the coiled and sleeping serpent, the impulses spontaneously arising within the individual when any one of his basic values or interests is challenged, will be characterized by self-centredness and egotism, by cold-blooded desirousness, and by disregard of other people and their needs. A well-bred and decent person, if he is so ruled by instinct, must be continuously on his guard lest he be taken unawares and fall into some asocial or unfeeling action that would not accord with his conscious attitude and character, and that he would deplore in himself and repent perhaps bitterly but to no purpose. For he has no guarantee that he will not on the next occasion find himself once more betrayed into a similar *faux pas* or similar sin. He is constantly obliged to compensate his instinctive impulses by a consciously adopted manner and carefully planned way of behaving, which naturally results in a guarded, quite unfree, frequently artificial attitude. The impression such a person creates is anything but whole. He is divided in himself and appears so to others, for he dare not act according to his impulse, and what he actually says or does represents only one side of himself.

Yet this is the only way in which the problem of the untransformed libido has generally been approached by those who are guided by the current attitudes of Western civilization and Christian ideals. I refer of course only to the collective ethic and morality, which rely for their effectiveness on discipline of the conscious individual. The Christianity of Paul and of the Gospels, in its deeper aspect, is centred upon a transformation of the libido through an inner, numinous experience entirely different both in nature and effect from conscious education.

But when these cultural holds, inadequate as they are because of their insecure foundation, are thrown off or become outworn and no longer act as a check on the instinctive impulses, all the unbridled desires and passions latent in the unconscious are lived out directly into life. When this happens to an individual, he loses himself, goes berserk. It may be only a transitory phenomenon, giving rise to a fit of anger or some other uncontrollable emotion; if it is more lasting, a state of criminality or of insanity may result. Where large numbers of people are affected, a crowd of decent citizens deteriorates into an uncontrollable and oblivious mob. Where a whole nation is overwhelmed by such instinctive forces, there are those who gladly say yes to the hurricane that is driving them along, while those who say no to it in consciousness may nevertheless be at its mercy. But their negation is all too often merely the protest of a helpless personal ego, for in them, too, the whirlwind sweeps through the unconscious, so that they are totally unable to restrain the madness of their fellows or to withstand the headlong stampede that can end only in universal disaster.

The crying need of the world today is obviously for a transformation of these dynamic instinctive forces. It is not enough that peace has been restored. If the unconscious spirit within man is not redeemed, it may well be that humanity as a whole will destroy itself. But so far as my experience as a physician of the psyche goes, the transformation process I have attempted to describe here pertains only to individuals. It is a solitary and individual undertaking, as was the alchemist's opus, and as is also the numinous experience of the truly religious person. It requires expenditure of both time and effort, and is rendered all the more difficult in view of the complete lack of understanding, on the part of the general social group, of its meaning and value.

Perhaps the most essential requisite for participating in the "great work" is an attitude of devotion, a seriousness of purpose in seeking to understand the full meaning of life, an utmost striving that the supreme value called the Self may be rescued from the darkness of the unconscious—like the precious gold of the philosophers that was lost in the blackness of the nigredo, which the *Aurora consurgens* likens to the "horrible darknesses of our mind" [62]—so that it may assume rule over the whole life. Our forefathers would have called this the search for God; the psychologist uses a more modest term, for he knows nothing about God as he is in himself. At the same time the attitude in undertaking this work must be one that can be described only as an attitude of religious devotion.

When a man has caught the cold-blooded, snakelike forces of the unconscious in his vessel, that is to say, in his own psyche, and has heated them through willed introversion, or, as the Buddhists say, through tapas or meditation, and they have thus been transformed by the well-directed processes of the great work, the very nature of his instinctive reactions undergoes a change. He is no longer impelled to speak or act self-

62. Jung, *Psychology and Alchemy* (C.W. 12), p. 261.

centredly, or to take revenge for his personal sufferings, or to snatch everything of value for himself, or to sweep relentlessly out of his way all beings whose interests conflict with his own. The other person's interest and point of view are as present to his consciousness as are his own, and seem equally important, so that he does not have to make a conscious effort to be tactful or considerate; indeed, he may not even realize that he is being so. He need only follow his impulses, and his action will really be appropriately related to the value concerned, his own or another's.

When such a change has taken place, even in small measure, within an individual who perhaps for years has consciously striven to live by decent standards that he has all too often failed to maintain, he experiences a great sense of freedom and release; life loses many of its complications, for now it is only necessary to act naturally for all to go well. The need for constant watchfulness against selfish or unthinking disregard of another no longer exists. The individual in whom this transformation has taken place has become truly a cultured person: body and spirit in him are no longer opposed.

The experience of such a change comes to most searchers after wholeness in small measure only, yet ever and anon a further installment of the libido becomes accessible to the process by which it can be transformed. In view of the present condition of the whole world, work on the nonpersonal forces within the individual takes on a new significance. The effort that any one person can make towards solution of the world's problems is small indeed; yet, when there is a real change in the nature of the instinctual forces functioning within one human being, there is a genuine contribution to civilization and peace.

Plans for control of the evil forces that have been loosed in the world, attempts to compensate the evil-doing by good works or sympathy for the victims, efforts to safeguard the peace or to effect ideal solutions of all the material problems involved, can do little to change the nature of the situation. The real problem, namely, the question of what can be done for civilization in face of the nonhuman forces arising from the collective unconscious in thousands or rather millions of individual persons, will remain untouched. However, if only one human being has met and solved the problem in himself, he will be a living demonstration of a solution. Such an individual carries within him the germ of a renaissance of the spiritual values of mankind.

BIBLIOGRAPHY

BIBLIOGRAPHY

*Aureum Vellus, oder Güldin Schatz und Kunstkammer . . . von
. . . Salomone Trismosino.* Rorschach, 1598. (Trismosin's
Splendor solis, pp. 3-59.)

Aurora consurgens. See JUNG, C. G., and MARIE-LOUISE VON
FRANZ.

AVALON, ARTHUR, pseud. (Sir John Woodroffe), ed. and tr. *The
Serpent Power.* Madras and London, 1935.

———. *Shiva and Shakti.* Madras and London, 1929.

BAYNES, H. G. *Mythology of the Soul.* London and Baltimore,
1940.

BERTHELOT, MARCELLIN, ed. *Collection des anciens alchimistes grecs.*
Paris, 1887-88. 3 vols.: *Introduction; Textes; Traductions.*

BERTINE, ELEANOR. *Human Relationships: in the Family, in Friendship, in Love.* New York, 1958.

Bhagavad-Gītā, The. Ed. and tr. by S. Radhakrishnan. London and
New York, 1948.

BRAINARD, D. L. *The Outpost of the Lost.* Indianapolis, 1929.

BRIFFAULT, ROBERT. *The Mothers.* New York and London, 1927.
3 vols.

BUDGE, SIR ERNEST A. T. WALLIS. *The Gods of the Egyptians; or,
Studies in Egyptian Mythology.* London and Chicago, 1904. 2
vols.

COLONNA, FRANCESCO. *Hypnerotomachia Poliphili.* Venice, 1499.
For French tr., see: (1) *Le Songe de Poliphile.* An anonymous
tr. adapted by Jean Martin. Paris, 1546; another edn., Paris, 1926.
(2) *Le Songe de Poliphile.* Tr. by Claude Popelin. Paris, 1883.
See also FIERZ-DAVID, LINDA.

DANTE ALIGHIERI. *The Divine Comedy.* Tr. by John Aitken Carlyle, Thomas Okey, and Philip H. Wicksteed. New York (Modern Library), 1932.

———. See also NORTON, CHARLES ELIOT.

DAVID-NEEL, ALEXANDRA. *With Mystics and Magicians in Tibet.* London, 1931.

DELPHINAS, NICHOLAS BARNAUD. "The Book of Lambspring." See WAITE, tr., *The Hermetic Museum,* I, 271-306.

ELIOT, T. S. *The Family Reunion.* London and New York, 1939.

Eranos-Jahrbuch 1938. "Vorträge über Gestalt und Kult der 'Grossen Mutter.'" Ed. by Olga Fröbe-Kapteyn. Zurich, 1939.

EVANS-WENTZ, W. Y. *The Tibetan Book of the Dead; or, The After-Death Experiences on the "Bardo" Plane.* London, 1927; 3rd edn., 1957, with a psychological commentary by C. G. Jung.

———. *Tibetan Yoga and Secret Doctrines, or, Seven Books of Wisdom of the Great Path, According to the late Lāma Kazi Dawa-Samdup's English Rendering.* London, 1935.

———. *Tibet's Great Yogī, Milarepa: a Biography from the Tibetan.* London, 1928.

[FIERZ-DAVID, LINDA.] *The Dream of Poliphilo.* Related and interpreted by Linda Fierz-David. Tr. by Mary Hottinger. New York (Bollingen Series XXV) and London, 1950.

FRAZER, SIR JAMES GEORGE. *The Golden Bough.* Abridged edn., London and New York, 1922.

FREUCHEN, PETER. *Arctic Adventure: My Life in the Frozen North.* New York, 1935.

FROBENIUS, LEO. *Das Zeitalter des Sonnengottes.* Vol. I (no more published). Berlin, 1904.

GEBER (Jabir ibn Hayyan). See HOLMYARD, E. J.

GRAHAM, GABRIELA CUNNINGHAME, tr. *The Dark Night of the Soul of San Juan of the Cross.* London, 1922.

GRAY, L. H., ed. *Mythology of All Races.* Boston, 1916-28. 12 vols. (III, Celtic; VI, Indian.)

GUEST, CHARLOTTE, tr. *The Mabinogion.* New York and London (Everyman's Library), 1906.

HAGGARD, SIR HENRY RIDER. *She, & King Solomon's Mines.* New York (1st Modern Library edn.), 1957.

HARDING, MARY ESTHER. *The Way of All Women.* New York, 1932.

———. *Woman's Mysteries, Ancient and Modern.* New York and London, 1935; new edn., 1955.

HARRISON, JANE ELLEN. *Prolegomena to the Study of Greek Religion.* London, 1908.

HASTINGS, JAMES, ed. *Encyclopaedia of Religion and Ethics.* Edinburgh and New York, 1908-26. 13 vols.

HESIOD. *Hesiod, The Homeric Hymns, and Homerica.* With an English tr. by Hugh G. Evelyn-White. London and New York (Loeb Library), 1920.

HIPPOLYTUS. *Philosophumena, or, The Refutation of All Heresies.* Tr. by F. Legge. London and New York, 1921. 2 vols.

HOLMYARD, E. J., ed. *The Works of Geber.* Englished by Richard Russell, 1678. New edn., London and New York, 1928. ("Summa Perfectionis, or The Sum of Perfection," pp. 23-197.)

HOPE, LAURENCE, pseud. (Mrs. Adela Florence [Cory] Nicolson). *India's Love Lyrics, including The Garden of Kama.* New York, 1912.

I Ching. The German tr. by Richard Wilhelm rendered into English by Cary F. Baynes. Princeton (Bollingen Series XIX) and London, 3rd edn., 1967.

JACOBI, JOLANDE. *Complex/Archetype/Symbol in the Psychology of C. G. Jung.* Tr. by Ralph Manheim. New York (Bollingen Series LVII) and London, 1959. (Paperback edn., Princeton, 1971.)

JOHN OF THE CROSS, ST. See GRAHAM, G. C.

JOHNSON, RICHARD. *The Famous Historie of the Seaven Champions of Christendome.* London, 1616.

JUNG, CARL GUSTAV.* *Aion.* CW, 9, ii.

———. "Analytical Psychology and *Weltanschauung.*" In CW, 8.

———. "Anima and Animus." In CW, 7.

———. *The Archetypes and the Collective Unconscious.* CW, 9, i.

———. "Archetypes of the Collective Unconscious." In CW, 9, i.

———. "The Dual Mother." In CW, 5.

———. *The Integration of the Personality.* Tr. by Stanley M. Dell. New York and London, 1939.

———. "The Mana Personality." In CW, 7.

———. "Marriage as a Psychological Relationship." In CW, 17.

———. "Mind and Earth." In CW, 10.

* CW = Collected Works, for which see list of relevant volumes at end of entry. For works not yet published in that edition, reference is made to currently available versions.

Jung, Carl Gustav. *Mysterium Coniunctionis.* CW, 14.

———. "On Psychic Energy." In CW, 8.

———. "On the Psychogenesis of Schizophrenia." In CW, 3.

———. "Problems of Modern Psychotherapy." In CW, 16.

———. "Psychological Aspects of the Mother Archetype." In CW, 9, i.

———. "Psychological Factors Determining Human Behaviour." In CW, 8.

———. *Psychological Types.* CW, 6.

———. *Psychology and Alchemy.* CW, 12.

———. "Psychology and Religion." In CW, 11.

———. "Psychology of the Transference." In CW, 16.

———. *Psychology of the Unconscious.* Tr. by Beatrice M. Hinkle. New York, 1919; London, 1921. (Cf. *Symbols of Transformation,* a revision of this work.)

———. "The Spirit Mercurius." In CW, 13.

———. "A Study in the Process of Individuation." In CW, 9, i.

———. *Symbols of Transformation.* CW, 5.

———. "Woman in Europe." In CW, 10.

———. *The Collected Works.* Tr. by R. F. C. Hull. Princeton (Bollingen Series XX) and London. The vols. referred to above are:

3. *The Psychogenesis of Mental Disease.* 1960.
5. *Symbols of Transformation.* 1956.
7. *Two Essays on Analytical Psychology.* 1953.
8. *The Structure and Dynamics of the Psyche.* 1960.
9, part i. *The Archetypes and the Collective Unconscious.* 1959.
9, part ii. *Aion.* 1959.
10. *Civilization in Transition.* 1964.
11. *Psychology and Religion: West and East.* 1958.
12. *Psychology and Alchemy.* 1953.
14. *Mysterium Coniunctionis.* 1963.
16. *The Practice of Psychotherapy.* 1954.
17. *The Development of Personality.* 1954.

———, and Marie-Louise von Franz. *Mysterium Coniunctionis.* Zurich, 1955-57. 3 vols. (Vols. I-II, by C. G. Jung = CW, 14. Vol. III, by M.-L. von Franz = *Aurora Consurgens.* Tr. by R. F. C. Hull and A. S. B. Glover. New York and London, 1966.)

———, and KARL KERÉNYI. *Essays on a Science of Mythology*. New York (Bollingen Series XXII), 1949. (Also pub. as *Introduction to a Science of Mythology*, London, 1950.) (Paperback edn., Princeton, 1969.)

KEITH, A. BERRIEDALE. *Indian Mythology*. See GRAY, L. H.

KHUNRATH, HEINRICH CONRAD. *Amphitheatrum sapientiae aeternae.* Hanau, 1604.

LANIER, SIDNEY. *Hymns of the Marshes*. New York, 1907.

LAYARD, JOHN. "The Incest Taboo and the Virgin Archetype," *Eranos-Jahrbuch XII* (Zurich, 1945), pp. 254-307.

LEAF, MUNRO. *The Story of Ferdinand*. New York, 1936.

LINDERMAN, FRANK BIRD. *American: the Life Story of a Great Indian, Plenty-Coups, Chief of the Crows*. New York and London, 1930.

Mabinogion, The. See GUEST, CHARLOTTE.

MacCULLOCH, J. A. "The Abode of the Blest," HASTINGS, *Encyclopaedia of Religion and Ethics* (q.v.), II, 680-710.

———. *Celtic Mythology*. See GRAY, L. H.

———. *The Religion of the Ancient Celts*. Edinburgh, 1911.

MAIER, MICHAEL. *Atalanta fugiens*. Oppenheim, 1618.

———. *De circulo physico quadrato*. Oppenheim, 1616.

———. *Secretioris naturae secretorum scrutinium chymicum*. Frankfort, 1687.

———. *Tripus aureus*. Frankfort, 1618. For tr., see WAITE, tr., *The Hermetic Museum*, I, 307-57 ("The Golden Tripod").

MANGETUS, JOANNES JACOBUS, ed. *Bibliotheca chemica curiosa*. Geneva, 1702. 2 vols.

MASTERMAN, E. G. W. "Saints and Martyrs, Syrian," HASTINGS, *Encyclopaedia of Religion and Ethics* (q.v.), XI, 81 ff.

MAX MÜLLER, FRIEDRICH, tr. *The Upanishads*. Parts I and II. (Sacred Books of the East, 1 and 15.) Oxford, 1879 and 1884.

MEAD, G. R. S. *Fragments of a Faith Forgotten*. 3rd edn., London, 1931.

———. *Thrice Greatest Hermes: Studies in Hellenistic Philosophy and Gnosis*. London and Benares, 1906. (New edn., London, 1949.) 3 vols.

MORGAN, CHARLES. *Sparkenbroke*. London and New York, 1936.

MORRIS, RICHARD, ed. *Early English Alliterative Poems*. (Early English Text Society Series, vol. I.) London, 1864.

MURRAY, MARGARET ALICE. *The Witch-cult in Western Europe.* Oxford, 1921.

Mutus liber. See MANGETUS, *Bibliotheca chemica curiosa,* I, 938-53.

NEIHARDT, JOHN G. *Black Elk Speaks: Being the Life Story of a Holy Man of the Ogalala Sioux.* New York, 1932.

NEUMANN, ERICH. *The Archetypal World of Henry Moore.* Tr. by R. F. C. Hull. New York (Bollingen Series LXVIII) and London, 1959.

———. *The Great Mother: an Analysis of the Archetype.* Tr. by Ralph Manheim. New York (Bollingen Series XLVII) and London, 1955. (Paperback edn., Princeton, 1972.)

NORTON, CHARLES ELIOT, tr. *The "New Life" of Dante.* Boston, 1920.

NORTON, THOMAS. *The Chemical Treatise . . . Called Believe-me or The Ordinal of Alchemy.* See WAITE, tr., *The Hermetic Museum,* II, 1-67.

ORANDUS, EIRENAEUS. *Nicholas Flammel: His Explanation of the Hieroglyphicall Figures, etc.* London, 1624.

OTTO, RUDOLF. *The Idea of the Holy.* Tr. by John W. Harvey. London, 1923; rev. edn., 1936.

PACKARD, VANCE. *The Hidden Persuaders.* New York, 1957.

Patience. See MORRIS, RICHARD.

PHILALETHES, EIRENAEUS. *A Short Vade Mecum or Guide to the Celestial Ruby.* See WAITE, tr., *The Hermetic Museum,* II, 246-60.

PLUTARCH. "Isis and Osiris." See MEAD, *Thrice Greatest Hermes.*

PONCINS, GONTRAN DE, with GALANTIÈRE, LEWIS. *Kabloona.* New York, 1941.

RADIN, PAUL. *The Trickster.* With commentaries by C. G. Jung and Karl Kerényi. London and New York, 1956.

READ, JOHN. *Prelude to Chemistry: an Outline of Alchemy, Its History and Relationships.* London and New York, 1937.

Rosarium Philosophorum. Frankfort, 1550.

SAINT-EXUPÉRY, ANTOINE DE. *Flight to Arras.* Tr. by Lewis Galantière. London and New York, 1942.

SPENCER, BALDWIN, and GILLEN, F. J. *The Northern Tribes of Central Australia.* London, 1904.

STEVENSON, ROBERT LOUIS. *Poems.* London and Glasgow, 1928.

STOLCIUS DE STOLCENBERG, DANIEL. *Viridarium chymicum.* Frankfort, 1624.

Tabula smaragdina. See "The Emerald Table of Hermes," in Waite, *The Lives of the Alchymistical Philosophers,* pp. 383-84.

TENNYSON, ALFRED. *Poetical Works, including the Plays.* London, New York, and Toronto, 1953.

Tripus aureus. See MAIER, MICHAEL.

TRISMOSIN, SOLOMON. *Splendor solis: Alchemical Treatises.* Reproduced from the MS. dated 1582 in the British Museum, with an introduction by J. K. London, 1920. See also *Aureum Vellus.*

VAN DYKE, HENRY. *Poems.* New York, 1930.

WACE, ALAN J. B. *Mycenae, an Archeological History and Guide.* Princeton, 1949.

WAITE, A. E., tr. *The Hermetic Museum, Restored and Enlarged.* London, 1893; repr. 1953. 2 vols.

———. *The Lives of the Alchymistical Philosophers.* London, 1899; repr., London, 1955.

———. *The Turba Philosophorum, or Assembly of the Sages.* London, 1896; repr. 1914.

WELLS, H. G. *Christina Alberta's Father.* London and New York, 1925.

[WILHELM, RICHARD.] *The Secret of the Golden Flower.* Tr. into German and explained by Richard Wilhelm, with a European commentary by C. G. Jung. Tr. into English by Cary F. Baynes. London and New York, 1931; 2nd edn., 1962. (1st edn. cited herein.)

ZIMMER, HEINRICH. "The Guidance of the Soul in Hindooism," *Spring* (New York: Analytical Psychology Club of New York), 1942.

———. "The Indian World Mother," *Spring* (New York: Analytical Psychology Club of New York), 1960.

———. *Myths and Symbols in Indian Art and Civilization.* Ed. by Joseph Campbell. New York (Bollingen Series VI), 1946. (Paperback edn., Princeton, 1972.)

INDEX

INDEX

world, 284, 288; as hero, 252; lamb
as symbol of, 256; in mandala, 390; as
reconciler, 373; and self-mutilation,
371 f; as stone, 442
Christianity / Christian culture: beginnings of, 7; concepts of, 28; and
ecstasy, 149 f, 155; esoteric aspects of,
28; lost influence of, 304 ff, 318; and
mana personality, 318; mandala in,
382, 390, 414; and mother worship,
174, 187, 191, 192; and Nazism, 6; and
numinous experience, 318; and self-
defence, 100; and self-mutilation,
371 ff; serpent in, 261, 264, 416; and
sloth, 39; symbolic stone in, 442; and
symbols, influence of, 6, 301, 319 ff;
and temptation to egotism, 233; see
also baptism; communion; Mass
circle: and cross, 383, 409; in magic,
383 f; as prophylactic against danger,
384; of psyche, 323 f, boundaries /
limits and centre of, 360 f, conflict
within, 386 f, and hermetic vessel, 430,
representations of, 323, 381, 401, as
symbol of individual, 324, symbolism
of, 383 ff, 418 f, 430; in spiritistic
seances, 384; and square, 388, 408; and
stupa, 408; as symbol, 360; taboo on
breaking, 384 f; in unconscious drawing, 345 ff; used in analogy of analytical procedure, 351, 359 f; see also
mandala
circulation / rotation: in alchemy, 434;
of light, 412-13, 434 f
city, as symbol of individuation, 414 f
civilization, 415
cock, as symbol of sexuality, 34 n, 159
collective unconscious, see psyche,
nonpersonal part of; unconscious
Colonna, Francesco, 458 f
combat: ritual, 111; in sexual play,
169
communion (meal), 23, 72, 83 f, 265
communism, 7 f
conditioned reflexes, formation of,
205
cone, 408
confession, 353
conflict: and birth of consciousness,
201; of conscious and unconscious
elements, 9, 18, 367, 386 f; in groups /
individuals / nations, 8 f, 92 ff, 102 f,
114 f; manifested in physical symptoms, 366; of opposites, 234 f, 364 ff,
381 f, 386 f, 410; parents as elements

in, 368 ff, 386; and reflection, 30 ff;
and regression, 115; and self-control,
343 f; and self- and race-preservation
instinct, 117; of world spirits, 8 f
coniunctio, 313, 431, 449, 456; alchemists and, 423, 446, 447; and
anima / animus, 453; body and spirit
in, 445 f, 450; by devouring, 449; as
incest, 199, 244; body (self-consciousness), 326 f; Buddhist doctrine of,
392 ff; concentration of, 215, 219; development in man, 35; ego as centre
of, 24, 203 f, 208, 210, 213 f, 220, 225,
254; elements unavailable to, 241 f;
evolution of, 84, 198 ff, 215, 224 f, 244,
328 f; invasion by unconscious elements, 284 f; nonpersonal, 24; object,
326; personal, formation of, 17; as
result of conflict, 18, 201; self as centre of, 24; stages of, 23 ff, 313; see
also All-Consciousness; autos; ego
container, see vessel
conversion, religious, 12
cooking, alchemists and, 423
Corinthians (I), 256 n
corn, as deity, 63; see also corn spirit
corn spirit, 63 ff; cultural significance
of, 72, 78 f; as god of harvest, 83; as
Mother, 63, 71; in psychological development of man, 80
Coventry, 256
cow, Hathor as, 179
creative instinct, 21
crescent, 408 f
Crete: bull fighting in, 109 f; phallic
art in, 126
cross: and circle, 383, 409; in mandala,
388; of St. George, 269; and serpent,
264 f, 416, 446
cross-cousin marriage, see marriage
Crow Indians, 97, 255
crucifixion of Christ, 416
cube, 408
cultural ideals, Eastern and Western,
226 f
culture, levels of, and consciousness,
386